Fundamentals of Educational Psychology

FUNDAMENTALS OF EDUCATIONAL PSYCHOLOGY

M. Dash
Neena Dash

ATLANTIC
PUBLISHERS & DISTRIBUTORS (P) LTD

ATLANTIC
PUBLISHERS & DISTRIBUTORS (P) LTD
7/22, Ansari Road, Darya Ganj, New Delhi
Tel.: +91-11-4077 5252, 2327 3880
E-mail: orders@atlanticbooks.com
Web: www.atlanticbooks.com

Published by Atlantic Publishers & Distributors (P) Ltd., 2024
Reprint 2006, 2012, 2022, 2024

Disclaimer

- The author and the publisher have taken every effort to the maximum of their skill, expertise and knowledge to provide correct material in the book. Even then if some mistakes persist in the content of the book, the publisher does not take responsibility for the same. The publisher shall have no liability to any person or entity with respect to any loss or damage caused, or alleged to have been caused directly or indirectly, by the information contained in this book.
- The author has fully tried to follow the copyright law. However, if any work is found to be similar, it is unintentional and the same should not be used as defamatory or to file legal suit against the author.
- If the readers find any mistakes, we shall be grateful to them for pointing out those to us so that these can be corrected in the next edition.
- All disputes are subject to the jurisdiction of Delhi courts only.

Printed & bound in India by Atlantic Print Services

Preface

Educational psychology is a vital subject of study for students of education and psychology in colleges and university departments. It is an essential subject in teacher education programmes at different levels. While there is complete agreement among experts about its study as a compulsory subject at Honours level, in B.Ed., M.Ed. and M.A. (Education) courses, there is no unanimous opinion about the contents to be studied at different levels. Moreover, educational psychology is a developing science. As new research findings are disseminated, its scope widens. Thus, it becomes difficult on the part of an author to incorporate all areas of study in a single textbook like the present one. Authors, therefore, tend to be selective in designing the contents of a book on educational psychology, and we are no exception to this.

In designing this book, we have delved deep into the recesses of libraries, our own experiences and those of other experts in the discipline. We have been immensely benefited by some outstanding work of great authors, past and present, whose books we have referred in giving a final shape to the book. We incur an indebtedness to these great authors and their publishers, institutes of excellence in education namely, Department of Psychology, Craigie College of Education, Ayr (Scotland), Scottish Council of Research in Education, Edinburgh, Moray House College of Education, Edinburgh, International Academy of Education, Geneva, Centre of Advanced Studies in Psychology, Utkal University, Department of Education, Kurukshetra University, R.N. Institute of Advanced Studies in Education, Cuttack, Dr. P.M. Institute of Advanced Studies in Education, Sambalpur, Academic Staff College, Sambalpur University and N.K.C. College of Teacher Education, Angul for the material help and feedback given to us.

We are grateful to Dr. K.R. Gupta, Managing Director and Shri Manish Gupta, Director, M/s Atlantic Publishers and Distributors, New Delhi for their sincere efforts to publish the book at a time when it was most needed by students.

M. Dash
Neena Dash

Contents

1
Concept of Educational Psychology

1. MEANING AND NATURE OF EDUCATIONAL PSYCHOLOGY

Meaning of Educational Psychology

(i) *Psychology of Education*

Educational psychology is the psychology that relates to education. It is the scientific study of human behaviour in educational situations. Educational psychology is that science which helps to provide a better background for understanding the total job of teaching in all its intricacies.

(ii) *Psychology of Learning and Instruction*

Educational psychology is a specialized field within the broad subject called psychology. The principles of psychology and information drawn from other social and biological sciences are combined in many ways as they are applied to learner, his learning, growth and adjustment. Learning and the learner are studied under a variety of conditions. This emphasis on learners, their learning, growth and adjustment is a key to the identity of the field. It is because of this emphasis on learning that some teachers call educational psychology as a psychology of learning. But learning as we all know, is greatly facilitated by planned instruction. Thus, educational psychology can be defined as a psychology of learning and instruction.

(iii) ***Study of Pupils, Learning and Teaching***

John F. Travers (1982) gives a working definition of educational psychology. According to him, educational psychology is best described as the systematic study of pupils, learning and teaching. Students, the learning process and teaching are related and interactive aspects of education. To teach effectively requires extensive knowledge about human beings, the means by which they learn, and the methods of communication.

In teacher training institutions, educational psychology is considered as a specialised and applied branch of pure psychology. Its subject matter is directly related to classroom learning and problems facing the classroom teacher.

Nature of Educational Psychology

(i) *Educational psychology is a science*: Science is a branch of study concerned with observation of facts and establishment of verifiable general laws. Science employs certain objective methods for collection of data. It has its objectives of understanding, explaining, predicting and control of facts. Like any other science, educational psychology has also developed objective methods of collection of data. It also aims at understanding, predicting and controlling human behaviour.

(ii) *Psychology, in the beginning, was a speculative science*: The psychologists were known as armchair psychologists. But psychology today has attained the status of a natural science. An educational psychologist conducts his investigations, gathers his data and reaches his conclusion in exactly the same manner as the physicist or the biologist.

(iii) *Educational psychology is a social science*: Like the sociologist, anthropologist, economist or political scientist, the educational psychologist studies human beings in social situations.

(iv) *Educational psychology is a positive science*: Normative science like Logic or Ethics deals with facts as they ought to be. A positive science deals with facts as they are or as they operate. Educational psychology studies the child's behaviour as it is, not, as it ought to be. So it is a positive science.

(v) *Educational psychology is an applied science or applied psychology*: It is the application of psychological principles in the field of education. It first developed as a branch of general psychology. As a branch of psychology, it is parallel to any other applied psychology. But these branches of psychology come into frequent contact with one another. For example, educational psychology draws heavily facts from such areas as developmental psychology, clinical psychology, abnormal psychology and social psychology.

(vi) *Educational psychology develops a critical attitude and approach towards general psychology*: It does not accept all the facts and principles of general psychology blindly but tests the validity of these principles in real living conditions of the school and then it either accepts or rejects a principle. That is to say, it selects from the whole field of general psychology those facts and principles which are of specific significance to learning and teaching.

(vii) *Educational psychology is narrower in scope than general psychology*: While general psychology deals with the behaviour of the individual in a general way, educational psychology is concerned with the behaviour of the individual in educational settings. It is interested with the behaviour of the child and adult behaviour does not receive much of its attention. While general psychology is academic in approach, educational psychology is professional in nature.

(viii) *Educational psychology is a developing or growing science*: It is concerned with new and ever new researches. As research findings accumulate, educational psychologists get better insight into the child's nature, and as refined methods of investigation are developed, its scope changes. They centre around new and new problems of education.

2. SCOPE OF EDUCATIONAL PSYCHOLOGY

According to Lindgren (1962), there are three aspects of education that concern the educational psychologist:

(a) the learner,
(b) the learning process, and
(c) the learning situation.

The Learner

By the word "learner" we mean the children or students, who individually and collectively comprise the classroom group and on whose behalf the educational programme exists and operates. A great deal of what happens in the classroom can be explained in terms of the personalities, developmental stages, adjustment and psycho-social problems of students, who comprise the class, individual differences in psychomotor abilities, cognitive ability, forces in and outside the school which influence children's learning, developments and adjustment. The learner or the child is the central theme in educational psychology.

The Learning Process

By "learning process" we mean what goes on when people learn. The teacher teaches and the child may learn. Sometimes the teacher teaches a subject but the child learns something else. At other times the teacher may not teach something but the child may learn it. These three instances indicate that children are learning something even though they may not be learning what the teacher wants them to learn or even when the teacher does not deliberately attempt to teach a subject. The educational psychologist is interested in what happens when a child learns, why he learns what teachers want him to learn, and why he learns what teachers do not want him to learn.

The Learning Situation

By "learning situation" we mean those factors or conditions that affect the learner and the learning process. The classroom setting, the attitude and behaviour of the teacher, the morale of the class and the emotional climate of the school are some of the significant factors that affect the learner and the learning process. Educational psychologists are interested in studying the learning situation with the aim of helping the learner in the learning process.

3. AIMS OF EDUCATIONAL PSYCHOLOGY

(i) One of the objectives of educational psychology is to study child development as it relates to learners and the learning process. Educational psychologists aim at studying heredity, growth and maturation, environmental influences, language and thinking, development of intelligence and the process of socialization in relation to their effect on the child as a learner.

(ii) Secondly, educational psychology studies learning and the educative process. Educational psychologists not only examine the several theories of learning but also the techniques of learning skills and problem-solving. They ask and try to answer questions such as: Why can one child learn a given skill and another not learn it? Is large or small-group instruction more desirable in a given subject or at a given age level? What is the best way to teach foreign language? It is obvious that the effective management of learning is a central problem in educational psychology.

(iii) The effective management of learning involves both input — the teaching process, and output — measuring what the learner has learned. Attempts to measure pupil's learning lead to the development of tests and other evaluation techniques. Thus, the development of tests and other methods of evaluation form another area of concern to educational psychologists.

(iv) Another area of real importance to the educational psychologists is the quality and quantity of teacher-pupil interaction. Teacher-pupil interaction has significant effects on pupil's learning. For this purpose, study of the teacher-learner relationship and the search for means of improving teacher effectiveness in this area are receiving continued attention and efforts. In fact, much of the educational psychologists' work is aimed at teaching teachers how best to help their pupils learn more effectively both in and out of class.

(v) The development of positive attitude towards learning is another objective of educational psychology. Teachers generally adopt reinforcement and other techniques to encourage positive attitude among learners to learning. Closely allied to this goal is the fostering of the spirit of enquiry and even skepticism. This is not an easy task.

(vi) Educational psychologists teach others about their field of study. This is done in the classroom and through textbooks and constitutes the academic practice of educational psychology. Since this is a key subject in the professional education curriculum, the teaching of it is obviously an objective of major importance.

(vii) Conducting research is another major objective of educational psychologists. Many educational psychologists, whether or not they teach, do research in the field. Their result published or not, frequently leads to further research. Knowledge in this field continues to develop from this practice of research.

Educational psychology not only encourages research in this field but also aims at the application of research findings in the learning situation.

(viii) A major objective of educational psychology is to give the teacher a sense of direction in his work. It aims at helping the teacher to relate more effectively to the learner. One course or text cannot provide the answer to every question or the solution to every problem. What is done is to present the principle from which application to a specific situation can be deducted.

In addition to the above objectives, educational psychology has following goals in relation to the learner:

(a) To study the most effective ways to teach specific materials to different children.

(b) To place the learner in the best possible learning situation — independent study, large or small group instruction, with one or several teachers for a given course.

(c) To estimate the optimal level or age at which subject matter should be presented.

(d) To determine what course material is appropriate to the needs, characteristics and goals of each learner.

However, educational psychology has two principal objectives: (i) to improve the understanding of how an individual obtains an education, and (ii) to improve current educational programmes. These objectives centre around the child as a learner, the learning process and the learning situation. But the main focus is on the study of the child as a learner.

4. RELEVANCE OF EDUCATIONAL PSYCHOLOGY FOR THE TEACHERS

Educational psychology has relevance for the classroom teacher in a number of ways. Its study is useful for the teacher to function as a behavioural scientist, to understand children, their development and adjustment, to understand instructional problems and to promote learning in and out of the classrooms. Its study is relevant to the teacher in the following broad areas:

(i) Understanding Educational Process

The purpose of educational psychology is to help teachers and prospective teachers develop a better, deeper, and more effective understanding of educational process. Everyone has some understanding of educational process. To a large extent, the understanding of educational process possessed by students is what might be termed as pre-scientific and incomplete. It is the special contribution of educational psychology to fill in the gaps in the student's understanding of educational process and to correct his misconceptions. A teacher who has acquired understanding of educational process is likely to become a more effective teacher than he would be if he had not undertaken the study of educational psychology.

(ii) Understanding Children

Children are at least as complex as automobiles. Thus it is just as important for teachers to understand children as it is for a driver or a mechanic to understand automobiles. A driver who does not understand autos very well is likely to abuse his car. A mechanic who does not understand autos is not only ineffective but can also cause damage to the motor and working parts of the car. Similarly, a teacher who does not understand children very well is an educational liability. At best, he is not as effective teacher as he could be. This does not mean that understanding children in and above makes a good teacher. Good teaching involves much more than understanding. But understanding is a basic requirement. The study of educational psychology helps a teacher to understand child behaviour which seems so complex and unpredictable.

(iii) General Competency

Today's teacher not only needs to know his subject-matter, but he also needs to have a good psychological understanding of what he is doing and what is happening as a result of his actions. He needs to be a behavioural scientist. The competency and general effectiveness of any teacher can be extended if he understands the psychological implications of what he is trying to accomplish, as well as of the events taking place in his classroom.

(iv) Self-analysis and Self-understanding

An improved understanding of both human behaviour and learning situations must imply a certain amount of self-analysis and self-understanding. It is hoped that teachers who study educational psychology will come to know and understand themselves better both as persons and as teachers. It is almost axiomatic that the understanding of the behaviour of other persons develops in direct proportion to the growth in understanding of our own behaviour.

(v) Scientific Points of View

It is hoped that teachers studying educational psychology will be encouraged to adopt what might be termed "the scientific points of view" with regard to the data of their professional lives. If teachers and teachers-to-be attain this point of view, it will mean that they have developed an interest in probing into the causes and effects of classroom problems and events. It means also that they will maintain an enlightened skepticism and an open-mindedness with regard to their own findings as well as to the claims and pronouncements of professionals and lay figures alike.

(vi) Role Perception

A teacher has to play many different roles in the classroom and the school. Roles are based on the expectations we have for ourselves, which in turn stem from the expectations that others have for us. A teacher is expected to play the role of an instructor, subject-matter expert, disciplinarian, youth group worker, interpreter to the public, artist in human relations, learner and scholar, parent figure, etc. Some of these roles are complementary and some are contradictory. There may be conflicts in roles, conflicts in expectations, and conflicts in loyalties. One of the key problems that face the teacher is that of integrating his roles and playing them effectively in different situations. The study of educational psychology will help a teacher for perceiving, integrating and playing his role effectively.

SELECTED QUESTIONS

1. Explain the concept of educational psychology and state its nature and scope.
2. Discuss the aims of educational psychology.
3. Discuss the relevance of educational psychology for the Secondary School teachers.
4. State three situations where the knowledge of educational psychology helps a teacher.

2
Methods of Studying Learner's Behaviour

The validity of any scientific findings about learner's behaviour depends on the validity of the methods employed in arriving at that finding. Crow and Crow (1973) said, "Successful educational practices are based upon formulated psychological principles that evolve from the application of scientific methods to the problems of human development and learning." Educational psychology uses the methods of science. Scientific methods of investigation are precise, objective and subject to verification. Educational psychologists approach their problems with a scientific attitude. There are many methods of studying learner's behaviour and development. The particular method to be used by teachers or educational psychologists is determined by the following factors:

(i) Nature of behaviour to be studied.
(ii) Training and experience of the teacher.
(iii) Availability of materials, time and financial resources.

Some of the methods of psychological investigation that have relevance for the teacher for studying learner's behaviour are as follows:

(i) The case-study method,
(ii) The observation method,
(iii) The experimental method,
(iv) The survey method, and
(v) The interview method.

1. THE CASE-STUDY METHOD

Definition, Nature and Characteristics

Case study is characterised as the detailed, realistic and concrete description and explanation of a case. In education and psychology, the case-study method gained momentum through the pioneering studies of persons like Sigmund Freud, H.A. Murray, Allport Gordan, Carl Rogers and Jean Piaget.

Case study can be defined as an in-depth study which is concerned with pertinent aspects of a particular case, unit, situation or behaviour. The case under study may be an individual child or an institution such as a school. The case may be some phase of life history of the individual or the institution, or it may represent the total life history or total functioning of the individual or the institution.

Case studies being conducted on the individuals may be linked with the biography of child development, mentally retarded child, psycho-analysis of a particular individual, growth and development pattern of a gifted child, etc.

Case studies of social institutions may include the various individual units like the family, marriage, school, college or university, etc.

In case of studies of the communities, a village, an industrial community, a factory setting, a slum area, a tribe, etc., can be considered as the units of studies.

The main purpose behind case studies is to discover all the variables which are important in the history, development and functioning of the individual unit. The enquiring terms like 'why,' 'what,' and 'how' come in the process of the study. For example, in a case study of a particular institution, the investigator may enquire about the aims and objectives behind the establishment of the institution, its functions, its present functioning, the environmental factors influencing its functioning, the type of interaction of different factors that is taking place in the institutional setting, etc. Such data regarding the history of institution, the present state, connected external environment and their interrelationship with one another enable the researchers to develop a clear picture of the institution.

Characteristics

The characteristics of well-organized case study can be mentioned as follows:

(i) *Continuity*: Like other methods of scientific inquiry, case study requires a continuous and systematic procedure of data collection.

(ii) *Completeness:* In case study several data gathering devices — observation, interview, tests, etc. — are needed to be used in such a way that the investigator can easily gather data regarding the complete picture of the case.

(iii) *Authenticity of Data:* As in case of historic research there is a strong need for authentic validation of data. Case-study method lays more emphasis on accuracy and adequacy of data collected through various sources. The researcher is to be more cautious about the problem of ethics regarding this issue.

(iv) *Confidential Recording:* Data in connection with personal nature, difficulties of teachers or pupils in relation to administration and discipline, achievement, mentality, etc., are required to be recorded and kept under secrecy.

(v) *Scientific Synthesis:* Along with the above-mentioned characteristics, case study depends upon scientific synthesis of diagnosis or identification of causal factors, with a prognosis that shows the means of remedial procedures.

Steps Involved in Case Studies

The cycle of case studies follows certain logical steps which are mentioned below:

(1) At first, the status of the phenomenon under investigation is to be determined. Direct observation or measurement or knowledge through other objective sources can lead the investigator to recognize the initial status or symptoms of the case. For example, a study is conducted over an "exceptionally talented child." The basis of labelling a child as exceptional must be determined by the investigator. Another case study of "Innovative Schools" would require the definition of the

innovative nature of the schools and on this basis institutions are to be identified. Other aspects of the study might be defined and determined in this stage.

(2) Secondly, data relating to the factors or circumstances associated with the phenomena to be studied are to be collected. In this stage, some tentative hypotheses must guide the researcher for collecting relevant data.

For collection of data, the investigator may use various instruments like tests, questionnaires, checklists, score cards and rating scales. Data relating to the case may be collected from various sources, such as the child, parents, peers, teachers and the headmaster in case of a child as the case may be, and library, records, registers, employer, employees, the trade union, etc. in case of an institution as the case may be.

Hypothesising in case studies differs from that in survey and experimental studies in that it does not involve explicit statements which could be tested statistically. Hypotheses in case studies are generally in the form of questions or statements related to the various aspects of the case which are tested mostly qualitatively. While conducting preliminary investigations on the case, the investigator may start with certain broad questions as he has limited experience of the case. However, in the process of investigation, the investigator's interaction with the situation or the case may generate many statements related to the specific case. For instance, in an investigation of the classroom dynamics of an instructional system taken as a case, the investigator may start with broad questions such as what is the interactional pattern in the class and how it is related to the academic achievement?

(3) The third step in case studies is objective analysis and interpretation of collected data. On the basis of such analysis and interpretation, the causal factors of the problem under study are identified and the hypotheses are tested.

Testing of hypotheses in case studies generally follows the qualitative approach. For this purpose, the investigator utilizes his insight into and impressionistic views about the process under study. Data processed in qualitative form along with the investigator's insight into the case would contribute toward the understanding of the case.

(4) The fourth step in case studies is writing a draft report about the case under study. Remedial or adjustment measures are also suggested in the draft report.

(5) The fifth step in a case study is introduction of remedial adjustment measures as suggested in the report. Subsequent follow-up must be conducted for evaluating the effectiveness of corrective measures applied. If the remedial measures do not work well, some other sets of hypotheses are to be framed and some further remedial measures are to be applied. Again follow-up would be done accordingly.

(6) The last step in case study is writing the final report about the case. This step which is very important for purpose of theorization and generalization is, at times, ignored by investigators. After the study is complete, the investigator should write a comprehensive report about the nature of the case, causal factors and the remediation/recommendations suggested. This is a theoretical framework which allows generalization for similar other cases. Adelman Jenkins and Kemmis (1976) state that "Case studies allow generalizations either about an instance or from an instance to a class."

An investigator studying similar other cases in future can study the findings of earlier case studies to be in a better position to study his case.

Uses and Limitations of Case Study

Uses

(i) The case study method has got its own status as a method of investigation.

(ii) This method proves very effective in the study of individual children and also social institutions.

(iii) Problem behaviours like delinquency, truancy, stealing, and other maladjusted behaviours, behaviour patterns of a talented child, growth and development of a social institution like a school or a university, etc., can be studied through case-study method. However, some doubts remain in the mind of the investigator regarding the scientific nature of this method.

Limitations

(i) It is very difficult to know the whole history of any child or an institution and to observe it objectively. The use of insights, direct and indirect observations, personal interpretations, etc. may be subjective and prejudicial.

(ii) Persons who provide the data about the unit may present a biased picture of the unit of study.

(iii) In case of small children it is difficult to know their history through them because their memory is neither strong nor reliable. It is also possible that the parents might not have observed something about the history of their children which would have been very important for the case study.

(iv) There is a tendency on the part of investigators to generalise facts about certain behaviour. But every individual or the institution is unique. It is, therefore, not right always to generalise the findings which are obtained through the study of one single and unique individual or the institution.

The main purpose of a case study is not to generalise but to get some knowledge about the unit of the study. If the method is to prove a success, the case study should present as accurate and as objective an account and as complete and as dynamic a picture as possible.

2. THE OBSERVATION METHOD

Everyone observes the actions of others. We look at other persons and listen to their talk. We infer what others mean when they say something, and we infer the characteristic motivations, feelings and intentions of others on the basis of these observations. We say, "He is a very shrewd judge of people" meaning that his observations of behaviour are keen and that we think his inferences of what lies behind the behaviour are valid.

This day-to-day kind of observation of most people is, however, unsatisfactory for science. The social scientist must observe human behaviour, but he must be dissatisfied with the inadequacy of uncontrolled observations. He seeks reliable and objective observations from which he can draw valid inferences.

He treats the observation of behaviour as part of a measurement procedure. Observation is, therefore, called "measurement without instrument."

Direct Observation and Indirect Observation

Basically, there are two modes of observations: We can watch people do and say things, and we can ask people about their own actions and the behaviour of others. The principal ways of getting information are by either experiencing something directly or by having someone tell us what happened. In this section we are mainly concerned with seeing and hearing events and observing behaviour.

Natural Observation and Participant Observation

Observation may be natural observation or participant observation. In natural observation, the observer observes the specific behavioural characteristics of children in natural settings like playground or any other social situation. In participant observation, the observer actually becomes an active participant in children's play or activities.

Controlled Observation and Free Observation

Observation may be conducted in a controlled situation or in an unstructured or free situation. Consequently, there are two types of observation: controlled observation and free observation. When the observer observes the behavioural characteristics of children in certain situations which have been controlled or structured by the observer for purpose of observing the specific behaviour patterns, it is called controlled observation. In free observation techniques, children's behaviour, feelings, actions and reactions are observed in free, natural and real life situations in the home, classroom, playground, etc.

Steps of Observation

The major steps of observation are as follows:

(i) Planning for observation,
(ii) Observing,
(iii) Drawing inferences and interpreting observed facts,
(iv) Reporting,

Planning for Observation

Planning is basic to all psychological investigations. The observer should, therefore, plan his observation very carefully. He should know clearly, precisely and unambiguously about the behaviour to be observed. He must decide about the time and place of observing the behaviour. In observation system, the observer may be required to use an observation schedule, record sheets or rating scales. The observer should keep these tools ready before he starts actual observation. If readymade tools are available, he can use them. If no such tool is readily available, he may develop tools which will serve his purposes. It is always advisable to consult two or three other persons about planning for the observation.

Observing

After planning for observation, the observer should start actual observation. He should be very careful and sincere to observe all details about the specific behaviour he is observing. If he is superfluous, he may miss certain details which are very important for the study. One important condition for an observer is that the observer takes note of facts in the observation record instantly. In developed countries video camera is used to record details about the behaviour being observed. Sometimes one-way screen is used in laboratory settings so that the observer can see the child but the child cannot see the observer. When a child knows that his behaviour is being observed by someone, he becomes conscious of the observer's presence and thus the original nature of his behaviour may be lost and some other behaviour may occur. That is why the child should not have any knowledge about the observation that is going on.

Drawing Inferences and Interpreting Observed Facts

The third step in observation system is to make inferences about the observed facts. Inferences about the causes and consequences of observed behaviour help to interpret facts.

Reporting

The fourth step is to prepare a report about the observation. This report should be comprehensive and complete in all respects so that others can use it for research and evaluation purposes.

Ensuring Objectivity in Observation

(i) The major problem of behavioural observation is the observer himself. In behavioural observation, the observer is both a crucial strength and a crucial weakness. Why? The observer must digest the information derived from his observations and then make inferences about causes or constructs. He observes a certain behaviour, say a child striking another child. He must process this observation and make an inference that the behaviour is a manifestation of aggression or hostility. Thus, the strength and weakness of the procedure is the observer's power of inference; if it were not so, a machine observer would be better than a man observer.

(ii) One of the difficulties of observation method is to bridge the gap between the behaviour and its causes. For this purpose, the observer must be a trained person and competent in relating behaviour to its causes.

(iii) The basic weakness of the observer is that he can make biased and incorrect inferences from observations. He may ignore important units of behaviour and their antecedents. This will make all observations subjective. Observation of human behaviour requires competent knowledge of behaviour and even the meaning of a particular behaviour.

(iv) The observer can also affect the objects of observation simply by being part of the observation situation. The observer can nullify this weakness only if he is unobtrusive and if the child being observed does not have the feeling that his behaviour is being judged by someone else.

(v) Another problem of observation is to ensure its reliability and validity. The common ways of ensuring reliability are to correlate the observations of two or more observers, to observe the same child two or more times and to determine common facts or points of agreement among observers. Similarly, validity of observation can be ensured by having a theoretical framework of the behaviour to be observed.

3. THE EXPERIMENTAL METHOD

Experimental method is a scientific method of investigation of social, psychological and educational problems. This method was first employed and then popularised by Wilhelm Wundt.

"An experiment is taken to mean a scientific investigation in which an investigator manipulates and controls one or more independent variables and observes the dependent variable or variables for variation concomitant to the manipulation of the independent variable" (Kerlinger, 1973). The main goal of an experiment is to discover relations among phenomena or variables, as for example, the relation between incentives and performance, pre-school education facilities and later cognitive development, etc. In an experiment, the investigator controls certain variables. He manipulates one or two variable; and he observes the effect of the manipulated variables on some other variable or the behaviour. Experimentation as a method of investigation will be made clear if we define certain fundamental concepts.

Experimental Group and Control Group

In an experiment it is sometimes desirable to have two groups — the experimental group and the control group. The experimental group is one which receives experimental treatment. This is the group on which the experiment is conducted. The control group is one which receives no such treatment. The experimental group is compared with the control group with reference to certain variables.

In modern research it is quite possible to have more than one experimental group and more than one control group.

Independent Variables, Dependent Variables and Controlled Variables

It has been mentioned earlier that the chief purpose of an experiment is to study the relation between phenomena or variables. A particular phenomenon, say, performance in a test, may be influenced by one or more factors like incentives, cognitive entry behaviours, teacher expectancy, etc. In studying the relation between variables, the experimenter may keep certain factors constant. He is said to have controlled the effect of these variables on some other variable. Human behaviour is so complex that it is difficult to control all the variables in a typical classroom experiment. For this reason, in simple classroom experiments one or two variables may be kept constant. The variable which is kept constant is called the controlled variable.

An independent variable is the presumed cause of the dependent variable. The independent variable is the antecedent, the dependent variable is the consequence. The terms "independent variable" and "dependent variable" come from mathematics where X is the independent variable and Y is the dependent variable. The investigator, thus, studies the relation between X and Y. There may be a number of independent variables XI, X2, X3... and a number of dependent variables Y1, Y2, Y3. In experimental groups, the independent variable is manipulated. The variable that is manipulated by the investigator is simply called X. When, for example, an investigator studies the effect of different teaching methods, he may manipulate method, by using different methods. Teaching method is the independent variable. For control group, the independent variable is not manipulated. The independent variable that is not manipulated in the control group is also termed as X.

The dependent variable is the variable predicted to, whereas, the independent variable is predicted from. The dependent variable Y is the presumed effect, which varies concomitantly with change or variation in the independent variable X. It is the variable that is not manipulated. Rather, change in the dependent variable as a result of the change in the independent variable is observed. Thus, the dependent variable is ordinarily the condition we are trying to explain. The most common examples of X and Y are methods of teaching and achievement of students respectively.

Sometimes the dependent variable is measured before the independent variable is manipulated. Dependent variable measured before the experiment is termed as 'Yb.' Dependent variable measured after the manipulation of independent variable is termed as 'Ya.'

Hypothesis

In an experiment, the investigator makes a statement about the relation between two or more variables. He anticipates the relation between variables and makes a declarative statement to that effect before the experiment begins. This declarative statement about the relation between X and Y is called the hypothesis. Sometimes the investigator tests the hypothesis. If his statement is found true, he accepts the hypothesis. If the statement is proved wrong, the hypothesis is rejected.

An Example

Suppose the investigator wants to study the relation between population education and attitude of high school students towards population issues. He may take 100 students of Class X. He allots 50 students to the experimental group and 50 students to the control group at random. The investigator then administers an Attitude Scale on both the groups to check the equality of two groups on attitude towards population issues. This forms the pre-test.

The experimental group is given population education for a certain period, say one year. The control group is given no such education during this period. At the end of the year, both the groups are again given the Attitude Scale to determine their scores on the scale. The investigator then applies a 't' test to measure the difference between the two groups on attitude towards population situation. If the experimental group is found better, it is said to be due to the effect of population education.

Uses and Limitations

The experimental method has certain limitations:

(i) All educational problems cannot be studied experimentally.

(ii) Many important variables cannot be studied experimentally, because they are not manipulable, *e.g.*, intelligence, religious values, home environment, etc.

(iii) All teachers are not competent to conduct experiments on school children.

(iv) The environment in most schools is not conducive for experimental investigations.

However, in spite of these limitations, experimental method has tremendous values for teachers:

(i) It is a scientific method.

(ii) It is the best method whenever independent variables are manipulable.
(iii) It lessens the effects of subjectivity in interpreting facts.
(iv) It creates and sustains the interests of the experimenter and the children if the procedure followed is systematic.

4. THE SURVEY METHOD

The survey method is one of the most commonly used methods of investigation of educational problems. It is followed in studying local as well as state, national and international trends. The survey method gathers data from a relatively large number of cases at a particular time. Thus, it is not concerned with a single individual or few individuals.

Every survey researcher is interested in the accurate assessment of the characteristics of the whole population. But very rarely, as in census operations, do survey researchers study the whole population. From these samples they infer the characteristics of the defined population. Surveys of this type are known as sample surveys. The study of sample from which inferences about population can be drawn is needed because of the difficulties of attempting to study the whole population.

Steps of Survey Research

The survey researcher must carefully follow the following steps:

1. First, the researcher must specify and clarify the problem to be studied. This means that he should specify the objectives of his research, the question he wants to answer. Suppose the researcher wants to study the educational backwardness of girls. His objectives may be:
   (a) To study the enrollment of boys and girls (6-14).
   (b) To study the enrollment of girls belong to S.C. and S.T. in the age group 6 to 14.
   (c) To study the rate of drop-outs among boys and girls (6-14).
   (d) To study the repetition rate among boys and girls (6-14).
   (e) To study the rate of drop-outs and repetition among girls belonging to S.C. and S.T.

(f) To study the causes of low enrollment among girls.
(g) To study the causes of drop-outs and repetition among girls.
(h) To suggest remedial measures.

2. The next step in the survey research is the selection of sample. The investigator first decides the universe to be sampled and studied. In our example on educational backwardness of girls, the investigator must decide and answer these questions:
   (i) Are all girls in the age-group 6-14 reading in the school to be included in the sample?
   (ii) Should I include in the sample those girls who are not attending school?
   (iii) Should I include in the sample parents, teachers and community members?

   Thus, the investigator must define the universe to be sampled and studied. It may not be possible to study the whole population of girls, parents and teachers. So the investigator must select a random sample of the population.
3. The next step in a survey is the preparation of interview schedules: Information blanks, forms and questionnaires for collection of necessary data. These forms and schedules may be in tabular form to elicit answers for various questions.
4. The first three steps constitute the planning side of survey. The important part of survey is the collection of data. The investigator or somebody trained in data collection collects pertinent data about the problem through interviews, on-the-spot enquiry, or door-to-door visit. Data may also be collected through telephonic talk, mailed questionnaires or information blanks. It is important to note that data are collected from those individuals or institutions which are randomly selected for the sample.
5. The next step of survey is tabulation and analysis of data. After collection of data, the investigator tabulates the data in tabular form and then analyses the data to facilitate interpretation.

6. The last step is interpretation of the findings. While interpreting data, the investigator may compare and contrast the data obtained through his survey with the findings of similar other surveys. Interpretation of findings has also implication for suggesting remedial measures or concluding remarks about the problem. It is advisable and necessary to interpret data and suggest remedial measures in terms of objectives of the survey.

Uses and Limitations of Survey Method

Uses

(i) Survey method is useful to collect information about 'what exists,' 'what we want,' and 'how to get there.'
(ii) It is useful to determine the present trend and solving current practical problems.
(iii) It contributes to the advancement of knowledge.
(iv) It helps in doing further research on the problem.

Limitations

(i) It is not a method of research of high order.
(ii) It ignores or pays little attention to the past condition which might have caused the present problem.
(iii) There is possibility of cheating or manipulation of data by the investigator.
(iv) The investigator may face difficulties in meeting people or visiting places for collection of data.
(v) This method involves more of clerical work and less of reasoning.

5. THE INTERVIEW METHOD

What is Interview?

Interview is a face-to-face or one-to-one situation in which one person (who is experienced, trained and qualified) or the interviewer gathers information about the behaviour or problems of the other(s) (less experienced) or the interviewee(s) for purpose of helping the latter to solve his or their problems or modify his or their behaviour. Interview is based on direct personal contact which is unique to the method of interview and not found in any other method of investigation.

Types of Interview

Interviews are conducted with definite design and specific purposes. Consequently, there are different types of interview according to the purpose for which they are used and according to their design or structure. When interview is used as a tool for gathering data for research purpose, it is called "research interview." When interview is used for clinical purposes, to secure information about an individual's problems, his past history, occupation and family adjustment for diagnosis and treatment purposes, it is called "clinical interview."

When the interviewer interviews one individual at one time, it is called "individual interview." When a group of individuals are interviewed, at one time, it is called "group interview." In group interview, the size of the group should not be too large nor too small. The optimum size of the group should be approximately 10. In group interview, some individuals may hesitate or feel shy to reveal some important facts concerning their problems in presence of others. For this purpose, individual interview is more effective than group interview.

Interviews are also classified as "structured" and "unstructured" interviews. In structured interview, the procedure, the type of questions, the order of questioning and the instructions are standardised and specified in advance. The interviewer has no freedom to alter the procedure or to rephrase the questions, or to add new questions. In unstructured interview, the interviewer is free to rephrase the questions, change the order of questions, time of interview and to add new questions. Thus, unstructured interview allows greater flexibility and freedom to the interviewer.

Techniques of Interview

If interview is to be effective as a technique for gathering useful information about the individual's problems, it must be conducted in a systematic way. The following techniques are useful for effective interviewing:

Preparation for the Interview

(i) The interview must be planned very carefully.
(ii) The types of questions to be asked, the order of questions, the timing and duration of the interview session, and the

ways of recording the data should be decided in advance with scope for flexibility.

(iii) It is advisable to try out the questions on another person before actual investigation starts. This will reveal the deficiencies in the questions and will help to modify them if necessary.

Conduct of the Interview

The interview should be conducted in the way it has been planned. The interviewer should possess the following qualities for successful conduct of the interview:

(i) The interviewer must maintain a harmonious relationship with the interviewee. A good rapport between the interviewer and the interviewee helps the interviewee to feel at ease and to express himself willingly.

(ii) He must create a friendly and relaxed atmosphere during the interview. The conversation should be pleasant and non-threatening in nature.

(iii) He should ask only one question at a time.

(iv) He should repeat a question if necessary.

(v) He should make sure that the interviewee understands the question. If necessary, he should rephrase the question.

(vi) He should listen patiently and carefully to what the interviewee says.

(vii) After putting a question, he should allow sufficient time to the interviewee to answer the question.

(viii) He should be able to observe the facial expressions, gestures and tone of voice of interviewee while he is giving the answers.

(ix) He should avoid suggesting answers to the questions.

(x) If the interviewee gives an unexpected answer, the interviewer should not show signs of surprise, shock, anger or other emotions.

(xi) He should maintain a neutral attitude with respect to controversial issues.

(xii) He should take note of answers that seem to be vague, or ambiguous.

(xiii) He should be tactful to bring the interviewee back to the point of question when the interviewee strays too far from the original questions.

(xiv) He should be prepared to redirect the interview to a more fruitful topic when he feels that the required information is not emerging.

(xv) He should wind up the interview before the interviewee gets tired.

Recording of the Interview

Useful information or data gathered through the interview should be recorded accurately and completely. Interview schedules, rating scale, notebooks or a tape recorder may be used to record the data. For all practical purposes, a tape recorder is a valuable asset for the interviewer. The interviewer is required to attend to the interviewee and record the information supplied by the interviewee simultaneously. While doing so, there is every possibility of omitting, distorting, modifying or exaggerating the information provided by the interviewee. A tape recorder helps the interviewer to avoid omissions, distortions, exaggerations or modifying the original information provided by the interviewee. It also saves much time required to record data by other means.

Advantages and Limitations of Interview

Advantages

(i) The interview method provides an opportunity to the interviewer to question thoroughly certain areas of inquiry.

(ii) It permits greater depth of response which is not possible through any other means.

(iii) It also enables the interviewer to get information concerning interviewee's feelings, attitudes or emotions in relation to certain questions.

Limitations

In spite of these advantages, the interview method has certain limitations.

(i) It is a time-consuming technique.

(ii) Many interviewers are not experienced, skillful and tactful as a result of which much useful information is not elicited and some also missed.

(iii) Moreover there is greater possibility of subjectivity in recording and interpreting the data.

(iv) Very often an interviewee fails to respond freely, frankly and accurately and this defeats the very purpose of the interview.

SELECTED QUESTIONS

1. What are the various methods of studying learner's behaviour? Discuss any one method most suitable for studying classroom behaviour of secondary school students.
2. Which method is most suitable for the following situations? Discuss
   (a) Problem behaviour of children.
   (b) Effectiveness of a method of teaching.
   (c) Educational backwardness of socially disadvantaged children.
3. Discuss the steps involved in survey method.
4. How can observation of children's behaviour be made more objective?
5. State five qualities of a good interviewer.
6. Discuss the techniques of interview.
7. Discuss the experimental method of studying learner's behaviour. State its uses and limitations.
8. What is observation method? State its advantages and disadvantages.
9. Discuss the characteristics of case-study method along with its merits and demerits.

3
Schools of Psychology

Men of thought have always been interested in human nature. Philosophers, artists, writers and theologists have sought to interpret human conduct from their particular points of view. But psychologists later took over the problem and questions about human nature. Since the science of human nature was launched upon the scientific world, psychologists have not always been in agreement as to just how they ought to proceed with their investigation. This eventually led to the formation of schools of psychology.

According to R.S. Woodworth (1976), the term 'school' suggests orthodoxy, followership, and uniformity. It refers to a body of persons of like opinions and beliefs. By 'schools of psychology' we, therefore, mean 'group of psychologists who associated themselves both geographically and systematically with the early leaders in the new science.' For the most part, the psychologists who formed a school worked on common problems and shared a common systematic orientation. Thus, the various schools of study were formed on two fundamental issues: (i) Area of study, and (ii) Methods of study.

The heyday of the schools passed with the end of the third decade of the twentieth century. With the rapid development of psychology and great increase in research findings, it became difficult for the psychologists to attempt to encompass the entire science of psychology in a single comprehensive system or school. Thus, psychologists became interested in specialization of a particular segment of psychology such as learning, perception or thought process. Thus a number of miniature systems of psychology developed in place of broad schools of psychology. But it must be remembered that these miniature systems developed out of these broad schools of psychology which are now of historical importance. We shall discuss them in the following sections of five schools, namely:

(1) Psychoanalytic School,
(2) Behaviouristic School,
(3) Gestalt School,
(4) Lewin's Field Theory, and
(5) Hormic School

1. PSYCHOANALYSIS

What is Psychoanalysis?

Some psychologists are of the opinion that psychoanalysis is neither a school nor a systematic theory of psychology compared to other schools of psychology. The psychoanalytic movement had never an academic background. It had never taken a systematic position on all of the mental processes. For example, the psychoanalysts have shown little interest in sensation, attention, perception and learning which have been the traditional areas of concern for the other schools. They neglected these academic fields primarily because their aim was the very practical one of providing therapeutic aid for neurotic patients. As a consequence, psychoanalysis as a theory was primarily concerned with the etymology, development and treatment of mental disorders. Psychoanalysis as a practice was a non-experimental clinical technique for treating patients suffering from psychological disorders.

The development of psychoanalysis is a story by itself. It has its origin in the medical practice of Sigmund Freud in Vienna around 1900. Freud was a practising physician who specialized in diseases of the nervous system. He became aware that many of his patients with nervous disease were, in reality, suffering from mental conflicts and neurotic states which manifested themselves as physical disorders like extreme fatigue, nervousness, insomnia and the like. Treating the patients' physical symptoms failed to get at the root of the problem. Clearly, what the patients needed was psychotherapy rather than physical therapy. While Freud was puzzling over these difficulties, Jeam Martin Charcot, a French practitioner, and Joseph Bewer, a German practitioner had been experiencing considerable success with the 'hypnotic treatment' of hysteria.

Free Association Technique

Freud was in touch with these results. He tried out hypnotic treatment on his patients. Soon he noticed that all patients could not be hypnotized. Moreover, hypnosis resulted only in a temporary alleviation of symptoms, not in permanent cure. He noticed that the real value of this treatment lay in a deeper, and more complicated analysis of the patients' problems which could be done even in the waking state of the patients. Thus, he changed over to a new technique called the 'free association technique'. In free association technique, the patient relaxes on a couch and freely tells whatever comes into his mind. The psychoanalyst listens to the patient and observes his emotional reaction, signs of distress, resistance to the treatment and the like. Following this session, the therapist discusses with the patient interpretation of the facts brought to light during the analytic period.

Dream Analysis

In course of his practice Freud became convinced that dreams were of special significance for the new therapy. The analysis of the dream revealed to him the hidden wishes, lost memories, and emotional attitude of the patient. Dream analysis also revealed repressed unconscious desires which were very important for the treatment of neurotic disorders. Freud considered dream interpretation as an important part of the theory and practice of psychoanalysis. He considered dream as a royal road to the interpretation of unconscious.

Upon analysis, dreams reveal two distinct types of contents — the *manifest content* and the *latent content.* The dream as remembered by the dreamer upon awakening is the manifest content. But the real or the hidden facts in the dream are the latent contents of the dream. The latent content may be quite different from the manifest content, because the former gets distorted and undergoes considerable modification by a certain process known as "dream work." Dream work operates through three ways, such as (i) condensation, (ii) displacement, and (iii) secondary elaboration.

In condensation, some elements of the dream are omitted altogether and others appear only in a fragmentary form. Sometimes also several elements may be blended into one. Generally unpleasant, unacceptable and harmful events in the dream are condensed. Most often, some elements of the dream may be replaced or displaced by other elements which are acceptable to the dreamer. Sometimes the latent content of the dream takes an opposite direction. For example, clothing often represents nakedness; love may be a disguise for hate. This process is known as displacement. Secondary elaboration is the process of hiding the real significance of the dream. Through this process, the dreamer, upon awakening, makes a good story out of the dream. He, therefore, adds new elements that were not in the original dream.

Dream analysis is designed to reverse these various processes and to reveal precisely what is repressed or hidden. This is done in two ways. First, the dreamer is required to associate around the various elements of the dream. Second, the dreams generally appear symbolically. Thus, an analysis of the various symbols in the dream reveals the real object of the dream.

Theory of Personality: The Id, the Ego, and the Super-ego

Freud's anatomy of personality is built around the concepts of the id, ego and the super-ego. These are three aspects of personality and each one is related to the other two—both genetically and functionally.

The id is the primary aspect of personality of which little is known. According to Freud, the id is somewhere in direct contact with the bodily process from which it derives its forces. It is dominated by infantile emotions and instincts. Thus, it has no logical organization.

The id has also no sense of time and values. Thus, it cannot distinguish between good and evil. It is guided by the pleasure principle.

The ego refers to the 'I' or the 'self that thinks, feels and does. It is the logical and orderly aspect of personality. The ego is that part of the id which has been modified by the influence of external world on it. Thus, the ego's power is derived entirely from the id and its ultimate goal is to satisfy the id desires. But it cannot do so always. Because, the id desires something which the super-ego does not permit. Moreover, there is the demand of the external reality, and the ego is governed by the reality principle.

The super-ego is the moral and judicial aspect of personality. It is the 'Conscience.' In it lie the feelings of 'do's and 'don'ts. Super-ego is the chief force that socialises a child. Freud further points out that the child's super-ego is modelled on the parent's super-ego. Thus, it becomes the vehicle of tradition which is handed down from generation to generation. It is the source of man's idealism. All striving for perfection arises out of the super-ego. Super-ego is critical of the relationship between the id and the ego.

As has been discussed earlier, the id demands satisfaction which the super-ego cannot 'tolerate.' Moreover, the ego must meet the demands of reality. Thus, the ego faces three sets of forces, such as:

(a) the desire of the id,
(b) the demands of the super ego, and
(c) the demands of external reality.

The ego tries to maintain a balance between these sets of forces. It does this either by postponement of id desires or by satisfying the id desires within limits set by the super-ego and the external reality. For example, a young man meets his sweetheart on the road. The id in the man desires to kiss the woman. But the super-ego advises, 'kissing is bad.' There are also social taboos and inhibitions about kissing on the road. At such a moment, the ego must reconcile the demands of these three sets of forces. The ego may advise the id 'Don't kiss now,' for you will be misunderstood and even punished for this (postponement of immediate gratification of id desires). The ego may also advise the id, 'wait, go home and kiss your dear one' (satisfaction of id desires within limits set by the super-ego and external reality).

If the ego fails to reconcile the demands of these three harsh masters, it experiences anxiety and a sense of guilt and inferiority. In order to get rid of anxiety and tension, the ego develops defence mechanisms. However, some psychologists are of the opinion that these aspects of personality are not real entities. According to Hall and Lindzey, the id may be considered as the biological component of personality, the ego as the psychological component and the super-ego as the social component of personality. Dash (1995) feels that the three components must be considered while studying personality.

The Conscious, the Sub-conscious and the Unconscious

Freud divided the mind into three imaginary layers such as the conscious, the sub-conscious and the unconscious. These three layers are otherwise known as the topographical aspects of mind. Conscious is that layer of the mind which contains memories, thoughts and desires of which we are aware at a given moment. Sub-conscious is that layer which we are not aware at the present moment but which are recallable through association and efforts. But the unconscious is that dark chamber or deeper layer of the mind which contains wishes, desires, thoughts, experiences and memories of which we are not aware at a given moment.

We cannot be conscious of these memories or thought ordinarily. Only through Freudian techniques, this dark layer can be brought to light. Unconscious is the storehouse of all our infantile and unsatisfied desires. A greater portion of our psychic life is dominated by the unconscious. Thus, the study of unconscious will help us to know the real roots and springs of human action.

It appeared to Freud that the unconscious consisted essentially of motives or wishes. The wishes, desires or memories which are painful and cannot be satisfied are forced down to the unconscious layer of the mind. Psychologically speaking, *whatever is strongly forbidden is strongly desired. Even whatever is strongly feared is really desired.* The forcing down of these desires into the unconscious layer of the mind is termed as repression. Repression is entirely an unconscious process. According to Freud, at times individuals may consciously suppress some of their desires. If repression is complete, the desires so repressed cannot ordinarily come into the conscious. But at times repression becomes incomplete. As a result of that, these repressed desires manifest themselves in thoughts, feelings and actions. The unconscious desires, which try to take possession of the conscious layer are prohibited to do so by a mechanism known as the 'Censor'. Censor is always vigilant about the unconscious desires. But during sleep, the censor lacks vigilant power and thus these desires appear in the form of dreams.

Psychic Determinism

Basing on a large number of studies of his patients, Freud developed a principle of psychic determinism. An event is said to be determined if it has a cause. It is fully determined if it has a sufficient cause. Every behaviour has a cause, a meaning and a significance. But the organism and the environment are so complex that we may fail to ascribe any particular cause to an individual's action. In that case we cannot say that the action is accidental. Rather it means that the cause or the motive behind his actions lies in the unconscious. Freud was of the opinion that "all behaviour is caused or motivated; even forgetting is also motivated."

Libido Theory

In his theory of motivation Freud emphasised the libidinal aspect of behaviour. The term libido is best understood as a psychophysical concept meaning both the bodily and mental aspects of the sex instinct. In other words, the libido is at once the raw sexuality and the mental desire or longing for sexual relations. Freud, however, emphasized the mental aspect of the libido in his writing. Moreover, Freud employed the term in a broader sense covering self-love, a mother's love for the child, religious love, in fact, any pleasurable activities in which the individual engages.

In his later writings, Freud recognized two aspects of libido — the life instinct or eros and the death instinct or the thanatos. Eros includes instinct for self-preservation, the desire to propagate the species, self-love, love for others and the tendency to grow and to realise one's potentialities, in short, eros is the creative force that underlies life itself. The thanatos is the urge to destroy the self and others. If the thanatos is drawn inward, it results in suicidal destruction; if this is drawn outward it results in hate, or aggression and even murder. Since eros and thanatos exist side by side, we are driven by conflicting unconscious motives. For example, we sometimes hate the person whom we love most. The elaboration of the eros and the thanatos determines the child's relationship with members of the society and his interpersonal relationship during his adult life.

Psychosexual Development

Freud recognised certain stages in the development of a child during early years. Each stage is characterized by a particular source of sexual pleasure. Each stage has certain psychological significance for the later development of the child. Freud named these stages as stages of psychosexual development.

For Freud, the sources of sexual pleasure during the first few years of childhood are the erotogenic zones of the body itself. The sex drive of the infant is not intense. It will have its intensity in adolescence, when the sex glands and hormones have matured. Sexuality during the early years does not have the definite aim of the sexually excited adults. It is diffuse rather than sharply focused. It aims simply at bodily pleasure from any organ — from the mouth, from the anus, from the genitals. It is auto-erotic, not yet being directed towards any other person as a love object. Freud called it 'infantile sexuality'.

The five stages of psychosexual development are:

(i) Oral stage,
(ii) Anal stage,
(iii) Phallic stage,
(iv) Latency period, and
(v) Genital period.

(i) The Oral Stage

This is the first stage of psychosexual development. This period lasts from birth to the end of first year. During this stage, sexual pleasure is localised in the oral zone. Thus, sexual pleasure is derived from the baby's oral activities. Consequently, there are two sub-stages of the oral stage: the *oral sucking stage* and the *oral biting stage.*

Oral sucking stage begins from birth and continues up to six months. The baby gets pleasure by sucking mother's breast, his own thumb or anything. This is assumed from the fact that when the baby is hungry, he may suck the breast. Sucking the mother's breast satiates his hunger. But when hunger is satiated, the baby may continue sucking the breast or even his own thumb. Sucking the breast or the thumb in this case is not driven by hunger but by pleasure seeking motive.

Oral biting stage begins after six months and continues up to the end of the first year. During this stage, biting begins to be a prominent feature of the infant's oral activities. Sucking behaviour continues during this stage, but the baby also gets pleasure by biting the mother's breast, putting anything into the mouth — the finger, the toy, and biting it. Mothers know it from their experiences that the baby at times bites the breast while sucking it. After his hunger is satisfied, the child bites the breast to derive pleasure from it.

Freud found that the successive phases of development would depend on how successfully the problems of the oral period have been met. This stage has psychological significance for the mothering care, feeding schedules and the methods and age of weaning. Frustration during this stage appears later in the form of smoking, chewing, nail biting and dependent, immature, pessimistic, suspicious, and aggressive behaviour.

(ii) The Anal Stage

At the end of the first year, the anal region becomes the predominant source of pleasure. During this stage, the main pleasure is derived from the activities of the organs of elimination. This stage has two sub-stages— the anal expulsion and the anal retention stage. During the anal expulsion stage, the main source of getting pleasure is the evacuation of stool and urine. The baby also derives pleasure by delaying that activity as long as possible.

The anal phase has significance for toilet training. The child learns toilet habits or delays his learning depending on his experiences and the training he receives from the mother. Fixation of sex energy at this stage leads to certain personality traits in later life such as obstinacy, miserliness, orderliness, etc.

(iii) The Phallic Stage

During this stage (from 3 years to 5 or 8 years), the genital region comes to be of absorbing interest for the child. The child gets pleasure by playing, handling or manipulating the genital organ. But there are restrictions and frustrations from the social environment. The child is also subject to harsher disciplines during this stage. The child may adjust himself adequately to social demands, or he may react by first intensifying and then repressing the particular activity leading to fixation of sex energy. Fixation of sex energy at this stage appears later in the form of self-love, exhibitionism, exposing the naked body to others, or looking at that of another person.

The Oedipus Complex and the Electra Complex: During the oral and the anal stages, the child's sex-energy was auto-erotic. In other words, the baby's sex urges were directed to his own body, rather than to any external object or person. But during the phallic stage, the sex energy begins to form some attachments. The first major attachment will be to the person, who takes care of the child's needs. That person is the mother. That is why young children love their mother most. Gradually the boy comes to have more and more attitude of possessiveness towards his mother and a strong resentment towards his father. The boy not only identifies himself with the father but also considers the father as rival for the mother's love. This love of the boy for the mother and resentment against the father is known as *Oedipus Complex*. The girl's reaction is somewhat different. She identifies herself with the mother and considers the mother as a rival to the father's love. This love of the girl for the father and her resentment against the mother is called *Electra Complex*. Oedipus complex and Electra complex appear after children identify their genital organ as similar to some others and different from some others.

Actually Oedipus complex and Electra complex do not appear in all cultures and societies. Oedipus complex or Electra complex may appear in the form of hostility against authority figures, but there is no sexual motive or competition between the children and the parents. Freud was criticized by later psychologists for his over emphasis on sex motive in explaining all behaviours.

Freud found that when the child does not find suitable subjects or persons for his love attachments, his love is directed into his own self. Self-love or narcissism is the result of directing the sex urge inward or to oneself. However, all this changes when the child reaches the next stage of development.

(iv) The Latency Period

Freud believes that during the latency period (between 6 and 12 years) the child's interest in sex becomes less active. The child seems to enjoy with members of his own sex rather than those of the opposite sex. Freud calls this homosexual stage. This is the stage when schooling begins. Thus, the child spends most of his time with peers of the same sex.

(v) The Genital Period

The oral, the anal, the phallic and the latency period taken together constitute the *pregenital* period. From the age of 11 or 12, the genital period begins and continues throughout the period of maturity. Although children feel safe in the company of friends of the same sex, heterosexual interests begin to develop in this period. Boys and girls take interest in opposite sex. True adult sexuality is characteristic of the later part of this period when sex urge becomes intense.

Freud gave much stress on the sex drive as the primary motivators for behaviour. Although he recognised the importance of early experiences in the child's later development, his explanation was biologically-oriented. Social interaction processes received very little consideration in his theory. It was Erik Erikson, a neo-Freudian, who expanded Freud's theory and advocated for certain stages of psychosocial developments.

Views of Adler and Jung

Alfred Adler and Carl Jung were the two outstanding associates of Freud who later differed from him on certain fundamental issues. Adler formed his 'Individual Psychology,' and Jung formed his 'Analytic Psychology.'

Adler does not deny the importance of sex impulse but he holds that sex impulse has not such a comprehensive importance in the child's life as Freud thinks. The mastery motive or self-assertive motive is the dominant motive of life. It is more thwarted by the social environment than the sex impulse. Inferiority complex or the feeling of inferiority is the cause of neurosis. According to Adler, in order to overcome the inferiority complex, the individual develops a life-style which determines the course of his future life. The unconscious inferiority complex and striving for power or will for power are complementary to each other and constitute a whole dynamic personality. Adler holds that dreams are not direct or symbolic fulfillments of old sex wishes. Dreams relate to the future rather than to the past. They are a sort of rehearsal of some important action to be performed in reality. They reveal the individual's style of life as to the approaching crisis. For Adler, the conscious and the unconscious are not separate and antagonistic entities in the individual. They are bound together as having the same desires and tendencies. For example, the unconscious inferiority complex and the conscious will-for-power constitute a dynamic unity. Unconscious is actually that part of our conscious which we have not understood and conscious is that which we have understood. Conscious helps in our progress and unconscious disturbs and obstructs. Like Freud, Adler also recognised the critical factors in the development of child's character structure. But he ignored the sex impulse in favour of interpersonal relationship during childhood as the main factor for the development of character structure.

Jung's major point of disagreement with Freud was over the nature of the libido. For Freud libido means the sex desire. For Jung libido means the life-urge. His concept of libido includes Freud's concept of sex, Adler's concept of will-for-power and in addition, a will to live. At first, it is manifested as life-urge, then as will-for-power and at last as sex desire.

Jung recognised two kinds of unconscious: the *personal unconscious* and the *collective unconscious*. The personal unconscious contains the individual's desires, emotions and impulses repressed in childhood, faint impressions of his past experience, subliminal sense impressions and unrealised potentialities. The collective unconscious contains the individual's primitive, symbolical, animistic, mythical ways of thinking and the primitive ways of behaving inherited from earlier generations. The contents of the personal unconscious can be made conscious by the removal of repression, but those of the collective unconscious cannot be made conscious.

Jung recognised two types of personality — *introverted and extroverted personalities* — which Freud did not admit. Jung holds that dreams indicate the patient's unconscious attitude towards his present problem. Dream analysis gives him an understanding of his present state as well as of the infantile past, and integrates his past experiences with his present experience.

Jung's theory of neurosis is different from that of Freud and Adler. According to him, neurosis is a present inadequate adjustment to the social environment. It is a poor attempt at a new synthesis. Merely unearthing past causes is the preliminary stage in the treatment. It cannot cure neurosis as Freud thinks. The neurosis can be cured by the psychoanalyst helping the patient along this new synthesis.

Educational Implications: Psychoanalysis does not have any direct implication for classroom learning. Psychoanalysis primarily developed as a method of treatment of neurotic patients. Later on, extension and application of psychoanalytic concepts and techniques in other areas of human behaviour appeared. A teacher is not expected to treat neurotic patients in his school nor to interpret the dreams of his students. A psychotherapist does that and a teacher is certainly not a therapist. Whenever a teacher encounters neurotic children, it is better for him to refer the cases to a therapist. But a teacher can do a lot to facilitate smooth functioning of children's personality:

(i) Psychoanalysis has emphasized the early years of life as critical for children's personality development. This implies that the early school years, especially the pre-school years and the elementary school years must be made as enjoyable and as productive as possible.

(ii) There must be healthy interpersonal relationship between teachers and students to ensure the development of a healthy lifestyle and to guard against children becoming neurotic.

(iii) The phenomenon of repression and the concept of unconscious have also implication for the teacher. If unpleasant experiences precede or follow the learning trial then children forget the learnt materials. In fact, any situation which is surrounded by painful experiences leads to motivated forgetting. Thus, in order to avoid that, learning situation must be followed by satisfying consequences.

(iv) Every behaviour has a cause, meaning and a significance. When a student misbehaves or if his behaviour does not come to the expected standard then it is proper to analyse the cause of such misbehaviour or failure than to punish him. Punishment for misbehaviour without due regard to its causes does more harm than good to the child.

(v) The unconscious inferiority complex and the conscious will-for-power constitute one dynamic unity. Teachers must provide such opportunities, activities and experiences in school so that the child will be able to satisfy his self-assertive motive.

(vi) Unhealthy comparison between one child and another should not be made in the school, as that will result in feeling of inferiority among the poor or unsuccessful students. Each child must be given the opportunity of achieving success in some field so that his assertive motive can be satisfied.

2. BEHAVIOURISM

What is Behaviourism?

Behaviourism refers to a group of psychologists who emphasize the objective study. Objective study of behaviour or psychological problems is less concerned with or ignores conscious processes. As a school of psychology, it developed as a reaction against structuralism and functionalism in America. J.B. Waston was the founder of this school. Around the year 1930, new forms of behaviourism emerged with new names coming into view. These later behaviourists were E.C. Tolman, C.L. Hull, E.R. Guthrie and B.F. Skinner.

Chief Features of the School

Emphasis on the Observable Behaviour

For behaviourists like Watson, psychology is the science of behaviour. By behaviour they mean the overt or observable behaviour only. They believe that anything that cannot be observed cannot be studied objectively. In the words of Waston, "Behavioural acts are to be described objectively in terms of stimulus and response, habit integration and the like." The aim of psychology is "given the stimulus to be able to predict the response and given the response to be able to predict the antecedent stimulus."

Opposed to Consciousness

Watson was not satisfied with the state of affairs in contemporary psychology. Contemporary psychologists defined psychology as the science of consciousness. This appeared absurd to Watson. He wanted to make psychology objective and thus for him mentalistic concepts such as mind, consciousness, image and the like had no place in an objective science. He was opposed to such mentalistic concepts — anything intangible and unapproachable.

According to Watson, "The existence of consciousness is a plain assumption. It cannot be proved by any scientific test. Even if it exists, it cannot be studied scientifically. If psychology is ever to become a science, it must follow the example of physical science; it must become materialistic, mechanistic and objective." With this purpose in mind, he discarded all references to consciousness.

Opposed to Introspection

The structuralists and the functionalists adopted the method of introspection which Watson found unsatisfactory. The introspective study of conscious process was subjective and resulted in disagreement and confusion. Again where introspection failed to obtain reliable results, the blame was misplaced on the observer. Watson argued that the fault was in reality with the method. Introspective study of conscious process could not be successfully employed by the structuralists and the functionalists in the study of animal behaviours. But Watson was more interested in animal behaviour. Watson's stand in this respect was acceptable to other early behaviourists.

Methods of Study

The methods proposed by Watson were four in number, such as:

(a) Observation Method,
(b) The Conditioned Reflex Method,
(c) The Verbal Report Method, and
(d) The Testing Method.

Observation is fundamental to all procedures, and scientific observation may be made either with or without instruments. When a behaviourist uses tests he regards them simply as measures of behaviour of the subject's responses, verbal or otherwise, to the objective situations that the tests present. Watson's conditioned reflex method was taken over from the Russian psychologist I.P. Pavolv. But he was largely responsible for its subsequent widespread usage in American psychological research. The verbal report method as propounded by Watson is also of special interest. Although Watson threw away the introspective study, his verbal report by the subjects was a kind of introspection. The only reason following verbal report in the laboratory is expediency. But critics point out that verbal report is not a behaviouristic method.

Emphasis on Environment

Watsonian behaviourism believes in environmentalism. Watson denied the existence of instincts, native intelligence, special abilities and gifts or talents. He emphatically denied that the human being is equipped with mental traits or has inherited instincts. It has inherited only its bodily structures and their modes of functioning. What we ordinarily call instincts or gifts or native abilities are really the results of environmental influence and training. It is in this connection that he made his much quoted statement, "Give him a dozen of healthy infants well-formed and my own specialised world to bring them up in and I will guarantee to take any one at random and train him to become any type of specialist... regardless of his talents, abilities and tendencies". Although this statement indicates his extreme environmentalism, it emphasizes the importance of infancy and early childhood as the most important formative period in human life.

In line with the behaviouristic aims and methods, Watson and his followers conducted experiments on different aspects of psychology and studied different segments of animal and human behaviour.

Sensation

In his earlier theory, Watson devoted considerable time in the study of sensory process. But he had to face certain methodological problems at the outset in his study of sensation in animals. According to him, since we cannot assume consciousness in animals we have no right to say that they see, hear or smell. But they demonstrably make motor responses to visual, auditory, and olfactory stimuli. Thus he avoided the word sensation and used such expressions as response to light, auditory response, olfactory response, etc. In studying the sensory capacities in animals, behaviourists must study the motor responses to different stimuli. For example, if the psychologist is interested in determining whether a certain animal can discriminate red from blue, he must arrange the experimental conditions in such a way that the animal can respond differentially to the two colours. Moreover, the animals must be motivated to learn discrimination either by reward for correct responses or punishment for incorrect responses.

Perception

Watson never used the term perception. Perception involves interpretation of meanings of sensory signs. To him, concepts such as meaning, perception, images are mentalistic and consequently unworthy of a scientific psychology. Watson and his followers were primarily interested in stimulus-response and learning. Because of their preoccupation with other aspects of psychology, they failed to make significant contributions in the field of perception.

Thinking

Watson's views on thinking are the most famous, challenging and controversial of all his doctrines. Watson believed in the peripheral theory of thinking as opposed to the centralist's theory of thinking. The centralists contend that thinking is exclusively a cerebral affair, *i.e.*, the function of the brain. But the peripheralists consider thinking to be a function of the body as a whole. It has been demonstrated without doubt that we do think with our entire body and not with our brains alone. The muscles of the arms, legs and trunk are in constant tension but during mental activity the tensions are increased — especially in those muscles, which are closely associated with the contents of the thought process. For example, if an individual imagines lifting a weight, strong bursts of action potentials can be recorded from his arms even though the limbs are apparently quiescent.

Watson and other behaviourists hold that thinking is not a mental process, and that it is identical with implicit speech movements or sub-vocal talking. We talk to ourselves, more or less while thinking. A child may talk about what he is doing or he may whisper to himself or talk silently. The implicit behaviour patterns or silent speech consist mostly of minute speech movements and gestures. Even in case of deaf and mute persons also, implicit speech movement, gestures and hand movements are noticed during the time of thinking. These implicit movements can be recorded by sensitive instruments. According to Watson, the better is the instrument, the more accurate will be the recording. Thus, according to him, when an individual thinks, minute changes or action currents are produced in the nerves, muscles and the body parts and more particularly in the larynx which is the organ of thought. Those action currents can be recorded by some sensitive apparatus. In case of individuals whose larynx had been surgically removed but who are still able to think, movements in the mouth and the tongue can be recorded.

Watson recognised the close relationship between thought and language and reduced thinking to laryngeal habits. Laryngeal habits are developed in early childhood out of vocalizations which all infants display during the first year of life. Through conditioning, such vocalization becomes words. For example, the child's 'da da' is attached to his father by conditioning and through selective reinforcement eventually becomes 'daddy.' As the child's verbal habits grow stronger, he no longer needs to speak the word 'daddy' but may simply think it when he sees his parent.

Learning

Watson's theory of learning belongs with the older associationism. It has something in common with Thorndike's connectionism and Pavolv's conditioning. But the later behaviourists like Tolman, Hull, Skinner and Guthrie differed from Watsonian learning theory.

Watson believed in the law of regency and frequency and the law of exercise advocated by Thorndike. But he discarded Thorndike's law of effect. Later Watson believed that all learning was conditioning. Through the technique of conditioning he was able to develop fear in a child.

Views of Tolman on Learning

Tolman also rejected the law of effect. He even differed from Watson when the latter maintained that behavioural acts should be described in terms of S-R. He introduced a new concept, intervening variable to explain learning. Thus, in place of S-R, he introduced S-O-R. According to him, certain processes intervene in between the stimulus (the independent variable) and the response (the dependent variable). What goes on in between the S and R is the intervening variable. Some of these intervening variables are demands, expectations, knowledge of the means and ends, readiness, and motivational state of the organism.

Views of Hull on Learning

Like Tolman, Hull also introduced similar intervening variables in between the independent variables and the dependent variables. He called these independent variables antecedent conditions or 'A factors' and the dependent variable 'R factor.' The intervening variables are also known as organism variables. Thus, his formula became A-O-R. In it elementary form, the total learning process is as follows.

A stimulus (S) acts upon the organism. The organism has a potential for reaction (SER). If the reaction reduces the drive (D), reinforcement (G) takes places. Reinforcement leads to a habit (SHR). If the reaction is not reinforced it is extinguished. Drive reduction and reinforcement are central concepts in his theory. Thus the tendency to react (SER) depends upon the drive (D) and habit strength (SHR) in terms of formula (SER) = D × SHR. Later on, Hull recognised the fact that the reaction potential is not constant always but varies from moment to moment depending upon the intensity of the stimulus (V), incentives (K) and the like. Thus, he revised his formula as SER = D × V × K × SHR.

Views of Guthrie on Learning

Guthrie was entirely different from Watson, Tolman, and Hull. But his theory follows the tradition of behaviourism. He rejected Thorndike's law of effect and even the old law of frequency. According to him, if a stimulus once elicits a response, this S-R association is established to the maximum in the first association itself. If the same stimulus recurs, it will again elicit the same response. Thus, learning is complete in one single trial. But gradual improvement is possible with practice or repetition. In different trials, the stimulus pattern is not identical. In one trial a particular movement gets conditioned to a particular stimulus. In another trial, due to change of situation, another movement may become conditioned. For example, in the basket ball game, the skill of getting the ball into the basket implies many acts and depends on many muscular movements under many circumstances. One movement may be learned in one trial and other movement in another trial, so that all the movements require practice in different situations sometimes near the basket, sometimes at a distance and so on.

If a stimulus, which was previously associated with a given response, accompanies with another incompatible response then this previous association is completely eliminated. Learning of incompatible responses leads to forgetting of previous responses. Guthrie's introduction of the concept of incompatible responses suggests the way to break bad habits and to form new habits. In forming habit or strengthening it, the same stimulus pattern should be associated with the desirable response. For breaking habits, Guthrie suggested three ways:

1. to change the stimulus situation;
2. to repeat the stimuli so that the original response is fatigued and the new response is associated with it, and
3. to introduce the stimulus when other aspects of the situation exhibit the undesirable response. For example, while training the dog not to eat chickens, a dead chicken may be tied around its neck so that on struggling to get rid of the same, the dog develops aversion to the chicken.

However, Guthrie recognised the importance of motives and intentions of the organism in the learning situation.

Views of Skinner on Learning

Skinner conducted series of experiments on rats, pigeons, and later on children to understand and explain behaviour or learning. But he did not recognize any intervening variable of Tolman or Hull. He followed the line of conditioning. But he favoured a special variety of conditioning known as operant conditioning or "Type-R conditioning" which was different from classical Pavlovian conditioning or "Type-S conditioning" as Skinner called it.

He emphasized the R-factors, or operant behaviour — as he called it. He believed that the organism has a tendency to act in a particular manner spontaneously in a problem situation. When a spontaneous behaviour or an operant is followed by reinforcement, *i.e.,* food, that behaviour is strengthened. Thus in Pavlovian conditioning, reinforcement is necessary to elicit a response. But in Skinner's operant conditioning, reinforcement is necessary to strengthen a response. However, Skinner recognised the importance of schedules of reinforcement (such as continuous or intermittent reinforcement), time of reinforcement (such as delayed reinforcement or immediate reinforcement) and type of reinforcement (such as positive or negative reinforcement) in learning. Skinner developed a special box known as "Skinner's Box" to conduct his experiments in learning by rats. He developed a special technique known as programmed learning or programmed instruction to understand and explain human learning. His programmed learning techniques have received wide recognition by psychologists in various parts of the world.

Feelings and Emotions

Watson was biologically and psychologically oriented in his study of feelings and emotions. He believed that feelings and emotions are not mental affairs but true sensorimotor phenomena. In case of feeling of pleasantness, sensory feelings come through sex organs or other erogenous zones and go out to muscles through motor impulses. The reverse is the condition in unpleasantness.

So far as emotions are concerned, Watson was definitely against the earlier centralistic theories like the James-Lange's theory. According to James-Lange's theory, when there is danger, perception of danger directly causes the bodily changes. The mass of such bodily sensations is the emotion as we experience it. But according to Watson, there is nothing like perception of situation. The presence of danger causes bodily changes. There are changes in the whole of the body at the time of emotions. But these changes are more prominent in the glandular and visceral systems. Each separate emotion leads to a particular pattern of such changes. There are many covert and overt expressions of these emotions such as changes in blood pressure, pulse rate, breathing, etc. There are accompanying facial expressions also.

Watson made pioneering efforts to study the growth and development of emotions among children. According to him, there are only three emotional reactions at birth. These are fear, rage and love. Other emotions are acquired through conditioning. There are appropriate stimuli for those emotions. But other stimuli can be associated with these emotional reactions by conditioning. Watson was able to develop fear in an infant for a harsh noise by conditioning.

Contribution of Behaviourism to Development of Modern Psychology and Education

Behaviourism had a great popular influence from the very beginning. But it has been criticised a lot:

(i) Some critics point out that Watson was not the first man to define psychology as the science of behaviour. The ground was well-prepared for him by contemporary psychologists like McKeen Cattell, William McDougall and Walter Bewers Pillsbury. The novelty with Watson lay with the methods of studying behaviour.

(ii) Watsonian behaviourism took a wrong view of psychology. Psychology cannot be the science of overt behaviour only. Behaviour is an expression of experience. Experience is known by introspection. Thus psychology cannot dispense with introspection. Psychology should be a science of both experience and behaviour of the organism.

(iii) Watson was an extreme environmentalist. There was little room for heredity in his school. But in reality, hereditary endowments cannot be ignored. A large number of researches conducted so far have proved the impact of nature on different mental capacities.

(iv) Watson regarded all behaviour as sensori-motor phenomena. He wanted to study human beings as machines. Thus his approach is mechanistic and materialistic. His explanations of perception and memory are absurd.

(v) Watson is not noted for any outstanding or specific discoveries in sensation. Whatever experiments he conducted were all in the field of animal sensation. Thus his chief contributions were in the direction of broadening the methodology and scope of sensory psychology.

(vi) Watson believed in the peripheral theory of thinking and opposed the centralist's theory. But the contemporary psychologists are inclined to take a middle ground on this issue. They recognise that both cortical and peripheral processes are involved in ideational activity. Moreover, he identified thinking with speech. But some psychologists did not agree with this. They point out that thinking is sometimes carried on without language. For example, in extempore speech our thinking runs ahead of the speech. Sometimes we read a passage without understanding a single syllable. Here thinking and reading do not go together. Sometimes we find difficulty in finding out a word required to express a meaning which we certainly have in the mind. All this indicates that thinking is not identical with speech. Even some psychologists failed to notice any implicit speech movements at the time of thinking.

(vii) Watson was also criticized for his analysis of learning. Critics point out that all learning is not conditioning. Human learning is mostly intelligent, rational and by insight. Watson completely ignored motivation. But actually no learning takes place without motivation. Watson emphasized the law of frequency in learning. Critics point out that if the animal learns the acts which occur more frequently then the wrong responses which also occur frequently should have been learned by the animal. But that is not the case. Through a little trial and error, the animal learns the correct responses and abandons the wrong responses. Here also motivation of some sort is necessary.

(viii) Watson's chief contribution lies with his emphasis on objective methods of studying children's behaviour. His interest and success with the observation method, experimental method, testing method and conditioning have provided tremendous inspiration to American psychologists and educators of various countries to use objective methods in the field of education and psychology.

(ix) One of the prominent characteristics of Watsonian behaviourism is its recognition of the importance of the period of infancy. Infancy is important from the standpoint of practical control of behaviour, because it is in infancy that the very foundations of behaviour are established. During this period, the child acquires attitudes and habits which will constitute the core of his personality. The establishment of modern nursery schools and kindergartens and the preparation of children's literature are in line with this attitude.

(x) Behaviourism, particularly the later behaviourism, contributed significantly towards the formation and breaking of habits, and control of defiant behaviour in children. Every action is purposive as Tolman emphasized. It satisfies a need as Hull put it. A habit can be broken with the change in the stimulus situation.

Thus, in breaking bad habits we have to understand the purpose, the need, and the motive and change the environment. These elementary principles are definite contributions of later behaviourists. Principles of behaviour modification are all based on behaviouristic explanation.

(xi) Tolman recognised that the child or the learner is not passive but an active participant in the learning process. Since every behaviour is purposive, the child must be made to understand the real value and purpose of education. The teacher must create a situation to ensure active participation of the child in the educative process.

(xii) Hull's theory threw new light on learning process and curriculum construction. The greatest contribution of Hull to contemporary education is that classroom activity and the curriculum should be related to the needs of children. Today we emphasise the need-based curriculum and learning.

(xiii) Later behaviourists recognised the importance of reinforcement, incentives and motivation in learning. Psychologists and educationists in modern days owe a great deal to them in emphasising the use of incentives and feedback in the teaching of learning processes.

(xvi) Skinner had a special contribution to contemporary educational methodology. His programmed instruction has received wide recognition all over the world by all educationists.

(xv) Previously it was believed that a child will develop in the direction determined by his heredity and that the efforts by teachers and parents matter very little. But with the advent of behaviourism, environment has been recognized as an important factor for the growth and development of children. Today while not ignoring the hereditary endowment of children, teachers and parents should try to provide a stimulating environment for the child for his maximum development.

3. GESTALT SCHOOL

What is Gestalt Psychology?

Gestalt school developed in Germany around the year 1912 under the leadership of Max Wertheimer, Kurt Koffka and Wolfgang Kohler. It developed as a revolt against structuralism and associationism. But when it gained momentum it also protested against Watsonian behaviourism. It must be noted here that both behaviourism and Gestalt psychology developed about the same time in two different countries, but neither party had any knowledge of the other's development. When the literature came out, they found their system opposed to the other's system. This anti-analytic, anti-structuralistic, and anti-behaviouristic school had its inception as a result of Wertheimer's interest in the 'phi-phenomenon', an illusion of movement. Wertheimer was interested in the perception of movement and he conducted a large number of experiments on 'phi-phenomenon.' In one such experiment he exposed a vertical line followed by a horizontal line with a very short interval, say 1/15 of the second (1_). The subjects should have perceived them as two different lines exposed one after the other. But they perceived only one line swinging around through (1_).

The word "Gestalt" is a German word which means form or configuration. The Gestalt psychology is sometimes called configuration psychology.

Salient Features and Areas of Study

The salient features and areas of study which distinguish Gestalt school from the behaviouristic school are as follows:

Both behaviourism and Gestalt school revolted against the analytic psychology, but they revolted in different ways.

(i) Behaviourism abandoned the study of conscious experiences. It confined itself to the study of overt behaviour only. But Gestalt psychology proposed to continue the study of experiences. According to its founders, excellent psychological data can be obtained from direct experiences. Experience is an important object of study in psychology. Thus Gestalt psychology aimed at studying both overt behaviour and experiences.

(ii) Behaviourism opposed the anlysis of the structure of conscious into its component elements. It emphasized the association of stimulus and response in behaviour. It reduced behaviour to S-R units. It was reductionistic and mechanistic. Gestalt psychology was opposed to analysis altogether. It was opposed to reductionism, elementalism, and the so-called brick-mortar psychology. According to this school, every experience carries with it a quality of wholeness. The whole dominates over its parts.

(iii) Behaviourism rejected introspection as a method of investigation. But Gestalt psychologists did not reject introspection altogether. They favoured phenomenological introspection.

(iv) Behaviourism rejects sensation because of methodological difficulties in studying sensory process. Gestalt psychology rejected sensation because sensations are atoms or elements of experiences.

(v) Behaviourists ignored the study of perception. But study of perception was the very heart of Gestalt psychology. Perhaps no other school contributed so much to the study of perception as the Gestalt school.

(vi) The analysis of behaviour by behaviourists is a molecular one. But the explanation of behaviour by Gestalt psychologists is a molar one. Molecular behaviour occurs in the organism in a given geographical environment. But according to Gestalt psychologists, behaviour occurs in a given geographical environment which is regulated by behavioural environment. They, therefore, differentiated between geographical environment and the behavioural environment. The environment as it exists in reality is the geographical environment. But the environment as perceived by the individual is the behavioural environment.

(vii) Watson's behaviourism reduced thinking to laryngeal habits. Watson identified thought with implicit speech movements. He interpreted thinking in the light of peripheral theory and psychological orientation. But Gestalt psychology discarded Watsonian explanation of the thought process. Gestalt psychologists presented a psychological approach to the study of the thought process. Gestalt psychologists were opposed to the association theory of thinking or piecemeal thinking. They insisted on the fact that when confronted with a problem, the individual must understand the essential structure of the whole situation and make an appropriate response. The individual must be able to organise or reorganise the materials so as to produce some results. These psychologists favour productive thinking.

Perception

For structuralists and functionalists like Wundt and Titchner, perception was a crucial problem. Watson, in keeping with his strict behaviourism, ignored perception. But the Gestalt psychologists want to make the study of the perceptual process the very heart of their system.

There is a general agreement among contemporary psychologists that the Gestalt school exerted a greater influence of the evolution of modern perceptual psychology than any other group. The leaders of the school devoted a great deal of their research efforts to the field of perception. This must not be taken as an implication that the Gestalt psychologists have failed to make significant contributions to other areas. Rather it means that the school's most significant and characteristic contributions were in the field of perception.

Gestalt psychology is form psychology. According to its proponents, our perceptual experiences arise as Gestalten or molar configurations which are not mere aggregations of sensations but organised and meaningful wholes. Gestalt psychologists apply the total approach as opposed to the part approach and say that individuals perceive objects as 'wholes' and not part by part. The whole approach provides meaningful perception because the whole is greater than the sum of its parts. For example, when we perceive a table we perceive it as a molar object, not a collection of colour patches, four legs, nuts, bolts and the like. After innumerable experiments on perception, these psychologists were able to formulate certain laws which govern the organisation of perception. These laws are: (a) the law of proximity, (b) the law of similarity, (c) the law of closure, (d) the law of good figure, (e) the law of continuation, and (f) the principle of figure and ground. However, the school's challenge in the area of perception was so successful that the Gestalt principles are now widely recognised as fundamental.

Learning

The Gestalt psychologists evidenced little interest in learning and made few significant contributions to learning theory. The school's chief interest was in the field of perception and learning remained a subordinate issue. Moreover Gestalt psychology from its very inception was antagonistic to the Thorndikian and Watsonian types of analysis of learning. The members of the school considered that one of their major contributions to psychology was the attack on associationistic theory or S.R. theory of learning.

The Gestalt psychologists did a number of experiments on chimpanzees, human infants and other animals to understand the phenomenon of learning. Through their experiments they demonstrated that animals and human beings learn not by trial and error or conditioning but by insight. We can discuss here some of the characteristics of insightful learning:

(i) Insight refers to the sudden, immediate, repeatable and transposable behaviour. It involves perception of the problem from different perspectives, so that the solution comes in a 'flash' all at once. Insight was originally defined as sudden reorganization of the perceptual process. This is possible only when the subject is aware of the relationship among various parts of the problem. According to English and English (1958), this suddenness of insight is not always necessary. It depends upon the problem and the way it is presented.

(ii) Prior experience with the various parts of the problem is useful in putting the various parts into a meaningful pattern.

(iii) Insightful solutions can be facilitated through imitation, verbalisation, demonstration and instruction.

(iv) Insight is possible only when the learning situation is purposive, goal-directed, and meaningful.

(v) Once the problem is solved by insight, subsequent behaviour shows immediacy and smoothness.

(vi) Once the problem is solved by insight, the subject is able to repeat solutions without error on successive presentation of original problems.

(vii) Once the problem is solved by insight, there is a high degree of transfer to similar problems.

(viii) Insight is not completely a human capacity. But it is related to the animal's intelligence.

Educational Implications

The Gestalt movement has significant implications for educational theory and practice:

(i) Whereas the earlier psychologists emphasized "what does a child do?" Gestalt psychologists emphasized "what does a child understand?" Traditional teachers gave importance to rote learning, learning by drill or repetition. But Gestalt psychologists accept learning by understanding. This understanding in learning facilitates retention and transfer.

(ii) The views of Gestalt psychologists imply that the teacher must present the material in such a way that children can perceive the relationships among various aspects of the problem. The teacher must try to develop problem-solving attitude among them.

(iii) If we accept that one of the ultimate objectives of education is to help children solve problems, then to permit children to operate at the mere trial and error stage would be extremely wasteful. They must be encouraged to develop insight into the problem. Of course, there are areas in education where insightful learning cannot take place. As R.M. Gagne (1970) says, "A child cannot learn the names of plants or stars in an insightful manner. He cannot learn to read by insight. A child cannot learn a foreign language by insight. A student of Biology does not learn the structure and functions of animals by insight. In short, insight cannot be prototype for a vast amount of learning that human beings ordinarily undertake."

(iv) Insightful learning is also not suitable for the teaching of literature, particularly reading.

(v) In the classroom, the teacher must ensure that children's past experience is known and utilised. The child must be encouraged to recall all the relevant information he has previously learnt and apply it to a new situation when required. Then he will be able to correlate these units of knowledge to one another and to apply them to the new principle he is attempting to understand. In order to facilitate these processes, some verbal instruction and demonstration by the teacher are essential.

(vi) Learning materials must be purposive and meaningful. School learning must be related to the daily life and living of the child so as to ensure maximum transfer. Learning situations must be properly structured and graded according to the intellectual development of the learner.

(vii) The teacher must encourage productive thinking as opposed to piecemeal thinking. The 'whole approach' must be adopted in solving problems. This whole approach will also prove beneficial in understanding the child. In other words, the teacher must try to understand the whole situation that might have led to the occurrence of a particular behaviour. This also implies that the whole child must be understood to plan the curriculum, instructional strategies, educational objectives, and outcomes.

4. LEWIN'S FIELD THEORY

Lewin may be considered as a member of the Gestalt school or as the founder of a separate system. But neither characterization is correct if taken literally, because Lewin's system is Gestalt-like in its orientation, yet at the same time differs strikingly from the orthodox Gestalt psychology in its emphasis on needs, will, personality and social factors. The founder of the Gestalt school stressed the study of perception and, to a lesser degree, learning. Lewin's orientation, on the other hand, is towards psychology as a social science. Lewin and his associates have emphasised the study of behaviour as a function of the total social and physical situation. Much of their research was carried out on children.

For Lewin, the aim of psychologists is to develop laws by means of which they can predict individual cases. Earlier psychologists tended to evolve laws basing on the statistical averages of the frequency with which a behaviour occurs in a given condition. Lewin says, "The proof of a law depends upon the purity of the case and not necessarily upon the frequency with which it occurs." Lewin's argument holds that psychological laws need not be formulated solely on the basis of statistical averages. Rather the individual case is equally important. Even if all general psychological laws are known, we still need to understand the concrete individual and the total situation in which that individual exits before we make any prediction about his behaviour. Thus Lewin favours a psychology in which the focus is on the individual as opposed to a system where the emphasis is on the statistical average. Lewin reduces his thesis to the formula:

$$B = f(P.E.),$$

where:

B, represents behaviour
P, the person
E, the total environment and f, function.

Fundamental Concepts

Lewin's system leans heavily on concepts derived from topology (a branch of higher mathematics), vector analysis (the mathematics of directed lines), and physics from which he borrowed such concepts as valence, equilibrium, field force and others. He used innumerable diagrams, signs, etc. and for this purpose it is said that Lewin's system grew out of his blackboard writings. Lewin has used two types of concepts such as structural concepts and the dynamic concepts.

Structural Concepts: Life Space

Lewin's system centres around his structural concept — the life space. Life space refers to the totality of all possible events that influence a person's behaviour. Life space has three aspects — a past, a present, and a future. Psychologically, each of these three aspects of life determines behaviour in a given situation. In other words, a person's behaviour is the function of his life space.

$$B = f\,(L.S.)$$

where:

B, means behaviour

f, means function, and

L.S., means life space of the person.

The goal directed individual looks to the future and is influenced in his present behaviour by the future life space towards which he is striving. The past, of course, influences the individual in terms of his experiences of success and failure, attitudes, etc., which are important in determining present goals, methods of approach to goals and reactions to failure. Sometimes the individual's life space may be entirely in the past as, for example, when he is thinking about his childhood. If he is imagining the pleasure of tomorrow's picnic, his life space is in the future. As the individual gradually matures and advances in age and experiences, differentiation of the life space takes place. The life space of the new-born infant is not well-differentiated. On the contrary, the highly educated and imaginative adult shows a well-differentiated life space.

Dynamic Concepts

Lewin's dynamic concepts deal with the motivational aspects of the system. The fundamental dynamic concepts are need, tension, valence, vector, barrier and equilibrium.

Need is Lewin's concept for any motivational state which can be brought about by a physiological condition, the desire for an environmental object or an intention to reach a goal. When a need arises, there is a state of tension. Tensions are emotional states which accompany needs.

Objects may have either positive valence or negative valence. Objects which are attractive and which satisfy needs have positive valence. Usually positive valence is indicated by a plus sign (+). Objects which threaten the individual or are repellent have negative valence. Negative valence is indicated by a minus sign (-). The same object may have positive valence for one individual and negative valence for another. Thus the valence of an object depends upon the individual's perception of the object as attractive or repellent. For example, sweets have positive valence for a young baby. To a diabetic patient, sweets have negative valence. Similarly, to a hungry child, an apple has positive valence. To a child who is experiencing the ill-effects of having eaten half a dozen green apples, the apple has negative valence.

Mathematically, a vector is a directed line. Lewin borrowed the concept to represent the direction and strength of attraction of objects. If only one vector impinges upon the individual, he will move in the direction indicated by the vector. If two or more vectors are impelling him in different directions, the effective movement will be resultant of all the forces. If two equally balanced vectors are operating, the result is a conflict. There are various types of conflict situations depending upon the valence and vector. The reader may refer to Chapter 20 of this book to understand the various types of conflicts.

The individual sometimes encounters barriers on his way to reach the goal. Barriers may be objects, people, and social codes — anything which thwarts the motivated individual as he is moving towards a goal. If the individual can overcome the barrier, he reaches the goal and the need is satisfied. If he fails to overcome the barrier, he experiences frustration. Thus the arousal of needs leads to a state of disequilibrium. The ultimate goal of all motivated behaviour is to return to a state of equilibrium in which the individual obtains relief from tension.

Learning and Group Dynamics

Lewin was influenced by Gestalt psychologists in his analysis of learning phenomenon. He was, therefore, opposed to S-R theories of learning. According to him, learning is a process of perceptual reorganization. As the child's perception undergoes change, learning occurs and the child is able to distinguish between reality and unreality. Like Gestalt psychologists, Lewin also explains learning in terms of insight.

Lewin applies the fundamental concept of his system — the life space — to the phenomenon of learning. He says that a child's life space has different regions. As the child moves from one region of the life space to another, the structure of the life space undergoes change. Due to this locomotion, restructuring or reorganisation of the life space takes place. Certain regions which have been connected are separated and certain regions which have been separated are connected. Learning involves differentiating and restructuring of the regions of the life space.

Learning involves a change in the cognitive structure. Changes in the cognitive structure are caused by forces in the psychological field like needs, aspirations, and valences. According to Lewin, learning results from a change in motivation. Change in motivation is caused by change in needs and the means of their satisfaction. Learning causes a change in valence of objects and attitude of the learner. Due to learning, an object which had negative valence earlier now acquires positive valence.

According to Lewin, all learning is influenced by the goal a person sets for himself. Level of aspiration is an important factor in learning. One's level of aspiration depends upon his capacities and previous experience of success and failure in reaching the goal. A person may set too low or too high level of aspiration. Too high or too low level of aspiration is detrimental to learning.

Lewin and his associates have conducted several characteristic experiments to explain the application of concepts and techniques of field theory in various areas of human behaviour.

According to the field theory, interrupting a subject in the middle of a task should have the effects of leaving him in a state of tension and disequilibrium. Moreover, the interruption should also serve as a barrier to the goal of completing the task and this should increase the subject's desire to finish the task. Applying this concept, Bluma Zeigarnik conducted an experiment on recall of finished versus unfinished tasks. His findings reveal that subjects recall more unfinished tasks than the finished tasks. Later researches revealed that learning and recall depend upon the interest and ego involvement of subjects in the tasks than on any interruption, tension, or barrier.

Barker, Dembo and Lewin conducted an experiment on effect of frustration on general standards of behaviour of children, like constructiveness of children's play. Their findings reveal that children, who demonstrate greater degree of frustration or disturbance show higher degree of regression or deterioration in their behaviour.

Lewin, Lippitt and White conducted an experiment to determine the effect of democratic and authoritarian atmosphere on the productiveness and general behaviour of small groups of boys. These groups of boys were exposed to various types of atmosphere — democratic, authoritarian and *Laissez Faire*. Their findings reveal that in general the democratic groups tend to be more productive, less demanding of the leader's time, more friendly in their approach to the leader, and less driven by internal dissension within the group. The democratic group's productiveness remains relatively high even when the leader is absent in the group. The authoritarian groups tend to be either more aggressive or apathetic than the democratic groups. The authoritarian group is also characterised by low morale.

Educational Implications

Lewin's system is essentially a theory of motivation and personality. Lewin favours the holistic approach in studying behaviour as propounded by Gestalt psychologists. But on the whole, the theoretical concepts of the field theory have been unimpressive in contrast to the experiments conducted by Lewin and his associates. Lewin also failed to develop a systematic theory of learning. The various implications of field theory to classroom practice are as follows:

(i) Lewin's main thesis that the B=f (P.E.) or that B=f (L.S.) implies that the child's behaviour at a given time is caused by a number of factors operating in the environment and that personal factors like needs, motivation, attitude and level of aspirations contribute significantly to the occurrence of a particular behaviour pattern. Thus in analysing, predicting and control of behaviour, teachers should consider the personal factors and the total situational factors which are responsible for the occurrence of that behaviour. This wholistic approach of Lewin has received much attention and acceptance by contemporary psychologists.

(ii) Since learning has been defined as a process of cognitive reorganisation or restructuring, the teacher should create conditions and opportunities which will facilitate the restructuring of the cognitive structure.

(iii) In motivating children to learn, the teacher should consider their need, the valence of various school subjects, and goal the child has set for himself.

(iv) The teacher should help children set realistic goals or level of aspiration depending upon their capacities and previous experience of success and failure.

(v) Since frustration leads to deterioration of behaviour, the situation surrounding the learning experiences should be such that the child will not experience disturbance or frustration of one type or the other.

(vi) The teacher should not be authoritarian in his approach. Because authoritarian approach of teaching and discipline leads to authoritarian personality syndromes. Democratic approach is better than authoritarian approach. Democratic approach is most desirable for training in leadership and ensuring the morale of the classroom.

5. HORMIC SCHOOL

What is Hormic School?

William McDougall, an Englishman by birth and education, a distinguished student of biology and an eminent psychologist of the past, was the chief exponent of Hormic School of psychology. As a school of psychology, Hormic School considered purpose as the motivating force in all our behaviour.

Purposive behaviour is the same as goal seeking. Purposive acts combine two factors: desire and foresight. We foresee the goal and desire to reach it. But foresight and desire do not always go together. For example, a truck driver may clearly foresee that he is going to dash against a tree without desiring it. Similarly, in some cases, there is a striving without any clear foresight of the goal. Hormic School emphasizes striving in behaviour rather than foresight. It is because of its emphasis on striving that McDougall adopted for his theory the name of hormic psychology.

As a school of psychology, Hormic School stressed the importance of objective observation. McDougall was one of the first few psychologists to define psychology as the science of behaviour. Thus, in line with his thinking McDougall accepted the method of objective observation for scientific study of behaviour. But he did not reject introspection completely. According to him, "If we limit ourselves rigidly to observation we get a mechanical view of an animal's behaviour. Even a human being appears like a machine. But we know our own behaviour from inside and know it to be purposive and not mechanical. Thus, there is no point in forgetting what we know by introspection."

Characteristics of Purposive Behaviour

McDougall cited several objective characteristics of goal seeking behaviour, as follows:

(i) It persists. An activity may start in response to a stimulus but continues after the stimulus has ceased. A rabbit scurrying to its hole after a momentary noise is an example.

(ii) With all the persistence, there is considerable variation of the activity. An obstacle is bypassed and the same goal is reached as if there had been no obstacle.

(iii) The activity terminates when the goal is reached and some other activity takes its place. For example, the cat makes a dash for a tree and up the trunk, but then sits down on a branch and calmly watches the dog.

(iv) The activity improves with repetition. Useless movements are eliminated, the whole performance becomes smoother and quicker with increased practice.

McDougall's criteria of purposive behaviour were later adopted by other behaviourists, particularly by Tolman.

Motives of Behaviour

Behaviour is purposive and goal-directed. What are the goals which animals and human beings seek for? What are the fundamental motives of behaviour which are common to human beings? When McDougall developed his new school, psychology had no specific answer to these questions. The motives of behaviour were explained differently by different groups of economists, anthropologists, and sociologists. Some psychologists also used to explain behaviour in terms of pleasure and pain. McDougall revolted against this existing state of affairs. He put a question and then answered it as follows: Why do we eat? We eat because it gives pleasure. When is eating pleasant? Eating is pleasant only when we are hungry, and have a desire for food. Thus the pleasure depends on the desire. Desire is more fundamental than the pleasure. Thus we must first find the natural desires and goals of men.

According to McDougall, there must be a number of fundamental motives which are natural and hereditary. All other motives must be derived from these natural motives. He called the primary motives by the name of "instincts." An instinct for him was not a mechanical affair like a reflex or chain of reflexes. He regarded an instinct as a complete mental process at the primitive level, capable of analysis into three parts:

1. On the receptive side, it is a predisposition to notice significant stimuli — like food odours when one is hungry;
2. On the executive side, it is a predisposition to make certain movements or to approach a certain goal, and
3. In between is the emotional impulse or striving.

McDougall later preferred to call these motives by the name of propensities. In 1908 McDougall listed twelve major human instincts. By 1932 his list included eighteen propensities as follows:

1. Food-seeking propensity,
2. Disgust propensity,
3. Sex propensity,
4. Fear propensity,
5. Curiosity propensity,
6. Protective or parental propensity,
7. Gregarious propensity,
8. Self-assertive propensity,
9. Submissive propensity,
10. Anger propensity,
11. Appeal propensity,
12. Constructive propensity,
13. Acquisitive propensity,
14. Laughter propensity,
15. Comfort propensity,
16. Rest or sleep propensity,

17. Migratory propensity, and
18. A group of very simple propensities serving bodily needs, such as coughing, sneezing, breathing, and evacuation.

Modification of Instincts

Although instincts or propensities are natural and hereditary in nature, they become modified by learning and experience. Remember the various ways a child expresses his angry impulse. Instincts are modified in two ways: it becomes attached to new stimuli and its mode of expression also varies.

Instincts are also modified in a still different way. The instinctive tendencies become combined into what McDougall called sentiments. They become combined by being attached to the same object. A man's love for a certain woman includes sex desire and also some of the tender, protective tendency called the parental propensity. These two natural tendencies and probably others as well are attached to that one love object and make up the sentiment of love, which is a powerful adult motive. Patriotism is also a sentiment. There is no single instinct of patriotism, but a man's native land becomes the object of several instincts.

According to McDougall, adult human behaviour is not directly motivated by the instincts. Human behaviour is motivated by sentiments which are derived from the instincts. For example, social behaviour is not based on a single social instinct, but on loyalties and interests resulting from the instincts combined into sentiments.

Reactions to the Hormic Psychology

One direct reaction to the Hormic psychology was the creation of social psychology as a branch of psychology in universities and colleges. Psychologists became interested on the themes of social institutions, social organisations and social behaviours and their instinctive aspects. But the sociologists could not accept the doctrine of instincts. According to these social critics, "We behave alike and behave like human beings not because of our instincts, but because of the social environment of the culture." The chief critic of Hormic psychology who emphasized the social environment in explaining human behaviour as against the instincts was L.L. Bernad.

Even psychologists who belong to the behaviouristic school did not accept McDougall's emphasis on innate propensities. Watson and Thorndike emphasized learning. According to them, human behaviour is learned or acquired and in rare cases they are innate.

An impartial view would indicate that some behaviour is innate while others are learned. Thus McDougall's view cannot be completely rejected, although his over-emphasis on native behaviour cannot be accepted unanimously.

Educational Implications

McDougall's theory is very little known and understood by contemporary psychologists. His theory is often considered as old and outdated with very little and no relevance for modern educational theory and practice. It is for this reason that Hormic School does not find a place in psychology and education courses in many universities.

(i) McDougall's emphasis on purposive nature of human behaviour has also been emphasized by other psychologists. This implies that a child's behaviour is motivated. Teachers must understand the fundamental motives — psychological, social and biological motives of behaviour. They must also know how different techniques can influence children's behaviour in the class.

(ii) Teachers should not put more emphasis on hereditary nature of behaviour, ability and/or performances. Behaviour is largely influenced by social environment, social expectations, social demands and opportunities. For example, learning in school depends not so much on innate capacities like intelligence or parental status but on such factors as the quality of instruction, teacher-pupil interaction, help in terms of time and material needed for learning.

(iii) Education should not aim at modification of instincts, as has been emphasized in old definitions of education. Education should aim at developing appropriate sentiments like patriotism among our young children and youth. Instructional materials should be prepared suitably to develop appropriate values and sentiments.

(iv) Opportunities should be provided to children to realize their propensities and to modify them, combine them into sentiments and behave accordingly.

SELECTED QUESTIONS

1. What is psychoanalysis? State its contribution to modern educational theory and practice.
2. Discuss the essential features of behaviourism. What are the educational implications of behaviouristic movement in psychology?
3. Discuss the contribution of Gestalt school to modern educational practice.
4. State the contribution of Gestalt school to learning. What are their educational implications?
5. Differentiate between the behaviouristic school and the Gestalt school.
6. What is field theory? State its contribution to learning theory.
7. Discuss the essential features of Lewin's Field Theory. What are their educational implications?
8. What are the various schools of psychology? Which school do you like the best and why?
9. What is Hormic School? State its contribution to modern educational theory and practice.

4
Growth and Development

1. MEANING OF GROWTH AND DEVELOPMENT

Meaning of Growth

Growth usually indicates physical development like height and weight. It means increase and enlargement of the body or some parts of the body. This also means that the body has become heavier and larger. Growth is a change in the organism which can be observed and measured in quantitative terms.

Meaning of Development

According to Hurlock (1980), the term development means "a progressive series of changes that occur as a result of maturation and experience." Development implies qualitative changes. But all changes in behaviour are not developments. Consider a 3-month-old infant lying quietly in his bed. When he becomes hungry, his behaviour changes: he begins to cry and thrash about. After he is fed, he becomes quiet again. These behavioural changes accompanying hunger and satisfaction are not developments because they are temporary and transient. As Mussen, Conger and Kagan (1979) have pointed out, "The term development is applied to alterations in behaviour or traits that appear to emerge in orderly ways and lasts for a reasonable period of time. Usually, these changes result in new, improved ways of reacting, that is, in behaviour that is more adaptive, healthier, more highly organised, more complex, more stable, more competent or more efficient." In this sense, the term development means more advancement, greater unfoldment, and going forward to greater maturity.

According to Peary London, "Development means the whole sequence of life from conception to death." It is not merely what happens but how it happens — the order of its unfolding, the rules which govern it and the variations and irregularities which separate individuals and cultures and whole species from one another.

In educational terminology, development is often described as psychobiological readiness. According to Ausubel (1969), "Readiness is the adequacy of the student's existing capacity in relation to some instructional objective." For example, reading readiness refers to performance the student must have acquired before he begins to read, the identification of different marks on the printed page as particular letters, the association of these letters into syllables and words, and so on. According to Dececco and Crawford (1975), "Readiness is identical with entering behaviour."

Differences between Growth and Development

Some authorities recognize the following differences between the two terms 'growth' and 'development:'

(i) Growth refers to changes in the particular aspect or aspects of the body. Development, on the other hand, implies the organisation as a whole. Thus, the term 'development' is more comprehensive than the term 'growth.'

(ii) Growth does not continue throughout life. But development means a progressive series of changes in an orderly and coherent pattern till the end of life. A person can develop even after physical growth stops and maturity is reached.

(iii) Usually growth contributes to development, but not always. A child may grow fat and heavier, but this growth may not be accompanied by any development.

(iv) Development may be possible without any significant growth. It is a fact that some children do not grow in size but they do develop ability.

(v) Growth is structural and development is functional. But a structure is of no use apart from its functions and function is a meaningless term without structure. These differences between 'growth' and 'development' are not real. The two terms are very much related and are interchangeable. In this book, these two terms are used to mean the same thing.

2. PRINCIPLES OF GROWTH AND DEVELOPMENT

The foregoing generalizations about the nature of growth and development are necessary for a detailed examination of the process of development.

(i) Development is a Product of Inheritance and Environment

Heredity supplies the potential which is acted upon by a dynamic environment. The child develops by using and interacting with his environment in biologically determined ways. Neither heredity nor environment is the sole factor in the development of a child. Both operate concurrently and co-operatively. Since the heredity of a child cannot be changed, an attempt should be made to provide a simulating environment for the child.

(ii) Development Follows a Pattern

Growth is not random and haphazard but a regular step by step process. Any trait or skill must have its antecedents and, in turn, it forms the foundations for the next level of growth. For example, the baby creeps before he crawls, and crawls before he walks. He walks before he runs, and runs before he dances. Thus the school curriculum must be based on the characteristic developmental patterns of pupils.

(iii) Each Individual has His Own Rate of Growth

Development involves both sameness and variety. Although every individual must have the same type of development at a particular stage or age as others yet there are individual differences in the rate of growth. As for example, some children grow rapidly and some grow slowly. Some reach maturity at an early date and some never become 'adult' in the broad sense of the term. Although there are individual differences in the rate of growth, the growth rate of a person tends to remain constant. A child who is tall for his age at two years will probably be tall as an adult. Individual differences in growth and development must be taken into account while preparing instructional practices for children.

(iv) Growth is Continuous and Gradual

Growth involves both change and continuity. Growth always brings about certain changes in the organism. But these changes do not take place suddenly. It is a continuous process. The principle of continuous and gradual development is worthy of constant attention at all educational levels. Educational achievement, vocational prominence, or mere competence in daily living is not achieved suddenly but they are the result of numerous successive steps. Teachers must know that they cannot expect sudden transformations of personality in their pupils.

(v) Growth Proceeds More Rapidly during Early Years

The child grows more rapidly during early years and slowly during the later years. Growth during early years is so rapid that it is easily noticeable. Various authorities believe that it is in the first five or six or eight years of life that the broad fundamental patterns of behaviour are developed. The idea is erroneous that personality is solidified in these early years and little changes will take place thereafter. It is important to recognise the tendency to make the early school years as enjoyable and productive as possible. Rapid early growth also necessitates concern for the child's health during the early school years. Although children seem to be ceaselessly active, they tire easily because of the immaturity of body tissues and because rapid growth demands large expenditure of energy. Fatigue may result in loss of appetite, low resistance to disease, restlessness, irritability and it contributes to slowness and even difficulty in learning. For these reasons, the child must have balanced programme of rest and activity both in the home and the school.

(vi) Each Part of the Body Develops at a Different Rate at Different Times

All parts of the body do not develop at the same rate and at the same time. For example, the head of the baby is fairly well-developed even at birth. The neural development is fastest in the early years, then the growth is gradually slowed down but there is a spurt again during adolescence. The growth of the genital organs, in contrast, is very slow initially but the rate becomes considerably faster around twelve or thirteen years of age. Thus, different parts of the body have different rates of maturation.

(vii) Rate of Growth of Male Children is Different from that of the Female Children

Girls and boys do not grow at the same rate. Girls are found to mature faster than boys. This is true even from the time of birth. Girls are found to do most of the developmental tasks a little earlier than boys. At certain stages of development, particularly in early adolescence, girls are found to be even taller and heavier than boys. This is because the growth spurt that is characteristic of adolescence occurs earlier for girls and, therefore, at this time they shoot up. Of course, boys catch up with them very fast and soon overtake them.

(viii) All Individuals do not Grow to the Same Extent

There are individual variations in the extent of growth. Some grow to be very tall and others remain short, while the majority are of average height. The average height will again differ from one face to another. There is a great deal of difference between the average height of the Europeans and the average height of the Japanese. Similarly, in mental growth too there are individual differences. Some have high levels of intellectual functioning while others remain at much lower levels.

(ix) There is a Process of Differentiation and Integration in Development

As an infant, the individual's movements are gross. From these movements emerge smaller, finer and more specific patterns of behaviour. These specific patterns are again integrated to form new and complex forms of activity. For example, look at the young child who is learning to eat by himself. He picks up the food with his hands, drops some, smears some all over his face in the process and then whatever remains is taken to the mouth. But as he grows older, it is not necessary for him to put in so much effort. He is able to pick up food by just using his fingers. He is then so dexterous that he does not drop anything. He is even able to converse, and read while he eats. The whole process becomes so integrated that it appears as though he is doing it almost automatically.

3. STAGES OF DEVELOPMENT

Human development takes place through various stages which are as follows:

Infancy (from birth to 3 years)
Pre-school years or
Early childhood (from 3 years to 6 years)
Later childhood (from 6 years to 12 years)
Adolescence (from 12 years to 18/19 years)
(In some case it starts at the age of 9)
Adulthood (from 18 years onwards)

Although each stage is different from the other, growth is not discontinuous. Rather growth and development take place through a continuous process. Each individual passes through these stages of development in his life.

4. DEVELOPMENTAL TASKS

Every individual passes through certain stages of development in his life. With each new stage of development, there are certain tasks — skills, attitudes, understanding — that must be met before a person can move on to a higher level of development. Havighurst (1963) calls these tasks as "developmental tasks." Developmental tasks refer to skills, attitudes, and understandings that occur at or about a certain period in the life of an individual. Successful achievements of these task leads to happiness and to success in later stages. Failure to achieve these tasks leads to unhappiness in the individual, disapproval by the society and difficulty with later tasks.

In a sense, these developmental tasks are the pre-requisite learnings and accomplishments necessary for successful adult living. The developmental tasks are not simply hurdles that must be jumped in some mechanical way. Each developmental task is a personal experience. Parents and teachers have strong influence on children to gain this personal experience of accomplishing each developmental task, resolving each problem successfully, meeting their individual needs in satisfying ways and reaching the next stage of development.

Developmental Tasks at Different Stages

Birth to 6 years

(i) Learning to walk,
(ii) Learning to take solid foods,
(iii) Learning to talk,
(iv) Learning to control the elimination of body wastes,
(v) Learning sex difference and sexual modesty,
(vi) Achieving physiological stability,
(vii) Forming simple concepts of social and physical reality,
(viii) Learning to relate oneself emotionally to parents, siblings and other people.
(ix) Learning to distinguish right and wrong and developing a conscience.

6 to 12 years

(i) Learning physical skills necessary for ordinary games.
(ii) Building wholesome attitudes towards oneself as a growing organism.
(iii) Learning to get along with age-mates.
(iv) Learning an appropriate masculine or feminine role.
(v) Developing fundamental skills in reading, writing and calculating.
(vi) Developing concepts necessary for everyday living.
(vii) Developing conscience, morality and scale of values.
(viii) Achieving personal independence.
(ix) Developing attitudes towards social groups and institutions.

12 to 18 years

(i) Achieving new and more mature relations with age-mates of both sexes.
(ii) Achieving a masculine or feminine social role.
(iii) Accepting one's physique and using the body effectively.
(iv) Achieving assurance of economic independence.
(v) Selecting and preparing for an occupation.

(vi) Preparing for marriage and family life.
(vii) Developing intellectual skills and concepts necessary for civic competence.
(viii) Desiring and achieving socially responsible behaviour
(ix) Acquiring a set of values and an ethical system as a guide to behaviour.
(x) Achieving emotional independence of parents and other adults.

Early Adulthood

(i) Selecting a mate,
(ii) Learning to live with a marriage partner,
(iii) Starting a family,
(iv) Rearing children,
(v) Managing a home,
(vi) Getting started in an occupation,
(vii) Taking on civic responsibility,
(viii) Finding a congenial social group.

Middle Age

(i) Achieving adult civic and social responsibility.
(ii) Establishing and maintaining an economic standard of living.
(iii) Assisting teenage children to become responsible and happy adults.
(iv) Developing adult leisure-time activities.
(v) Relating oneself to one's spouse as a person.
(vi) Accepting and adjusting to the physiological changes of middle age.
(vii) Adjusting to ageing parents.

Later Maturity

(i) Adjusting to decreasing physical strength and health.
(ii) Adjusting to retirement and reduced income.
(iii) Adjusting to death of spouse.
(iv) Establishing an explicit affiliation with one's age group.
(v) Meeting social and civic obligations.
(vi) Establishing satisfactory physical living arrangements.

5. FACTORS INFLUENCING DEVELOPMENT

A child's development depends on certain factors or forces. These factors or forces which determine a child's development can be classified under three heads:

(i) Genetic factors (heredity)
(ii) Physiological factors (maturation)
(iii) Environmental forces (learning, experience, etc.)

Influence of Genetic Factors (Heredity)

Every child is born with certain potentialities or characteristics. These innate potentialities or characteristics are inherited from his parents at the moment of conception. This complicated process of passing on biological and even mental characteristics from parents to their children or from one generation to another is called heredity. In other words, heredity refers to what nature contributes to the individual. How does hereditary transmission take place?

Life begins from the moment of conception. By conception we mean the union of two germ cells (one germ cell from the mother called the ovum or the egg and one germ cell from the father called the sperm). The union of the particular ovum of the mother and the particular sperm of the father lays the foundation for the characteristic development of the child.

Each of these germ cells has a nucleus which contains long threadlike structures called the chromosomes. The pairing of chromosomes at the moment of conception occurs purely by chance and varies from conception to conception. This is why children in the same family differ from each other so widely.

Each chromosome contains thousands of tiny structures called the genes. The genes are the real carriers of hereditary characteristics. There are millions of genes in a single chromosome. Each gene carries a specific trait or characteristic, such as the colour of the eye, the shape of the nose, the height of the body, the spread of fingers, the chin, the forehead hair, etc. Children inherit characteristics from their parents through combination of genes. Combination of genes varies from conception to conception and this produces variation in children's growth and development.

In the process of gene combination, some genes are dominant and some are recessive. Either the father's genes are dominant or the mother's genes are dominant. It happens that some genes of the father and some genes of the mother are dominant. The dominant genes will determine the characteristics of the child. Suppose the father is tall, and the mother is short. If the father's gene is dominant, the child will be tall; if the mother's gene is dominant, the child will be short. This is why tall fathers have tall children and at times tall fathers have short children.

The child inherits traits not only from his near parents but also from his ancestors. This is why a child has the chin of his mother, the forehead of his father, the eyes from his grandfather, the nose from his grandmother. A child may not resemble any near parent but he may inherit his traits from some remote member of his ancestry. In fact, a child owes 1/2 of his original equipment to his parents, 1/4 to his grandparents, 1/8 to his great-grandparents and so on.

How does heredity determine the sex of a child? The sex of the baby-to-be-born is determined from the moment of conception. As has been pointed out earlier, the germ cell of the father has twenty-three pairs of chromosomes and the germ cell of the mother has also twenty-three pairs of chromosomes. One pair of chromosomes of the father is called sex chromosomes and is named as XY chromosomes. The sex chromosomes of the mother are named XX. If the X chromosome of the father unites with the X chromosome of the mother, the child will be a male child. If the Y chromosome of the father unites with the X chromosome of the mother, the child will be a female child.

The above discussion is a rough indication of the role of heredity in the growth and development of a child. In a later chapter we will discuss how heredity influences intelligence. In a later chapter on personality we shall again discuss the influence of heredity on personality development of the child.

Influence of Physiological Factors (Maturation)

Maturation refers to development of physiological and anatomical structures of the body. Maturation plays an important role in the development of specific behaviour patterns. For example, the first time the baby walks or talks is an indication that maturation is at work. The swimming of tadpoles and the flying of birds also demonstrate the effect of maturation on behaviour. The child first creeps, then crawls and then walks. The first behaviour creeping takes place only when the infant is mature to do so. Similarly, whatever training you may provide to an infant of six-month old, he cannot climb the staircase; when his body is mature he can do it. All these examples make it clear that maturation leads to development of some specific behaviour patterns.

Several studies indicate that training is largely wasted if the child has not reached the appropriate level of maturation. The classical study of Myrtle McGraw on toilet training has established this fact. In one study, McGraw used two pairs of identical twins to see whether she could speed up their toilet training. One member of each pair was given training from the second month of life. They were taken to the toilet room at intervals of one hour for seven hours a day. Their partners received similar training at fourteen and twenty-four months respectively. At the end of twenty-eighth month McGraw found that the boys whose training was delayed had achieved as much control as the boys who received training earlier. She concluded that the maturation of certain muscles must precede effective toilet training.

Influence of Environmental Forces

Genetic factor such as hereditary transmission and physiological factor such as maturation are no doubt important factors of a child's development. But these are not the only factors which determine a child's development. Environment is equally important in the development of a child. The term environment is a broader one which includes the home, social and moral surrounding, all types of events, circumstances and influences, all types of stimulations, encouragement, guidance, opportunities, enrichment activities and deprivations, training, education and experiences, and in fact, everything that is externally operated either consciously or unconsciously by parents, teachers, community and others to influence or help the child to develop along the desired line.

A young plant inherits its basic features from its seed. The seed determines the characteristic growth of the plant. But the young plant will not grow into a healthy plant if it is undernourished or short of light and water. In the same way, a child will grow in the direction determined by his heredity. But he will not be able to realise or develop his potentialities to the fullest extent if he is deprived of appropriate environmental stimulation. Genetic factors determine the base; physiological factors determine the time, sequence or order of development and environmental factors influence the pace and limit of development. Again genetic and physiological factors are responsible for development of certain traits like colour of the eye, colour of the hair, etc. Environment is responsible for some other qualities. Growth and development are the result of interaction and interplay of genetic, physiological and environmental factors.

The relative influence of genetic, physiological and environmental factors on development will be discussed again in subsequent sections or chapters on intelligence and personality.

6. IMPORTANCE OF STUDYING GROWTH AND DEVELOPMENT

The study of growth and development of children is essential for the teacher for various reasons.

Teachers interact with very young children who are always changing and always growing. Teachers must know-how children grow and how they change so that they can interact with them effectively. The teacher can study the behaviour of children, guide their learning, help them realise their capacities, and provide a stimulating environment or advice parents on matters of child rearing practices, and early childhood, education only if he has a knowledge of the stages of development. A study of growth and development helps in the professional competence of a teacher. To be specific, study of growth and development is important for the teacher for the following reasons:

(i) The teacher can know-how children grow physically and what he can do to facilitate physical development of children. He can plan suitable educational programmes for the physically handicapped children.

(ii) The teacher can understand the process of social development of children and guide them in their socialization. He can help the socially maladjusted children to resolve their conflicts and lead a happy life.

(iii) The teacher can know-how children develop emotionally and help the emotionally disturbed children through appropriate school programmes.

(iv) The teacher can understand the cognitive development of children at different ages and plan the instruction accordingly.

(v) The teacher can know the developmental needs, problems and tasks at different stages and organise the school activities and atmosphere to help children maintain a sound mental health.

(vi) The teacher can organise his instruction and the school programmes in accordance with the needs and requirements of exceptional children (the gifted, the slow learner, and the socially disadvantaged children, etc.).

SELECTED QUESTIONS

1. Explain the terms 'growth' and 'development.' State the differences between the two terms.
2. State the principles of development and their implications for educational practices.
3. What are the different stages of development? Write the developmental tasks for each stage of development.
4. Discuss the factors influencing development.
5. State the importance of studying growth and development for the teacher.

5
Physical Growth

The story of physical growth of the individual is the most fascinating and perhaps the most important one. It indicates what anatomical and physiological changes take place from conception to death; how the foetus becomes a man or a woman; and how other aspects of development are dependent upon physical growth. The study of physical growth has educational significance for parents and teachers; it will make clear the duty and responsibility of the school and teachers for the physically handicapped children. In this chapter, we will discuss physical growth during infancy, pre-school years, childhood and adolescence.

1. INFANCY

Incomplete Development at Birth

When we consider the physical development of a new-born infant we find him far from being a fully formed and functioning human organism. Although the infant's body structure is almost complete at birth, his bones are softer than those of older children. His bones are also shaped differently. For example, the bones of the skull are not fully joined together. For this reason, there is a soft spot on the top of the infant's head. These bones will be joined together somewhere between nine months and a year. The feet are also incomplete at birth.

Rapid Physical Development

During the first year, the infant makes a remarkable progress in physical development and motor co-ordination. In fact, growth during the first year is very rapid. At birth, the average weight of the baby is 3 Kg. and the average height is 50 cm. By the end of twelve months, the baby has tripled his birth weight and has grown one-third taller. Growth slows down gradually after that.

Head-to-Tail Development

At the time of birth, the infant shows a few reflexes such as the startle and grasp reflexes. By the end of the year, the infant learns to crawl, stand and take a few steps. Development during this period illustrates the "head to tail" direction of growth. In other words, growth proceeds from the head downward and from the centre of the body out to the periphery. The brain develops more rapidly than any other part of the body.

Rapid Motor Development

Along with physical development, motor development also takes place rapidly. Motor development refers to the development of strength, speed and accuracy in the use of muscular parts of the body and coordination of muscular movements. It is due to the motor development of the baby that he sits, stands, creeps, crawls and walks. The sequence of motor development during infancy is presented in Table 1.

Table 1: Sequence of Motor Development

Age	Development
1 Month	Chin up
2 Months	Chest up
4 Months	Sits with support
7 Months	Sits alone
8 Months	Stands with help
9 Months	Stands with support
10 Months	Creeps
11 Months	Walks when led
12 Months	Pulls self-up to stand by furniture
13 Months	Climbs staircase
14 Months	Stands alone
15 Months	Walks alone

This sequence does not mean that every baby must have these developments at the specified ages. Rather some children may have late developments or abnormal developments due to various reasons.

After children learn to walk, they move into a stage called 'toddlerhood.' Within a few years they will begin to jump, run and hop as well as play. When children first attempt to walk, their feet are wide apart and their movement is irregular. With increased practice, children bring their feet closer together and their steps become more even and rhythmical. They also begin to do variations and occasionally walk straight. Once children have confidence about walking, they begin to do variations and occasionally walk side way and backward. Towards the middle of the second year, children may have a 'hurried walk' that looks something like running. But it is not true running because they do not have the leg power and balance to do so.

2. PRE-SCHOOL YEARS

Development is More Gradual

The pre-school years are much less dramatic than the first two years of life with respect to physical and motor developments. This is not to say that development stops during the pre-school years, but just that it is more varied and more closely related to specific patterns of experience and practice than it was in infancy.

Less Rapid Development

Growth in height and weight is less rapid during the pre-school years than in infancy, but both height and weight continue to increase at faster pace than in middle childhood. By 5 the average child is 108 cm. to 109 cm. in height. During the first 2 years of life, infants grow about 10 cm. a year whereas from age 2 to 5 they grow only 7 cm. per year. Weight gain also slows down and may even stop for a while in some cases. That is why children become taller and thinner without gaining much weight during the pre-school years.

Toilet Training

One of the major motor accomplishments of the pre-school years is toilet training. Typically bowel training precedes bladder training mainly because it is easier for children to control their bowel movements than it is for them to hold their urine. That is why most children are capable of bowel control before they stop bed-wetting especially at night. Girls generally achieve toilet training earlier than boys. Thus, boys are more likely to continue to wet the bed for a longer time than girls. The age of toilet training depends upon how soon the parents begin training and how vigorously they pursue it.

Maturing Motor Abilities

The pre-school child also shows further advancement in motor development like balancing, climbing and throwing a ball. Even when children show balancing and climbing behaviours, there is always a fear of falling. This is so because pre-school children have not accomplished motor developments completely. Play activities also reflect pre-school children's maturing motor abilities. The ability of holding pencils and drawing also indicates clear progression in motor development.

3. CHILDHOOD

Leisurely Growth

Childhood is a time of leisurely growth. By age 6, most children have lost their soft contours and their top heavy stature that make pre-schoolers so appealing to adults. In childhood the arms and legs grow faster than the trunk so that in this period many youngsters appear tall and thin and usually weak. Boys remain taller and heavier than girls until about the age of 10. In general by the time a child reaches this period, his relative size is fairly stable and predictable. A child who is short or tall in relation to his peers will probably have the same position in adulthood.

Loss of Baby Appearance

Changes in body proportions at this time are accompanied by changes in the shape of the face. Children lose their baby appearance. Their face becomes slimmer and narrower. Children lose their baby-teeth and permanent teeth begin to develop. At 5 years of age, the eyes have not yet reached their size and shape. Many children between 6 and 8 years of age are slightly far-sighted, but this condition usually corrects itself spontaneously between the ages of 8 and 10 when their eyes reach about adult eye size and shape.

Co-ordination of Muscles

During the pre-school years, children learn the smooth co-ordination of small and large muscles. During childhood this co-ordination is further refined and used in many activities ranging from reading and writing to playing team games.

Development of Body Image

As children progressively grow they develop a body image. Body image not only includes an awareness of the body and its parts but it also involves an evaluation of the adequacy of one's physical appearance and motor skill in comparison with one's peers. Although body image begins to be formed in infancy and early childhood, it becomes more conscious during childhood when the youngster can compare himself with others. This body image is a factor for later development of self-concept.

4. ADOLESCENCE

Adolescence is a period in which marked physical, and physiological developments take place and which transform children into young adults.

Onset of Puberty

This occurs in boys around the age of 13½ — the normal range being 12-15. In girls the first changes happen about 2 years earlier, at around 11½ — the normal range being 10-17. The changes take about 2 years to complete and at that point sexual maturity has been reached.

Secular Trend in Rate of Growth and Time of Adolescence

Data from many countries confirm that, compared with children 50 years ago, children today are both heavier and taller and reach adolescence sooner. For example, an average child of 10 years, 30 years ago had the height and weight of a child of 9 at present. The age of menarche has been getting earlier by some 4 months per decade in Western European countries during the period 1930-60. Similar studies in boys show the same trend, the peak height velocity in the year 1800 occurring as late as 17. It is known that malnutrition during childhood can delay the onset of adolescence and conversely it is thought that the secular trends described above may be the result of better nutrition.

Growth Spurt

This is a constant phenomenon. In boys it takes place from 12-15 with a peak height velocity of 10 cm per year around 14 years. In girls the spurt begins 2 years earlier between 10 and 13 with a peak height velocity of 8 cm per year around 12 years. The growth spurt is accompanied by an increase in appetite which in some cases may seem excessive but is in fact physiological.

Secondary Sexual Characteristics (Boys)

Fine hair appears at the root of the penis, becoming gradually coarser and curlier. This is followed by auxiliary and facial hair including bushier eyebrows. Abdominal, chest, leg and arm hair appears in varied amounts. Some recession of temple hair is a normal feature of late adolescence. In 40 per cent of boys some breast development may be noted — often unilateral. This regresses usually within a year. The voice deepens due to enlargement of the larynx. The sweat glands around the axilla, genital, and anal areas become active and the appearance of acne (blackheads) on the face, chest, or upper back is a feature in 75 per cent of boys. The penis and the testicles enlarge and ejaculation of semen may occur.

Secondary Sexual Characteristics (Girls)

The first signs of breast enlargement may be noted about 2 years before the start of menstruation. This is accompanied by darkening of the nipples and surrounding area of skin (the areola). Pubic and auxiliary hair appears — the former usually preceding the latter. The hips widen due to skeletal changes in the pelvis to accommodate child bearing.

The skin changes include sweat gland activity and a tendency to acne although less marked than in boys. In addition, a thick layer of fat is deposited which, in contrast to the male, produces the softer contours of female. It enables girls to survive longer than boys in conditions of extreme cold.

The vagina, womb and ovaries increase in size and menstruation begins. This may be scanty and irregular at first and ovulation may not occur for the first year of menstruation.

Evaluation of Physical Characteristics

Adolescents tend to evaluate themselves largely in terms of their physical characteristics. In evaluating their bodies, young people often compare themselves with certain ideal concepts that prevail in the society. Sometimes their body image is influenced by certain stereotypes.

For example, some young people believe that if a girl of 16 does not have 32-24-32 figure and a button nose, she is ugly. Similarly, some young people believe that hairiness, muscularity, and large genitals are signs of virility among men. Depending upon the body image, the ideal concepts, and stereotypes that prevail in the society, an adolescent derives satisfaction or dissatisfaction with his body. All this contributes positively or negatively to the development of self-concept in adolescents.

5. EDUCATIONAL SIGNIFICANCE

Parent Education

Physical and motor development of children has implications for parent education programmes. Such programmes are necessary on the assumption that most modern parents have not had the opportunity to observe a wide variety of child-rearing practices. Effective parenting is critical during infancy for the healthy growth and development of the child, and effective parenting can be taught. Programmes of parent education try to promote better interaction between parents and children during the formative years. The goal of such programmes is to facilitate rather than to accelerate growth.

Parental education with reference to physical development must include instruction in prenatal and post-natal care, health and hygiene, first-aid, food habits and many such facts.

Handedness

As the child gradually matures he learns to use his hands. But some children develop preference for a particular hand. Thus, they develop handedness. For example, use of right hand is considered normal for taking food, or writing or performing similar acts. But some children tend to use the left hand for performing those acts. We call them left-handed. Such handedness is not an inborn tendency of the child. It is learned. It is the result of practice. Such left-handedness can be changed by encouraging the child to use the right hand and to practise doing that. This can be accomplished in the beginning stage of handedness. But once the habit is established, it is of no use to force the child to learn to use the right hand.

Motor Tasks

Parents should give opportunity to children for manipulating and handling objects, to play with blocks, and to perform simple motor tasks. In schools, various types of activities such as handicrafts, woodcrafts, building and gardening activities should be organised.

Confusion *versus* Self-confidence

As children mature and reach adolescence, special attention must be given for their physical development and the accompanying sexual urge. During adolescence, rapid physical development may be accompanied by a feeling of confusion. It may be taught to them that it is a normal part of development and that every one passes through it. Heterosexual interests can be dealt with through providing opportunities for participation in various social activities like drama, debate, club activities, etc. where both boys and girls can participate. Outdoor experiences can be provided which will facilitate both physical and mental development.

Inclusive Education

All children have the right to education. This implies equality of educational opportunity for all children — whether they are disabled or non-disabled.

Some children may be physically handicapped. There are visually impaired, hearing impaired and orthopaedically handicapped children. Their handicaps may be mild, moderate, severe or profound. Mild-to-moderately handicapped children should be encouraged to receive education along with non-disabled children in inclusive schools. Severely and profoundly handicapped children should be educated in special schools (Please refer to the book *Education of Exceptional Children* by M. Dash for discussion on education of disabled in regular schools).

SELECTED QUESTIONS

1. Discuss the physical growth of the child during childhood.
2. Discuss the physical growth that takes place during adolescence.
3. Discuss the physical growth during infancy. State the educational implications of physical growth.

6
Emotional Development

1. MEANING OF EMOTION

Emotion and motivation are known as the 'dynamics of behaviour.' The term 'dynamics' refers to the energies or forces that initiate activity. The term 'emotion' is derived from a Latin word 'emovere' which means to stir up, agitate, excite and move.

According to modern psychologists, emotion refers to 'an activating or energizing state of the organism'. The degree of activation varies depending upon the level of emotionality. A mild level of emotional arousal tends to produce alertness and interest in the task at hand. When emotions become intense, they result in some decrement in performance.

Emotion does not refer to a specific behaviour pattern but it stands for a wide range of behaviour like love, anger, jealousy, etc.

Emotion is the fuel that fires the human spirit that gives passion and urgency to what we do. Emotion is that internal force which intensifies motivated activity. For example, anger promotes attack; anxiety stimulates fight.

All emotions can be divided into those that are pleasant (joy, love) and those that are unpleasant (anger, fear).

2. NATURE OF EMOTION

Emotion is a Form of Energy Mobilisation

Emotions activate and direct behaviour in the same way as motives. The degree of activation or energy mobilisation varies depending upon the level of emotionality. But a state of intense emotion is disruptive whereas a state of moderate emotion is adaptive.

The Basic Ways of Expressing Emotions are Inborn

The basic ways of expressing emotions develop through maturation. Children all over the world cry when hurt or sad and laugh when happy. Even the emotional expressions of deaf and blind children are also inborn. Children who are blind and deaf from the time of birth have no opportunity to hear or see emotional expressions of other children.

But at appropriate ages, particular emotional expressions are noticed in them. So we can say that emotions are largely innate.

Emotional Expressions are Modified by Learning

Although certain emotional expressions may be largely innate, many modifications occur through learning. Anger, for example, may be expressed by fighting, by using abusive language, or by leaving the room. Leaving the room is not an expression of emotion that is known at birth. Similarly using abusive language under the state of anger is not found at birth. These are definitely learned ways of expressing anger.

Certain Facial Expressions of Emotions have Universal Meaning

Facial expressions that characterize certain emotions are found in every culture. This has been proved by a reputed investigator, P. Ekman (1971). Ekman showed photographs of facial expressions of happiness, anger, sadness, disgust, fear and surprise to members of different cultures (United States, Brazil, Argentina, Chile and Japan). The members of these cultures could easily identify the emotions expressed in the photographs. This study indicates that certain facial expressions of emotions have a universal meaning regardless of the culture in which the individual is raised.

Every Emotion is Accompanied by a Feeling

The feeling that accompanies an emotion is one's private experience. The same emotion-provoking stimulus may lead to different emotions in different individuals.

Every Emotion has a Behavioural Aspect

An emotional reaction leads to certain behavioural expressions such as smile, tears, gestures and other facial expressions and overt actions.

Emotions are Aroused by External Stimuli or Learned Symbols

Whereas motivation is aroused by internal stimuli and external stimuli, emotions are largely aroused by external objects, events or situations.

An Emotion can be Virtually Attached to Anything

Love is an emotion. Love can be attached to God, teacher, humanity, children or one's sweetheart. The objects or stimuli to which a particular emotion will be attached depend upon learning.

Emotions are Flexible

Emotions are not permanent states or static states of the organism. They are flexible in nature. They are temporary states of the organism. Children's emotions are more flexible than the emotions of adults. The emotion of a child changes suddenly and frequently. At one time a baby may cry, the next moment he laughs.

Every Emotion is Accompanied by Certain Physiological or Bodily Changes

When we experience an intense emotion such as fear or anger, we notice a number of bodily changes. Some of these bodily changes are as follows:

Rapid heart-beat and breathing,
Dryness of the throat and mouth,
Increased muscle tension,
Perspiration,
Trembling of hands and legs, and
A sinking feeling in the stomach.

Most of the physiological changes that occur during intense emotion result from activation of the sympathetic division of the autonomic nervous system. The sympathetic division of the autonomic nervous system prepares the body for emergency action. The sympathetic system is responsible for the following changes:

Blood pressure and heart-beat increases,

Respiration becomes more rapid,

The pupils of the eyes dilate,

Electrical resistance of the skin decreases,

Blood sugar level increases to provide more energy,

The blood becomes able to clot more quickly in case of wounds.

The hairs on the skin stand on their ends.

The sympathetic system gears the organism for energy output. As the emotion subsides, the parasympathetic system, the energy conserving system, takes over and returns the organism to its normal state.

3. DEVELOPMENT OF EMOTIONAL BEHAVIOUR

If parents and teachers are to help the child develop emotionally so that emotions will be beneficial, they must know the normal pattern of emotional development. Almost everyone has his characteristic emotional development as he passes from infancy to adulthood. But during this transition from infancy to adulthood, great changes take place in his emotions. There are always individual differences in emotional development among children.

Several psychologists have studied emotional development that takes place during infancy, childhood and later. Some of these psychologists are K.M.B. Bridges, W.E. Blatz and his colleagues and John B. Watson. Bridges (1932) studied emotional development in early infancy and his views are still widely accepted. Bridges proposed a scheme of emotional development which is given in Table 2. According to her, new-born infants have no differentiated emotional responses to emotional stimuli. The emotions of infants are uncoordinated, undifferentiated, diffused and gross. As he develops and matures, various emotions begin to differentiate. These various emotions appear as the child advances in years. For example, at birth, the infant shows generalised excitement. At the age of 3 months, excitement is further differentiated into distress and delight.

Table 2: Bridge's Scheme of the Development of Emotions in Children

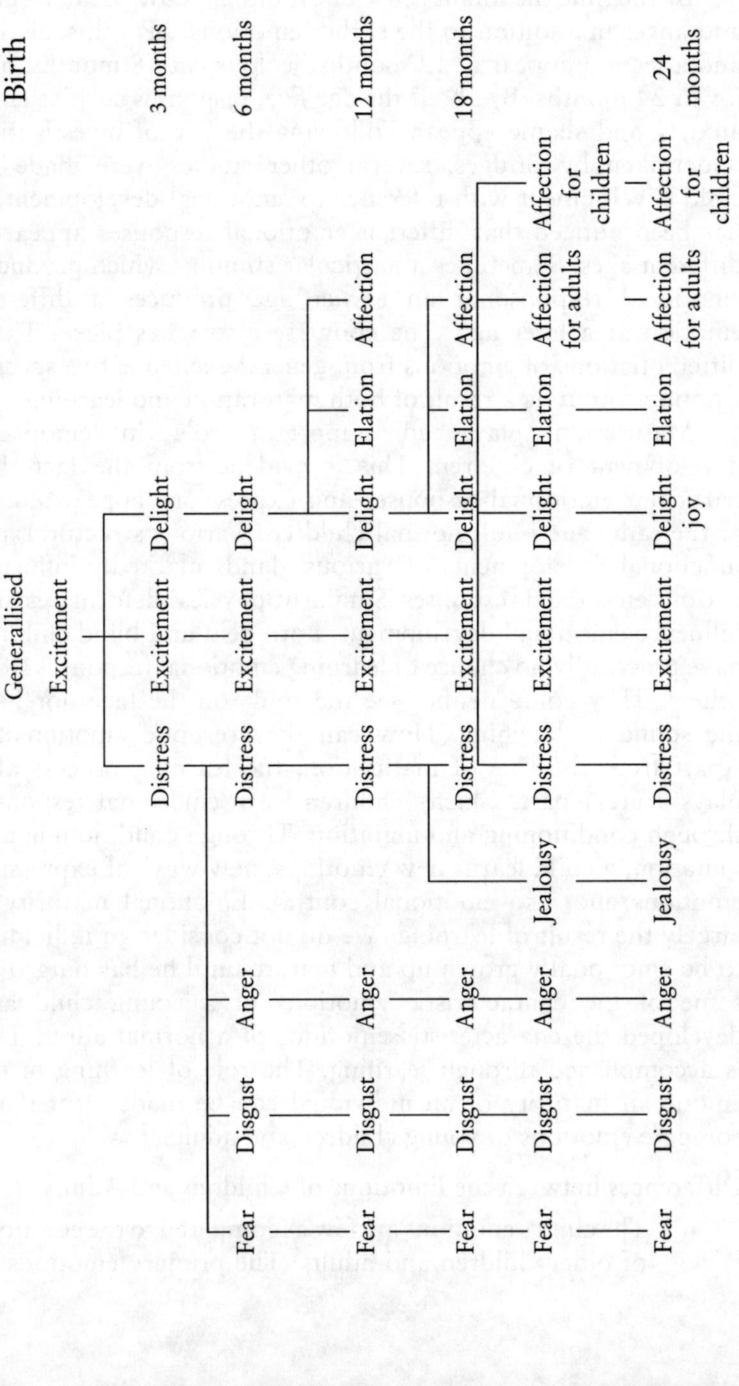

By the time the infant is 6 months old, he shows fear, disgust and anger in addition to the earlier emotions. Like this, elation and affection appear at 12 months, jealousy at 18 months, and joy at 24 months. By about the age five, responses such as envy, anxiety and shame appear. Following the line of investigation undertaken by Bridges, several other studies were made on child development with reference to emotional development. It has been noticed that different emotional responses appear at different ages. Sometimes a particular stimulus which produced emotional response at an earlier age produces a different emotion at a later age. The converse also takes place. These differentiations of emotions from general excitement to specific emotions occur as a result of both maturation and learning.

Maturation plays an important role in emotional development of children. This is evident from the fact that particular emotional responses and expressions appear almost at the same age in all normal children. Various structural and functional developments of various glands markedly influence various emotional responses. Similarly, physical deformities also influence emotional development. Born deaf and blind children have practically no chance of learning emotional responses from others. They could neither see the smile on the face nor hear the sound of laughing. How can they respond emotionally? Apart from the role of maturation, the learning process also plays a great part. Chiefly children learn emotional responses through conditioning and imitation. Through conditioning and imitation, a child learns new emotions, new ways of expressing emotions and also emotional control. Emotional maturity is largely the result of learning. We do not consider an individual to be emotionally grown up and mature until he has outgrown some of the characteristic emotions of a young child and developed the characteristic emotions of a normal adult. This is accomplished through learning. The role of learning in the emotional maturity of an individual can be made clear if we compare emotions of young children and adults.

Differences between the Emotions of Children and Adults

(i) The child's emotions are few as compared to the emotions of older children and adults. The primary emotions of a child are love, fear and anger. Other emotions like jealousy, wonder and admiration that characterise the older children are learned by the child.

(ii) During the earlier years, the stimuli that arouse emotional reactions are very few. These stimuli relate to the immediate environment and certain biological needs of the child. As the child grows up, it learns to be afraid of many more things and situations. A concrete example is fear for snake. The young infant does not have any fear for the snake. He may even touch it when it is encountered. But grown-up children are definitely afraid of snakes.

(iii) Another important difference is that the child freely expresses his emotions much more than the adult. If he is angry he kicks about, rolls on the ground, tears the clothes, etc. But a grown-up child does not do that way. Grown-up children gradually learn to control some of the overt expressions of their emotions according to the accepted standards of their culture.

(iv) The child may get upset and behave emotionally even to weak and insignificant stimuli. For example, not getting a piece of chalk or chocolate may evoke anger in the child. But as the child grows up, he learns to adjust the strength of his emotions to the strength of the stimulus.

(v) The emotions of a grown-up child are balanced, organised and steady. But the emotions of a young child are not organised and balanced. Quick changes can be noticed in the emotional response of a child. At one time he cries the next time he laughs and the like.

4. SOME EMOTIONAL REACTIONS

Anger

Anger is one of the most powerful emotions with which the parents and teachers have to deal with.

As the child matures he/she changes the manner of expressing his/her anger. The young child becomes angry when his physical movement is restricted. He expresses his anger by crying, stiffening his body, getting red in the face, and thrashing around.

The pre-school child becomes more tolerant if physical restraint is for a brief period. He may resent if he is asked to go to the toilet, or wash his face, or do something else while he is playing. The anger is expressed by vehement protest, scramming, jerking away from the adult and by the temper tantrum. Later on, anger becomes more socialized and the child starts quarrelling, *e.g.*, for possession of toy/eatables, etc.

Responses to anger can be roughly divided into two major categories: Impulsive and Inhibited. Impulsive responses are called aggression. They are directed against persons, animals or objects. Children do not hesitate to hurt others by any method at their disposal, namely, hitting, spitting, kicking, punching or pulling. Language, as an angry response, is used around the age of four years.

Inhibited responses are called withdrawal. Children may withdraw into themselves by fleeing from the person or object offending them.

Factors Contributing to Arousal of Anger

Many factors may arouse anger. Some of them are:

(a) Needless interference in the child's everyday affairs,
(b) Assignments or tasks beyond his ability,
(c) Lengthy period of confinement,
(d) Demanding children to do a job in which they are not interested,
(e) Favouritism,
(f) Fatigue and illness,
(g) Over personal possessions.

The parents and teachers facing temper tantrums may react in different ways, but three main patterns are:

1. Punishment — verbal and physical
2. "Giving in"
3. Over solicitous behaviour

How to Handle Anger?

A few useful hints to handle emotional reactions of anger are suggested here:

(a) For older children, when the child regains composure, talk over the situation that arose anger and help the child to have a correct view of the situation.
(b) Avoid needless restraints, tedious repetition and inconsistent demands.
(c) Do not punish physically or do not give reprimands when there is no likelihood that they will improve behaviour.
(d) Cultivate skills and competencies which make possible for the child to solve those problems which provoked anger previously.
(e) Promote pleasant feelings on issues outside the field of conflict and tension.
(f) Try to find out clues to the underlying motives of anger by inquiring, 'Why did he act like that?'
(g) Help children to make self analysis.

Fear

A child in the beginning is afraid of only a loud noise, a sudden flash of light, a sudden movement of the body, and a rough push but later on he acquires new fears.

The most common fears between 2 and 6 years of age, centre round darkness, thunderstorm, and animals especially dogs, "bad people," doctors, etc. Between 6 and 13 years of age, the fears take on a different quality, *e.g.*, fear of ghosts, witches, fear of dangers that have not actually threatened them, fear of doorbells, people hiding under the cot, fear of being late in school, school examination, etc.

Factors Contributing to Arousal of Fear

(i) The child may actually be threatened by an object or situation (accident, bullying, a chase by a dog, etc.).
(ii) Warnings given by the elders. For example:
  (a) "Don't talk to strangers. They will put you in the bag and take you away."
  (b) "Don't go there alone, spirits live there."
  (c) "Don't touch the dog, cat," etc.
(iii) Unconscious imitation of the fears of the parents or elder siblings.
(iv) Weak-development of the child's personality.

Fear-related Emotional Patterns

There are a number of emotional patterns that are fear-related in that the dominant aspect of these patterns is fear. The most important are shyness, embarrassment, worry, and prevention of fear.

Shyness

Children may be shy in the presence of guests or strangers — especially when they are to sing, recite or participate in a school play. The shyness comes from uncertainty about how others will react to them or fear that others will laugh at them.

Pre-school children show their shyness by blushing, by stuttering, by talking as little as possible, by nervous mannerism — such as pulling the ears or clothing, shifting from one foot to the other and bending the head to one side and then raising it slowly to look at the stranger.

Embarrassment

It develops later than shyness and it is usually not present in a child less than 5 or 6 years of age because it is heightened by memories of experiences in which their behaviours fall below social expectations.

Most of the common responses in shyness are also characteristics of embarrassment but one major difference is that shy children speak as little as possible even when asked a question. Embarrassed children, on the other hand, usually speak out; they try to explain and justify their behaviour in the hope of dispelling the unfavourable social adjustment that caused their embarrassment.

Worry

Worry is usually described as "imaginary fear" or "borrowing trouble." Unlike fear, it is the product of child's own mind. The child imagines that a dangerous situation could arise. Generally children below 3 years of age do not worry. It becomes more frequent and more intense as childhood progresses.

The children worry about those things that, they think, are significant for them at that time. The most common worries centre round the home, family and peer relationship, school problems, etc.

Worry is expressed in different ways by children depending upon the personality patterns. Children who feel inferior or inadequate have the tendency to internalise their worries. Better adjusted children are more likely to discuss their worries with people who, they think, will be sympathetic. Insecure and rejected children tend to verbalize their worries hoping that of winning sympathy and improving social acceptance.

Prevention of Fear

Fears are valuable and at the same time must be prevented. In normal cases, fears provide safeguards against harm, and promote caution. But there are irrational or baseless fears which also cause much suffering to the individual. Complete prevention of fear is not possible because all feared objects cannot be eliminated for all time to come. The following techniques may prove effective in specific situations:

(a) *Verbal Reassurance:* By this method we have to build up confidence in the child and give all encouragement to the child to make efforts to give up fear.

(b) *Negative Adaptation:* In this method the child learns to give an opposite response to the fear response (*e.g.*, overcoming the fear for a dog by learning to play with it).

(c) *Reconditioning:* In this method, the child is helped to give up feared response and learn fearless response by associating pleasant experiences with the feared object.

(d) *Use of Distraction:* The use of distraction as a technique to overcome fear requires drawing the attention of the child to some interesting features of the feared objects.

(e) *Forewarning*. It means to tell about the evil consequences beforehand on the basis of close cause and effect relationships.

(f) *Social Imitation:* It requires observing friends and relatives acting in a fearless way towards the feared object or situation.

Jealousy

Jealousy is common in children. It is a normal response to actual, supposed, or threatened loss of affection. The child who is jealous feels insecure in relationship with a loved one and is afraid of losing it. The three major situational sources of jealousy are:

1. *Home Environment*: "Sibling rivalry" is a classical example. The new-born baby takes much of the time and attention of the mother.
   The earlier born child feels threatened with the loss of parental love. He does not want to share his exclusive possession, *i.e.*, the mother. Parental favouritism also results in jealousy. The non-preferred child is quick to perceive the differential treatment and resentment begins.
2. Social situations in the school.
3. Situations in which children feel that they have been deprived of material possession.

Jealousy Responses

The jealousy responses depend on the situation. The child may attack in one situation while in another situation the same child may try to win the favour of the persons concerned. The main causes of jealousy are: feeling of insecurity and uncertainty. Direct responses of jealousy may be aggressive behaviour—biting, kicking, hitting, pushing, punching, and scratching or socially acceptable behaviour like attempts to outdo one's rivals. Indirect responses are difficult to recognise. They include: bed-wetting and thumb-sucking, general naughtiness, destructiveness, and verbal expressions such as name calling, giving vent to the feeling on toys or animals.

Prevention of Jealousy

(a) Do not pamper the child and make him a showpiece before other children.
(b) Avoid making comparison between one child and another.
(c) Be objective in praising children for their achievements.
(d) Inculcate in children an objective attitude towards their problems.
(e) Encourage children to strive for self-improvement by making self-efforts.

Joy, Pleasure and Delight

Joy is a pleasant emotion. Psychologists call it pleasure, delight and happiness when it exists in its milder form. Pre-school children derive pleasure mainly from activities in which others are involved particularly their age mates, and they are extremely happy when they do much better than others. Happiness also comes through physical well-being, incongruous situations, and play on words.

The children jump up and down, roll on the floor, clap their hands, hug the person, animal or object that has given rise to their joy and laugh uproariously.

How to Provide Pleasure?

Pleasure is a positive emotion. So every effort should be made at home and in school to provide the child those experiences which are most satisfying and sources of enjoyment to him. A few suggestions in this respect are mentioned here:

(a) The activities should be so graded that they provide some challenge to one's abilities, but at the same time do not over task them.

(b) The activities are so varied that it is possible to provide experience of success to every child.

(c) Every child should be given a chance to perform those activities in which he is most competent.

(d) The child should be given more freedom in choosing and pursuing his activities.

(e) A child who has done well should be praised, and his efforts should be commended.

Affection

Affection is a positive emotional reaction directed towards people, animals or objects. The child shows affection for those people, objects or animals with whom he has pleasurable experiences. The child not only seeks the love and affection of others, but also he gives it. In fact, love or affection is a two-way process. It grows best only when it is both given and received. Learning plays a dominant role in the selection of a person to whom affection is directed. Parents and teachers who care for the child, who show their love to the child not by words but by dealings, receive the affection of the child. It is not enough to say 'I love you,' but how you say it, what you do, and how you do it means a great difference.

Children who enjoy the love and affection of their parents and teachers develop a healthy behaviour pattern. Children who are deprived of love and affection have no chance to learn to show love and affection to others. They develop ill-health.

How to Help Develop Affection?

(a) Children desire acceptance and affection from their teachers. The teacher who shows such qualities as kindness, sympathy, and a genuine interest in children is highly liked by his students. Hence, a teacher should show his affection for children in the class, as well as he should also try to receive affection from them.

(b) It is not sufficient for the teacher to have a feeling for the children, but this feeling should be expressed in a warm-hearted manner.

(c) Expression of affection should not take the form of self-indulgence or displayed too much. Otherwise it may mean interference in child's activities and may make him lose self-initiative.

(d) Care should be taken to find out that the child is not extremely preoccupied with himself. If it is so he will be incapable of extending his affection to others.

(e) Encourage children to mix freely with other children and adults and thereby widen their circle of friends.

5. EDUCATIONAL PROGRAMMES FOR EMOTIONALLY DISTURBED CHILDREN

How should disturbed children be educated? There are many different answers to the question of educating disturbed children. This is natural because disturbed behaviours range from aggression to withdrawal and from mild to profound category. There are different approaches to the education of disturbed children such as:

Psychoanalytic approach,
Psycho-educational approach,
Humanistic approach,

Ecological approach, and

Behavioural approach.

We will not go deep into the differences in these approaches but, instead, highlight the essential points of these approaches.

(i) Emotional disturbance is the result of some inner conflict. Hence before any educational programme is designed for these children, psychologists and psychiatrists must help to uncover the underlying inner conflict in an effort to improve the psychological functioning as well as behaviour and achievement of the child.

(ii) Emphasis should be placed on teacher-pupil relationship in which the child feels accepted and free to act out his impulses in a permissive environment. Initially little emphasis should be given on academic achievement or to change the 'surface behaviour' of the child. If the teacher can uncover the mental conflict, half of his work is achieved.

(iii) Once the underlying pathology is revealed, the teacher should gradually move more towards managing the disturbed behaviour and academic achievement. There should be emphasis on meeting the individual needs of children and most teaching should be done through projects or the creative areas like music, art, dance, etc.

(iv) Educational programmes should be designed to enhance children's self-direction, self-evaluation and active involvement in the learning environment. Teachers should be non-authoritarian, open and personal in their approach towards the child.

(v) The roots of emotional disturbance may lie in the social environment of the child in which the child lives, grows and interacts. Hence the entire social system — the school, family, community and other social agencies — must be altered as far as practicable. Hence the teacher's concern should not be just effective teaching in the classroom but to work with the child's family, neighbourhood, and community agencies as well. Teacher's rapport with parents, community members and other adults will help to achieve his goal — altering the social system.

(vi) Educational practices must emphasize the behaviour modification strategies. School authorities must remember that every behaviour is learned. The disturbed child has failed to learn desirable behaviour and has learned inappropriate behaviours. Following the behaviour modification techniques, the teacher can modify the undesirable behaviour of the child, teach desirable behaviour through praise, reward and recognition and develop in him the ability and confidence in learning essential academic and other skills.

(vii) The mildly and moderately disturbed children should be kept in the mainstream as much as possible. If it is not feasible to keep the disturbed child in regular classes all the time then he may be removed to the resource room or the special class for a part of the day with the goal of reintegration in the regular classes.

(viii) The curriculum for such children will be the same as for normal children with emphasis on basic academic skills (reading, writing and arithmetic), arts, music, dance, social skills, and affective experiences. How to manage his own feelings and behaviour and how to get along with other people are essential skills which are no less important as academic schools. Teachers are expected to adopt novel teaching methods based on their experiences for teaching these skills.

(ix) The basic idea in the education of disturbed children is that they can be re-educated if the social system is changed and if teachers play their role with sincerity and dedication.

Role of the Teacher

There are specially trained resource teachers for all categories of disabled children but trained resource teachers are not available for teaching emotionally disturbed children. It is, therefore, obvious that disturbed children are to be educated in regular classrooms by regular teachers. Regular teachers are, thus, to play a very befitting role in managing such children.

(i) If there is an emotionally disturbed child in the regular class, the regular teacher must ask the special educator or any other special education personnel for advice concerning behaviour management, behaviour modification and teaching technique.

(ii) The regular teacher should let the child know from the first contact that he expects a reasonable standard of conduct to be maintained. The sooner the child knows the limits of permissible conduct, the better.

(iii) It is essential that the teacher communicates his expectations to the child clearly and firmly. Nothing is to be gained by beating about the bush or keeping the child guessing about what the teacher has in mind regarding behaviour and goals.

(iv) The teacher must have realistic expectations concerning the child's behaviour and academic performance. His tasks should be well within his capacity, but still challenging. The child must feel success and pride in what he accomplishes.

(v) It is important that the teacher empathises with the child and understands how negative aspects of his social environment (abuse at home, peers who taunt him, teachers who criticise him) may contribute to his inappropriate behaviour. If negative environmental influences can be identified, he should try to change them, if possible.

(vi) The teacher must be able to tolerate a great deal of unpleasantness and rejection. He should not be counter-aggressive or withdrawing himself. Some disturbed children change dramatically by the kind gesture of the teacher. But this may not be the case always. Kind gestures, caring attitude and decent behaviour of the teacher are not always reciprocated by his pupils. Still then, the teacher needs to maintain considerable patience which most teachers are not capable of.

(vii) There must be consistent and appropriate consequence for behaviour. The child's desirable behaviour should be immediately recognized and rewarded with praise and signs of approval. Inappropriate behaviour is to be consistently ignored, or, if necessary with mild punishment. Recognition and praise for good behaviour should be given openly so that other students can see and hear the teacher's approval. If it is necessary to correct or reprimand the child, this should be done as quietly and privately as possible.

(viii) The teacher managing emotionally disturbed children should remember that good behaviour management for disturbed children has lot in common with good behaviour management for all children. The best preventive action any teacher can take is to make sure that the classroom is a happy place where children take pride in their work and learn to treat others with respect.

(ix) Most behaviour problems in the classroom are noticed when children do not find interest in their education, when they fail to get any real meaning of their schooling, when the quality of teaching is poor. Good teachers do not encounter much problem behaviour in their classroom. Good teachers are not simply teachers; they are teacher-counsellors. They impress upon the students through their qualitative teaching, effective counselling and pleasing personality.

A teacher-counsellor is a decent adult, educated, well-trained; able to give and receive affection, to live relaxed; and to be firm; a professional through and through; a person with a sense of the significance of time, of the usefulness of today, and the promise of tomorrow; a person of hope, quiet confidence, and joy; one who has committed himself to children and to the proposition that children who are emotionally disturbed can be helped by the process of re-education.

SELECTED QUESTIONS

1. What is meant by emotion? State its nature.
2. State the development of emotional behaviour during infancy.
3. Differentiate between the emotions of children and adults.
4. State the factors contributing to arousal of fear. Give examples of some fear-related emotional patterns among children.

5. Why do young children develop fear? How can they be prevented?
6. Answer the following:
   (a) How can you prevent jealousy among children?
   (b) What strategies are to be adopted in the home and the school to provide pleasure to young children?
7. State the role of the teacher in dealing with emotionally disturbed children.

7
Cognitive Development (Piaget's View)

1. WHAT IS COGNITIVE DEVELOPMENT?

Cognitive development means intellectual development or mental development. It includes mental processes such as knowing, reasoning, memorizing, imagining, language acquisition and thinking. The speed with which a child learns new words, names and places, his ability to notice differences and similarities, the ability to communicate in the language, learning of mathematical principles, the child's curiosity to know and understand his world — all these indicate the child's progress in cognitive development. The most outstanding work on cognitive development has been done by a Swiss biologist, Jean Piaget. According to Piaget, the child is daily confronted with change. As he grows and as his world expands beyond the home to school and community, the child encounters new ideas, new experiences, and new challenges.

Substitution and Integration

According to Piaget, there are two paths of mental development: Substitution and Integration. Substitution is a process whereby the child replaces a less mature idea with a more mature one. Integration is a process whereby less mature ideas are brought together to arrive at more complex and abstract concepts.

Assimilation and Accommodation

Piaget's work has shown that as the child grows, he learns to adapt to the world around him. This adaption becomes possible through two ways: Assimilation and Accommodation. When placed in a new or familiar situation, the child tries to adapt by behaving in his established pattern. If his behaviour is found successful, the child does not change his behaviour. This is what Piaget calls assimilation. However, if the child's established behaviour pattern is not adequate or appropriate, he must change his behaviour in the new situation. This is what Piaget calls accommodation. In other words, accommodation means changing an existing behaviour pattern that does not work in the new situation.

Cognitive development proceeds through substitution and integration, assimilation and accommodation.

According to Piaget, cognitive development proceeds along with physical development or maturation. There are ages and stages of a child's cognitive development. These stages are not independent of an unrelated to one another. Cognitive development is both continuous and discontinuous. It is continuous in the sense that each subsequent development depends on its previous development. It is discontinuous in the sense that qualitative changes take place from stage to stage. The age ranges for each period are the average ages at which children generally demonstrate the characteristics of the period. But there are individual differences in the ages at which children enter each stage. Piaget himself admits that the sequence of development is more important than the particular age at which such development takes place.

2. STAGES OF COGNITIVE DEVELOPMENT

Cognitive development, like all other developments is a continuous process. Piaget divides cognitive development into four broad periods or stages. These are:

1. The Sensorimotor period (from birth to 1½ years),
2. The Pre-operational period (from 1½ years to 7 years),
3. The Concrete operational period (from 7 to 12 years),
4. The Formal operational period (from 12 years onwards).

Sensorimotor Period

Piaget's account of sensorimotor period or infancy is novel and sometimes surprising. His views offer a strong contrast to the common conception of infants as a predominantly helpless and inactive creature who is capable of learning almost nothing. Piaget characterizes the new-born baby as active and an initiator of behaviour. The infant quickly learns to distinguish among various features of the immediate environment and he modifies his behaviour in accordance with its demands. In fact, his activities reveal the origin of intelligence. Piaget's account of the sensorimotor period can be best understood by examining the characteristics of infants.

(i) ***Development from Reflex Activity to Sensorimotor Solutions to Problems:*** During the sensorimotor period, much of the behaviour of the new-born infant is reflexive in nature. The baby can suck, grasp, cry and otherwise respond on a reflex level. The baby depends heavily on his reflexes or inherited abilities for his interaction with the environment. Sensorimotor reflexes become modified and, as a result of this, behaviours not present at birth begin to emerge. The hungry infant begins to differentiate between a milk producing nipple and other objects that his mouth encounters. This shows infant's primitive recognition. When the infant is not too hungry he may suck anything — the fingers, the blanket, etc. But when hunger is strong, the infant shows selectivity or discrimination in choosing object. While rejecting the skin surrounding the nipple, the infant seizes immediately upon the nipple itself. He may suck the nipple so rapidly that we may call his behaviour a crude form of recognition. The evidence of discrimination or recognition is an indication of sensorimotor intelligence which is a necessary first step in the development of later thinking and intelligence.

(ii) ***Co-ordination of Sensorimotor Actions:*** Hand-mouth and hand-eye co-ordinations appear at this stage. The infant is able to grasp an object, move towards a goal, and imitate sounds and actions. Sensory experiences — sight, sound, touch and taste — become co-ordinated. Infants gradually learn to touch what they can see and to look at what they hear. By the end of this period, young children's motor actions are well-coordinated. For example, they can pick up toys by performing several simultaneous actions bending their knees, still retaining their balance, reaching towards the toy and grasping it. Co-ordination of sensorimotor actions enables the infant to understand the world and its reality in the most elementary form.

(iii) ***Primitive Ways of Anticipating Future Events***: The infant learns in a primitive way to anticipate future events. When placed in the appropriate position, the infant anticipates nursing by initiating sucking movements.

(iv) ***The First Signs of Curiosity***: The infant shows an interest on moderately novel events, objects or people. But infants may not show curiosity for too familiar or too new objects. Curiosity is a function of the relation between the new object and his previous experience. C=f (NXE), where C means curiosity, N means novelty of objects, E means experience with the object and 'f' means function. For example, a given toy may elicit interest in one child and boredom in another.

(v) ***Tendency to Imitate or Repeat Behaviour or Actions of Models***: Piaget considers imitation as another expression of the infant's endeavour to understand reality and interact effectively with the world. But an infant's imitation is restricted to elementary, vocal and visual movements.

(vi) ***Perception of Objects and People***: For the new-born baby, objects and people have no permanence and hence transitory. But around the second year of life, a child regards objects as having permanence and therefore seeks toys and other objects that disappeared from view. If a four-month-old baby plays with a ball and the ball is rolled out of sight, he will not search for it even if it is easily within the reach. It is as if the ball has ceased to exist once it leaves his field of vision.

(vii) ***Practical Intelligence***: Although the infant cannot think as adults do, he thinks with his body, sensory experiences and motor actions. Thus, this period is known as the sensorimotor period.

Pre-operational Period

This is the second stage of cognitive development. This is a crucial period of cognitive development of the child. This period is called the pre-operational period because the operations of logical thinking are not yet fully developed. This is the pre-logical or partly logical period. During this stage, development proceeds from sensorimotor representations to pre-logical thought and solutions to problems. There are two sub-stages, such as (1) Egocentric stage (one and half years to four years), (2) Intuitive stage (five years to seven years).

(i) ***During the First-half of This Stage, Extremely Rapid Development of Spoken Language Occurs***: By four years of age, the average child in any culture has mastered much of his native language. Typically he understands and uses a great number of words arid the grammar of the language. Educationally it is interesting that all children learn their native language without any formal instruction. If children are raised in a bilingual home, they learn two languages with little difficulty.

(ii) ***The Child's Thought is Dominated by Perception***: In order to understand the thought process of children during this stage, Piaget conducted a number of experiments on conservation. The conservation principle states that a substance is not changed when its shape is changed or when it is divided into parts. For example, the total weight of an object will remain the same even if it is packaged differently; or the volume of a liquid will not become different simply if it is poured in different containers with different shapes. But children at this stage are not capable of solving conservation problems logically. It takes several years for children to learn the principles of conservation.

(iii) ***Thinking in the Pre-operational Period is marked by Egocentrism, Animism and Realism***: Egocentrism refers to the inability of children to look at a problem from the point of view of others. The child thinks that everyone thinks the same way he does; that everyone thinks the same thing he does and quite logically that everything he thinks is 'right'. Egocentrism of thought diminishes slowly through the child's interaction with his peers.

Another characteristic of pre-operational thought is what Piaget calls animism. Animism implies the belief of the child that things are alive because they move. "If it moves, it is alive, if it does not move, then it is not alive." Thus, the moon as well as clouds, stars and the trees are all alive because they move.

Concrete Operational Period

Beginning at the age of seven, children are able to engage in activities of the mind which Piaget calls 'operations.' Piaget uses the term 'operations' to describe cognitive actions closely organised into a strong network or system. They are actions on objects that can be carried out mentally without being carried out physically. The major change in this period is that development proceeds from pre-logical thought to logical solutions to concrete problems. The chief characteristics of this period are as follows:

(i) ***Logical Thinking Using Concrete Objects Occurs During This Stage***: The pre-operational child's thought is dominated by perception rather than logic. But during the concrete operational period, perception no longer dominates. The child is capable of logical thinking. But his logical thinking is confined to concrete objects and actions. The child has, therefore, difficulty in applying his logic to abstract problems, hypothetical problems, and problems dealing with future, and complex verbal problems. For example, if a 7 or 8-year-old child is given three blocks, say X, Y and Z differing in size, he can tell by looking at them that if X is larger than Y and Y is larger than Z then X is larger than Z. He can do this logically without directly comparing each pair of blocks. However, if he was asked the same problem in abstract terms, he would have great difficulty in responding correctly. If told, Mitu is taller than Riku and Riku is taller than Pinku, he would find it difficult to indicate the tallest of the three boys. Nevertheless, this state does represent an advance in child's logical thinking.

(ii) ***The Child's Egocentrism Waves and He is Able to Take Other's Viewpoints***: The child begins to understand changing points of view. His speech becomes increasingly socialised and communicative.

(iii) ***The Concrete Operational Child Understands Conservation of Numerousness, Length, Area and Ultimately Volume***: This understanding of conservation marks the difference between pre-operational thinking and concrete operational thinking. For example, with regard to the length, the pre-operational child contends that a winding path and a straight path have the same length if they begin and end at the same point. But the concrete operational child does not contend in that way. Let us take another example involving conservation of liquids. Bring three bottles — one narrow, one wide and one still wider. Pour the same quantity of water in all bottles. When asked which bottle contains more of water, the pre-operational child will say that the narrow bottle contains more water. He does not understand that the amount of water remains the same although the height may change depending upon the shape of the bottle. But the concrete operational child understands the relationship of the shape of the bottle to the quantity of water.

(iv) ***Decentering and Reversibility of his Thought*:** During this stage, the child's thinking no longer centres about himself, *i.e.*, the child's thought is no longer egocentric. During this stage, the child is able to think of multiple dimensions of a single subject. Reversibility is the ability to reverse thought, to carry a thought backward and forward in time. For example, the concrete operational child can tell the numbers backward from 10 to 1.

(v) ***Capacity to classify Group and Arrange Objects Serially*:** For example, the child can group chickens as living animals and fried food. He is able to understand the relation among things and classes of things. He can also understand changes in the objects and the environment.

Although the child during the concrete operational period makes marked progress in developing concepts, his thinking is still limited to concrete objects and things that can be perceived and manipulated. Thus direct experiences play an important part in forming concepts.

Formal Operational Period

According to Piaget, the final period of intellectual development is the period of formal operations which begins at about the age 12 and is consolidated during adolescence. But in some cases the period may extend beyond the age 16. Individual differences are greater during this period than during other periods.

(i) ***The Adolescent's System of Mental Operations has Reached a Degree of Equilibrium*:** This means, among other things, that the adolescent's thought is flexible and effective. He can deal efficiently with the complex problems of reasoning. He can imagine the many possibilities of solving a problem. Unlike the concrete operational child whose thought is limited to concrete objects and events, the adolescent can deal with hypothetical propositions.

(ii) ***The Adolescent is Able to Apply Logical Thoughts to All Classes of Problems*:** The fact that the adolescent is logical in his approach does not mean that he no longer thinks illogically. Rather it is a fact that the adolescent shows further advancement in his intellectual development with increasing ages. But he cannot differentiate between logic and reality. He cannot distinguish between what is real and what is logical. That is why, many adolescents appear to be very idealistic in their thinking. Piaget says that the adolescent's idealism is temporary. This false idealism will change during subsequent years when he will confront the real world. False idealism is not a negative development. Rather it is a necessary and normal part of development. False idealism is a necessary prior development to realistic thought.

(iii) ***The Adolescent is Able to Use Abstract Rules to Solve a Whole Class of Problems***: For example, consider the problem "What number is 30 less than 3 times itself?" The concrete operational child is likely to begin the problem by trial and error. The adolescent has learned a higher-order operation and may set up the equation $X + 30 = 3X$ and quickly find the answer of 15.

(iv) ***Formal Thought is Rational and Systematic***: Piaget did a number of experiments taking problems of physics, chemistry and mathematics. In all these experiments he wanted to know how the adolescent solves them, what plans he follows, what rules he applies, what hypothesis he forms and in what way he differs from the concrete operational child. He found that the concrete operational child begins his experiments with little foresight and does not have a detailed plan for carrying them out. He does not consider all of the possibilities before he begins. On the contrary, the adolescent deals with propositions, not objects. He plans the tests adequately or designs the experiments properly. He observes the results accurately. He draws proper logical conclusions from his observations. Thus formal thought is rational and systematic.

(v) ***The Adolescent becomes Concerned with the Hypothetical, Abstract and the Future***: The child in the concrete operational period deals largely with concrete objects and with the present. It is for the first time that the adolescent begins to think about himself, his role in life, his plans and the validity of his beliefs.

3. EDUCATIONAL IMPLICATIONS OF SENSORIMOTOR AND PRE-OPERATIONAL PERIODS

(i) The first two periods of cognitive development have practically very little implications for teachers. During these two periods (from birth to 6 years), the child spends most of his time in the home and the peer groups or at best in pre-school centres. The parents and pre-school guides have a major role to play in the cognitive development of children.

(ii) The first duty of parents and pre-school teachers is to understand the normal development of children during sensorimotor period and pre-operational period. Such understanding will help them to appreciate the behaviour of children and guide them successfully along the path of cognitive development.

(iii) Imitations and repetitive behaviours are characteristic features of children during these stages. Children should be encouraged and given the opportunity for learning and strengthening behaviours through information and repetition. This is particularly important for learning certain social manners, exploring the environment, language and other habits.

(iv) Children should be exposed to different varieties of objects so that they will know about them. Young infant's play activities can centre on these objects. Very interesting plays can be organised by parents and older children in the family in relation to the objects, their appearance and disappearance, and this will give pleasure to the infant while at the same time learning about the transitory nature of objects.

(v) During the pre-operational period young children very often ask innumerable questions which appear fantastic, absurd and difficult for older persons. But these questions indicate the child's curiosity to know about his environment. For the young child, parents are all-knowing persons. When parents fail or avoid to answer the child's questions, this adversely affects his curiosity to explore the environment. As a matter of fact, children's questions should be answered directly depending on the level of their understanding. Children's questions can be taken as a starting point for telling interesting stories about people, events and animals.

(vi) The pre-operation stage is the period of pre-school instruction or early childhood education. The pre-school period is critical for intellectual growth. If we leave this period devoted to fun and games, we are lowering the individual's ultimate level of intellectual attainment. This does not mean that we should start formal academic instruction from age 3 or 4 in nursery schools or kindergarten. A study by Bloom (1964) indicates that "About 50% of the intellectual development takes place between conception and age 4, about 30% between ages 4 and 8 and about 20% between ages 8 and seventeen." Thus, if the child has only 50 per cent of his intellectual ability at age 4 but 80 per cent at age 8, it might be better to delay formal education three years so that he can profit more fully from instruction. With 80 per cent of his ability he is likely to learn more quickly and efficiently. Bloom's findings imply that formal academic instruction should not be introduced into the pre-school programme. Rather pre-school should prepare the child for life in the primary school, develop in him the basic social skills, language skills and motor skills. Pre-school education should be as enjoyable for the child as possible. Pre-school education is very useful to compensate the deficiency of children, who come from disadvantaged communities.

4. EDUCATIONAL IMPLICATIONS OF CONCRETE OPERATIONAL AND FORMAL OPERATIONAL PERIODS

Piaget does not consider himself as an educator. He has also never passed an examination in psychology. But his work had its greatest impact upon education and educators. His periods of concrete operational thinking and formal operational thinking have wide implications for teachers. The school and the teachers have important duties and responsibilities for the child during these two stages.

(i) According to Piaget, "The principal aim of education is to create men who are capable of doing new things, not simply of repeating what other generations have done — men who are creative, inventive and discoverers. The second goal of education is to form minds which can be critical, can verify and not accept everything they are offered." The great danger today is of slogans, collective opinion, ready-made trends of thought. We have to be able to resist individually, to enhance, to distinguish between what is proved and what is not. So we need pupils who are active, who learn early to find out by themselves, partly by their own spontaneous activity and partly through materials we set up for them.

(ii) Piaget states that the child, like the persons from a foreign country, thinks less efficiently and differently. This implies that teachers must have knowledge of how children think and why they think so. The child's mind is not an empty slate. Quite the contrary, the child has a host of ideas about the physical and natural world, but these ideas differ from those of adults and are expressed in a different linguistic mode. The first prerequisite for educating children is developing effective modes of communication with them. We must learn to comprehend what the concrete operational children are saying and to respond in the same mode of discourse.

(iii) The stage of concrete operational thinking is the beginning of formal schooling. It is also called the age of reason. The child comes to school with his own ideas about the space, time, quantity and number. His ideas are no doubt incomplete. Education must help children for the modification of their existing knowledge and to learn new materials.

(iv) The child is by nature a knowing creature. The child has ideas about his world through his spontaneous interactions with the environment. But his ideas are limited because of his limited abilities and experiences. Education should not dull the child's eagerness to know by rigid curricula. Curricula should be rich and varied to provide adequate experiences to the child so that he will have a complete view of the world.

Piaget believes that in modern complex societies, communication gaps between the teacher and the child, and the rigid curricula are responsible for cognitive failures and stagnation among children.

(v) Piaget distinguishes between two modes of experiences that result in behaviour modification. One mode occurs when things act upon us. Piaget calls it physical experience or 'P.' Another mode occurs as a result of our actions upon things. He calls it the logicomathematical experience or 'LM.' Piaget puts more emphasis on LM learning. In other words, "to know an object, the child must act upon it." This means:
The child hears — and he forgets
The child sees — and he remembers
The child acts — and he understands

(vi) According to Piaget, teaching at all levels must be founded on the activities of the learners. Cognitive development does not proceed as a consequence of child's talking, listening to other's talk, reading or watching the television. Cognitive development arises out of the activity of the child. Thus, the best methods of education are those that foster the activity or activity learning of the child. But the activities of the child must be spontaneous. The motivation and initiation must flow from within the child. The teacher should create an environment and atmosphere in which children will be active and initiate and complete their own activities. They must be provided with time and materials. Teachers must act as initiators of group activities, arranger of environment, assessor of children's thinking and supplier of materials. The author has noticed this type of teaching situations in all the "Open-Plan Schools" of England and Scotland.

(vii) Piaget's sequence of cognitive development is more important than the ages at which each development takes place. According to him, concrete operational stage precedes the formal operational stage. This implies that a learner must have concrete experiences about concepts and processes before he understands their abstract forms. Teachers must understand whether children are at the concrete operational stage or at the formal stage and plan teaching accordingly. Learning failures are the result of forcing the child to learn beyond his capacity to comprehend facts and teaching abstract concepts before providing concrete experiences. The curriculum and the instructional materials should be distinctly prepared for the concrete operational children and the formal operational children. This is more truer for subjects like mathematics, physics and chemistry.

(viii) Once children enter the formal operational stage, the teacher must encourage problem-solving behaviour among them. They should be guided to plan, to hypothesise, to experiment, to verily and to generalize in problem situations. Guided discovery should be the basis of teaching and learning.

(ix) Piaget has observed that education has long tended to be test-oriented. In testing children's learning, teachers usually value in terms of 'right' and 'wrong' answers. This is wrong evaluation, because children's answers cannot be right or wrong. On the contrary, they indicate the level of their understanding of concepts, rules or principles. Evaluation programmes should therefore aim at broadening their understanding and modifying the quality of instruction to help the slow learners to make up the deficiencies in their understanding.

SELECTED QUESTIONS

1. What is cognitive development? State, in brief, the various stages of cognitive development.
2. State the characteristics of cognitive development during the sensorimotor period/pre-operational period. What are their implications for teachers?
3. State the characteristics of cognitive development during the concrete operational period/formal operational period. What are their implications for the teacher?

8
Development of Language and Play

Although as proud parents or loving relatives, adults often notice how babies grow up physically turning and lifting their head, crawling, standing, walking, etc. and how they learn several tricks from saying 'bye-bye' (ta-ta) to showing their body parts in response to commands, the manner in which the child acquires his first language is hardly ever noticed except when he utters some initial words ('mama,' 'papa,' etc.) or when he says something funny. But, in fact, the flowing ease with which a new-born infant, capable of producing the only sound in crying, soon grows up to be a competent speaker of his mother language is perhaps the most striking language feature of his growth.

1. LANGUAGE DEVELOPMENT

1. What is Language?

Language is man's finest asset. To the philosopher, language may be an instrument of thought, for we think through language. When we think we talk to ourselves. Thought involves sub-vocal speech. To the sociologist, language is a form of behaviour — a behaviour of mind in a social context. To the psychologist, language is a form of activity, an activity of mind of basically four types — listening, speaking, reading and writing.

Webster says, "Language is audible, articulate human speech as produced by the action of the tongue and adjacent vocal organs." Webster also gives a second definition of language as "any means, vocal or otherwise, of expressing or communicating feeling or thought." The first definition limits language to speech and to human beings. The second definition is more inclusive, implying that waving of an arm (to say Tata or bye, bye) or the furrowing of a brow is language, as is writing. For school purposes we ordinarily think of language as verbal symbols, that are associated with ideas and objects and that are produced in systematic patterns to convey meaning from one person to another. The symbols may be graphic (letters and combinations of letters) or they may be vocal (separate sounds or combinations of sounds).

Language does not mean a collection of words strung together in sentences, each word having a separate identity and meaning. In fact, the words are brought together in special ways to give a highly systematic order from which we get a meaning. Similarly, there is no one meaning for each word in a sentence. The meaning we ascribe to a sentence or a word can change from one context to another. Altering the position of words in a sentence alters the sense of the sentence. "The sun is shining" is not the same as "Is the sun shining?" Language, then is not random behaviour, but is systematic, where certain orderings are accepted as having prescribed meanings. Language has form, substance and context. The raw materials of language are the basic sounds which are called phoneme. The phonemic utterances are put together to form morphemes which are the smallest units of a language having a grammatical purpose. For example, in the word 'plans' there are two morphemes — 'plan' and 's.' Prefixes, suffixes and word endings which change the singular to plural or alter the tense are, therefore, morphemes. The sentence "The girl liked to dress her dolls" broken into morphemes would be "The + girl + like + ed + to + dress + her + doll + s." Each morpheme has a particular function in a sentence.

2. Characteristics of Language

John Savage (1973)[1] has described five characteristics of language:

1. Language is human, and only humans can employ oral and written language symbols to represent their thought.

1. Savage, John, *Linguistics for Teachers*, Chicago: Science Research Associates, 1973.

2. Language is speech, which is uniquely human. By school age, most children have mastered their language; they can efficiently use the sounds of their language (phonology); they know the meanings of various sounds (morphology); and they have learned how to arrange language units (syntax).
3. Language is symbolic and arbitrary. Language symbols represent reality so that you can discuss ideas and convey meanings not immediately apparent. For example, teachers ask children what they did last summer and, using symbols, children explain experiences not presently observable. But the symbols are arbitrary; there is no natural connection between letters and reality, only commonly shared agreement about usage.
4. Language is systematic, dynamic, and complete. While language changes (new words and new standards are accepted), it is systematic (for example, the formation of plurals and the arrangement of elements) and complete (we can communicate all our ideas and experiences through language).
5. Language is a cultural phenomenon. Any language reflects the culture of the people who speak it and thus serves their needs, values, and customs.

3. Young Children and Language Usage

Although communication is the ultimate purpose of language, there are several details which Joan Tough (1974)[2] calls the framework of language uses. If you observe young children in play situations in and out of school, you will find the following uses of language:

1. *Self-maintaining*: When a child is protecting his own interests, justifying his claims or behaviour, criticizing or even threatening others.
2. *Directing*: When a child is monitoring his own actions, or telling someone else what to do.
3. *Reporting on Present or Past Experiences*: When a child is labelling, referring to incidents, relating what has happened.

2 Tough, Joan, *Listening to Children Talking*, HMSO, London, 1974.

4. ***Towards Logical Reasoning***: When a child is explaining a process, recognising causal relationships, drawing conclusions.
5. ***Predicting***: When a child is beginning to anticipate what will happen next, anticipate a sequence of events, predict the consequences of actions.
6. ***Projecting***: When a child is projecting into the experiences of others, projecting into the feelings of others.
7. ***Imagining***: When a child is developing an imaginary situation based on real life, developing an imaginary situation based on fantasy.

In order to identify the uses of language, parents and teachers should encourage children and give them time to speak, to talk, to converse. In doing so, one should not be in a hurry, or over-ambitious, but have patience. In pre-school centres, the teacher may organise "structured play" situations like small word play, role playing or doll play, play in the garden, etc. The teacher may get children out for a little bit of expedition. Parents can also do the same thing. All this will give children opportunity to use language.

4. Acquisition of Language

How does a verbally helpless infant develop into an articulate adult? Scholars have proposed many, often conflicting, theories or models to explain how humans acquire language. For example, B.F. Skinner argues that language is a learned behaviour. Jean Piaget and Jerome Bruner believe that language is an integral part of the individual's cognitive development. It is the result of maturation and environmental influences. Noam Chomsky stresses that language is the result of one's innate capacity. A teacher is not concerned with the debate or the conflicting views about language acquisition. But a knowledge of these theories will undoubtedly help the teacher to understand how children acquire language, the sequence of development of language structure and how he can facilitate children's acquisition of language.

Views of Piaget

According to Piaget, language is a symptom of existing cognitive structures of the child. There are four major cognitive stages:

sensorimotor, pre-operational, concrete operations, and formal operations. Language acquisition varies depending upon the particular stage of cognitive development. During the sensorimotor period (age 0-2) language is almost absent until the final months of the period. During pre-operational period (age 2-7) two categories of speech are noticed: egocentric speech and socialized speech. In egocentric speech children do not care to whom they are speaking or if anyone is listening. There are three sub-divisions of egocentric speech:

1. Repetition, which is not communication and is used for pleasurable purposes; it has no social character.
2. Monologue, in which the child does not address anyone but talks to himself or herself; again, this is not communication.
3. Collective monologue, in which no one listens to the child, although other young children are present; the child's egocentric speech precludes others from participating. In socialized speech, the child exchanges thoughts with others, criticizes someone, questions another, and definitely attempts to interact with others. Socialized speech follows egocentric speech. Even though the 6-year-old is capable of socialized speech, it is still limited, that is, there is no effort to explain or to search for causes; most of socialized speech consists of commands and criticisms.

It is not until children are about 7 or 8 that there is any genuine verbal understanding between them. But their understanding is limited to concrete objects. That is, children use language in relation to concrete objects. They cannot use language for abstract ideas. It is only during the formal operation period that children's language is freed from the concrete. Now children develop the verbal ability to express abstract ideas, *e.g.*, the possible consequences of an action.

Views of Bruner

For Bruner, language is crucial for mental development and is not merely a symptom of underlying cognitive structures. He believes that language has a strong influence on thought. The child acquires not only a way of saying something but also a powerful instrument for combining experiences and organizing thoughts about things. He further believes that language has six distinct functions:

1. *The Referential Function:* The child uses language to give a message, *e.g.*, "Bharati is coming."
2. *The Emotive Function:* The child uses language to express his feelings, *e.g.*, "Damn; I cut my finger."
3. *The Conative Function:* Language indicates the intent of the message, *e.g.*, "Will you give my toy, please?"
4. *The Phatic Function:* Language is expressed in a way to maintain contact with the listener, *e.g.*, "Yeah, yeah, yeah", during a telephone conversation.
5. *The Politic Function:* Sometimes the word combinations and not rules are emphasized, *e.g.*, "Where you going?"
6. *The Metalingual Function:* When verbal precision is emphasized, *e.g.*, "Is war or fight the better word?"

Bruner concludes that language serves many functions, pursues many aims, and employs many voices. It commands as it refers, describes as it makes poetry, adjudicates as it expresses, creates beauty as it clarifies, and serves multiple needs as it maintains contact.

For Bruner, language instruction should be an integral part of school curriculum. But some precautions are necessary if language is to be an attractive subject. For example, teachers should avoid initially teaching children what language should be and having them memorize the grammar of the language.

Views of Chomsky

Contrary to the cognitive explanation of language acquisition, psycholinguists believe that children possess an innate competence for language acquisition just as they possess an innate capacity for walking. No one has to tell children how to walk; they talk and walk without consciously knowing how they did so. Not only do children quickly manifest this competence, they also display an ability to produce and understand at an amazing rate sentences they have not heard previously. According to Chomsky, this innate capacity to acquire language is the result of our uniquely human biological inheritance. He calls it our Language Acquisition Device (LAD).

Chomsky states that no one acquires a language by learning all the possible sentences of that language. Instead of learning billions of sentences, a child unconsciously acquires a grammar that can generate an infinite number of sentences in his own native language. Not every human being can play the violin, do calculus, jump high hurdles, or sail boats, no matter how excellent his teachers are. But every person constantly creates utterances, never before spoken on earth. The person's ability to generate new sentences, grammatically correct, is called the generative transformational grammar. Chomsky believes that the sentences that are the result of the generative transformational grammar have both surface and deep structures. For example, a sentence may have a single deep structure:

> "The infant ate the chocolate quickly and this bothered her mother."

But there may be many different surface structures:

> "The mother was bothered by the infant eating the chocolate quickly.
>
> That the infant ate the chocolate quickly bothered the mother.
>
> The infant, eating the chocolate quickly, bothered the mother."

Chomsky makes a distinction between language competence and language performance. The speaker's innate ability and knowledge of language are called his competence. The speaker's use of language is called performance. In every speaker, the competence is greater than his performance. But if the gap is very big, language acquisition is affected and blocked.

Views of Skinner

"Men act upon the word, and change it and are changed in turn by the consequences of their actions," with these words, B.F. Skinner began his analysis of language in his famous book *Social Behaviour.* Skinner explains language acquisition in terms of learning principles or more particularly his operant conditioning techniques. A child must first make a response. If the response is reinforced it is strengthened, repeated, or occurs again. Thus the child makes a sound, utters a word or a sentence. The sound or the utterance is reinforced (approved by the parents in some way).

As a result of this, the child repeats the sound or the utterance in similar situation. If the utterance is not reinforced or reinforced negatively (disapproved) that utterance is not repeated again. It is through this sequence of response-consequences that the child acquires language.

The views of scholars like Piaget, Bruner, Chomsky and Skinner are definitely conflicting. But in the light of the knowledge we have gained from these scholars, we can explain the sequence of language development. There may be individual differences so far as the age of development is concerned, but the sequence remains the same for all.

1. At birth language is practically absent.
2. At about 4 weeks small throaty sounds are noticed.
3. The starting point in language development is the child's cry or noises, smiles and cooing at the age of 16 weeks.
4. Around 28 weeks, the babbling stage begins. Now, the baby makes sounds such as 'dadadada.' The baby also vocalizes to toys. Initially the babbling sounds have no symbolic meaning. But the baby soon discovers that people, dada in the above instance, pay particular attention to him when he makes certain sounds. This reinforces the baby's sounds and he repeats these sounds.
5. Around 40 weeks, the baby imitates sounds made by adults and takes these sounds into his own system. Now the baby says one word.
6. Around 52 weeks, the baby says two or more words.
7. Around 18 months, the baby combines words to form basic sentence patterns.
8. Around 24 months, the baby uses simple phrases and understands simple directions.
9. Around 36 months, the child's vocabulary tremendously increases. Now he talks in sentences, and answers simple questions. The vocabulary explosion at 3 years occurs at about the same age in every healthy child throughout the world. It is at this age that some children are sent to the kindergarten, play groups, day-care centres or pre-school centres.
10. Around 4 years, the child uses conjunctions and understands prepositions.

11. Around 5 years, the child speaks without infantile articulation. He asks "why?" By their fifth birthday, almost all the normal children can speak and understand all kinds of sentences (such as simple, complex, active, passive, negative, interrogative, etc.) which any other adult speaker of their language is capable of using.

Thus, to grow up into a competent user of mother tongue, a child only takes 3½ to 4 years. This is an amazing fact considering the difficulty the adults face in acquiring a second language even after much longer periods of deliberate training and effort. Even more striking is the fact that a child born here can be taken to any place in the world and he/she would acquire the language used by adults in the place with the same ease and speed as other children throughout the world. Further, it has been observed that children all over the world acquiring different languages do so in quite similar ways suggesting common universal features of languages. Regardless of cultural and linguistic variations, major milestones of language development unfold in universally similar ways closely corresponding to major milestones of physical and motor development of children. These and many other observations by linguists and child psychologists clearly suggest that humans have species-specific propensity to acquire language without any deliberate training. All that human children need to acquire a language is to hear the adults around them speak it. So powerful is this capacity that children in bilingual and multilingual environments learn all the languages they hear and become fluent in each one of them. Children's capacity in this respect is much greater and efficient compared to that of adults who find it quite hard to acquire native-like competence in a second language to which they are exposed during their adulthood.

5. Factors Influencing Language Development

Several factors influence language development of children. These are given below:

Child's Maturity Pattern

The child's maturity level, or more particularly, his physical and motor development, influences his language development. The child cannot make any sound, the first step in language development, until his vocal apparatus is mature. Again as we have discussed earlier, at different ages different types of linguistic behaviour occur. There may be individual differences in respect of age at which a particular linguistic behaviour occurs, but the sequence of language development closely corresponds to the child's physical and motor development.

Family Environment

The family environment is the most important factor other than the child's maturity pattern in determining the language facility he develops and the speed with which he develops it. For instance, an only child may have closer association with adults than one who has brothers and sisters. This closeness may result in the development of a larger vocabulary and more maturity in expression. Similarly, the child whose parents talk with him a great deal develops language facility earlier than one who grows up in a family in which he is ignored or told to "be quiet." In addition to providing the child with language experiences, the family provides the language model — the kind of language he is going to imitate.

Child's Mental Development

A child's mental development and his progress in using language move along together. Every experience a child has bears upon his development, especially his intellectual and language development. Each new experience or enrichment of an earlier one results in his gaining greater knowledge and understanding. A child soon learns that language is important to the gaining of knowledge and understanding, and he makes use of it as he explores things around him.

Objects around the Child

The things a child encounters in his exploration determine the language he uses, the words he learns, and the meaning he attaches to those words. A pre-school child living in a city apartment house certainly has different experiences from those of the farm child. One will certainly know the words *woods, pig, pasture,* and *hedge,* and the other will certainly know *taxi, auto, elevator,* etc. Of course, each will know some words in both lists, or they may have different meanings attached since words, lexical items, have meaning only as they are used in context.

School

Besides the above four factors, the school has also a powerful influence upon the language development of children. The term school is used here to refer to pre-school and primary schools. So far as the home language is concerned, the first four factors are very important. But there are great differences in language used at home and language used outside. Generally, children who attend nursery schools, kindergarten or other pre-school centres and primary schools both at the formal and non-formal sectors have greater vocabulary and functionally they are better than those who do not attend such schools. This happens so because the children in pre-schools and primary schools are exposed to a richer linguistic environment with enough reading materials.

6. Language Training in Pre-School Years[3]

From the preceding discussion it may appear that children need no training for language development. While this may be largely true for development of home language or of language for social use, the same is not true of developing language readiness for school purpose. The primary education of the three R's — reading, writing and arithmetic skills — are primarily a language-based instruction programme. Children in early school years are required to follow instruction of teachers, read, comprehend written language and demonstrate expressive skills — oral and written. There are some basic differences between the characteristics of the home language and language used in schools. In home and other social situations, use of language is usually context embedded. For example, the meaning of a child's utterance "Mammy, milk" varies greatly with the context in which it occurs. Depending on the context of use, the same utterances may mean "I want to drink milk," "There is milk on the table," "Mammy spilled some milk," etc. But the language used in classrooms and textbook language are relatively context

3. Mohanty, A.K., "Language Training in Pre-school Years," a paper presented in the Orientation Programme for CDPOs and *Anganwadi* Supervisors on Pre-school Education — Bhubaneswar (1985).

free; their meanings are much less dependent on the social context of their use. Further, whereas the home language is mostly here and now type, the school and textbook language is abstract and mostly refers to concepts, ideas, events and things not present in the immediate conscious environment; references are mostly to past and future. Whereas in home language the sentences need not be fully formed, complete grammatical ones, this is a necessary condition for good language use in classrooms. Thus, there are significant differences between the language that the child acquires and the one he would be required to use in school. The situation is even more complicated for a large number of children for whom the school language is unrelated to the language they grow up with. In any case, children need to be prepared for school language use and the requirement for such preparation is even greater with children from lower socio-economic strata where the home language is much more different from the school language compared to such differences among the urban middle class children. To the extent that the primary objective of pre-school training is to develop school readiness among 3 to 5-year old children, pre-schools must emphasize language training so that children can derive maximum benefit from regular schooling.

Language use in school is primarily a communication process and developing competence in such communicative arts has five aspects: (i) listening (with attentiveness), (ii) speaking, (iii) reading, (iv) writing, and (v) use of language for abstract reasoning. It has been found that those children who have better competence in these aspects of communication arts are more successful in school compared to other children. Thus, to prepare children for high achievement in schools, pre-school experience must focus on language training and on providing a rich linguistic environment for the child. Generally, some simple but basic rules have to be followed in pre-schools towards these objectives.

Talk to the Children in the Pre-schools

An important difference has been noticed between competent children who grow up to do well in schools and less competent ones who fail to gain from schooling — the mothers (as well as fathers and other adults) of competent children talk to their children more often than the mothers of the less competent ones.

In pre-schools also children need to be talked to. While talking to children *talk slowly, clearly and in simple sentences. Avoid baby talk with children.* The comprehension or understanding of any child or language user is always ahead of his own expressive capacity. So, although a child himself talks in a childlike manner, he is capable of understanding normal adult speech. If you talk to children as they talk to you, there is no propeller for furthering language growth which becomes slower, as a result.

Provide Language Experience through Stories and Songs

Stories and nursery rhymes are essential activities for enhancing children's expressive and receptive (understanding) skills. Children can be encouraged to tell a story from memory or to narrate a story from pictures. Children do not lose interest in a story told several times or singing a known song over and again. Rather, they find a known story or song more interesting than an unknown one. Telling stories from a book and allowing children to look into the pictures in the book at the same time is desirable since this encourages children's interest in books — something that is essential in creating good pre-reading habit. Dramatization of a story or a song while saying it helps keep children's attention uninterrupted.

Listening with Attention

A major aspect of children's language development during pre-school years and their language readiness for schools is attentive listening to conversation and other sounds around them. In a regular classroom children have to hear their teacher talk which takes at least 75 per cent of the class time. So classroom achievement depends largely on children's ability to listen and follow teachers' instructions. Children have to attend to only relevant and necessary sounds and talk, picking them up from a host of other noises. Thus, there has to be purposeful and attentive listening rather than simple indifferent hearing of sounds. The listening skills in pre-school children have to be cultivated through a number of planned activities such as locating the source of a sound or imitation of various sounds, etc. Teacher's behaviour in pre-schools provides a model for children to follow. As such, the pre-school teacher herself must listen to the children attentively in order to encourage attentive listening among them. If children are given instruction in the pre-schools clearly but only once without any repetition as far as practicable, they will quickly learn not to miss the talk of the teacher and to attend to that carefully. But, the teacher may repeat an instruction if specifically requested by any child and while doing so, the teacher should also remind the children to be more careful in listening. It has, however, to be remembered that how much, at a time, pre-school children can attend to and listen with comprehension has a limit and teacher's language use in pre-school must be within the listening span of the children.

Provide Ample Opportunity for the Children to Speak and to Express

Often, adults and pre-school teachers guess what a child wants to speak even before he expresses himself and act accordingly. As a result, the child is not encouraged to speak and to try to express himself. In order to foster expressive skills, the child has to be carefully and attentively heard without putting too much pressure on him to speak something often against his will. The pre-school environment must be such that children feel quite relaxed and self-confident in expressing themselves.

Care in Correcting Mistakes in Children's Utterances

Mistakes and mispronunciation, stuttering, stammering, and hesitation are normal phenomena in children's language use during the pre-school years and should be accepted as such. Creating much fuss over them and prompt correction particularly in front of others only serves to reduce children's motivation to express themselves.

Instead of direct and blunt correction, any error in their speech can be indirectly corrected by providing the correct form in subsequent conversation. Sometimes mistakes are natural course in language development and may occur as a result of over-generalization of certain rules. For example, it is quite common among the English speaking children at a stage of their language development to say something like, "I goed there," as a result of over-generalisation of the rule for past tense marking. To point to the error, telling the children that they are wrong usually serves no purpose. The correct form ('went') can be given to the child by the teacher in his/her own conversation. Children need to hear a correct form several times before they begin to use it in their utterances. Telling the children, "don't say like this," only generates disinterestedness and unwillingness in them for fluent and relaxed language use and results in a variety of speech disorders particularly in conditions of heightened emotionality such as anger and excitement.

With proper care and observance of these principles, it should not be difficult to accelerate adequate language development among pre-school children and to create readiness in them to meet the challenge of school language. With adequate receptive and expressive skills, transition to reading and writing instruction is not a problem. Reading readiness depends on communicative skills, knowledge of vocabulary and interest in books. The following symptoms can be observed to determine the extent of reading readiness in a child:

1. The child should be able to comprehend a simple picture;
2. He should be able to talk so as to make himself understood;
3. He should be able to demonstrate his conceptualisation of the left-to-right orientation in written forms in the books;
4. He should be able to discriminate between different shapes, patterns and alphabets;
5. He should have knowledge of sound discrimination and a sensibility for rhythm;
6. He should have perception of sequences in stories and other events;
7. He should demonstrate ability to follow verbal instructions; and above all,
8. He should have interest in books and reading from them.
   In pre-schools, training for school language and reading readiness can be effectively provided through stories, songs, games and a variety of interesting activities.

2. PLAY

1. Meaning and Characteristics of Play

Meaning

Every child plays. Children would not be children if they did not play. Play is the chief business in a child's life. What is play? Why do children play?

Play has been defined differently by different authorities but a satisfactory definition has not been found yet. Dennis Child (1976) has said, "Play is a universally spontaneous activity especially among young children." This spontaneous activity of the child is directed towards specific purposes (which may vary from situation to situation or from time to time) or is performed for its own sake. Jerome Bruner (1965)[4] held the opinion that "play must be understood as practice in coping with the environment." Play can be viewed as an opportunity for children to manipulate the materials of their environment, and to assist them in differentiating the real from the imaginary. We will accept this meaning of play for purpose of educating children.

Purposes

Many theories have arisen to explain the purposes of play, but we are still not certain. Amongst the theories, we find the 'surplus energy' theory which regards play as the inevitable outlet for the abundant energy of youth made available for the survival of the species. Once the business of survival has been catered for, the surplus is used in exploratory activities. 'Recreative' theories emphasize the hedonistic aspects of play. We play for pure joy, pleasure and relaxation. The 'preparatory' theory considers play as a rehearsal for adult roles (girl and doll — mother with baby) in which life are played out in miniature.

One theory also considers 'achievement-mastery' and a desire to have physical mastery over the environment as having some bearing on the motivation to play, Stamm (1976)5 states that if you were to ask, "why do children play," you would

4. Bruner, J.S., "Towards a Theory of Instruction," Belknap and Harvard, p. 118.
5. Stamm, Ira, "The Multiple Functions of Play," in *The New Children,* edited by J.F. Travers, Stamford, Conn, Greylock Publishers, 1976.

receive an amazing variety of responses, but they would fall into three main categories:

1. Play is fun.
2. Children learn about themselves and their world through play.
3. Play permits children to cope with intense emotional reactions.

Characteristics

Play is not easy to define. Its purposes are not easily understood. However, if you examine the meaning of play, its purposes and the various forms of activity which we call play, certain general characteristics of play can be identified. The characteristics of play are as follows:

Play is Instinctive: Every child breathes, sucks, and moves his arms without being aware of it. Similarly, he throws, runs, jumps and talks. All these activities are instinctive. Children have a natural inborn desire and ability to do them and with practice their ability develops into skill. These activities are the starting point of play. Play is the most natural and spontaneous activity of a child. Although play is natural and spontaneous, different forms or types of play are noticed at different periods depending upon the dominant impulses and interests at different times. Similarly, the forms and types of play at different periods in life depend upon learning. Thus play is instinctive in nature but is influenced by learning experiences.

Play is Activity: For young children play is just the opposite of idleness. Play involves activity — bodily activity, sensory activity or cognitive activity. When children play hop-step-and-jump or at chasing and shouting, their activity is essentially bodily. When they play at searching, pointing out distant objects or counting birds, stars in the sky — their activity is sensory. When they play at solving riddles, telling or listening to stories, reciting rhymes, manipulating blocks and materials, their activity is mental or cognitive. A particular play may also combine different activities.

Play Absorbs All Attention and Strong Interests of a Child

At play, children are so deeply absorbed in and their attention is so deeply concentrated on what they are doing that they are hardly aware of what is happening just near them. At play children are full of enthusiasm, inspiration, will and purpose so much so that they forget their mother's call, their mealtime or the school bell.

Play is engaged in for its Own Sake

There is no ultimate goal or end of play; children play for the sake of play. The only motive behind play is joy or pleasure that is derived from play.

To sum up, we can say:

Play is natural
Play is spontaneous
Play is freedom
Play is activity
Play is fun
Play involves self-expression
Play is practice in coping with the present and future environment.
Play is a relief from excessive energy and emotions.

2. Development of Play Activities

Pre-school Years

The development of play follows the same pattern of development of social behaviour of children. If you observe the play of pre-school children, you can classify them into six forms or levels. These are:

Unoccupied behaviour,
Onlooker behaviour,
Solitary independent play,
Parallel play,
Associative play and
Co-operative or organized supplementary play.

Play behaviour of children proceeds from unoccupied behaviour to co-operative play. During first few months after birth, the infant shows some reflex activity such as moving the arms and the legs. The infant is not occupied with any specific play behaviour. Gradually, he develops onlooker behaviour. He observes other children in play situations, but his immature growth does not permit him to play. Children under three years of age are principally involved in being onlookers, solitary play and parallel play. In solitary play, the child plays alone with nobody around him. Parallel activity describes situations in which a child plays beside other children but not with them. Generally solitary play precedes parallel play. But the same child may be involved in solitary play at one time and parallel play at other times. In parallel play, the child does not openly influence other children, nor do they try to influence him. Children over four are still occupied with parallel play but engage in far more associative group play and co-operative play than younger children. In associative play, the child is more actively involved in the play of others. The children engage in activities that are identical or similar. They borrow toys and other materials and imitate one another. But associative play lacks the team spirit. In cooperative play the child is a member of the group that plays a game, or makes a product, or engages in role playing. Co-operative play is generally the characteristic of older children.

Pre-school children are likely to be individualistic. They are not very much concerned with developing group relationships in play. When they play together co-operatively, it does not last very long. Pre-school children will usually accept any child as a playmate, provided he wants to play what they are playing. Even adults are also accepted as playmates. There are exceptions to this, of course. Sometimes two or three pre-schoolers in a nursery school will choose to play with one another and with no one else, and such an association may continue for months. More usually, however, their choice of playmates will change from day to day and week to week.

Primary School Years

Before the child enters school, the number of his companions is limited. At school he meets many new playmates and finds himself wanting their friendship and approval. To win them he soon realizes that he must learn to share games and toys, to take turns, to give and take.

After six, imitation tends to be replaced by self-assertion and children begin doing things on their own initiative. Running, dodging, chasing and the like are more in evidence and self-assertion is so strong that more time is lost in disputing than in playing. Passion for self-display and pride in achievements is strong and interest in competitive games is entirely individual. It is just at this stage that the school and the home should co-operate to provide ample opportunity for individual contests in games and sports. Till twelve, the spirit continues to be dominant, muscular control and skill grow, interest in physical activity is vigorous and varied, and co-operation and team spirit begin to dawn though still at a low level.

After twelve, the child becomes more and more interested in organized games and co-operative play. The gang spirit begins to develop and team games are more popular. Groups begin to divide into 'teams,' 'sides' and 'gangs' and individual competition makes way for cooperation and group rivalry. From 'pairs,' 'sides' and 'teams' grow the spirit of co-operation and fellowship, the subordination of personal glory to that of the team. Ideals of self-sacrifice and heroism appeal strongly to them and interests in club activities are sharpened.

In later childhood, the national games of hockey, football and cricket dominate the interests of many a boy. Children play such games incessantly, saving their pocket expenses to buy equipments. Girls almost give up playing as soon as they reach the age of twelve or thirteen. But they may play indoor games and take interest in stories about personal achievements, glory, life's problems and adventures. Girls who come from progressive families still continue to play games like badminton, hockey, running, jumping and even cricket too.

3. Some Activities for Younger Children

In the previous sections we discussed how play behaviour develops at different ages and stages. This implies that suitable play activities can be organised for younger children depending upon their characteristic behaviour patterns. Rajagopal and Narayan[6] have compiled 87 different types of common Indian games for pre-school children and seven types of games for physically

---

6. For more about play activities, see the following book:
—"Here we play" compiled by V. Rajagopal and J. Narayan on behalf of Indian Association for 'Pre-school Education,' Coimbatore Branch (undated).

handicapped children. Mina Swaminathan* has also suggested different categories of play activities for young children.

Children grow, develop and learn through play. Play is useful for all aspects of a child's development — physical, social, emotional and intellectual. Thus different play activities can be organised for different aspects of development. Of course, some play activities are useful for various developments. Examples of some play activities are given below:

Physical Development	*Play activities*	
	running	balancing
	jumping	rocking
	hopping	pushing and pulling
	skipping	building
	throwing	swimming
	crawling	splashing
	stretching	dancing
	rolling	
	swinging	
	bouncing	
	sliding	

The same activity can be performed in different ways. For example:

Jumping: Jumping off a low wall, a stool, a step, or a rock.
Jumping over a brick, a stone, a pole, or a rope.
Jumping in and out of a tyre, a hoop, a circle, or a tub.
Jumping along a line, a rope, or a stick.
Jumping between two stones, two lines or two ropes.
Jumping while holding or carrying something.

Language Development: *Play Activities*

Games and activities that give children the opportunity to sing, speak, listen and have fun; acting games like 'Statues,' 'Do as I say,' 'The colour game,' 'Blindfold race;' puzzles (picture puzzles, word puzzles, sound puzzles, etc.) story-telling; and puppet play.

---

* —"Play activities for young children" prepared by Mina Swaminathan, on behalf of UNICEF, New Delhi (undated).

4. Organising Play Activities in Schools

There are different play activities for different aspects of development. A balanced programme will include:

Something for the body,
Something for social adjustment,
Something for the mind,
Something for creative expression,
Something for the hands,
Something for the emotions,
Something for the senses,
Something for the curiosity.

For the above purposes, the teacher should plan time, space, equipment and materials.

Children are subject to different moods. Sometimes they need to play alone. The teacher should be able to recognise this need and allow them the freedom to play with whatever they please. At other times they will be eager to play in a group and then they will need careful instruction from the teacher and guidance on how to follow directions. The teacher must provide for both individual activity and group activity. Here are some of the different types of play that the teacher must consider when planning his day. He needs to balance both sides in order to enjoy wholehearted participation:

Physically active and noisy	Physically quiet and restful indoors, outdoors
Individual play/work	Group activity/work
Free play	Structured or guided activity
Usual daily routine	New activity or event

Children need space for physical movement and activity, an environment that stimulates variety and change in the environment, and a sense of order in the environment. If the school can provide these essentials, they can learn while they play. Ideally the school should have:

A room for a group of up to 30 children,
a verandah or courtyard,
a small compound, garden or open space,
a kitchen to cook and store food,
a latrine,

a clean water supply for drinking water,

containers for storage of all the materials.

Perhaps most schools do not have all or some of the above. In that case, the teacher must make the best use of what he has. The teacher must learn to adapt his limited facilities. If the school has nothing like extra space, but classrooms only, then one corner of each classroom may be utilized as 'toy corner' or 'play corner' for very young children and for arranging and storing play materials.

It will be desirable to display clearly materials to play and work with, pictures, charts and other objects, samples of children's work in the classroom. Display not only makes the place attractive and cheerful but is also an aid to learning. Display gives children an opportunity to develop a sense of achievement and a desire to perform better.

In order to organise a worthwhile programme of play activities, the teacher needs some simple materials and basic equipments. The teacher needs same outdoor play equipments such as swings, slides and seesaws; furniture, such as mats, *durries;* storage, such as trunks, boxes, tins, etc. He needs materials that are free, such as sand, earth, clay, leaves, flowers, stones and other natural materials; things that he can collect, such as used boxes, cartoons, books, cardboard, cigarette packets, matchboxes; things that he must buy, such as paints, slates, story-book, picture books, dolls, toys, tools and musical instruments.

5. Play and Cognitive Development

Most homes do not have a right environment, ample space and adequate materials for play activities of young children. Even some parents do not allow children to go out and play with other children. Our schools are also handicapped in this regard. We, as parents and teachers, must recognise the tremendous power of play in facilitating or accelerating cognitive development of children. Play-way techniques can be adopted by teachers and parents to help children learn through their experiences and the experiences of others.

When children play with blocks, household objects and other simple materials, they can be encouraged to compare and classify objects, identify the similarities and differences between objects, arrange objects in terms of their shape, size and colour. Seriation, classification, discrimination, generalization, etc. can be learnt while children play. These also help in concept learning and language learning.

Piaget has observed that cognitive development proceeds by stages. Each stage is characterized by specific cognitive behaviours. This implies that play activities should be suitably organised for children of different age-groups. In order to facilitate the cognitive development of young children, suitable play materials should be available to children. The following play materials may be provided to children for the above purpose:

picture pairs	cards: associated pairs;
picture families	cards in series/graded;
dominoes	pictures;
sequence cards	number cards;
bingo board	board games counters;
jigsaws	dice;
puzzles	assembly and constructional materials;
puzzle and activity books	board games;
problem-solving toys	mosaic shapes and tiles
slates and pencils	

SELECTED QUESTIONS

1. What are the characteristics of language? How does a young child use language?
2. How do children acquire language? What factors influence the acquisition of language?
3. State the duties and responsibilities of the pre-schools in the language training of young children.
4. What is play? State the characteristics of play.
5. Discuss the development of play behaviours of young children during the pre-school and primary school years.
6. How does play influence the cognitive development of children?

9
Social and Moral Development

1. MEANING OF SOCIAL AND MORAL DEVELOPMENT

Social development refers to the development of social behaviours among children. It refers to how the infant becomes a socialized individual: how he learns to relate to others; how he interacts with others; how he conforms to the social rules and regulations of the community and society to which he belongs. Moral development proceeds along with social development.

Moral development includes moral behaviour and moral concepts. Moral behaviour means behaviour in conformity with moral code of the social group. 'Moral' comes from the Latin word 'mores' meaning manners, customs and folkways. Moral concepts are the rules of behaviour to which the members of a culture become accustomed and which determine the expected behaviour patterns of all group members.

An individual whose social development has been disturbed due to some or the other reasons, and the individual who is socially maladjusted develop immoral behaviour. Immoral behaviour is behaviour that fails to conform to social expectations. Such behaviour arises not due to ignorance of social expectations but due to intentional disapproval of social standards or lack of feeling of obligation to conform. Similarly, an individual who has been deprived of the opportunity to learn social behaviours develops immoral or non-moral behaviour. immoral or non-moral behaviour arises due to ignorance of what the social group expects rather than intentional violation of the group's standards.

Moral behaviour not only conforms to social standards but also it is carried out voluntarily. It is always accompanied by feeling of responsibility for one's acts. It involves giving primary consideration to the welfare of the group and considering personal gain or desires as having secondary importance. True morality is rarely found in children; it appears during the adolescence period. This does not mean that the child is immoral, because most of the behaviour of young children is due to ignorance of social expectations. Thus, a young child is unmoral, not immoral.

2. SOCIAL DEVELOPMENT DURING INFANCY

(i) Development of Expressive Behaviour

Social development of an individual begins in infancy with the appearance of expressive behaviours. At first, expressive behaviour consists of *gazing* which is an orienting behaviour and *crying, smiling, babbling,* and *imitation,* which are signalling behaviours. Thus, infants make social contact chiefly through five orienting and signalling behaviours. These behaviours appear of their own accord in all infants. Over time, however, each of these behaviours becomes directed towards people rather than objects, and towards certain people rather than others. Each behaviour is also influenced by how these people respond.

Early expressive behaviours tend to be repeated when parents and others, who are caring for children provide them with pleasant stimulation such as by smiling at them, talking to them or picking them up. There is a strong relationship between the amount for stimulation infants receive in response to their expressive behaviour and amount of expressive behaviour they show. Without such stimulation, infants may be slow to develop this behaviour and thus lag in making social contacts with others.

(ii) Selective Attachment to Parents

At about 6 to 8 months of age, infants begin to form special attachments to their parents and other familiar persons in their world. These attachments are not necessary to those who spend

In some homes, children are discouraged by their parents for performing various activities. Such children fail to co-operate in various school programmes. A child who has been discouraged in his home does not understand the significance of co-operative behaviour in the school. Rather he demonstrates "attention-getting mechanism" to draw other's attention towards him.

School Environment

In addition to the home environment, the school environment is largely responsible for behaviour problems of children.

The school policy, the social, moral and psychological climate of the school, teacher's behaviour and attitude towards the problem child, and interpersonal relationship among children in the school, etc. lead to problem behaviour or aggravate the problem behaviour of children.

Some children notice differences in the behaviour acceptable in the school and those that are encouraged in the home. Generally in most schools, middle class behavioural standards are accepted. If a child from low social class imitates the behaviour of middle class and behaves accordingly in his home, parents discourage it. If the child behaves according to the low class standard, he is punished in the school. This creates confusion in the child's mind. Behaviour problems arise out of such confusion. Children who express their confusion adopt defence mechanisms. Children who do not express their confusion or conflict but keep it within themselves remain unhappy or moody most of the time.

The child learns in the school that adults are always right and that children are wrong. He also finds a gap between what adults say and what they do. For example, a teacher who himself smokes advises children not to smoke. Thus, the child starts defying the teacher. Defiance is a problem behaviour.

Children are forced to abide by the rules and regulations of the school. But they do not find any meaning or justification of the school policy. Thus they begin to defy or violate school policy, and consequently are punished for violating school discipline. The punished child may later follow school policy or he may continue to violate the discipline.

the most time with infants or who take care of their physical needs. Rather, the attachments are to those persons who are most responsive to an infant's needs for social attention and stimulation. Hence, it is the quality and not the quantity of parental care that is crucial for infant's personality development.

(iii) Stranger Anxiety and Separation Anxiety

After infants have formed selective attachments, they often develop stranger anxiety. Stranger anxiety usually reaches its height at around one year of age and then gradually diminishes, as infants learn that they do not have to fear people just because they are unfamiliar. Beginning at around 8 months of age, infants are also likely to become upset when they are separated from those to whom they have become attached. This separation anxiety, which reaches a peak between 13 and 18 months of age is expressed through crying and search for the absent person. If the separation is relatively long, infants may lose interest in having social contact with anyone. However, these reactions usually disappear soon after the absent person returns or when the infants are placed in familiar surroundings and with familiar people.

(iv) Assertions of Independence

As children near the age of two, they begin to detach themselves from their parents and to assert themselves as independent persons. This detachment becomes clear as children start to say 'no' and do what they please regardless of what their parents may want. Since this is a normal part of social development, parents must allow and encourage these assertions of independence.

(v) General Attitude Towards the World

Two-year olds also begin to form general attitudes towards their world. They begin to consider the world as a safe and friendly place, if parents are sensitive to children's needs and if they are affectionate, responsive and stimulating; on the contrary, they feel insecure if parents do not provide this kind of care. Not only infants are influenced by their parents but also they affect other's behaviour towards them.

Although research evidences suggest that many of the social behaviours, like extroversion, introversion, placidity and activity and other temperaments are inherited, later experiences influence many new kinds of behaviour and change the social behaviours of infants.

3. SOCIAL DEVELOPMENT DURING PRE-SCHOOL YEARS

(i) Development of Self-awareness

Between the ages of 2 and 5, children become increasingly aware of themselves as people. They experience many new kinds of interpersonal relationships and they begin to recognize and adopt socially approved patterns of behaviour. In the process, they form many distinctive attitudes, preferences, and ways of acting.

Pre-schoolers become aware of their bodies and learn their sexual identities as male or female. They become also aware of what others think about their bodies. Thus, self-awareness contributes to the development of either positive or negative self-attitudes.

(ii) Development of New Relationships

It is during pre-school years that children develop new interpersonal relationships. Parents especially fathers appear to play important role in helping children maintain positive interpersonal and sex-appropriate relationships with others. Most pre-schoolers learn during this stage to share with siblings. At times also sibling rivalries develop among pre-schoolers. Young children also learn to share and compete with peers whom they meet in neighbourhood play groups, and *chhatsalis*. It is in such groups that the child learns either to be a leader or a follower. Opportunities to meet and play with many different children and to be away from home for brief periods of time help prepare children for entering kindergarten.

(iii) Beginning of Socialisation

Early childhood is a crucial period for socialisation. Socialisation is the process by which children acquire the social judgment and self-control necessary for becoming responsible adults in their society. Children are socialised primarily through discipline and identification. Discipline is most effective when parents administer it consistently, when they attempt to teach rather than merely punish their children with it. Such discipline ordinarily helps young people develop a sense of adopting the feelings, attitudes and actions of others as one's own. Usually children, first of all, identify with parents. Strong identifications help the socialisation process, because the more children attempt to be like their parent, the more they tend to imitate parental codes of conduct. Besides their parents, children also model themselves after other adults, siblings, playmates, and TV characters.

4. SOCIAL DEVELOPMENT DURING CHILDHOOD

(i) The Golden Years of Life

Children enter middle childhood as semi-socialised little boys and girls. During this stage social development is slow and steady. Since the strains are relatively few, the pleasures are many. The child is no longer in need of close parental supervision. He spends most of his time in playing, exploring his world and learning about people and things. Since they do not have major responsibilities, they are free to live for the joys of the moment. Most important aspect of this period is that it is the period of entry into school. The early school years are often referred to as the golden years of childhood, and most adults recall this period of their life fondly and with vivid memories of friends known and things done. As children start school and become less dependent on their families, the focus of their interpersonal relationships gradually shifts from their parents to their peers and the larger community. School-age children begin to spend more time with their peers than with their family.

(ii) New Challenges and Opportunities

Entry into school confronts children with a host of new challenges and opportunities. Most children look forward eagerly to beginning school because it gives them a feeling of importance and maturity and a chance to learn and do many new things. Sometimes overly dependent children are fearful of going to school because they dread being separated from their parents. But majority of children are enthusiastic about school for it plays a major role in their intellectual and social development.

Here they come to understand more about their culture and their environment; they develop social relationships with large number of adults and age-mates, and they are challenged to exercise their initiative and mastery.

(iii) A Desire for Popularity

It is during this period that a desire for popularity develops among children. This desire for popularity is satisfied through peer-group interactions. Children who become popular tend to be well-adjusted, friendly, sociable and outgoing; they are kind and accepting towards others, and they accept the prevailing group standards. Unpopular children, on the other hand, tend to be shy, withdrawn, and not well-adjusted, they do not participate in group activities and do not accept the group's standards of conduct, and they are hostile and rejecting towards others.

(iv) A Sense of Belonging/Alienation

Interpersonal experiences also determine whether elementary-school children develop an attitude of belongingness or of alienation. A sense of belongingness is a feeling that one is an integral part of a larger society. This feeling emerges from enjoyable participation in neighbourhood and community as well as peer group activities. A sense of alienation is the reverse of a sense of belonging. This arises when children are not accepted by their peer group and have no opportunity to participate in neighbourhood, community and peer-group activities.

Peer groups are informal at age 5 or 6. But the peer groups at age 10 or 11 are well-organised and highly structured. This helps prepare children for more complex interpersonal relationship that begins during adolescence.

(v) Sex-role Identity

Elementary-school children begin to develop a psychological identity as members of either one sex or the other. Sex-role identity arises from a number of factors — from biological differences between the sexes, from differences in the way parents socialise their sons and daughters, and from children's identification with their same-sexed parent.

5. SOCIAL DEVELOPMENT DURING ADOLESCENCE

(i) A Period of Recapitulation

Adolescence recapitulates many of the developmental highlights of earlier years. Like infancy, adolescence is a period of rapid physical growth and major changes in bodily appearance. Like the pre-school years, it is a time of expanding social relation. Like middle childhood, it is marked by increasing liberation from the family and a shift from home-centered activities to peer-group and community activities.

(ii) Striving for Independence

The most important aspect of adolescent's social development is striving for independence. Adolescents strive for total psychological freedom from their parents. They want freedom to be their own person, to determine their own values, to plan their own future, to choose their own clothes, friends and recreation activities and to preserve the privacy of their room, belongings, thoughts and feelings. Adolescents want to establish their independence partly because they have reached most of their adult physical and mental growth and partly because it is expected by others. Even though adolescents press for independence and their parents encourage it, both groups experience some ambivalent feelings about it. This ambivalence occasionally leads to inconsistent behaviour on both sides. For example, adolescents want independence, but they also hesitate to take responsibilities. Similarly, although parents like to see their children grow up as independent adults, they also worry about the possible dangers, frustration and disappointments their children might face.

(iii) Feelings about Parents

Parents differ in their attempts to exert authority over their adolescent children. Some are autocratic, imposing their own views on important issues and policies on their youngsters and some are permissive, allowing their children to make all of their own decisions. Democratically reared adolescents generally have more positive feelings about their parents and their own capacity to be independent than those who have autocratic or permissive parents.

(iv) Peer Group Acceptance

Because adolescents are no longer children but not yet adults, they rely heavily on peer-group acceptance for a sense of belongingness. Popularity comes most rapidly to young people who are physically attractive, bright, talented, self-confident, energetic and comfortable in interpersonal situations.

(v) Heterosexual Relationship

During adolescence, heterosexual relationship begins most prominently. First, there are separate groups of boys and girls who have little to do with each other. Then young people move towards mixed boy-girl social functions, and then they take interest in one another. Boys and girls learn how to cope in heterosexual relationship.

(vi) A Sense of Identity and Value Systems

During this stage, adolescents develop a sense of identity or self-concept or an image of themselves more clearly and consistently than during the earlier years. It is because of this self-image that adolescents consider and try out various sex appropriate roles and value systems. Adolescents' value systems, roles and attitudes towards the general community are influenced more by their peer groups than their parents. In fact, most adolescents find them in conflict with their parents in relation to these value systems. Social critics call this tendency of adolescents as adolescent rebellion. Adolescent rebellion is not noticed in all families. Only in those cases where there is generation gap or communication gap between parents and children that adolescents develop rebellion against their parents.

6. MORAL DEVELOPMENT AT DIFFERENT STAGES

Several psychologists have discussed moral development from their own points of view. One such notable child psychologist is Jean Piaget. For Piaget, moral development takes place along with cognitive development. Thus, from a Piagetian point of view, moral development can be discussed under the same stage of cognitive development, namely:

(a) The sensorimotor period,

(b) The pre-operational period,

(c) The concrete operational period, and
(d) The formal operational period.

But Piaget's discussion of moral development has now been considerably modified by Lawrence Kohlberg. In Kohlberg's view, moral development takes place through three levels, namely:

(a) The pre-moral level,
(b) The level of conventional morality and
(c) The level of morality of self-accepted principles.

Kohlberg further says that there are two stages in each level of development. Thus there are six stages of moral development. Elizabeth B. Hurlock has also discussed moral development through a different approach. In this section we shall discuss moral development with reference to infancy, pre-school years, middle childhood, and adolescence. While discussing through this approach we shall keep in mind views of Piaget and Kohlberg on moral development.

7. INFANCY

During infancy the child is not capable of thinking efficiently. He has no conscience and no scale of values. He cannot distinguish between what is good and what is bad. So no significant moral development takes place during this stage. But he is not immoral. Rather he is unmoral or non-moral. The wrong acts performed by the infant are not intentional. They are caused due to ignorance and his inability to understand what is good or what is bad. Some psychologists like Hurlock have the opinion that since the infant has no conscience, it is no use teaching him moral behaviour and moral concepts. Parents must, therefore, wait until the child develops his conscience and is able to understand what the society expects.

8. PRE-SCHOOL YEARS AND CHILDHOOD

Before a child can behave in a moral way, he must learn what the group regards as right and wrong. He learns this from his relationship with parents, older siblings and through identification, imitation and direct teaching.

Before the child enters school, he is expected to distinguish right from wrong or do's from don'ts in simple situations and to lay the foundation for the development of a conscience. Moral concepts during this period are specific at first and relate to specific situations in which they were learned. The Piagetian view is that since the pre-school child is incapable of abstract thinking and generalization, he considers good behaviour in terms of specific acts, such as obeying the mother or helping the mother and 'bad behaviour' in terms of not doing what his mother or father wants him to do. Kohlberg says that during this stage, conduct is determined by external factors like approval and disapproval or rewards and punishment. Thus, the child's behaviour is oriented towards obedience and punishment. His behaviour is hedonistic in the sense that he considers acts as right that satisfy the self and sometimes his parents. If a certain behaviour brings him pleasure, comfort, or some satisfaction, and at times if a certain behaviour pleases his parents, particularly mother, he repeats that behaviour.

As a child approaches middle childhood, his capacity to understand relationships increases. Thus, his concepts of right and wrong in different but related situations emerge. As a result, he moves from specific response to a generalised response. By the time a child is 8 or 9 years old, his concepts become more generalised. For example, he realises that stealing is bad, rather than 'it is wrong to steal a ball' as in pre-school years.

According to Kohlberg morality, during this stage, is defined as performing good acts and maintaining the conventional social order. Morality is held to be maintaining good relations and oriented towards getting approval, and pleasing and helping others. During the last part of this stage, moral behaviour is oriented towards authority, law, duty and maintaining the *status quo* which is assumed to be a primary value. However, the moral values of the child change as he associates with more people and with people whose values differ from those of his parents.

9. ADOLESCENCE

By the time the child reaches adolescence, his moral code is fairly well-formed. During the earlier years when a child does things that the group regards as wrong, it is often assumed that his parents have not taught him how to behave. But as the child reaches adolescence, society expects him to behave in accordance with the mores of the group, because during adolescence he will be better capable of understanding what is right and what is wrong.

Moral development is an important aspect of the adolescent's development. Most adolescents learn to behave in a socially approved manner. But few others are socially stupid. They violate the mores of the group. But society does not condone violations of its mores. Thus, such adolescents pay the penalty in the form of social rejection.

During the adolescence period, morality is defined as conforming to common standards — rights or duties. The adolescent is oriented towards existing rules and standards. But he no longer wants to accept all that is imposed on him. Rather he applies his own conscience and individual rights in accepting moral behaviour. Adolescents prefer democratic techniques in teaching and learning moral behaviour. Adolescents who are trained through autocratic techniques resent those who teach him moral behaviour. Sometimes parental expectations come in conflict with peer group standards. The adolescent in his attempts to conform to peer group standards ignores or revolts against the parent. Such adolescent reactions are usually known as adolescent rebellion. Adolescent rebellion is generally expressed in choice of friends, hours of coming in and going out of home, leisure time activities, dress and interpersonal relationship with members of the opposite sex. Adolescents who are successful as moral beings have a smooth transition to adulthood. Failure to do so may lead to excessive worries, anxieties, feelings of inferiority and general sense of frustration.

10. DUTIES AND RESPONSIBILITIES OF PARENTS AND TEACHERS

Learning of social behaviour and moral behaviour is a long, slow process. Socialization has both an intellectual aspect and an impulsive aspect. The child must learn what is right and what is wrong, and as soon as he is old enough he must understand why it is so. In addition, he must develop the desire to do what is right, to act for the common good and to avoid doing what is wrong. The intellectual aspect of social development is accomplished by participating in group activities so that the child can learn what the group expects. The impulsive aspect is accomplished by associating pleasant reactions such as reward and approval with what is right and unpleasant reactions such as punishment and disapproval with what is wrong. The child can learn to behave in a socially approved manner through trial and error, through direct teaching and identification. Trial and error learning is time-consuming and energy-consuming and the end results are often far from satisfactory.

Direct Teaching

Parents must teach the child what is right and what is wrong and persuade him to act as society expects. The child must first learn to make correct specific responses in specific situations. If the standards learned in the home are in consistent with those in the schools and play group, it will be easy for the child to see the similarity, and in time, develop abstract concepts of right and wrong. If standards differ from one situation to another, the child is confused and wonders why he is punished for an act which was ignored or looked upon as especially acceptable in another situation. Thus a consistent approach must be followed in teaching social and moral behaviours to young children.

Identification

The child also learns social and moral behaviours through identification. In identification, the child takes over the values of another — parents, siblings, peers — and models his behaviour after the behaviour of that person. This he does unconsciously. The child learns to do what the adult does and what the adult tells him to do. When a child identifies with a person he admires without any pressure or direct teaching, he will imitate the patterns of behaviour he observes in that person.

Discipline

Whether the child learns social and moral behaviour through direct teaching or through identification, parents and teachers use discipline to shape behaviour. Discipline consists of habit formation. The functions of discipline are:

(a) To teach the child that certain behaviour will always be followed by approval while others will be followed by disapproval;

(b) to teach the child reasonable degree of conformity but not too much conformity, and
(c) to help the child develop self-control and self-direction so that he can develop a conscience to guide his actions.

In disciplining the child, parents and teachers can use any one of the three techniques:

(a) Authoritarian technique,
(b) Democratic technique,
(c) Permissive technique.

Authoritarian technique of discipline refers to strict rules and regulations about the behaviour. It means control through external force in the form of punishment. In this technique, the parents do not encourage the child to make decisions regarding his act; they tell him how to act.

Democratic technique implies explanation, discussion and reasoning to help the child understand why he is expected to behave in a certain way. If the child comes up to expected standard, parents reward him with praise, approval, etc. Punishment is occasionally used only when the child intentionally does the wrong act.

Permissive discipline is really little or no discipline at all. Through this technique, the child is permitted to make his own decisions and act on them in practically any way he wishes. This technique does not guide the child into socially approved patterns of behaviour. In this technique, neither punishment is given for wrong act nor rewards for good act. On the whole, democratic discipline is the best one, although authoritarian technique is better than a permissive one.

Over-protection *versus* Under-protection

Sometimes children are over-protected by their parents. Such children are not allowed to go out, play and interact with peers. They are not given the opportunity to make mistakes and learn through their experiences. Parents always keep a close watch over their movements. The under-protected child is given all the freedom; he is neither disciplined nor guided by parents in his social relationships. He is very often a rejected child in the home. Nobody bothers about him nor cares for him. The process of socialization requires a delicate balance between over-protection, discipline and freedom and autocratic and democratic attitudes which must be consistently maintained to produce a healthy normal child.

SELECTED QUESTIONS

1. State the relationship between social development and moral development. Explain the characteristics of social development during childhood.
2. Discuss the essential features of social development during adolescence.
3. What are the various stages of moral development? State the moral development of children during pre-school years.
4. Discuss the role of the teacher to facilitate social and moral development of children.

10
Behaviour Problems at Different Stages of Development

1. WHAT IS BEHAVIOUR PROBLEM?

Every teacher encounters behaviour problems of children in his classroom. There is nothing new in it. Every child shows some behaviour problem at a particular stage or at different stages of development in his life. But in case of some children, behaviour problems occur more frequently; some of these problems persist over a period of time like a chronic disease; and these problems become more and more serious in nature. In most cases these problems interfere with their normal day-to-day activities and the activities of the classroom.

By problem we mean those behaviours of the child which create or which are likely to create difficulties in the learning activities of the child, and the instructional programme and discipline of the classroom. About 2 to 4 per cent of children in the classroom demonstrate behaviour problems. The occurrence of behaviour problems is more in case of boys than in case of girls. Girls also experience problem behaviour. Since they are more capable of socially adaptable behaviour, their problems do not come to focus.

2. EXAMPLES OF SOME BEHAVIOUR PROBLEMS

A child may show one or more than one problem behaviour during his period of development. Some behaviour problems may occur at a specific stage of development while some behaviour problems occur at different stages. For example, revolt against parents, teachers, and other authority figures is characteristic feature of adolescence. Similarly, stranger anxiety is a problem of infancy. Lack of interest in studies or negligence of duties may occur at any stage of development.

M. Dash (1995) conducted a study on behaviour problems of children. His findings reveal the following behaviour problems occurring at various stages of development:

Stages of Development	Behaviour Problems
Infancy	(i) Crying
	(ii) Lack of appetite
	(iii) Stranger anxiety
	(iv) Separation anxiety
	(v) Sibling rivalry
	(vi) Jealousy
	(vii) Bed-wetting
Early childhood	(i) Excessive shyness
	(ii) Unhappiness
	(iii) Temper tantrums
	(iv) Obstinacy
	(v) Jealousy
	(vi) Bed-wetting
	(vii) Laziness
	(viii) Bullying and teasing
	(ix) Cheating
Late childhood	(i) Excessive shyness
	(ii) Unhappiness
	(iii) Temper tantrums
	(iv) Obstinacy
	(v) Laziness
	(vi) Bullying and teasing
	(vii) Cheating
	(viii) Stealing
	(ix) Defiance
	(x) Day-dreaming
	(xi) Truancy
	(xii) Telling lie
	(xiii) Vulgarity

(xiv) Destroying school property
(xv) Getting nervous and feeling disappointed over petty matters

Adolescence
(i) Rebellion against parents, teachers and authority
(ii) Unhappiness and excessively moody
(iii) Laziness
(iv) Bullying and teasing
(v) Cheating
(vi) Telling lie
(vii) Stealing
(viii) Destroying school property
(ix) Defiance and disobedience
(x) Excessive day-dreaming
(xi) Truancy
(xii) Vulgarity
(xiii) Objectionable behaviour towards girls
(xiv) Getting disappointed over petty matters
(xv) Excessively thoughtful
(xvi) Excessive carelessness

3. CAUSES OF BEHAVIOUR PROBLEM

Every behaviour has a cause. The problem behaviour of a child has also a cause or a number of causes. The manner in which the child behaves is clear enough to suggest that he has a problem. This external manifestation of the child's problem through his typical behaviour may not indicate the real cause or causes of his problem. For example, a child of Class V steals money from the schoolbag of his classmates. But why does he steal money? There may be a number of causes of his stealing money. Stealing money is a symptom of an underlying problem. The causes of his problem behaviour cannot be ascertained from its symptom. The causes of his problem behaviour can only be ascertained through a psychological analysis. Sometimes the causes of problem behaviour as reported by the child himself may be different from the causes ascertained through a psychological analysis of his problem. But one thing is certain that the child's behaviour has a cause.

The child behaves in a specific way to meet his basic needs and to avoid or to get rid of frustrating circumstances or the impending danger which may arise out of the failure to satisfy his basic needs. If his behaviour is not socially acceptable, it is considered as problem behaviour.

Behaviour problems are not hereditary in nature. They are caused by social and psychological environment of the child. The environment which causes problem behaviour may be the home environment or the school environment of the child.

Home Environment

Some children come from families with low socio-economic status. The way such children are brought up, the care, education and stimulation which they receive in their homes cause behaviour problems in such children. It is generally noticed that the occurrence of behaviour problems is more in case of children who come from low societies than those children who belong to middle class or high class societies. For example, a child from low class society may learn that stealing is acceptable until it is detected. But a child from high class society may learn that stealing is bad.

In some homes, parents exert authority over their children. Children who are brought up by authoritarian parents generally show bullying and teasing behaviour towards their classmates. Some children are rebuked, scolded, insulted, blamed and punished very frequently by their parents. They are considered as 'useless' by their parents. In some cases these children are rejected and neglected by their parents. Such children show behaviour problems in future.

Parents teach social and moral values to their children. Children also learn values from their peers. Very often parental values come in conflict with the value system of peers. If the child fails to appreciate the parental values and behave accordingly and if his behaviour is predominantly influenced by the value system of peer's behaviour problem may occur. This is particularly noticed during adolescence. We call it adolescent rebellion.

The curriculum load of the school becomes unbearable for some children. Continuous teaching in the classroom, load of homework, and undue emphasis on examination make the child distracted and disinterested in studies. If such a child does not get academic help from parents or elders, he becomes a truant. A truant leaves his home in time, but he does not go to school. He spends his school time in the playground, parks, cinema hall and watches TV somewhere with some of his friends. Then he reaches his home in time.

4. REMEDIAL MEASURES

If we have to help the problem child to proceed along correct lines and to maximize his potentialities, the following remedial measures are to be taken:

(i) Teacher's Attitude Towards His Job

Some teachers believe that teaching is the only duty which they have to perform and that remediation of behaviour problem is not their responsibility. Thus they lack concern in behaviour problems of children. In worst cases they refer a problem child to the headmaster. In reality, showing lack of concern or referring problem cases to the headmaster is an instance of avoiding or shifting responsibility.

A teacher may live in peace for sometime by keeping himself aloof from the problem situation but this does not bring permanent solution of the problem. The teacher fails to understand the child. His problem becomes more and more serious. A time comes when his instruction is bound to be interrupted. Due to lack of a sense of responsibility on the part of the teacher, other children in the classroom are also affected.

(ii) Change in the Teacher's Attitude Towards the Problem Child

The school and its teachers should be dedicated to the welfare of children. The school should aim at all-round development of the problem child. Unless the problems of the typical child are solved, the teaching — learning process in the classroom cannot be effective. This necessitates change in the teacher's attitude towards the problem child. The child should not only be viewed as a learner but also as a human being, He should be treated as a human being who does not need sympathy but understanding on the part of the teacher.

(iii) Abolition of Physical Punishment

Some teachers use physical punishment like beating to help the child correct his behavioural abnormality. Some teachers drive the child out of the classroom. Asking the problem child to stand on the bench, lean down, detaining the child after the school hour or rebuking, blaming or insulting the child are common remedial measures adopted by most teachers. These direct and drastic measures do not bring any satisfying results. Rather the problem child becomes reactive and loses his honour for the teacher. Thus these direct and drastic measures are never considered as acceptable remedial measures.

Before adopting physical punishment, the teacher should think and decide carefully as to whether the behaviour of the child is punishable or not; whether his behaviour interferes with the learning activity of the class; whether other remedial measures can be adopted in place of physical punishment. The primary objective of the teacher should be promotion of learning and learning can be promoted through modification of his behaviour.

(iv) Opportunity to Learn Good Behaviour

The problem behaviour of the child also implies that he has not learned correct behaviour. Opportunity should be created in the school so that children interact with one another and play together. Emphasis should be given on cooperative life and cooperative activities in the school. Every child has freedom to think, acquire experiences and perform activities. The child should be helped to learn to express his feelings and experiences in such a way that this does not hurt others' feelings or sentiments. The school atmosphere should be made healthy, joyful and secured. There should be healthy relationships, free exchange of feelings and experiences, mutual trust and respect between the teacher and students. Children should be helped to develop strong determination and self-confidence to learn desirable behaviour.

(v) Good Teaching

It is generally observed that the problem child does not create problems in all periods and for all teachers. Problem behaviour is noticed in certain classes and for some teachers. Teachers who are good, who make their teaching interesting and joyful, who are successful in developing social and moral values among children do not encounter behaviour problems in their classrooms. Teachers whose teaching becomes unpleasant, ineffective and meaningless encounter behaviour problems very frequently. It is rightly said that good teachers have good students and bad teachers have problem students. Thus behaviour problems can largely be prevented by making teaching effective, joyful and interesting.

(vi) Motherly Attitude of Teachers

Problem children are usually deprived of the love, care and advice of parents. A teacher is viewed as a parent figure for the child. A problem child expects a great deal of love and care from the teacher. A little love, some care, a kind attitude and few pleasing words from the teacher can prevent problem behaviour of children. Thus, it is rightly said that the teacher should act as a mother for the child.

(vii) Appointment of Lady Teachers

It is generally observed that problem behaviour is more frequent in the classroom of male teachers than in case of female teachers. Young children tend to perceive the female teacher as their mother. Female teachers have more patience in problem situation as compared to male teachers. Prevention and remediation of problem behaviour require patience on the part of the teacher. Considered from this point of view, it is suggested that more female teachers should be appointed in schools, particularly in primary schools.

(viii) Behaviour Modification Techniques

Teachers should adopt behaviour modification techniques for remediation of behaviour problems. This requires careful planning and consultation with other teachers. The important steps of behaviour modification techniques are as follows:

— Identification, explanation and clarification of problem behaviour of the child:
When does the child show problem behaviour? How frequently does the problem behaviour occur? What is the circumstance or environment of the child when he shows problem behaviour? What reinforcement does the child get when he shows problem behaviour?

— Determining the causes of problem behaviour:
What do the parents, friends and teachers say about the causes of child's behaviour? What does the child himself say about his behaviour? What is the finding of psychological analysis of the child's problem behaviour (if possible)?

— Suggesting tentative remedial measures:
Advice to parents,
Advice to teachers,
Instruction to friends,

— Application of remedial measures,

— Studying the effect of remedied measures on behaviour of the child;

— Change in the measures taken or accepting the suggested measures depending upon their effects on the child,

— Remediation of behaviour problems.

SELECTED QUESTIONS

1. Discuss the behaviour problems of children at different stages of development. How can they be prevented/ remedied?
2. What are the causes of behaviour problems of children? How can these behaviour problems be prevented?
3. What is behaviour problem? Give some examples of behaviour problems at different stages of development.

11
Adolescence Development

1. WHAT IS ADOLESCENCE?

"Adolescence is that span of years during which boys and girls move from childhood to adulthood mentally, emotionally, socially and physically." The rate at which individuals progress through adolescence stage varies widely. But there is an orderly sequence of physiological development through which different adolescents pass in their own time and at their own rate. Psychological development may lag behind physical development by years. For example, a youth of nineteen may be physically matured but he may remain much more dependent economically and emotionally on his family.

The concept of "adolescence" has both a biological connotation and a psychological connotation. Biologically, this period is associated with physical maturation. The onset of puberty marks the beginning of adolescence. In case of girls, puberty occurs sometime between the ages of twelve and seventeen. In case of boys, puberty occurs between the ages of fourteen and seventeen. But there are individual differences among boys and girls. Some may be early matures and some may attain maturity late. One girl of 12 may attain maturity and may confine herself in her study room, but another girl of the same age may be still playing hide-and-seek game with her boyfriend. In some cases adolescence begins at the age of 9.

In a purely psychological sense, adolescence means a state of mind, an attitude, a style of existence that begins with puberty, and ends when one is relatively independent of parental control.

Along with biological maturity, social, emotional and intellectual maturation takes place during this period. An adolescent, who has matured biologically and psychologically has a smooth transition to adulthood.

Adolescence has been divided into two periods — early adolescence and late adolescence. The dividing line between early and late adolescence is somewhat arbitrarily placed at around seventeen years. Because boys mature later than girls, they have a shorter period of early adolescence. Early adolescence extends roughly from twelve or thirteen to sixteen or seventeen, and late adolescence covers the period from sixteen or seventeen to eighteen. Late adolescence is thus a very short period.

2. CHARACTERISTICS OF ADOLESCENCE

As is true of every period, adolescence has certain characteristics that distinguish it from the periods that preceded it and the periods that will follow it. Hurlock outlines these characteristics as follows:

(i) Adolescence is an Important Period

Adolescence is an important period because the short-term effects and the long-term effects of this period on the individual are important. It is also important because the physical and psychological effects of this period on the individual are important.

(ii) Adolescence is a Transitional Period

Adolescence is a period when an individual is neither a child nor an adult. The individual has crossed childhood and yet to reach the stage of adulthood. He is in a stage of transition. During any stage of transition, the individual's status is vague and there is confusion about the roles the individual is expected to play. If an adolescent behaves like a child he is said to be 'childish.' If he acts like an adult, he is accused of being too big for his age.

(iii) Adolescence is a Period of Change

Adolescence is a period when rapid physical changes are accompanied by changes in attitudes, values, interests and behaviours. It is a period when physical and psychological changes take place rapidly.

(iv) Adolescence is a Problematic Period

The rapid changes that take place during this stage create problems which are often difficult for boys and girls to cope with. Every age has its own problems. But during childhood their problems were met and solved in part by parents and teachers. During adolescence, boys and girls are expected to meet and solve their problems on their own. But they do not have the capacity nor the experience to solve their problems. The solutions which they devise do not always come up to their expectations. Adolescents want to solve their problems independent of their parents but they are often incapable of doing that. This itself creates a problem.

(v) Adolescence is a Time of Search for Identity

During childhood conformity to peer group standards is far more important to children. Children want to be, as nearly as possible, like their gang-mates in dress, speech, and behaviour. In early adolescence, conformity to group standards is still important to boys and girls. But gradually adolescents begin to search for their identity. They no longer want to be like their peers in all respects. They begin to develop individuality in their dress, manners, behaviour, personal style and possessions. This search for identity sometimes leads to identity crisis in some adolescents.

(vi) Adolescence is a Time of Unrealism

Adolescents have a tendency to look at life through rose-tinted glasses. They see themselves and others as they would like them to be rather than as they are. Their aspirations are more idealistic and less realistic. The more unrealistic their aspirations are, the more angry, hurt and disappointed they will be. With increased personal and social experiences and with greater maturity and rationality, older adolescents see themselves, their life, family and friends more realistically. As false idealism disappears, they suffer less from disappointments.

3. GROWTH AND DEVELOPMENT DURING ADOLESCENCE

Adolescence is that period which is characterized by rapid physical, emotional, social, moral and intellectual developments and changes.

Physical Changes during Adolescence

Physical changes during adolescence are marked by onset of puberty, growth spurt, sexual maturation and acceleration of hormone secretions. Physical changes during this period are both interned and external.

(i) Puberty

Puberty means "age of manhood". It begins in early adolescence. Boys and girls during this stage grow rapidly as young men and young women. Puberty begins with the gradual enlargement of ovaries and uterus in girls. In case of boys, puberty refers to enlargement of the prostate gland and seminal vesicles. These changes are internal and thus cannot be observed outwardly. For practical purpose, puberty in girls is marked by breast development or the bud stage of breast development. In case of boys, growth of pubic hair marks the onset of puberty.

Sexual Maturation: As we discussed earlier, puberty marks the beginning of sexual maturation. The first outward indication of sexual maturity in boys is usually an increase in the rate of growth of the testes and scrotum. There may be beginning of growth of pubic hair at about the same time or shortly thereafter. A year later the penis grows in size.

In girls, the elevation of the breast (the bud stage of breast development) is usually the first sign of sexual maturity. In some girls, the initial appearance of pubic hair may precede breast development. Growth of the uterus and vagina occur simultaneously with breast development. The labia and clitoris also enlarge. Menstruation may occur after growth spurt slows down. Menstruation is a symbol of sexual maturity — of her future status as a woman.

(ii) Growth Spurt

The term growth spurt refers to the accelerated rate of increase in height and weight that occurs with the onset of adolescence. During this period, there is a swift increase in body size, a change in the shape of body composition and a rapid development of reproductive organs.

The age of onset and duration of the spurt varies from one child to another. Girls attain their adult height and weight about two years earlier than boys. But boys increase only slightly more than girls in height.

(iii) Acceleration of Hormone Secretions

Many of the physical changes that occur during adolescence are due to increased output of hormones from the pituitary gland which is located in the brain. The pituitary gland is responsible for growth and serves to monitor the hormone balance of the body.

In girls hormones from the-ovaries stimulate development of the breasts, uterus, fallopian tubes and vagina. In addition, they produce the secondary sex characteristics including the growth of pubic hair, and a broadening of the hips.

In boys, hormones from the testes stimulate growth of the prostate gland, seminal vesicles, penis and such secondary sex characteristics as broadened shoulders, deeper voice, growth of pubic and auxiliary hair.

Social Development and Emotionality during Adolescence

Adolescence is a period of expanding social relations and heightened emotionality. Since emotionality during adolescence is largely the result of social factors, these two developments will be discussed simultaneously.

(i) Striving for Independence

The most important aspect of adolescent's social development is striving for independence. Adolescents strive for psychological separation or freedom from their parents. They want freedom to be their own person, to determine their own values, to plan their own future, to choose their own clothes; friends and recreation activities and to preserve the privacy of their room, belongings, thoughts and feelings. Adolescents want to establish their independence partly because they have reached most of their adult physical and mental growth and partly because it is expected by others.

While striving for emotional independence and psychological separation from parents, most adolescents experience confusion and anxiety. The adolescent wants to be self-sufficient but he is inexperienced and incapable of taking responsibility for his security and comforts which he gets from parents. This is reflected in his inconsistent bahaviour and attitude which we call adolescent rebellion. Similarly, although parents like to see their children grow up as independent adults, they also worry about the possible dangers, frustrations and disappointments their children might face. Adolescent rebellion becomes more intense when there is a communication gap between parents and the child. However, with experience, insight and increased maturation, adolescent rebellion can be gradually resolved into mature and responsible behaviours. The feelings of adolescents towards their parents vary depending on whether parents are autocratic, permissive or democratic. Democratically reared adolescents have more positive feelings about their parents.

(ii) Peer Group Relationship and Acceptance

Adolescents have a strong tendency for peer group relationship. Usually peers who are attractive in appearance, cheerful, comfortable, cooperative, responsible, resourceful, true to their words, trustworthy and who have similar interest and abilities are chosen as friends.

(iii) Heterosexual Relationships

During early adolescence, there are separate groups of boys and girls, who have little to do with each other. The early adolescent involves himself in intense relationships with members of the same sex. He typically finds and relates himself to others who have some qualities, he himself admires. The mid-adolescent's love is highly narcissistic and frequently one-sided and intense. The object of love is admired at times passively and yet passionately. This idealisation serves temporarily to keep the adolescent unaware of the erotic and homosexual component of the friendship. As sexual interest and fantasy are intensified, they may like to belong to social groups and to be accepted by the groups. The adolescent's social groupings include close friends, cliques, crowds and gangs. The adolescent is no longer interested in large number of friends. He has two or three close friends or confidants. They are of the same sex and have similar interests and abilities. Close friends have a marked influence on one another, though they may quarrel occasionally. Cliques are usually made up of groups of close friends. At first they consist of members of the same sex, but later include both boys and girls. Adolescents also take interest in crowd which is made up of cliques and groups of close friends. In crowds adolescents join in parties, excursion and picnics. Adolescents who have no close friends or who do not belong to cliques join a gang. Gang members are usually of the same sex, and their main interest is to compensate for peer rejection through delinquent activities accompanied by sexual explorations, breaking through inhibitions and 'testing capacities' than any interest in intimacy. This rather contributes to the sudden disruption of their relationships. Girls are more involved in romantic love relationships than boys. During late adolescence, boys and girls are not interested in expanding social relations or in number of friends but in close intimate friendship. They are interested not in quantity but in quality of relationships. Relationships with members of the opposite sex begin to develop in late adolescence. Boys and girls try to look attractive and acceptable to members of the opposite sex.

(iv) A Sense of Identity

During late childhood and early adolescence, boys and girls tend to identify themselves with peers. Such identification may be manifested in dress, manners, speech, etc. But during late adolescence, boys and girls are no longer satisfied in identifying and imitating. They want to be their own. They search for their identity: Who am I? What is the aim of my life? In what way I am different from others? Now the adolescent has a self-image: he wants his own clothes, own private room and other personal possessions which he considers to be exclusively his own and different from others.

Development of Moral Values

By the time the child reaches adolescence, his moral code is fairly well-formed. During the earlier years when a child does things that the community regards as wrong, it is often assumed that his parents have not taught him how to behave. But as the child reaches adolescence, society expects him to behave in accordance with the mores of the group, because during adolescence he is better capable of understanding what is right and what is wrong.

Most adolescents learn to behave in a socially approved manner. But society does not condone violations of its mores. Thus such adolescents pay the penalty in the form of social rejection, isolation, criticism and disapproval.

During this period, morality is defined as conforming to common standards — rights or duties. The adolescent is oriented towards existing rules, standards and values. But he no longer wants to accept all that is imposed on him. He applies his own conscience and individual rights in choosing standards and values. His values are influenced more by peer group value than by parental value system. Sometimes parental value system comes in conflict with peer group standards. The adolescent in his attempt to conform to peer group standards ignores or revolts against the parents. Such reactions are usually called adolescent rebellion. Adolescent rebellion is generally expressed in choice of friends, hours of coming in and going out of home, leisure time activities, clothing and interpersonal relationships with members of the opposite sex. Adolescents who are successful as moral beings have a smooth transition to adulthood. Failure to do so may lead to excessive worries, anxieties, feeling of inferiority and a general sense of frustration.

Cognitive Development (Intellectual Maturation)

During and following puberty, the adolescent attains intellectual maturation. Piaget associates intellectual maturation with what he calls formal operation. During and following this stage, the adolescent's thoughts are flexible and effective. He can deal with abstract and hypothetical propositions. The mental structure of the adolescent has reached a high degree of equilibrium. He can apply logical thought to all classes of problems. The adolescent's thought is logical. This does not mean that he never thinks illogically. Rather it is a fact that the adolescent is capable of logical thinking with increasing ages. But he cannot distinguish between what is real and what is logical. That is why many adolescents appear to be very idealistic in their thinking. The adolescent's idealism is temporary. This false idealism will change during subsequent years when he will confront the real world. False idealism is not a negative characteristic of adolescent's development. It is necessary and normal characteristic of development. Problem-solving behaviour also appears at this stage. The adolescent can plan carefully, design an experiment appropriately, observe the results accurately and draw conclusions rightly. This means that the adolescent thinks about himself, his role in life, his plans and the validity of his beliefs. Thus, he is now concerned with his future. Intellectual maturation is the result of interaction between maturation, experiences, education and training.

4. BASIC NEEDS AND PROBLEMS OF ADOLESCENTS

Every child has certain needs. Adolescents have also certain basic needs. The needs of adolescents are similar to those of earlier stages; they are also different from the needs of earlier stages. The differences in the needs of adolescents and younger children arise due to rapid and major changes that take place during adolescence. These needs are likely to be accompanied by potential difficulties and problems. It is because of the peculiar needs, difficulties and problems that adolescence has often been called a period of stress and strain. It is a fact that the adolescent faces the same problems as faced by others. But the problems of adolescence vary in complexity and mode of expression. Problems which remained unsolved during early years appear again at this stage. During childhood the child's needs were met and his problems were solved mostly by parents and teachers. But during adolescence, boys and girls have to solve their own problems. The basic needs and problems of adolescent boys and girls are as follows:

(i) Need for Status

Adolescents are growing up very fast as young men and young women. They are in a stage of transition when they are no longer children and at the same time they are yet to become adults. Where does an adolescent boy or girl stand? Because of their rapid physical changes and sexual maturation and because of social and parental expectations, the adolescent boy or girl is confused about his/her status as an individual. If he or she behaves or acts in an immature way, society regards it as childish. If he or she behaves or acts or thinks like an adult, society calls it 'too big for the age'. What is his or her status then? Although boys and girls during this stage are young men and young women they are not granted such status. The adolescent's need for status should be understood by parents and teachers and they should be given the opportunity for participating in all decision-making in home, school and the community. When their need for status is not met satisfactorily in the family or the school, it may lead to confusion, ambiguity and disappointment in them.

(ii) Need for Approval and Recognition

In conformity with social and parental expectations, the adolescent boy or girl wants to play sex appropriate roles for which he or she needs approval of parents. Adolescents have a tendency towards adventurous activities. They want to plan for their own future — education, occupation and family relations. They choose their own friends and clothes. They want privacy of their own. Although they are not mentally matured enough to plan for their own future, they need approval from parents. If parents and their adolescent boys and girls sit and discuss together and if their plans are approved, they have a sense of satisfaction. If they succeed in performing certain tasks independently they need to be recognised. If their success is not recognised in home or in school, they begin to lose interest in such activities.

(iii) Need for Advice

Adolescence is a period of rapid physical and sexual maturation. It is also a period of intellectual maturation. The adolescent should be prepared and trained to accept these rapid changes. This is particularly important for adolescent girls. Some girls are prepared to welcome and accept these changes which they perceive as normal part of development. But some girls become hesitant and are confused. They need advice to accept their bodily changes and to make proper use of their body. Such advice relates to menstruation, heightened sexual urge and emotionality, heterosexual relationships, sex appropriate roles and similar other characteristics. Boys and girls need advice for education, preparation for an occupation and personal problems. Girls, particularly, need to know a lot of things about their bodies. Sometimes questions are answered by parents and elders, but most often their questions remain a mystery. In fact, correct information is less dangerous than mystery. When boys and girls do not have the answers to their questions, they look for "other ways" of knowing their bodies. Adolescents who get such advice from parents, teachers, elders and peers have a happy ending of adolescence and a promising beginning of adulthood.

(iv) Need for Independence

Adolescents need independence — economic independence and emotional independence. Boys and girls during this stage strive for emotional independence and psychological separation from parents. During childhood they were completely dependent on their parents. Now they no longer want to depend on their parents for all that they want. They no longer want to be treated as "children." They want to be self-supporting and self-sufficient. While striving for emotional and economic independence, most adolescents experience confusion, anxiety, frustration, and ambivalence in behaviour and attitude. They strive for independence but they are inexperienced and incapable of taking responsibility for their security and comforts which they get from their parents. Parents also like to see their children grow up as independent adults, but at the same time they worry about the possible dangers and disappointments their children might face.

(v) Need for Intimate Friendship

The adolescent has a strong need for intimate friendship with two or three members of the same sex. These intimate friends are his confidants with whom he or she can discuss secret, private or confidential matters. The adolescent does not want a number of friends. He wants two or three close friends. He is not interested in the quantity of relationship, but in the quality of relationship. Intimate relationship with members of the opposite sex begins to develop in late adolescence.

Adolescents sometimes clash with their parents in matters of choosing friends, hours spent with friends and relationship with members of the opposite sex. But this gradually vanishes as adolescents gain insight and greater understanding.

(vi) Need for Family Life Education

Adolescents, particularly adolescent girls need family life education. They need instruction on matters relating to sex, relationship in the family, duties and responsibilities of various members of the family, and such other matters relating to family life. Adolescent girls who are given such instruction by their mothers and other elderly members in the family are able to adjust successfully and lead a happy family of their own in future. Such education enables them to think rationally and develops in them the capability to take a decision and behave as responsible parents in future. Adolescents who are deprived of such education or knowledge may encounter innumerable problems in family life in future.

(vii) Need for Recreation Activities

Adolescents need to spend their recreation in useful activities. The recreational interests of adolescents vary depending on their sex, their intelligence, environment, opportunities available, interests of peers, interests of their families, and many other factors. Some of the adolescent interests centre around spectator sports, intellectual games, relaxing, travelling, making clothes, repairing radios, dancing, reading newspapers and books, going to the movies, listening to radio and records, watching television, etc. Sometimes they are so much engaged in such activities particularly watching television and listening to cricket commentaries that their studies are hampered. Parents and teachers should guide the adolescents in proper use of time in studies and recreational activities.

5. FACTORS INFLUENCING ADOLESCENT'S DEVELOPMENT AND ADJUSTMENT AT HOME AND SCHOOL

Factors in the Home

Every adolescent boy or girl is expected to make healthy adjustment and progress towards greater self-sufficiency and self-direction. The home, particularly the parents, can contribute either to promote or to hinder the adjustment of adolescent boys and girls. The following factors are important:

(i) Relationship between father and mother.

(ii) Relationship between parents and their adolescent sons and daughters: Parental lag and rigidity.

(iii) Relationship between the adolescents and their elder siblings.

(iv) Differential treatment of parents towards their sons and daughters.

(v) Attitude of parents towards their adolescent sons and daughters: Under-protection and over-protection.
Affection and control,
Autocratic and democratic attitude,

(vi) Involvement of parents in the life and activities of adolescents.

(vii) Autonomy for adolescents.

(viii) Recognition and respect for adolescent's status.

The factors just mentioned above are so much interlinked and overlapping in nature that they cannot be discussed separately. A global picture of the influence of these factors on adolescent's adjustment or maladjustment is presented below.

(i) The adolescent has need for physical and emotional security. He needs to be loved and also to love. Physical security may be available in most homes. But emotional security is not granted in most homes. The factor which promotes the sense of emotional security is the happy and harmonious relationship between the parents and other members of the family. The adolescent's sense of emotional security is badly affected if the family tie is broken or if there are frequent quarrels between the father and the mother. The adolescent must have the love and affection of parents. It is not sufficient to say "we love you." The adolescent must himself feel that he is loved, liked and wanted in the family. Once the adolescent develops a feeling that he is unwanted in the family (as in case of an illegitimate child) or that he is not liked by the parents, problems of mental health and adjustment arise then and there. Adolescents in broken homes become socialized aggressive or unsocialized aggressive.

(ii) The relationship between the father and the mother is as important as the relationship between parents and their adolescent sons and daughters. Adolescent sons and daughters are young men and young women. The relationship between parents and their sons and daughters should be based on friendly and sympathetic understanding. It is, therefore, rightly said: *Praptesu sodasha barshe putram mitramiba charet*. If there is a strained relationship between the parents and their adolescent sons and daughters, this will develop in the adolescent a hostile and aggressive attitude towards the parents and authority figures.

(iii) Another phenomenon that interferes with the development of healthy adolescent independence is the existence of a parental lag in many parent-child relationships. Many parents find it difficult to change their behaviour towards the children as the children grow older. Adolescent sons and daughters are not given independent responsibilities in family affairs because they are still considered by many parents as too immature. Confidence and self-esteem are highest among those adolescents who are given opportunity for independent responsibility and active participation in family affairs. Parents are considered as old-fashioned and conservative if they show rigidity in their behaviour and relationship with their adolescent sons and daughters. Considered in this sense, the relationship between the adolescent boy or girl and the elder siblings is also equally important.

(iv) In most homes, sons and daughters are treated differently by their parents, and this contributes significantly to how the adolescent views himself. For example, affection and punishment are used differently for sons and daughters. Girls are subjected more to 'love-oriented' child-rearing techniques. Boys are subjected to physical punishment. Independence and achievement are encouraged among boys. In case of boys, parent-child interaction seems to be focused more on directing him "towards the environment," while with girls the emphasis is more on "protecting her from the environment." This is why girls are usually found to be more obedient, cooperative, and in general better socially adjusted than boys of the same ages. Adolescent girls also tend to be more anxious, dependent and sensitive to loss of affection. Characteristics such as a independence, self-confidence, initiative, and self-sufficiency require for their development a balance of authority and affection than simply love-oriented strategy.

(v) Parental attitude and protection affect the adolescent's adjustment at home and later in school. Parents should not unnecessarily criticise the adolescent son or daughter. They should never make unhealthy comparison between their own children and other children in front of others. This rather damages the self-concept of the adolescent and develops in him a feeling of inferiority which is a major cause of maladjustment. Parents should not be over anxious about their children's scholastic performance. Overestimating the child's capacities and expecting too much are serious causes of maladjustment. Sometimes over-protection or under-protection by parents creates serious problems of adjustment among adolescents. An over-protected adolescent becomes shy, withdrawing, dependent and lacks initiative. An under protected adolescent may become delinquent, irresponsible, and fail to adjust properly with the demands of peers and teachers. Thus there must be a healthy balance of affection and control, freedom and discipline in the home.

(vi) Some parents become excessively involved in all affairs of their adolescent sons and daughters. Although their children have grown up, they consider them to be immature and thus their children are not given any opportunity to act, think, or behave independently. This stifles their independence training. Such adolescents lack social qualities, initiative and the ability to carry on a task independently. Parents should grant autonomy to their adolescent sons and daughters within limits; recognise their status as grown-up individuals in their families; give them an opportunity to participate in family affairs. This will contribute to their growing up as independent adults.

Factors in the School

The development and adjustment of adolescents are influenced by factors in home and in school. The home has primary responsibility of promoting the development and adjustment of adolescent boys and girls. But due to a number of reasons, the home has failed or at least not been completely in position to discharge its responsibilities properly. The school can therefore contribute significantly to the promotion of development and adjustment of adolescents. It is to be emphasized here that the school is not a substitute for the home. It can supplement or complement the contribution of home.

In some schools, the development and adjustment of adolescent boys and girls are hindered by the following factors:

(i) Unsuitable curriculum,
(ii) Teacher-centred instructional strategies,
(iii) Undue emphasis on examination and competition,
(iv) Improper disciplinary measures,
(v) Lack of teacher-pupil interaction and communication,
(vi) Improper behaviour of male teachers towards adolescent girls,
(vii) Lack of boy-girl interaction,
(viii) Lack of opportunity for success and recognition,
(ix) Inability of the teacher to pay individual attention to students in a crowded classroom,
(x) Misunderstanding of teachers about students' behaviour and problems,
(xi) Favouritism of teachers,
(xii) Classroom climate,
(xiii) Lack of guidance for stress management.

The school is in a favourable position to promote the development and adjustment of adolescent boys and girls. By working with adolescents day by day, it can help them to develop wholesome attitudes, values and habits and to consolidate these in an effective pattern of life. It provides a variety of opportunities for them to learn satisfying ways of working together. It also provides knowledge and skills that enable them to develop into competent, self-dependent individuals, capable of meeting social and vocational demands.

The social and emotional climate of the school should be one based on mutual give-and-take, sharing responsibilities, affection and control, mutual respect and understanding. Every teacher has to become a mother for younger adolescents. Teacher's interaction with adolescent girls should be based on sympathetic understanding.

Different types of curricular activities should be organised in the school — some exclusively for girls, some exclusively for boys and some with the participation of both boys and girls. When boys and girls participate in certain activities, they have opportunity of knowing each other's capabilities, interests and limitations, appreciating each other, and this helps them to adjust with members of the opposite sex.

Teacher's expectations of children's behaviour and performance should be realistic and based on what they can do and what they cannot do. Unhealthy comparison between boys and girls, unhealthy criticism of adolescents in presence of members of the opposite sex, lack of opportunity for boys and girls to work together, etc. hinder their development and adjustment. Teachers play a significant role in facilitating the development and adjustment of adolescent boys and girls.

6. ROLE OF THE TEACHER

Adolescence is a period of transition. It is during this period of transition that most individuals face a lot of difficulties and certain problems. Teachers can help boys and girls to have a smooth and successful transition from childhood to adulthood. The manner with which they are handled may do much to determine both the continuing nature of their relationships in the school and the home and the character of the adolescents as they enter adult life.

(i) Assessing the Developmental Level

Teachers must recognise that an adolescent is neither a child nor an adult. Thus, they should avoid being authoritarian in their approach and should not have too much expectations. Different circumstances call for different strengths and abilities and consideration must be given to the adolescent's ability to cope with the particular situation.

(ii) Maintaining Objectivity

The adolescent's problem frequently presents itself in a dramatic fashion. Teachers must show objectivity in understanding the problems of adolescents. A thorough understanding of the situation before judging or acting assists in maintaining objectivity. Information from the family members, school and the social agencies will help in maintaining an accurate and balanced assessment of adolescent's capacity and problems.

(iii) Avoiding over Involvement

Very often the dependency of the adolescent is unnecessarily and inappropriately increased by teachers. Thus, they should avoid, as far as possible, being over involved in the life and activities of the adolescent.

(iv) Developing Trust

If teachers expect respect and trust from the adolescent, they must first give it. Trust is built on clear and matter-of-fact communication. One should not be vague and misleading. Everything must be made clear to him.

(v) Establishing Confidence

The adolescent must be treated as the situation demands. Thus, teachers should not be authoritarian unnecessarily. They must have openness and willingness to listen.

(vi) Facilitating Individuation

The adolescent must be given opportunity to achieve successfully the goals of emotional independence and the formation of individual identity.

(vii) Clarifying Confidentiality

The adolescent may require some information about confidential or private matters. An adolescent girl, for example, needs instruction about sex. Thus, depending on age, nature of relationship between the adolescent and the teacher and the subject under consideration, teachers can discuss with her fully and frankly leaving no doubt. Such instruction must be idealistic, positive and constructive. Correct information is less dangerous than silence and mystery. When such information cannot be given by parents and teachers, it is advisable to take the help of movies, books and friends.

(viii) Providing Co-curricular Activities

A great variety of co-curricular activities must be organised in school. Organisation of games and sports will enable the adolescent to channelize his excessive energy. Provision of self-government and other activities will encourage in him leadership behaviour. Participation in creative works will lead to sublimation of his sex urge. Group discussion, library activities, study circle and club activities will meet his intellectual requirements.

(ix) Providing a Varied Curriculum and Suitable Books

Since an adolescent is expected to attain intellectual maturity, the school curriculum must be varied to meet his intellectual needs. Suitable books on adventures, travels and biography must be provided to him so that good reading habits and high and noble ideals can be developed in him.

(x) Providing Educational, Vocational and Personal Guidance

During this stage, the adolescent has to take decisions of lifelong importance like choosing an educational career or a vocation. He also needs to solve many problems of his personal life. In all these areas, wise and sympathetic guidance must be provided to him.

(xi) A Busy and Hard Routine

An idle mind is a devil's workshop. For this reason, some authorities also prescribe a busy and hard routine with opportunity for delight for the adolescent.

7. THE GIFTED ADOLESCENT

1. Who are the Gifted Adolescents?

There is no unanimous agreement about the definition of giftedness. The profusion of definitions of giftedness is great which is probably due to the fact there are many kinds of gifted children. Moreover, each culture defines giftedness in its own image, in terms of the abilities that the culture values. For example, ancient Greeks honoured the philosopher and the orator and Romans valued the engineer and the soldier.

Giftedness has been traditionally associated with intellectual superiority — a very high IQ score on a standardized test of intelligence. Over the past few decades, periodic efforts have been made to broaden the definition of giftedness to include more than abilities directly related to school work. As for instance, Maryland (1972) defined gifted students as follows: "Gifted and talented children are those, identified by professionally qualified persons, who, by virtue of outstanding abilities, are capable of high performance." These are children who require differentiated programmes and services beyond those normally provided by the regular school programmes in order to realize their contributions to self and society. Adolescents capable of high performance include those with demonstrated achievement and/or potential ability in any one of the following areas:

(i) General intellectual ability,
(ii) Specific academic aptitude,
(iii) Creative or productive thinking,
(iv) Leadership ability,
(v) Visual and performing arts.

One of the latest definitions of giftedness has been given by Ross (1993). According to Ross, "Children and youth with outstanding talent perform, or show the potential for performing, at reasonably high levels of accomplishments when compared with others of their age, experience, or environment. These children and youth exhibit high performance capability in intellectual, creative and/or artistic areas, possess an unusual leadership capacity or excel in specific academic fields. They require services or activities not ordinarily provided by the schools. Outstanding talents are present in children and youth from all cultural groups, across all economic strata, and in all areas of human endeavour."

Other definitions of giftedness try to include the way an individual define and then tackles a problem — the ability to *problem-find* and *problem-solve*. In the real world, problems do not come in neat packages ready for solving. Usually they are hard to define and organise. Problems in the real world are ill-structured. The ability to take an ill-structured problem and organise it so that the issue is clear is one indicator of giftedness. Thus, "Gifted students are those who demonstrate or show the potential for outstanding performance in academic, creative, artistic, leadership or problem-solving areas and who require special education and related services to actualize their potentialities and maximize their capacities."

2. Identification of Gifted Children

Our society has a special interest in children who are gifted. As individuals they have the same right to appropriate education as do all children. In addition, many of the leaders, scientists, engineers and doctors of the twentieth century came from the current group of gifted children. This necessitates early identification of gifted children and provision of suitable education and other services for them.

Gifted adolescents are usually identified by subjective and objective methods, such as the following:

Intelligence Scores,
Creativity Measures,
Achievement Measures,
Measures of Special Aptitude (such as in Mathematics),
Nomination of Peers,
Nomination by Parents,
Self-nomination.

It is important to note that no single method can identify all gifted and talented children. A combination of subjective and objective methods is desirable for identifying gifted and talented children.

Identification Checklist for Parents: Parents can identify their gifted children before they enter the primary school with the help of the following checklist as suggested by Witty (1955). Such identification/nomination by parents should be followed by systematic assessment by specialists:

(i) The early use of a large and accurately employed vocabulary.
(ii) The use of entire sentences and ability to tell or reproduce a story at an early date.
(iii) Keen observation and retention of information about things observed.
(iv) Interest in and liking for books.
(v) Early interest in calendars, telling time, and clocks.
(vi) The ability to attend or concentrate for a longer period than is usual for children.
(vii) Demonstration of proficiency in drawing, music, or other art form.
(viii) Interest in exploration and discovery of cause and effect relationships.
(ix) The early development of ability to read.

Identification Checklist for Teachers: The classroom teacher has the primary responsibility of identifying the gifted adolescents. He is in a better position than anyone else to observe the classroom behaviour of adolescents. In order to make the teacher's observation/nomination more systematic, Koogh and De Haan (1955) have suggested the following checklist:

(i) Learns rapidly and easily,
(ii) Uses a lot of common sense and practical knowledge,
(iii) Reasons things out, thinks clearly, recognizes relationships and comprehends meanings,
(iv) Retains what he has heard or read without much drill,
(v) Knows about many things of which other children are unaware,
(vi) Can read books that are one to two years in advance of the rest of the class,
(vii) Performs difficult mental tasks,
(viii) Asks many questions,
(ix) Does some academic work one to two years in advance of the rest of the class,
(x) Is original, uses good but unusual methods or ideas,
(xi) Is alert, keenly observant and responds quickly.

It is important to note that nomination by a group of teachers is more valid than nomination by a single teacher. In any case identification/nomination by teachers should be followed by objective methods of identification and assessment by specialists.

3. Characteristics of Gifted Children

Giftedness is a complex concept covering a wide range of abilities and traits. Some children have special talents. They may not be outstanding in academics, but they may have special abilities in areas such as music, art, dance, or leadership. Other children may have intellectual abilities found only in one child out of 1,000 children.

Clark (1988)* describes the characteristics of gifted children across five domains: cognitive, affective, physical, intuitive, and societal. There are individual differences among gifted children relating to these characteristics. These characteristics are given below:

I. The Cognitive Domain

- — Extraordinary quantity of information; unusual retentiveness,
- — Advanced comprehension,
- — Unusually varied interests and curiosity,
- — High level of language development,
- — High level of verbal ability,
- — Unusual capacity for processing information,
- — Accelerated pace of thought process,
- — Flexible thought process,
- — Comprehensive synthesis,
- — Early ability to delay closure,
- — Heightened capacity for seeing unusual and diverse relationships and overall gestalt,
- — Ability to generate original ideas and solutions,
- — Early differential patterns for thought processing (*e.g.*, thinking in alternatives and abstract terms, sensing consequences, making generalizations),
- — Early ability to use and form conceptual frameworks,
- — An evaluative approach toward oneself and others,
- — Persistent goal-directed behaviour

II. The Affective Domain

- — Large accumulation of information about emotions that have not been brought to awareness,
- — Unusual sensitivity to the expectations and feelings of others,
- — Keen sense of humour — may be gentle or hostile,
- — Heightened self-awareness, accompanied by feelings of being "different",
- — Idealism and a sense of justice that appear at an early age,
- — Earlier development of an inner locus of control and satisfaction,
- — Advanced level on moral judgment,
- — High expectations of self and others, which often lead to high levels of frustration with self, others, and situations,
- — Unusual emotional depth and intensity,
- — Sensitivity to inconsistency between ideals and behaviour.

III. The Physical Domain

— Unusual discrepancy between physical and intellectual development,
— Low tolerance for the lag between their standards and their physical capacity,
— Cartesian split — can include neglect of physical well-being and avoidance of physical activity.

IV. The Intuitive Domain

— Early involvement and concern for intuitive knowing, psychic and metaphysical phenomena,
— Open to experiences in this area; will experiment with and metaphysical phenomena,
— Creativity apparent in all areas of endeavour,
— Acceptance and expression of a high level of intuitive ability, especially with the highly gifted.

V. The Societal Domain

— Strongly motivated by self-actualization needs,
— Advanced cognitive and affective capacity for conceptualizing and solving societal problems.

Source: *From growing up gifted: Developing the potential of children at home and at school* (3rd ed.) (pp. 253, 260, 264, 268, 271) by B. Clark, Columbus, OH: Merrill.

4. Underachieving Gifted Adolescents

Some adolescents with superior intellectual ability don't perform well in the school. Some gifted students actually fail in the school. In such cases, there is a discrepancy between their potentialities and their actual performance. They are called the underachieving gifted adolescents.

Terman and Oden (1947) found four major factors of underachievement of gifted students:

(i) Greater feelings of inferiority,
(ii) Less self-confidence,
(iii) Less perseverance,
(iv) Less of a sense of life goals.

Gowan (1987) has summarized the research findings and concluded that the following factors are related to underachievement:

(i) Lack of clear and definite academic and occupational choice,
(ii) Weak ego control,
(iii) Withdrawal tendency and feelings of self-sufficiency,
(iv) Poor use of time and money,
(v) Neurotic tendencies,
(vi) Authoritarianism by parents,
(vii) Impossible demands by parents,
(viii) A sense of irresponsibility,
(ix) Lack of self-confidence,
(x) Apathetic view of life.

Gallagher (1960) presents a combination of events which lead to underachievement among children of superior intelligence:

(i) The underachieving child grows up in, or belongs to, a cultural group which does not value education, independence or individual achievement.
(ii) The underachieving child has parents (especially the father) who show limited interest in academic matters or try to put undue pressure on their children to succeed.
(iii) Faced with impossible demands by parents in home and teachers in the school, the child rejects their programmes.
(iv) The strict and repressive measures of the school turn the child even more emphatically against the school.
(v) Unable to obtain satisfaction from parental contacts, the child seeks out his peer group for satisfying human relationships. He often finds himself in rebellious and angry groups.

Whitmore (1980) found the following personality and behaviour traits that describe many underachieving gifted children:

(i) A negative self-concept,
(ii) A low self-esteem,
(iii) Expectation of academic and social failure,
(iv) A sense of inability to control or determine outcomes of one's own efforts,
(v) Emotional disturbance.

Most of the factors that lead to underachievement lie outside the school. What can the school do to help the underachieving gifted child?

Kirk (1972) suggests the following measures:

(i) Identifying underachieving gifted children during the early years in school.
(ii) Assigning tutors who will support and motivate the children through success in academic fields.
(iii) Counselling parents concerning the problems of the child and better human relations in the family.
(iv) Rewarding the child by praise and recognition in school for efforts and achievements in school work.
(v) Organising small group sessions/special classes for underachieving gifted children with support from specialist teachers.

Whitmore (1980) points out that the creation of a warm, accepting environment can overcome the signs of emotional disturbance of such children. Whitmore (1980) and Butler-Por (1987) have shown that carefully designed programmes over an extended period of time can make a positive difference in the academic and social performance of underachievers.

5. Educational Programmes for the Gifted

***Aims of Education of the Gifted*:** In a broader sense, the aims of education of the gifted are no different from those for all other children. Feelings of self-worth, self-sufficiency, civic responsibilities, and vocational competence are important for everyone. There are, however, some additional goals which are specially desirable for gifted and talented children. Gallagher (1981) has suggested two major objectives of educational programmes for the gifted and talented children:

(i) Mastering the knowledge structure of disciplines which includes basic principles and systems of knowledge.
(ii) Heuristic skills which include problem-solving, creativity, and use of the scientific methods.

Setting educational goals for gifted children means little, unless these children are given appropriate learning opportunities, or unless the school programmes are modified to match their special needs. The school programme for the gifted can be modified in three areas: learning environments, content, and cognitive strategies (Kirk, Gallagher and Anastasia (1996).

Modification in the Learning Environment: The learning environment can be modified for the gifted and talented students in three ways. These are:

(i) Flexible pacing,
(ii) Grouping, and
(iii) Special courses.

(i) *Flexible Pacing:* Flexible pacing is a strategy that accelerates the student to a level in the school programme that is higher than the level of his/her age-mates. This strategy involves the following:

— Early admission in the school or college,
— Continuous progress at one's own rate,
— Skipping (bypassing) subjects and receiving some instruction at a higher level with another group of students while remaining with the peer group for most of the instruction.
— Skipping grades (double promotion),
— Concurrent (dual) enrollment at two levels — secondary and post-secondary,
— Giving credit on satisfactory completion of an examination,
— Covering the course in a shortened period of time and pursuing special courses during the rest of the time.

(ii) *Grouping*: Students can be grouped on the basis of performance or aptitude. Having all students with high performance ability in one group allows the teacher to proceed much more swiftly and in greater depth. Grouping can be of various types:

— Cross-age or multi-age grouping of students on the basis of similar interests or skills.
— Homogeneous grouping of students in a particular class on the basis of similar skill level.
— Cluster grouping within a regular class in which a cluster group (4 to 10) of students receives academic support from the cluster teacher.
— Subject grouping in which students are grouped for specific subjects on the basis of their performance or aptitude in that subject.

— Part-time placement in the regular class with part-time placement in a special class for specialized instruction.

— Full-time placement in a special class.

(iii) *Special Courses:* At the secondary level, special courses can be organised for gifted and talented students. These include:

— Honours courses,

— Advanced placement courses or college-level courses,

— International courses and foreign languages,

— Special school courses,

— Residential high school courses not available in most high schools.

Modification of Content

Boredom is a real problem for gifted students because they are forced to learn material they already know. For this reason, the teacher needs to:

— Find out what the students know before instruction,

— Arrange to teach, in a brief fashion, the remaining concepts or skills, and

— Provide a different set of experiences to enrich or advance the students.

Content modification involves the following:

Content acceleration,

Content enrichment,

Content sophistication, and

Content novelty.

(i) *Content Acceleration:* This process allows students to master increasingly complex set of ideas at a faster rate. For example, by learning calculus in ninth grade, students have the foundation to begin physics and chemistry which require the skills of calculus.

(ii) *Content Enrichment:* This process gives students the opportunity for a greater appreciation of the topic under study by expanding the material — exploring additional examples, using specific illustration, taking additional assignments, referring to encyclopaedia, etc.

(iii) *Content Sophistication:* This process involves challenging students who are gifted to use higher levels of thinking to understand ideas that average students of the same age would find difficult or impossible to comprehend. The objective is to encourage gifted children to understand important abstractions, scientific laws, and general principles that can be applied in many circumstances.

(iv) *Content Novelty*: Content novelty is the introduction of material that normally would not appear in the general curriculum because of time constraints or the abstract nature of the content. Computers can be used to introduce content novelty into the curriculum.

Teaching Cognitive Strategies

One objective of all educators of gifted and talented students is to increase or enhance their capability in problem-finding and problem-solving. Problem-finding is the ability to review an area of study and to perceive those elements worthy of further analysis and study. Problem-solving is the ability to reach a previously determined answer by organising and processing the available information in a logical and systematic fashion. Along with enhancing their problem-finding and problem-solving skills, gifted and talented students should be guided to extend their intellectual fluency through brainstorming. The four ground rules for *brainstorming* are as follows:

(i) No criticism should be allowed when a student presents an idea.
(ii) The more ideas, the better.
(iii) Students should be encouraged to integrate and combine ideas.
(vi) Evaluation should take place after all ideas have been presented.

6. Role of the Teacher

No educational programme is more important than the teacher, who implements it. Most schools do not get the services of a specialist teacher for educating gifted and talented students. Hence, the regular teacher has to play an important role in identifying children who are gifted, assessing their potentialities, modifying the learning environment, providing acceleration and enrichment and organise brainstorming sessions for gifted students.

One of the first questions most people ask is whether the teacher must be gifted to teach gifted children effectively. The answer is "Not necessarily." In fact, all teachers must be gifted, regardless of whom they teach. They should be gifted in different ways to teach different children. Nonetheless, teachers of gifted children do need some particular qualities. They must:

— be willing to accept unusual and diverse questions, answers and projects;
— be intellectually curious;
— be systematic and business-like;
— be well-prepared in instructional techniques;
— be well-prepared in content areas;
— have a variety of interests;
— appreciate achievements;
— realize that they may not know as much about some topics as the children, and be comfortable with that situation.

(*Heward and Orlansky, 1992*)

8. THE ADOLESCENT SLOW LEARNERS

Who is a Slow Learner?

It is a known fact that all children experience school-related problems at one time or another during their school years. A teacher on any working day may have to deal with problems ranging from aggressive behaviour to disinterest in the learning task. The cause of such difficulties may vary from an unknown conflict at home to simple headache. Such situations may result in poor academic performance and aggressive behaviour temporarily. Effective teachers tackle such problems easily. There is, however, another group of children who display prolonged learning difficulties. These are the children whose scholastic performance is below the average expected of their age-group. Most teachers who deal with average and below-average pupils meet children who do not seem to profit from the usual educational methods and content provided. The term 'backward' or 'slow learner' is reserved for these children who are not coping with the work normally expected of their age-group (Burt, 1937) or whose scholastic performance is below the average expected of their age group (Kirman, 1975).

For Kirk (1962), rate of learning is the basis of identifying a child as slow learner, average or gifted. For Kirk, the slow-learning child is not considered mentally retarded because he is capable of achieving a moderate degree of academic success even though at a slower rate than the average child. He is educated in the regular classes without special provisions except an adaptation of the regular class programme to fit his slower learning ability. At the adult level, he is usually self-supporting, independent and socially adjusted.

There are some children who have borderline retardation and some who have mild retardation. Individuals with borderline mental retardation blend with the normal population, and with proper training can achieve social and vocational adequacy. This group and those mild mental retardates, who remain undetected in a class are often called 'slow learners.' The child we call a slow learner is one who is not necessarily retarded or in need of special education but is likely to need some extra time and help in a regular classroom. He is capable of learning just about anything that the average child is capable of; it just takes him longer. In other words, a slow learner is one who learns or is learning at a slower than average rate.

Causes of Slow Learning

Every behaviour has a cause, meaning and significance. The behavioural characteristics of slow learners are symptoms of conditions or some factors present either within the child or outside the child. Slow learning is caused by a variety of factors such as:

(i) Low intellectual abilities such as subnormal intelligence.

(ii) Personal factors such as:
long illness,
long absence from school,
undetected physical defects,
poor cognitive entry characteristics.

(iii) Environmental variables such as:
poor home facilities for learning skills,
low quality and quantity of food,
shortage of sleep,
adverse parental attitudes towards education,

poor or inappropriate opportunities in school (large classes),
poor quality of teaching,
choosing inadequate or advanced materials,
incompatibility between home and the school,
repeated changes of school and consequent changes in teaching styles and content.

(iv) Emotional factors such as:
dislike of teacher through classes of personality,
negative parental attitudes to school creating in the child similar adverse attitudes,
feeling of inadequacy,
lack of confidence in self and need to achieve,
extreme timidity and anxiety giving rise to poor levels of attainment.

Identification of Slow Learners

In every classroom, a large number of slow learners are noticed. These children with borderline or mild handicaps who attend the regular class are likely to drop out if their needs are not met. It is, therefore, necessary that these children are identified early and helped in their learning. A competent teacher should be alert to general characteristics of the associated classroom behaviour relating to learning difficulties of a child. For example, the slow learner requires more help and time to acquire the skill than his average peer. The slow learner will rely on concrete learning rather than abstract learning.

Slow learners are to be identified by employing various procedures and using various tools and techniques. These are as follows:

(i) Day-to-day observation of classroom behaviour of children by the teacher.
(ii) Assessment of children's performance in specific subjects based on the Cumulative Record Card or school marks.
(iii) Opinion of parents about the child's progress and difficulties in learning various subjects, doing homework, his language difficulties, emotional problems, illness, injuries and physical defects and problems.
(iv) Measures of intellectual ability or IQ scores.

(v) Competence-based tests and diagnostic tests in various subjects.

However, if slow learners are to be helped in their learning difficulties, they must be identified early in schools, because prolonged learning difficulties may imply placement of such children in special schools which are very rare in India.

Educational Programmes for the Slow Learner

The slow learner is capable of achieving a moderate degree of academic success though with additional time and help. They are capable of being educated in the regular class with few adaptations. As adults, they are self-supporting, independent, and socially adjusted. If the needs of such children are not met, they experience failure and drop out prematurely from school. The difficulty is that most of these children are not diagnosed as slow learners until they attend school and begin to fail. This calls for early identification, diagnosis of their learning difficulties and proper instructional provisions for them.

Adolescent slow learners are usually benefited from the following plans:

Carefully Guided Instruction

Slow learners work best with a carefully designed, step by step technique, and additional time and help. Considerable repetition is usually necessary and the material should be adapted appropriately for the slow learner. Positive reinforcement technique should be used as much as possible. The following recommendations are useful for the teacher:

(i) The teacher needs to emphasize the concrete and the specific with regard to the problems and materials.

(ii) Instruction should be directed towards satisfying those needs that are more immediate and more easily recognised and identified.

(iii) Slow learners should be given more time, attention and guidance by the teacher until they reach the expected average standard.

(iv) Instruction should be less dependent on conventional printed materials.

(v) Out-of-school resources like the field trip should be used more frequently.

(vi) There is need for greater utilization of audio-visual aids.

(vii) Learning units should be organised around life's problems more than around academic subjects.

(viii) Teachers should avoid any kind of competition or comparison between normal or gifted students and slow learners.

(ix) All types of labelling such as 'stupid,' 'idiot,' the 'slow learner,' 'the dull,' 'the back bencher' should be avoided by the teacher as this may lower the child's self-concept, self-esteem and lead to greater frustration, anxiety, withdrawal and delinquent tendencies.

(x) Teachers should discover any specific skills slow learners may possess. If possible, let them demonstrate their skills for other students.

(xi) Teachers should be careful about the number of things taught and the abstractness of the material. Sheer numbers can overwhelm any one, especially the slow learners. The more abstract the material, the greater difficulty the slow learner will have with it.

Individualized Instruction

Slow learners can learn as well as fast learners if instruction is approached systematically and sensitively, if they are given extra time and if they are helped in their learning difficulties. This was the proposition maintained by Bloom (1965). Bruner, a cognitive psychologist, also held similar views. Any concept can be taught to any child if appropriate instructional methods and procedures are utilized. Individualized instruction is most useful in the education of slow learners.

In individualized instruction, the methods and materials of instruction are adjusted to the needs and abilities of individual learners. There are mainly three forms of individualised instruction, such as:

(i) Tutoring,

(ii) Individually Prescribed Instruction (IPI), and

(iii) Individually Guided Education (IGE).

Of these three forms, tutoring is a popular programme in schools and homes. The IPI and the IGE are new developments.

Tutoring

Tutoring is a face-to-face, one-to-one relationship or situation in which the tutor has the primary responsibility of helping a child in his learning difficulty. Tutoring may be also done in a small group consisting of four to five children, but the essence of the situation remains the same in a small group as in one-to-one situation: individual help, attention and time. Thus instruction that is individualised, whether in one-to-one situation or small group situation is called tutoring.

Usually teachers act as tutors, but able classmates, older students and adult volunteers can also be tutors. Older children can talk their language and can provide excellent models for them. Children teaching children are not a new idea; it is very popular in homes and schools.

Remedial Instruction

Slow learners are benefited mostly from remedial instruction. Remedial instruction for slow learners refers to two types of programmes:

(i) Eliminating ineffective habits and unwholesome attitudes and re-teaching skills which have been incorrectly learned. This refers to remediation of defects.

(ii) Teaching for the first time those habits, skills and attitudes which have never been learned but should have been and which are needed by such children. This refers to developmental teaching or developing increased competence.

Remedial programme involves taking a child where he is and from that point leading him to greater achievement. Remedial teaching is just good teaching concerned with two types of deficiencies — the presence of bad habits and the absence of good habits.

Remedial instruction requires proper diagnosis of their specific difficulties in various subjects and understanding their problems before actual instruction begins. In certain cases, slow learning is caused by factors other than low intellectual ability. For example, visual defects may cause reading difficulties; emotional factors may cause general academic failure. In such cases, interview with parents and the classroom teacher or a simple medical examination may solve the problem.

Remedial instruction can be given by the regular teacher, full-time remedial teacher or visiting remedial teacher. In Scotland and England, a large number of schools are utilising the services of visiting remedial teacher, who visits a number of schools in a single day and provides remedial instruction to the students, who need it on a part-time basis. The remedial teacher is a specialist teacher who uses alternate learning materials, methods, audio-visual aids and workbooks in tutoring situation.

SELECTED QUESTIONS

1. Explain the concept and characteristics of adolescence.
2. Discuss the basic needs and problems of adolescents with special reference to their developmental tasks.
3. State the influence of home in the development and adjustment of adolescents.
4. State the role of the school in promoting adolescent development and adjustment.
5. Discuss the social and emotional development during adolescence.
6. Discuss the cognitive development during adolescence.
7. State the role of the teacher in facilitating adolescent development.
8. Discuss the identification and education of adolescent slow learners/gifted adolescent.

12
Individual Differences

1. MEANING, NATURE AND TYPES

Although human beings possess certain universal common characteristics such as a physical body, intellectual capacities, emotions and feelings, they differ in respect of their quantitative aspects. Thus there may be qualitative similarities among individuals, but there are quantitative differences among them. The concept of individual differences refers to quantitative differences found among individuals in respect of specific trait or various traits. Individual differences are a matter of degree, not of kind.

Studies in the field of psychology and education have thrown adequate light on the nature and extent of individual differences. These studies have indicated that individuals cannot fall into distinct categories in respect of any physical or mental trait. For example, in respect of intelligence we cannot group individuals as: (i) those having intelligence, and (ii) those having no intelligence at all. If we measure any trait of a group of individuals, we will find that they are distributed according to the law of normal probability curve in respect of that trait.

Types of Individual Differences

Individuals differ from one another in respect of a specific trait or a number of traits. For example, individuals differ from one another in respect of height, weight, intelligence, personality traits, and other physical and psychological areas. This is what we call inter-individual differences. In addition to inter-individual differences, there are also intra-individual differences.

Differences are noticed within the same individual when he is studied in respect of various traits. For example, an individual may possess a good height, but he may have a very low weight. A student may demonstrate superior performance in school-related subjects, but at the same time he may experience failure in dramatics. A girl student may look attractive and beautiful, but she may be an average student in relation to studies. Even differences may also be noticed in the same individual with respect to his performance on a particular task at different times. Runners differ in running the same distance. The same runner may cover the same distance taking different times on different occasions. This is what we call intraindividual differences.

2. AREAS OF INDIVIDUAL DIFFERENCES

Individuals differ almost in every respect. They differ in age, height, weight, sensory and motor-powers, intelligence, aptitude, attitudes, emotional reactions, interests, appreciations and educational attainments. In other words, individuals differ in physical, physiological, cognitive and personality traits.

Physical and Physiological Areas

Individuals vary in physical and physiological characteristics. They vary in their physical appearance, colour and curliness of their hair, colour of their eyes (brown eyes and blue eyes), pigmentations and colour of their skin (fair skin and black skin), shape of their nose (hooked nose and straight nose), their height and weight. They also vary in their body build. Some have pyknic type body; some have aesthetic type; and some have athletic type body. Similarly some are late matures and some are early matures. Some of these physical and physiological characteristics do not have any influence on their personality characteristics or their learning. But some characteristics have positive correlation with personality characteristics, on what they can do and what they cannot do, on how they interact with others and how they are accepted by others. Children of the same age-group vary in their strength of grip, handwriting, physical fitness such as speed, strength, agility, muscles, skeletal system, etc., which indicate to a great extent their readiness, participation, progress and success in school-related subjects, skills, games and sports and other physical activities. Similarly, boys and girls who are taller, stronger and attractive are more popular, have more friends and are more likely to be selected as leaders. There are children who are physically handicapped. Unless special provisions are made for such children, they cannot profit from education in general schools.

Cognitive Areas

Children vary in their general intellectual abilities, specific intellectual abilities, and their level of educational achievements. Most children possess average intelligence and very few children demonstrate high degree of intelligence. There may be some children who possess low intellectual ability. Children possessing low level of intelligence will not be successful in learning school-related subjects. Even children who possess the lowest level of intelligence will not attend regular schools and will require constant help throughout their lives for performing even the simplest tasks like eating, dressing, toileting, etc. Children at the top end of the scale will show superior performance in all types of academic work.

Children also vary in their level of educational achievement. There is a high correlation between achievement at earlier grades and achievements at later grades. Thus the present level of achievement is a good indicator of future achievement. This also means that children vary in their present academic achievement mainly because of their earlier achievements in school. Thus a teacher cannot estimate accurately how well a student is achieving before knowing his intellectual level or his previous achievement.

Personality Characteristics

Individuals not only vary in their physical, physiological and cognitive characteristics, they also vary in their personality characteristics. Individuals vary in their social adaptability, emotional balance and control, personal tempo and other personality traits. Some individuals are able to adapt to social situations more easily than others. Mentally retarded individuals have poor social adaptability. Some are emotionally stable whereas others are emotionally disturbed. Emotionally disturbed children have learning problems. Some are sober and some are exuberant. Children also vary in their passivity-activity in relation to the world of people and objects. Some are introverts and some others are extroverts. Introverts are more inhibited, timid, shy and withdrawn. Extroverts are more active, friendly, outgoing and spontaneous. In the learning situation, extroverts are more motivated by constructive and friendly criticism. Introverts are motivated more by praise than blame.

In addition to the above traits, children also vary in their attitudes, needs, values and interests. There are two fundamental needs of school children — the need to achieve success and the need to avoid failure. Children vary in these needs and this variability markedly influences their tendency to undertake or to avoid activities. Children who have a high need to achieve success have high achievement motivation. Children who have a high need to avoid failure have high achievement anxiety. A child with a high need to achieve success and a low need to avoid failure undertakes an activity with vigour. On the contrary, a student with a high need to avoid failure does not participate at all in the activity—or puts off the task for fear of experiencing failure. Children likewise vary in other motives such as for love and belongingness, self-esteem and self-actualisation. They vary in their recreational interests, interests for and attitude towards various subjects, institutions and their value systems.

3. SIGNIFICANCE OF THE STUDY OF INDIVIDUAL DIFFERENCES

The study of individual differences is significant for the teacher for the following reasons:

(i) Learners differ from one another in almost all respects. Some are bright, some are average, and some are below average in respect of their cognitive abilities. Even some are fast learners and some are slow learners. If learners are distributed normally and if they are given the same instruction, individual differences in the ability to learn and the rate of learning will tend to increase further. Under the system of uniform instruction for all learners, bright learners will continue to remain as bright and slow learners will also continue to learn at much slower rates. Conversely if teachers are able to provide appropriate instruction to each and every learner then individual differences in the rate of learning and the ability to learn will tend to decrease and all learners will be able to learn the desired competencies excellently. The study of individual differences will help teachers to plan instruction systematically and sensitively to enable learners to learn skills, attitudes and behaviours excellently and this will reduce individual differences among learners.

(ii) Individual differences in children's aptitude, interest and attitudes have significance for teachers to plan different types of in-school and out-of-school activities to help children progress along the desired line and maximize their potentialities.

(iii) The study of individual differences is significant for curriculum planning and curriculum transactions at different stages of schooling.

(iv) Children attending schools differ in respect of their prerequisite learning. Children coming from socially disadvantaged communities have very little or no previous learning in their homes. Children who lack prerequisite learning required for learning school-related subjects experience failure and later drop out from the school. The study of individual differences will give the teacher the knowledge and skills required for providing compensatory education or remedial education to those who need it. This will also reduce the number of failures, drop-out cases and contribute to the success of the programme of *Sarva Sikshya*.

(v) The study of individual differences is also useful for the teacher to measure children's abilities or traits and to provide educational and vocational guidance to them.

(vi) The study of individual differences among boys and girls is also significant for teachers for gaining a better understanding of children, what they are capable of doing and what they are not and this will create in them the needed confidence and skills for professional growth.

4. CAUSES OF INDIVIDUAL DIFFERENCES

In attempting to understand the causes of individual differences, many factors must be considered. Even the simplest behaviour is often the result of many different influences. Basically, these influences fall into five major categories such as:

(i) Genetically determined biological variables (for example, heredity);

(ii) Non-genetic biological variables (for example, lack of oxygen during the birth process, malnutrition);

(iii) The child's past learning;

(iv) The immediate social-psychological environment (for example, parents, siblings, peers and teachers), and

(v) The general social and cultural milieu in which the child develops.

Individual differences in the behaviour, intelligence, and personality are, at any one time, a product of continuing interaction of nature and nurture or heredity and environment. In practice, one cannot easily determine how much each set of forces contributes to a particular trait. Both genetic and environmental factors interact continually to produce a given effect. Consider the analogy of a snowfall. Cold temperature and a high proportion of moisture in the air are both required to produce snow. It is not possible to say that the cold temperature was 60 per cent responsible and the moisture 40 per cent responsible for the snowflakes. Although we speak of genetic and environmental determinants of behaviour, we always acknowledge that they act in unison. Scientists try to discover the specific genetic and environmental forces that are controlling a specific behaviour; they do not ask which influence is more important. This realization of the intimate interaction of genes and environment is relatively recent.

(1) Influence of Genetic Factors

Life begins at conception. Conception occurs when a sperm from the father unites with the ovum from the mother. At this moment, the sperm of the father releases 23 tiny particles called the chromosomes. At approximately the same time, the ovum of the mother also releases 23 chromosomes. The chromosomes contain even smaller particles called genes. Genes are the real carriers of heredity. There are about 20,000 genes per chromosome. Combinations of genes vary from conception to conception. This is why two children of the same parents are so different physically and mentally. If each child received all of both parents' genes, we could not explain individual genetic differences between siblings, as all brothers and sisters would then have identical heredities. The fact, however, is that each child inherits only half of each parent's genes. Moreover, different children in a family inherit different combinations of their mother's and father's genes. This results in individual differences among children of the same parents. Genetic differences cause differences in intelligence, personality, physical features and psychological traits among children. Let us take few studies to prove that individual differences are caused by genetic factor or heredity.

Goddard's Study

H.H. Goddard (1921) studied one Kallikak family. Martin Kallikak (false name) had children by two women: one woman was feeble-minded and the other was of normal intelligence. The feeble-minded mother gave birth to feeble-minded children while the mother with normal intelligence had no feeble-minded children. This study proved that mental retardation was caused by hereditary or genetic factors.

Galton's Study

Sir Francis Galton (1892) was the first to study the possible relationship between intelligence and heredity. Galton first demonstrated that there is a great deal of individual variation in intelligence — that all people are not equally bright or capable. Then he also tried to show that these differences in mental ability were largely inherited, mostly by arguing that eminent men tended to be related to one another. As evidence he presented the family trees of prominent men in the fields of law, science, art and military indicating that greatness ran in certain families.

Erlenmeyer-Kimling and Jarvik Study

L. Erlenmeyer-Kimling and L.F. Jarvik (1963) studied genetic relationships and IQ. Their findings based on 52 studies are presented in table 3.

Table 3: IQ Correlation between Persons of Various Relationships based on the Results of 52 Studies

Relationship	Range of Correlation
Unrelated children reared apart	0-.30
Unrelated children reared together	.13-.38
Foster parent-child	.20-.50
Parent-child	.24-.81
Siblings reared apart	.30-.40
Siblings reared together	.25-.70
Fraternal twins (opposite sex)	.30-.60
Fraternal twins (same sex)	.33-.83
Identical twins reared apart	.60-.88
Identical twins reared together	.72-1

Interpretation of Kimling and Jarvik's Findings

(i) If genetic factors have great influence on the intellectual abilities of children then arbitrarily picked up pairs of children, who are not biologically related and who are reared in different environments will not be similar in IQ at all. The correlation of IQ scores of such pairs of 'unrelated children reared apart' will be very negligible or even zero. This has been proved by Kimling and Jarvik.

(ii) If heredity has an important influence on the intellectual abilities of children, then children's IQ scores will correlate positively with those of their biological parents. Kimling and Jarvik found a positive correlation between the IQ scores of children and those of their biological parents which ranges from .24 to .81.

(iii) Children and their biological parents have similar heredity in contrast to the children and their foster-parents. Thus the IQ correlation of parents and their children should be higher than the IQ correlation of children and their foster-parents. Kimling and Jarvik found IQ correlation of children and their foster-parents ranging from .20 to .50 which is less than the IQ correlation of children and their biological parents which ranges from .24 to .81.

(iv) The IQ correlations of identical and fraternal twins indicate the genetic influence on intelligence. Identical twins have identical heredity whereas fraternal twins may be as dissimilar as two siblings born to the same parents at different times. Thus the IQ correlation of twins should be very high and that the identical twins should have a higher correlation than that of fraternal twins. This has also been proved by Kimling and Jarvik.

Jensen's Study

Arthur Jensen (1969) conducted very important studies on inheritance of intelligence. His studies show that intelligence is 80 per cent genetically determined. Based on studies conducted over the past 50 years, Jensen says that genetic factors are far more important than environmental influences in explaining individual differences in IQ scores.

Wilson's Study

R.S. Wilson (1975) conducted a study on pattern of cognitive development of identical and non-identical twins using the Wechler Pre-school and Primary Scale of intelligence. The correlations of over 100 pairs of twins comparing their test results on the Wechler scale are given in Table 4. As you will find, the scores of identical twins are more similar than the scores of non-identical twins resulting in higher correlations for scores of identical twins. This also shows the influence of genetic factors on intellectual functioning of children.

Table 4: Correlations of Test Scores of Twins

Subject	Identical Twins	Non-identical Twins (Same sex)
Information	.81	.47
Vocabulary	.71	.27
Arithmetic	.65	.57
Similarities	.73	.40
Comprehension	.80	.40
Animal house	.82	.42
Picture completion	.69	.38
Mazes	.61	.43
Geometric design	.72	.36
Block design	.68	.34

Physical Features

Our physical features depend heavily upon heredity. For example, the colour of our eyes, the pigmentation of our skin, and the colour and curliness of our hair are typically a function of the genes we inherit. Some features, such as eye colour, depend upon simple combination of genes. Other features such as skin colour are more complex and involve many sets of genes acting together.

Personality Characteristics

Although it is difficult to demonstrate the influence of genetic factors on personality traits, a number of studies indicate that certain personality characteristics such as introversion — extroversion, affective disorders, passivity—activity, body build, personal tempo, etc., are at least partially genetically determined. We will return to our discussion on personality characteristics again in a later chapter on 'Personality.'

2. Influence of Environment Factors

In addition to genetic factors, environmental factors also cause individual differences among children.

Kimling and Jarvik's studies not only indicate genetic influence on intelligence, but these studies also establish the importance of environmental influences on intelligence. For example, unrelated children raised in the same environment have different heredity but similar environment. Thus, any similarity in IQ scores of such children must be due to environmental influences. Studies of Kimling and Jarvik indicate a correlation of .13 to .38 between the IQ scores of unrelated children reared together.

Similarly foster-parents and their children have different heredity. A positive correlation of their IQ scores (.20 to .50) indicates the role of environment.

If environment has important influence on intelligences, then identical twins reared together should be more similar in IQ scores than identical twins reared apart. Identical twins who are reared together have identical heredity and similar environment. By contrast, identical twins reared apart have identical heredity but different environment. For this purpose, identical twins reared together have very high correlation of their IQ (.72 to 1} as compared to identical twins reared apart (.60 to .88).

Several studies also indicate that children who are exposed to pre-school education, rich language experiences, large vocabulary of adults, children's literature and other forms of stimulating environment and opportunities during early years of their life have better cognitive development than children who are deprived of such opportunities, experiences, encouragement and guidance from parents and other adults. Similarly, if children born in lower class families are shifted to and brought up in middle class and upper class families then they show clear gain in their IQ scores.

Environmental influences are not only responsible for individual differences in intelligence but also they cause differences in personality and adjustment. In relation to personality traits and adjustment, environmental forces include interpersonal relationship in the family, peer group influences, cultural and social forces, including the emotional climate of the school. Certain personality traits like extroversion and introversion, friendliness, aggressiveness, certain mental disorders, maladjustment, delinquent tendencies, truancy, stress tolerance, social interaction styles, gestures and other non-verbal signs, etc. are largely determined by social, cultural and other environmental forces.

3. Influence of Physiological Factors

In addition to genetic and environmental influences, certain physiological factors also cause individual differences among children. For example, individual differences among children are caused by maturation process — late maturation and early maturation. Studies indicate that late matures are rated as less attractive in physique, less well-poised, more affected and more tense in manner, and more eager. They tend to engage in more attention-getting behaviour, are more restless, talkative and bossy; are less popular with their peers, and fewer of them are selected as leaders. In contrast, early matures emerge as more reserved, more self-assured, more matter-of-fact, and more likely to engage in socially appropriate behaviour. Many of these differences appear to persist over long periods of time.

Early matures are more likely to be selected for leadership and supervision work.

Early and late maturation makes a great deal of differences in boys than girls because of social expectations.

Maturation influences one's height, weight, and strength. Children who are taller, heavier and stronger are more likely to be rated high on social traits than those shorter and weaker. Similarly, children with greater strength have more participation in in-school and out-of-school activities than children who are shorter and weaker.

Body build also leads to great differences in personality traits of children. Kretschmer found significant relationship between different types of physique and character. Sheldon also found relationship between body types and temperament (Please refer to the concerned chapter on Personality for detailed discussion).

We have examined how genetic, environmental and physiological factors cause individual differences in intelligence and personality. As is evident now, individual differences are caused not by any single factor, but by the interplay of genetic, environmental and physiological factors. Some differences are largely controlled by genetic factors. Others are controlled by environmental or physiological factors.

Teachers should not over-emphasize the importance of any single factor. If a teacher believes that environment is the complete force and that heredity is little or nothing, then his efforts will be directed almost equally for all children. In that way, he will misdirect much of his energy. There are teachers who believe that every child is a diamond in the rough which needs only polishing in order to reflect the light of intelligence.

On the contrary, if a teacher believes that children differ in respect of their potentialities, he will feel that his efforts will bring different results with different children and he will have different expectations for different children. Such teachers believe that a child will develop in the direction determined by his heredity and that the guidance and training by parents and teachers matter very little. A teacher with such beliefs will miss many opportunities to develop the latent capacities of his pupils. It is, therefore, necessary to accept the importance of all the factors — genetic, environmental and physiological — as causes of individual differences among children.

5. EDUCATIONAL PROVISIONS FOR MEETING INDIVIDUAL DIFFERENCES

Children differ in their learning abilities. Schools have important duties and responsibilities to make provisions to meet individual differences in the classrooms so that every child is helped to rise to a height commensurate with his own abilities. The following are a few of the important steps that a school might take up in this direction:

(i) Every Individual's Ability should be Assessed as Accurately as Possible

Since individuals possess cognitive and psychomotor abilities ranging from a very low to a very high degree and since they do not fall into distinct types, it becomes difficult to locate the exact standing of a child. Hence, it is imperative that the abilities of children should be accurately assessed. The more reliable is the assessment, better will be the provision.

(ii) A Good Environment and Proper Education are Necessary

Though heredity is important in determining eventual adult performance, environment also plays a vital role as demonstrated by experiments. Hence a good environment and proper education are necessary for all. Younger children must have rich opportunities to express themselves and they must have proper guidance for their emerging abilities. Kindergarten education and nursery school attendance must be provided to all children.

(iii) Identification of Special Talents

We need to spend considerably more effort than we do at present in identifying abilities starting early in school years with the help of standardised tests. Such identification will be more authentic. The identified talents should be properly nurtured.

(iv) Educational Provision must be Continuous

In order to provide well for children of the entire range of abilities, educational provisions must be continuous. The continuity must be ensured especially when children pass from one stage of education to another, or from one school system to another.

(v) Adequate Facilities and Materials are Needed

Bright children need some instructional materials more advanced than those for the other children. The slow learners also require reading materials different from the rest of the group. The sensori-handicapped and emotionally disturbed children also require special materials, equipment and space. In order to provide all the facilities for individual differences, every school should be properly equipped with such facilities and materials as will be needed by all kinds of children.

(vi) Competent School Staff is Needed

Even the best facilities for the education of children cannot be better than the school personnel doing the work. Hence the society should recognise the importance of well-educated and competent school staff and give the necessary financial support to schools. Every school should have competent teachers, school psychologists, guidance workers, curriculum supervisors and administrators.

(vii) Special Provisions should be Made for Children with Special Needs

There may be some children in the school who have special needs. The visually handicapped, the hearing handicapped, the mentally retarded, the learning disabled and the emotionally disturbed have special needs. Provisions should be made in the regular schools and special schools for identification, assessment, placement, care and training of such children.

(viii) Special Provisions should be Made for Socially Disadvantaged Children

In order to help children to overcome the restrictive influence of disadvantaged social conditions and to reduce the differences between advantaged and disadvantaged children, provisions like enrichment programmes, school readiness programmes, remedial instruction and incentives should be made available to disadvantaged children.

(ix) Special Provisions are Necessary for Gifted Children

We have already discussed educational programmes for the gifted adolescent. To recapitulate here, enrichment activities, homogeneous grouping, acceleration programmes and other provisions are necessary for maximizing the potentialities of gifted children.

(x) Individualisation of Instruction is Necessary

The principal means of meeting individual differences in the classroom is individualisation of instruction. This refers to adapting instructional methods and materials to the needs and abilities of individual students. The open learning system, self-learning system, programmed instruction, tutoring, individually prescribed instruction, individually guided instruction are examples of individualising instruction. A more detailed discussion is presented in the next section of this chapter.

6. INDIVIDUALISED INSTRUCTION

Individualised instruction is a planned and systematic procedure in which the materials and methods of instruction are adapted to the needs and abilities of individual learners of a given age. It takes many forms such as:

(i) Alternative forms of classroom organisation such as ability grouping, non-graded classes, programme of rapid promotion, open classrooms, tutoring, etc.

(ii) Individualising technological aids such as programmed instruction, computer-based teaching, audio-visual instruction.

(iii) Individualising the pace of learning such as individual assignment, learning contracts, individual projects, self-learning, personalised system of instruction, individually guided education, individually prescribed instruction, learning for mastery and programme for learning in accordance with needs (PLAN).

We shall discuss three forms of individualised instruction programmes here.

Personalised System of Instruction

The Personalised System of Instruction (PSI) was first propounded by Fred Keller in the year 1964. Keller along with his colleagues

Sherman, Azzi and Bari prepared and presented a personalized course for college level students in the University of Brasillia in Brazil in the year 1964. They called it Personalised System of Instruction (PSI). The PSI was defined as "an individually paced, mastery-oriented teaching method for college level education."

There are five essential features of the PSI model (Keller, 1968). These are:

(i) Individual Rate of Progress: In PSI model, each student learns at his own rate taking his own time.

(ii) A Mastery Requirement: Each student in a PSI model is required to attain mastery over the task. Thus learning for excellence or learning for mastery is a basic requirement of the PSI model.

(iii) An Emphasis on Printed Study Guide: In PSI model, printed study guides are provided to each student. The printed study guides are supplied to students for communication of information.

(iv) Use of Proctors or Tutors: Each student in a PSI model is attached with a proctor or tutor (teacher). The proctor or the tutor meets the student at regular intervals, helps him in his learning activity and evaluates his performance.

(v) Inclusion of Only a Few Lectures in Each Course: Even if printed study materials are supplied to each student, few lectures in each subject are organised. The purpose of organising lectures is not transmission of information but stimulation and motivation of students.

In PSI model, the course in each subject is divided into certain units. Each unit in a course corresponds to a chapter in the book. The various units are arranged in a graded way. The student is required to learn one unit at his own rate and taking his own time. After learning the first unit, the proctor evaluates the performance and progress of the student in relation to that unit. If required, the student attends few lectures on that unit. If he attains mastery over the unit, he is allowed to proceed to the next unit. If he has deficiency in that unit, he re-learns the unit adopting alternative learning materials. In this way he masters all the units. At the end of the course, the proctor evaluates his performance and awards grade to the students.

Open Learning

Open learning system is a non-conventional, non-traditional innovative programme of teaching and learning. It is defined and named differently by various thinkers in different countries. In India even knowledgeable persons use the following terms interchangeably:

Correspondence Education,
Distance Education,
Off-campus Study,
Extended-degree Programme,
Open Education,
Open School,
Open University,
Open Learning, etc.

Whenever any new educational programme is planned, it is always based on certain considerations and assumptions regarding the nature of the learners. As an innovative educational programme, open learning is based on the assumption that:

(i) A learner is an active and self-directed agent.
(ii) The learner is capable of making choices, taking decisions and assuming responsibilities.
(iii) He can direct the process of teaching quantitatively and qualitatively.
(iv) He is not simply a passive recipient of knowledge, but a self-monitor, self-evaluator, self-feedbacker and self-improver.

Essential Features of Open Learning

(i) In open learning system, learning is made more independent of instructors. There is very little face-to-face contact between the students and the teacher.
(ii) It gives greater flexibility in schedules and location of classes. There is no fixed time table or fixed classroom.
(iii) It is a form of individualised instruction. Instruction for those is arranged according to the convenience of the learner. The learner can take his own time to complete a course. It leads to self-learning.
(iv) It provides alternative modes of instruction for those who do not learn well in conventional classes.

(v) It is available to each student who is deprived of formal education in schools and colleges due to various reasons. It is available at all levels of education such as secondary, higher secondary, college, university and for all types of education such as formal, non-formal, technical and vocational education. It is also available to each student whether in urban area, rural area, industrial area or slum area. It is available to each student whether SC, ST, disadvantaged and disturbed, disabled and normal.

(vi) It uses multi-media approach. Instruction is provided through contact services, postal services, newspaper, TV, radio, computer, printed materials (learning package), etc.

(vii) It is part-time education. An individual can work in a farm, industry, office or any organisation and at the same time participate in a course. Hence, it is less expensive.

(viii) It is flexible with regard to qualifications for entry.

(ix) It is meant for any student who is willing to be educated.

(x) It is committed to "education for each" as against "education for all" in conventional system of instruction.

The National Open School, New Delhi, Indira Gandhi National Open University (IGNOU) and Andhra Pradesh Open University are three distinguished organisations dedicated to open learning system.

Self-learning

Self-learning strategies are gaining popularity as forms of individualised instruction. As the name suggests, self-learning is a systematic procedure in which the child learns independently without constant help from the teacher. In this procedure, diagnosis is first made about the child's existing knowledge and skills. Self-learning materials are provided to the child. These materials are prepared in a graded and sequential way. Each material is based on certain objectives and followed by objective-based test items. The child is also provided with alternative learning materials. The child learns one material. Then he answers the test items pertaining to that material. Immediate feedback is provided to the child about his progress and deficiencies relating to that material of learning. If deficiencies are noticed in his learning he is allowed extra time to re-learn the material adopting alternate learning materials and methods. In this way, the process continues until he attains the objectives of learning the material. Once he attains the objectives specified for the piece of material, he is allowed to proceed to the next material in the sequence. Programmed instruction, computer-assisted instruction, individually-prescribed instruction (IPI) and individually guided education (IGE) are examples of self-learning strategies.

SELECTED QUESTIONS

1. State the meaning and nature of individual differences. Discuss, educational provisions to meet individual differences in the classroom.
2. Discuss the areas of individual differences and the educational significance of individual differences.
3. Discuss the causes of individual differences.
4. Write short notes on:
   (a) Concept of individual differences,
   (b) Intra- and Inter-individual differences,
   (c) Individual differences in cognitive areas,
   (d) Educational significance of individual differences,
   (e) Genetic causes of individual differences,
   (f) Environmental causes of individual differences,
   (g) Individualised instruction,
   (h) Self-learning strategies,
   (i) Open learning system,
   (j) Personalized System of Instruction.

13
Intelligence, Problem-solving and Creativity

1. MEANING AND NATURE OF INTELLIGENCE

Meaning of Intelligence

To define intelligence is really a difficult task. Psychologists all over the world have made attempts to define intelligence in their best possible language but a definition which is universally accepted has not yet been noticed in any literature on intelligence. For example, intelligence has been defined as an ability of the individual. But there is no agreement as to (i) what kind of ability it is, and (ii) the ability to do what. Like the blind men appraising the size of an elephant, psychologists have defined intelligence in their own way. While the psychologists try to measure intelligence and the teachers try to cultivate intelligence, nobody seems to know precisely what intelligence is. It is worthwhile to quote some of the definitions here to arrive at a meaning of intelligence:

"Intelligence manifests in purposive direction, active adaptation and conscious correction. It is the ability to take and maintain a given mental set, the capacity to make adaptations for purpose of attaining the desired end and the power of self-criticism." — *Alfred Binet* (1916)

"An individual is intelligent in proportion to as he is able to carry on abstract thinking." — *L.M. Terman* (1921)

"Intelligence is the global or aggregate capacity of an individual to act purposively, to think rationally and to deal effectively with his environment." — *David Weschler (1944)*

"Intelligence is the analytic and synthetic ability of mind."

— *Charles Spearman (1923)*

"Intelligent activity consists of grasping the essentials in a given situation and responding appropriately to them."

— *A.W. Heim (1970)*

"Intelligence refers to a general level of cognitive functioning as reflected in the ability to understand ideas and to utilise abstract symbols (verbal, mathematical or spatial) in the solution of intellectual problems."

— *D.P. Ausubel and F.F. Robinson (1969)*

P.E. Vernon (1960) perceived three broad categories for defining intelligence. These were: (a) biological, (b) psychological, and (c) operational. Biological definitions emphasize the individual's capacity to adjust or adapt to environmental stimuli. Adaption, here, refers to modifying behaviour either overtly or covertly as a result of experience. Psychological definitions stress mental efficiency and the capacity for abstract thinking. Operational definitions involve making detailed specifications of intelligent behaviour and then finding measures of these specifications. Intelligent behaviour is thus expressed in terms of these measures. The expression "Intelligence is what intelligence tests measure" is often used to describe the operational definition.

An analysis of various definitions reveals the following facts:

Intelligence is—

(i) the ability to profit from experience,
(ii) the ability to solve problems,
(iii) the ability to adjust and relate to one's environment,
(iv) the ability to perceive relationship,
(v) the ability to think abstractly,
(vi) the ability to behave competently and effectively,
(vii) the ability to learn.

All these meanings are not mutually exclusive. Rather they are interrelated. For example, if an individual can perceive relationship, he can learn. If he can learn, he profits from experiences. This helps him to behave competently and effectively, to think abstractly and to solve problems. He is now able to adjust and relate to his environment.

Nature of Intelligence

Is intelligence an innate trait? Is intelligence a single ability or does it consist of more than one ability? Is it a stable characteristic of the individual or does it change over time? There are innumerable questions regarding the nature of intelligence. There are also several viewpoints regarding the nature of intelligence:

(i) Growth of intelligence is orderly and cumulative. Intelligence is made up of more than one ability. It is a succession of constantly developing functions. The successful development of each new function depends on the combination of a number of simpler ones that have matured earlier. Intelligence, like other developing functions and skills, proceeds in more or less orderly fashion. For example, reasonably correct and accurate copying of a square by a three-year-old child depends on the extent to which he has learned certain lower level functions such as:
  (a) gripping a pencil;
  (b) holding it in an upright position;
  (c) perceiving the relationship between moving it along the paper and producing a mark;
  (d) sensory awareness of the relation between the visual image of four corners, four straight lines and
  (e) necessary eye-hand co-ordination to produce this same picture on paper.

(ii) Intelligence is related to learning. Wherever learning is, intelligence is too. But the reverse is not always true, *i.e.*, wherever intelligence is, learning is not sure to follow. For example, we know young and old persons, who are no doubt intelligent, but who, for one reason or other, simply refuse to learn from their own experience or from the experience of others. Intelligent students do not always use their capacity for learning. They are frequently underachievers.

(iii) Intelligence is an inborn personal quality of an individual. Although it is genetically determined, environment has tremendous influence on it. The role of heredity and environment on intelligence has already been discussed in the previous chapter.

(iv) Intelligence is distributed according to the law of normal probability curve. Very few individuals possess a high degree of intelligence, very few individuals possess very low intelligence, but majority of individuals possess average intelligence.

(v) In respect of the degree of intelligence possessed by men and women, it has been found that there is a greater diversity in case of men than in case of women. But the average IQ is the same in both cases.

(vi) Some interesting facts are noticed about the growth and decline of intelligence over time. Studies by Jones and Conrad (1944) indicate that intellectual development is most rapid during the early years and slows down with increasing age. Mental growth follows a rather shallow, steeply slanted S- shaped path. This means that growth occurs very rapidly during infancy and the pre-school years and then gradually slows down after that point. It may be added here that intellectual growth or power (ability to think; solve problems, understand complex issues) does not necessarily stop at some magical age.

(vii) Crystallized and fluid intelligence differs in rate of decline. Crystallized intelligence includes such abilities as verbal, numerical, and reasoning skills. This intellectual capacity is enhanced through experience and education. It increases over time with new experiences and educational opportunities. In other words, it does not deteriorate over time. But fluid intelligence slows down and decreases with age. It is genetically determined and relatively independent of formal education and experience. It includes abilities such as perceptual or manual speed, close attention to details and long periods of concentration. It is for this reason, older persons receive lower scores than younger persons on those items of an intelligence test which emphasize these abilities. In conclusion, we may say that crystallized intelligence increases throughout most of adulthood. Older persons use crystallized intelligence in place of fluid intelligence. Although they may be short on speed and brilliance, they may be long on insight and wisdom.

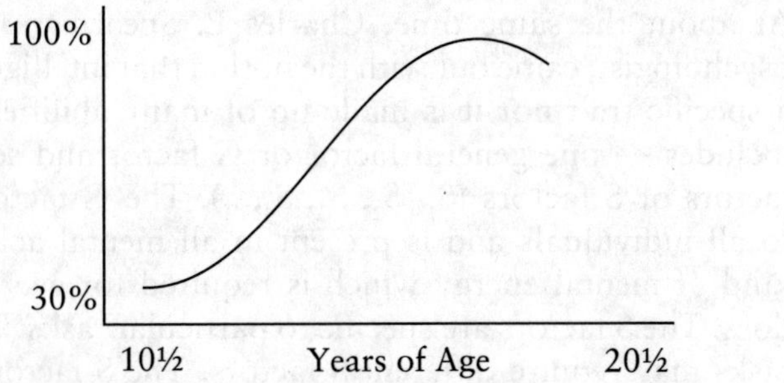

Fig. 1: Intellectual growth from ten and one-half to twenty and one-half years age. From H.E. Jones and M.S. Conard, "Mental Development in Adolescence." National Society for the Study of Education, 43rd Yearbook. Partl, 1944, pp. 146-63.

An old dog cannot only be taught new tricks, but he may even understand them better.

(viii) Intelligence is not a specific trait of the individual. It is a composite of many abilities. Many different abilities or components are tied up in a package that we label as intelligence. Various psychologists have found out various components of intelligence ranging from 2 to 120 separate abilities which compose intellectual ability of an individual. Various theories have been developed on this issue also. Mainly there are four theories of intelligence such as:

(a) The Two-factor Theory of Spearman,

(b) The Three-factor Theory of Thorndike or The Theory of Neural Connections,

(c) The Theory of Primary Mental Abilities of Thurstone, and

(d) The Theory of Three-dimensional Structure of Intellect of Guilford.

2. THEORIES OF INTELLIGENCE

As discussed above there are mainly four theories of intelligence. A brief discussion of these theories is presented below:

(i) The Two-factor Theory

Alfred Binet, the father of intelligence tests, was the first to conceptualise that intelligence is a composite of many abilities.

At about the same time, Charles E. Spearman, an American psychologist, came out with the notion that intelligence is neither a specific trait nor it is made up of many abilities. Intelligence includes — one general factor or G factor and several specific factors or S factors (S_1, S_2, S_3, S_4,...). The G factor is common to all individuals and is present in all mental activities. It is a kind of mental energy which is required for everything a man does. The S factors are specific to particular tasks. Thus different tasks may require different S factors. The S factor required for arithmetic is not the same as those required for reading and spelling. S factors vary from task to task. S factors also vary from individual to individual. Thus, two students may have a high level of general intelligence. But one student may be less capable in arithmetic than the other who has high S factor required for arithmetic. Usually persons having high general intelligence have more S factors at their command, but these are exceptions. This is why persons with above average (or below average) general intelligence tend to be above average (or below average) in most things they do.

(ii) The Three-factor Theory or The Theory of Neural Connections

Edward L. Thorndike differed sharply with Spearman by asserting that there are no such things as general intelligence or general mental ability. Thorndike's theory was a more abstract one. His theory is based on the idea that intelligence is due to the number and kind of neural connections. Thus, a bright person has more neural connections of an adequate nature than a dull person. According to him, every mental act is different from the other. But there are common elements in all mental acts. Based on these common elements, he identified three components of intelligence such as: (a) concrete thinking (the ability to deal with things), (b) social thinking (the ability to deal with people, and (c) abstract thinking (the ability to deal with ideas).

(iii) The Theory of Primary Mental Abilities

A somewhat better known theory of intelligence is the theory of primary mental abilities propounded by T.G. Thurstone. According to Thurstone, intelligence is made up of seven components or seven primary mental abilities. These seven primary mental abilities are as follows:

(a) *Space Factor*: The ability to visualise objects in space. It is the ability, for example, to judge whether or not we have time and room to pass a car when another car is approaching in the other lane. Although most intelligent people have this ability, some highly intelligent people are lacking in this primary ability. That is why, some intelligent people have trouble in parking a car.
(b) *Number Factor*: The ability to manipulate numbers (*e.g.*, making change, maintaining accounts, etc.). Accountants and cashiers are expected to be high on this ability.
(c) *Verbal Comprehension:* The ability to read and understand what is read, interpret language and vocabularies.
(d) *Word Fluency:* The ability to use words.
(e) *Ability to memorize.*
(f) *Inductive Reasoning:* The ability to discover the underlying rule or principle in the material one is working with, the ability to arrive at useful generalizations from limited information.
(g) *Perceptual Speeds:* The ability to identify objects quickly, the ability to understand entire sentences without having to examine each word carefully, the ability to comprehend the entire paragraph without looking at each sentence thoroughly.

These abilities are thought to be relatively independent. Thus a person proficient in one is not necessarily proficient in another. But some studies show a positive relationship among these abilities. Thus a person who is average (or above or below) in one ability is usually average (or above or below) in the others. This is evident to suggest that different types of mental activities share something in common and that they may all be influenced in part by general intellectual ability.

(iv) The Theory of Three-dimensional Structure of Intellect

Perhaps the most comprehensive theory of intelligence is the one developed by J.P. Guilford. Guilford developed a three-dimensional structure of intellect. According to him, intellectual activity has three dimensions — operations, contents, and product. The operation dimension refers to the particular cognitive process being used such as cognition (thinking), memory, divergent production, convergent production, and evaluation. The content dimension refers to the particular medium in which a person happens to be operating at the moment. It may be visual, auditory, symbolic, semantic and behavioural. The product dimension is the result of operations and contents. It includes units, classes, relations, systems, transformations and implications. Thus Guilford's components of intelligence include 5 intellectual operations, 5 contents and 6 products which interact to produce 150 separate abilities (5 operations x 5 contents x 6 products).

Guilford's model offers a valuable framework for exploring and further defining the many components that make up intelligence. Among other things it suggests that in relatively complex forms of learning, such as problem-solving, several combinations of abilities may be required depending upon the nature of the problem being solved. This mode also explains why a particular student is good at solving mathematical problems and very poor in memorizing historical dates and names.

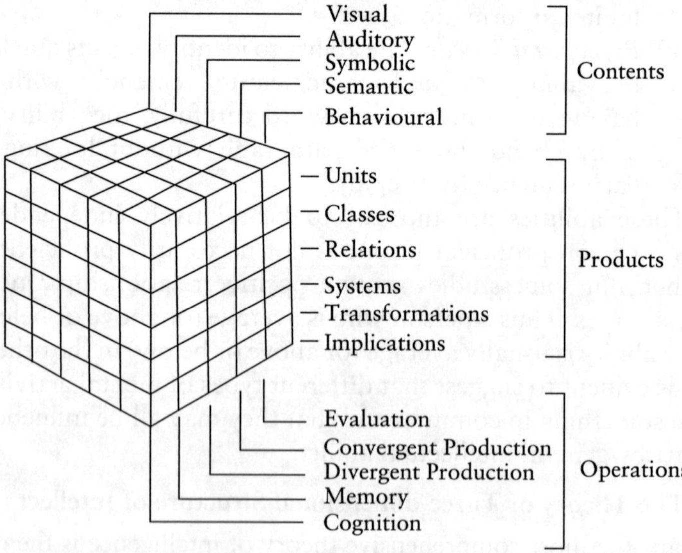

Fig. 2: Guilford's Structure of Intellect (1967).

3. MEASUREMENT OF INTELLIGENCE

Intelligence is measured through standardized tests of intelligence. These tests of intelligence can be grouped under two heads depending upon the contents of the test. These are:

Verbal Tests of Intelligence and

Non-verbal Tests of Intelligence.

Intelligence tests are also grouped under two heads depending upon the number of children tested at a given time. These are:

Individual Tests of Intelligence, and

Group Tests of Intelligence.

Verbal and Non-verbal Tests

Some intelligence tests require the use of language or verbal ability, the ability to read, write or understand words. A test which requires the use of verbal ability of the subjects is called a verbal test. On the contrary, there are tests of intelligence which require no use of language in its administration or in the subject's answers. In some of these only the test tasks are non-language in character; in others, the instructions can be given by pantomime and no language need be used at any point during the testing. Such tests which are non-language in character are known as non-verbal tests. Non-verbal tests may be pictorial or performance type.

Some non-verbal tests of intelligence are as follows:

(i) *Raven's Progressive Matrices*: It consists of geometric figures and designs. In this test, the subject has to apprehend relationship between figures and selects appropriate parts for completion of each pattern. It is a widely used test.

(ii) *Lorge-Thorndike Intelligence Test*: The test consists of identification of animal and human figures, classification of pictures, and association of objects shown in the picture. It is meant for grades 2 and 3.

(iii) *Cattell's Culture-free Intelligence Test*: We will discuss about this test later.

Most of the widely used intelligence tests depend to some degree upon language and include tasks presented in verbal terms. This is natural, since the bulk of our learning and thinking makes use of language. For the usual person and in relation to the usual type of academic learnings, aptitude for learning can be tested more efficiently by tasks that involve language than by those that do not. However, for some groups or situations this is not so. The most obvious example is that of groups which do not speak the language or speak it only slightly. When an individual has limited command of English, results from a verbal test in English are in large measure meaningless. Children who have had little opportunity to attend school may suffer a special handicap on a test that relies upon materials close to school learning. For such children, non-verbal tests are useful.

Examples of some verbal tests are as follows:

(i) *Jalota's Test of General Mental Ability*: This test is in Hindi and is meant for children of 12 to 16 years of age.

(ii) *Patel's Group Test of Intelligence*: This test is in Gujarati and has items from the area of analogy, synthesis, and completion.

(iii) *Upadhayay's Verbal Test of Intelligence*: It is a group test for children in the age group 8+. It is standardised in Indian conditions.

(iv) *Mishra's Group Test of Intelligence*: It is a verbal test meant for children in the age group of 12+ to 15+.

Performance Tests of Intelligence

There are some categories of children and adults such as the deaf, the dumb, illiterates, shy and withdrawn children, educationally deficient children, and children speaking foreign languages who cannot be tested with the help of verbal tests of intelligence. Such children and adults can be tested with the help of performance test of intelligence. A performance test is one which requires the subject to perform something or to manipulate some concrete material without much use of language. Such tests are more useful in clinical work. Since these tests are administered individually, they provide an opportunity for close observation of the behaviour of the subject in test situation and his own method of solving problems. Generally performance tests are used to supplement other tests of intelligence. Some performance tests are as follows:

(i) The Pinter-Paterson Scale of Intelligence for deaf and dumb children.

(ii) The Draw-a-Man Test for children in the age group 3+ to 13+.
(iii) Patel's Performance Test for grades 2 to 11.
(iv) Prabha Ram Linga Swami's adaptation of the performance scale of WAIS for the age-group 15+ to 45+.
(v) Pathak's Adoption of the Draw-a-Man Test for Indian children in the age-group 6+ to 8+.

Individual and Group Tests

Intelligence tests can also be grouped into individual and group tests. Individual intelligence tests can be applied to one individual at a time. But group tests of intelligence are applied to a group of individuals at a time.

There is no difference in purpose between group tests and individual tests of intelligence. Both aim at measuring the intelligence. But the differences lie in methods. These differences are summarised as follows:

1. In group tests, the problems are presented in a printed booklet. The examiner has to read them first. Thus the group test requires the reading ability among testees. Of course, some group tests are non-verbal in nature. In individual intelligence tests, problems are presented orally by the examiner. Thus, the individual intelligence tests can be administered on children who have lagged behind other children in reading skills.
2. In group tests, a large number of individuals are tested at one session. Thus minimum personal contacts can be established between the examiner and the examinee. But the individual intelligence test is a face-to-face situation like interview. Thus, rapport may be established between the examiner and the examinee. The examiner can motivate the examinee. He can create confidence in the examinee. The test can be adapted to slow learners also.
3. In group test, there is a specified time-limit for the test on the various sub-tests. The whole test is presented as a unit. But in individual tests, problems are presented one at a time. There is no indication of time limit. In

group test there is possibility of lapses of interest and effort. But in individual tests, lapses of interest and effort can be re-established. But individual tests are time consuming.

4. Scoring of group test is objective, rapid and there is possibility of number of errors. Generally there is a key table for scoring and interpretation. But the scoring and interpretation of individual tests are time-taking.
5. There is also a difference in construction of test items. In individual test, the examinee responds freely giving whatever response seems appropriate to him. This gives rise to the possibility of subjectivity in scoring unless a manual is available. But in group test, the questions are of multiple choice types which fosters objectivity in scoring.
6. In group test, sometimes an examinee fails to understand the directions or to co-operate. Thus, a low score on group test is not always due to deficiency in intelligence. In group test also there is possibility of cheating by the examinee.
7. Individual tests can be better applied to young children and children below school age. But group tests are suitable for large number of individuals and grown-up children or individuals. Since individual tests are very costly, they are not always practicable. Thus group tests of intelligence are now used more frequently.

4. THE CONCEPT OF MENTAL AGE

Mental development of children is measured in terms of mental age or M.A. A large representative group of children who are, say, exactly 10 years of age, would automatically have a mental age of 10, *i.e.*, the mental development that is average for 10 years old. In the same way, an M.A. of 6 represents the mental development that is average for children who are 6 years old and so on.

The child's mental age is obtained from his performance on an intelligence test. His success on the various items of the tests is added and the total is converted into mental age. Suppose there are six sub-tests in a test of intelligence meant for children of a particular age-group. Success in passing one sub-test means a credit of 2 months. If a child passes all the six sub-tests he gets a credit of 12 months. There are specific tests for children of various age groups. The level at which and below which a child passes all the sub-tests and beyond which he fails to pass all the sub-tests is termed as the basal age.

A child's mental age is calculated by adding the basal age and the credits (in terms of months) obtained by him in subsequent levels.

Suppose a child takes a test of intelligence. His success and credits earned at various levels are given below:

Passed all tasks at 6-year level	6 years (Basal age)
Passed 3 out of 6 tasks at 7-year level	3×2 = 6 months credit
Passed 1 out of 6 tasks at 8-year level	1×2 = 2 months credit
Failed all tasks at 9-year level	0 credit
	6 years 8 months

His mental age would be 6 years 8 months.

Intelligence is, however, a relative term. A child is not bright or dull but rather is brighter or duller than other children of his chronological age. To state that a child has a mental age of 6 years 8 months is relatively meaningless since it would be important to know if he is chronologically 7, 9 or 12. Thus mental age has to be considered in terms of mental age of children of a particular chronological age. This relationship or ratio between one's mental age and chronological age is known as the intelligence quotient or IQ.

5. THE CONCEPT OF IQ

Although Binet was the father of intelligence tests, a German psychologist, Wilhelm Stern, was the first man to formulate the concept of IQ in 1912. Today, IQ is the generally accepted means of expressing intelligence.

IQ is determined by the ratio of mental age or mental level to the chronological age. Thus, a child whose mental age is equivalent to his chronological age has an IQ of 100.

Since the IQ represents the ratio of mental age to chronological age or the rate of mental development compared to age, it varies from child to child in the same age group. For example, a child of eight whose M.A. is 10 has an IQ of 125.

$$\text{I.Q.} = \frac{\text{M.A.}}{\text{C.A.}} \times 100 = \frac{10}{8} \times 100 = 25$$

Similarly, a child of eight whose M.A. is 8 has an IQ of 100 (8/8 × 100 = 100).

Individuals have been classified into different categories according to the IQ possessed by them:

IQ 130 and above	Genius
IQ 120-129	Superior
IQ 110-119	High average
IQ 90-109	Normal or average
IQ 80-89	Low average
IQ 70-79	Borderline defective
IQ 70 and less	Mentally retarded

However, one criticism of the IQ concept is that IQs are not comparable from one test to another. A child may have an IQ of 116 on one of the tests and 120 on another. Of course, this difference is mainly due to difference in the tests themselves. Another criticism is that it does not have the same meaning at all levels. For example, a child of 5 has an M.A. of 6. His IQ is 120. A child of 10 has an M.A. of 12. His IQ is also 120. But in the former case, the difference between M.A. and C.A. is only one year, but in second case the difference is two years.

There is a misconception that intelligence reaches its maximum limit about the same time physical maturity is reached. But experience shows that a person may not grow taller or acquire more teeth once he is mature. But he may gain in wisdom or stature as long as he lives. But as per the ratio of IQ, if an individual's M.A. ceases to increase after a certain age, IQ value declines. But actually in most cases M.A. does not remain constant or decrease. It is presumed that M.A. remains constant after the age of 16 or 20. In this case, IQ of a man of 25 would be 16/25 × 100 = 64. This is wrong. It is therefore customary not to calculate the IQ of a man beyond 16 years of age, but to express his relative position in his age group by percentile ranks or by standard score or by deviation IQ. Deviation IQ is a standard score with an arbitrary mean and S.D. For adults S.D. is taken as 16 and Mean is taken as 100.

Constancy of IQ Scores

Is IQ constant? Can IQ be changed? How stable are IQ scores? Various studies (Wellman, 1945; Holloway, 1945; Lorge, 1945; R.L. Thorndike, 1948) indicate some gain in IQ scores over a period of years. In summarizing the findings of these studies, one can conclude that the little gain in IQ scores is mainly due to educational experiences in kindergarten or pre-school centres, environmental stimulation, specific practice in taking the test and continued schooling. On the contrary, a progressive decline in IQ scores can be noticed when children are placed in non-stimulating environments. It is found that the longer children remain in orphanages or with mentally retarded mothers, the progressively lower their IQs become in comparison with the IQs of comparable children reared in a more favourable environment (Skeels, 1966; Skeels and Fillmore, 1937). Similar evidence is found in reports of a progressive decline in intelligence test scores of isolated mountain and canal boat children who may be also considered to be immersed in an intellectually non-stimulating and unchallenging environment (Gordon, 1923; Sherman and Key, 1932; Wheeler, 1942). Studies by Skeels (1996) indicate that if children are removed from extremely unstimulating environment and placed in a better environment, they show high gain in IQ scores. Studies by Bloom (1964) also indicate positive support for IQ gain as a result of better environmental stimulation.

Our discussion so far centres on the constancy of IQ. It is now clear that an individual's IQ does not remain constant. It can be changed with changes in the environmental stimulation. But environmental stimulation is not the only factor which causes fluctuation in IQ scores. Even when the individual remains in the same environment, his IQ may be found unstable at different points of time in his life cycle. Suppose you measure the IQ of a child at age 6 and again at age 12, you may notice fluctuation in his IQ score. Fluctuations in IQ scores of an individual at different points of time may be due to the following factors:

1. Measurement Factors

(a) Variation in test items;

(b) Errors of test administration and scoring;
(c) Variation in situations such as personality of the test administrator, rapport between the administrator and the student, fatigue, general attitude, motivation, attention span, self-confidence, level of aspiration, etc. and
(d) Exposure to practice and coaching on intelligence tests.

2. Genetic Factors

The pattern of intellectual growth varies at different points of time in the life cycle of an individual. Cornell and Armstrong (1955) observed three main patterns of mental growth:
(a) A continuous growth curve from age five to age eighteen;
(b) a step-like curve consisting of alternate spurts and pauses, and
(c) a discontinuous curve thereafter.

To summarize, a whole host of factors can influence the stability of IQ scores of children in essentially normal environments over the long or short term. For this reason, the most consistent estimates of IQ will be those obtained from tests given in close proximity. As the time interval between successive tests increases, fluctuation in IQ scores becomes more evident. Again intelligence test scores obtained below the age of six are not very useful for making predictions. It is therefore obvious that important decisions utilizing IQ data should be based on current estimates of mental ability.

6. EDUCATIONAL SIGNIFICANCE OF INTELLIGENCE TESTS

Intelligence tests are of manifold use for educational purposes.

(i) For Measuring General Learning Readiness

The scores on intelligence reveal the mental age or mental level of a child. It indicates the educability or readiness of a child for learning. If intelligence tests are administered in the beginning of primary, secondary and college level education then the teacher can know whether the student is capable of reading in that stage or not.

(ii) For Indicating Individual Differences in Capacities of Children of Same Chronological Age

Children differ from one another in respect of capacities. The test results will indicate the need for providing teaching materials at different levels of difficulty. The teacher can also guide students to choose subjects according to their capacities.

(iii) For Identifying the Degree of Mental Retardation

Intelligence tests can be used to identify more accurately the levels of mental retardation. On the basis of such identification, the retarded children can be properly instructed. Special provisions can be made for them.

(iv) For Identifying the Gifted Children

From the result of intelligence tests, gifted children or children with high IQs are identified. Instruction, syllabus and teaching aids are specially provided to meet their requirements.

(v) For Educational Guidance

Intelligence tests are also useful for guidance work. Children can be given guidance in pursuing higher studies, choosing subjects of study and getting scholarships. Intelligence tests are also useful in locating strong and weak points in children. The syllabus can be made interesting and suitable for their intellectual level.

(vi) For Vocational Guidance

An important use of intelligence tests lies in giving vocational guidance to students. Occupational success is related to intelligence. Thus intelligence test scores can indicate the possibility of entering into an occupation and succeeding in it in future.

(vii) For Homogeneous Grouping

Teachers generally face the difficulty of teaching a group of children possessing different degrees of capacity. If his teaching suits the average children, it bores the bright children and creates confusion in the dull children. To remedy the situation, homogeneous grouping of children is needed. Intelligence tests help teachers in having homogeneous grouping among children.

7. LIMITATIONS OF INTELLIGENCE TESTS

(i) The calculation of IQ requires the chronological age of the child. But sometimes parents hide the real age of the child. Thus IQ becomes unreliable.

(ii) Verbal intelligence tests require the use of language or the reading ability of the child. For children who are handicapped in the use of language, these tests cannot be applied.

(iii) Unless experienced and trained persons are available, the scoring and interpretation become invalid.

(iv) In some tests, items are not chosen properly. Thus, the purpose of testing is lost.

(v) Intelligence tests especially individual tests are too costly. Thus, ordinary teachers cannot purchase and make use of such tests.

(vi) It is also useless to rely completely on the result of one testing because scores on a test are influenced by so many factors and not merely by intellectual ability of the child.

Critics of intelligence testing have marshalled an impressive array of arguments against intelligence tests. These criticisms may be classified under three headings:

(i) What the tests measure,

(ii) Psychometric or technical properties of the tests and

(iii) How test results are used.

In terms of what intelligence tests measure, critics have noted:

— Measurement experts are unable to define the intelligence in a way which satisfies every one, and it is illogical to measure something we cannot define.

— IQ tests do not measure real intelligence (they only sample intelligent behaviours).

— IQ tests assess abilities that are too narrow and tell nothing about creativity, motivation, honesty, friendliness, and other human traits and characteristics.

— IQ tests are only achievement tests that measure what the child has already learned, rather than his innate capacity to learn.

Criticisms regarding psychometric or technical properties of the test include:

— It is not unusual for an individual's IQ to show extreme fluctuation from one test administration to the next.

— The standardization sample fails to include all ethnic, racial, regional and socio-economic groups.

IQ tests suffer from content bias that is related to inappropriate vocabulary that is not related to the purpose.

Criticism regarding the use of test results may include:

— Administrators do not ask for IQ scores for admission to schools and colleges or for employment purpose.

8. DESCRIPTION OF A TEST OF INTELLIGENCE

There are a large number of tests of intelligence to measure the intelligence of children and adults. Some of these tests are verbal in nature, while others are non-verbal in nature. Non-verbal tests are largely of performance type. Some tests have been developed in India which can be administered on Indian children. Rathor's Non-verbal Test of Intelligence (1984) is one such test. Cattell's Culture Free Intelligence Test can also be used with Indian children. In the following paragraphs, a brief introduction about Cattell's Culture Free Intelligence Test is presented.

Cattell's Culture Free Intelligence Test

Cattell's Culture Free Scales were first published in 1930. In 1935, 1940, 1949 and 1961 revisions of the original scales were made as a result of which the test became more refined and more comprehensive. Cattell's tests are non-verbal in nature and are so designed to reduce the influence of verbal factors, cultural climate and educational level.

There are three scales in the culture free series. Scale 1 was designed for use with children of 4-8 years of age. The scale may also be used with older and mentally handicapped individuals. There are eight subtests in this scale. It is not wholly grouped administrable. It also requires the examinee to understand and respond to verbal instructions.

Scales 2 and 3 are wholly grouped administrable. Nevertheless occasions may arise for individual testing to enable the individual being tested to perform most effectively.

There are four sub-tests in scale 2 and 4 sub-tests in scale 3. These sub-tests are called:

Test 1 Series
Test 2 Classifications
Test 3 Matrices
Test 4 Conditions (topology)

The number of items in each sub-test and the time required to administer the sub-tests are given in table 5.

Table 5

	Scale 2 Form A or B		Scale 3 Form A or B	
	Number of Items	Time Allotted	Number of Items	Time Allotted
Test 1 (Series)	12	3 minutes	13	3 minutes
Test 2 (Classification)	14	4 minutes	14	4 minutes
Test 3 (Matrices)	12	3 minutes	13	3 minutes
Test 4 (Conditions)	8	2 minutes	10	2 minutes
Total	**46**	**12 minutes**	**50**	**12 minutes**

It must be mentioned here that each scale has two forms (Forms A or B) which make the full test. But at times it becomes difficult to administer the full test in single session. It also needs extra time. For this purpose, the test administrator can administer only the Form A in one session and after a rest interval administer the Form B.

Discussion of various items in the sub-test is beyond the scope of this chapter. The reader may refer to the original scales to know about the items. It must be mentioned that before each sub-test is given, the test administrator gives examples so that the task requirements become clear to the examinee.

A question which occasionally arises among test users: Which scale (2 or 3) is more appropriately used in a given situation? Scale 2 can appropriately be used with older children and adults. From age 13 or 14 onwards, either scale 2 or scale 3 can be employed. Scale 2 is unusable in all cases but greater refinement in the higher intelligence ranges is obtained with scale 3. Scale 3 would be called for with college students and other individuals generally considered higher in ability level. Whether one uses scale 2 or scale 3, instruction given in the manual of the test should be strictly followed in respect of administration and scoring of the test. After the tests have been administered, the test administrator will get some raw scores for each individual. Following the manual, those raw scores can be converted into IQ scores, and a clear and accurate picture of the individual's intelligence is obtained.

The Culture Free Tests are valuable instruments for all uses to which an intelligence test is rationally applied notably:

(1) Discovering whether the achievement of each individual is what would be expected from his intelligence;
(2) assessing an applicant's potential to perform a job-relevant task that involves cognitive ability;
(3) making a more reliable and informed decision — whether a particular child may require special educational facilities or a programme of cultural enrichment;
(4) selecting students for accelerated educational programmes within an age-group or a grade;
(5) advising students in regard to probable success in college or the chance of winning a scholarship and
(6) increasing the effectiveness of vocational guidance both for students and adults.

9. PROBLEM-SOLVING

1. What is Problem-solving?

In schools and colleges, students learn concepts, rules and principles. Learning rules and principles helps them to learn new and higher order rules and principles in future. Learning rules and principles helps in solving problems of various types. The activity of problem-solving is thus a natural extension of rule learning. Robert M. Gagne (1976) states, "Problem-solving may be viewed as a process by which the learner discovers a combination of previously learned rules which can be applied to achieve a solution for a novel situation."

Problem-solving is not simply a matter of applying learned rules. It is also a process that yields new learning. The learners are placed in a problem situation, or find themselves in one such situation. They recall previously acquired rules in the attempt to find a solution. In carrying out such a thinking process, they find a particular combination of rules that fits the situation. They not only solve the problem but also learn something new.

In fact, all learning is problem-solving. There may be different forms of learning — psychomotor, verbal or affective. But these are differences in form, the core remains identical. Problem-solving is a complex form of learning. It is at the apex of hierarchies of human learning.

Solution to problems is not an easy or a sudden process. The individual may encounter difficulties or obstacles in achieving a solution to problems. Problem-solving behaviour involves a process of overcoming difficulties that appear to interfere with the attainment of a goal — the solution to a problem.

We can also view problem-solving as a form of transfer of learning. When experience in one task influences performance in another task, transfer of learning is said to have occurred. Similarly experience in solving one problem helps in solving similar other problems. Successful solution of similar problems is the evidence for positive transfer of learning as well as for successful problem-solving behaviour.

Problem-solving, Discovery and Creativity

Problem-solving as a method of learning requires that the learners discover the higher-order rule in their own idiosyncratic manners. This does not mean that the learners will arrive at solution by 'pure discovery' without any guidance or verbal instruction. Problem-solving behaviour occurs when the learners get some verbal instruction or guidance. Verbal instruction does not include a 'verbally stated solution' but some hints about the nature of the problem.

The processes involved in problem-solving and creativity are so similar that it is difficult to differentiate problem-solving from creativity. A great scientific discovery or a great work of art is surely the result of problem-solving activity. As problem-solving behaviour, these creative acts are based on a tremendous amount of previously acquired knowledge. Many creative thinkers testify that they have previously immersed themselves deeply in the subject-matter of the problem, often over considerable periods. The steps in creative thinking are almost similar to the steps in problem-solving.

2. Conditions Influencing Problem-solving

The following are some of the conditions which influence problem-solving behaviour:

Principle Learning

Problem-solving is closely related to principle learning since it combines two or more previously learned principles into a higher order rule or principle. Thus, one essential condition of problem-solving is that the student must learn principles before he is able to solve problems. For example, a student has to solve a problem hitting an underwater target. To do this, he must have learned the principles of refraction.

A Period of Initial Efforts

There are two views regarding the means of solving problems. One view is that the solution to problem is arrived at suddenly after some initial efforts. Another view is that a problem gets solved through gradually eliminating errors and putting together correct responses. Although considerable arguments have occurred concerning which is the correct interpretation, we can accept the view that certain problems which are easy for the learner are solved with fewer trials and difficult problems take more trials for a solution.

Intelligence

Intelligence has been defined as the ability of an individual to solve problems. Thus other things being equal, an older and more intelligent person can solve a problem with less fumbling and fewer errors than a younger and less intelligent child. Teachers can arrange learning situations to facilitate achieving the correct solutions with fewer errors.

Experience with Success and Failure

Problem-solving is related to one's experience with success or failures in solving problems previously. Repeated failures result in giving up, substituting a different goal, or showing other forms of unproductive behaviour. The problem-solving processes of a student after experience of failure are significantly inferior to those following successful experiences. Thus successful experiences in solving problems are easily transferred to solving similar new problems.

Set

Set influences problem-solving. Set is usually defined as a predisposition to react to a situation in a certain way. That set influences problem-solving has been demonstrated in a number of situations. It was found that when individuals were taught to solve a series of related problems by one method, they persisted in using that method in solving other problems even when the method did not work. Persons taught by a single method and having experienced success repeatedly in solving series of related problems cling to that method, even when repeated trials with it are found not to work in solving new problems of different types. The influence of set on problem-solving points out the fact that we should not be rigid in applying a particular and already established method in solving problems. We should be better flexible in our approach.

Group Work

Teachers generally work with groups as well as individuals. How do groups perform on problem-solving in comparison with individuals? Most researches find the average performance of small groups to be superior to that of individuals. Sometimes the best individuals exceed the averages of groups. It is possible that group members would perform better after experience in working together and after instruction. Why is the average performance of small group superior to that of individuals in problem-solving situations? During the initial learning, the small groups collectively arrive at an understanding of the problem more quickly than individuals, secure information more rapidly, cognize them more effectively, remember the relevant information better, bring a larger variety of methods to bear upon the solution, pose more solutions, and verify the solutions more reliably.

Productive and Reproductive Thinking

Problem-solving involves both productive and reproductive thinking. When one is confronted with a problem, the problem is brought to focus. He then organises his present and past experiences in order to reach a solution. If he is satisfied with his present meaning and organisations and solves the problem accordingly, reproductive thinking has occurred. If he is not satisfied with present experiences or meaning, he needs to restructure his meaning, experiences or cognitive structure. This restructuring of the cognitive structure is the occurrence of productive thinking.

Convergent and Divergent Thinking

Problem-solving also involves convergent and divergent thinking. In divergent thinking, we think in different directions and search for more than one answer to solutions. But in convergent thinking, the information leads to one answer or to a recognised or conventional answer. Convergent thinking is synonymous with reasoning and divergent thinking is associated with creativity. Thus, Skinner said, "Problem-solving is the framework or pattern within which creative thinking and reasoning take place."

3. The Steps in Problem-solving

There are many viewpoints regarding the steps of problem-solving. It is not therefore easy to resolve problem-solving into a series of orderly steps. Nevertheless, it is helpful to understand what the steps are, even though they are taken in reverse or mixed order. These steps are:

First — A felt need,
Second — Locating or recognizing the problem situation,
Third — Accumulation of data,
Fourth — Formulating a hypothesis,
Fifth — Testing the hypothesis,
Sixth — Making a generalization.

A Felt Need

The first step in problem-solving is a felt need. The problem solver must first feel the difficulty with sufficient definiteness and speculate the probable solution.

Locating or Recognizing Problem Situation

After the difficulty is felt, the next step is to locate or understand the nature of the problem. The more clearly an individual can state the nature of the problem, the more likely he is to solve it. In locating the problem, the teacher may help students save time.

The Accumulation of Data

The third step in problem-solving is to gather relevant information about the problem. Gathering data to solve a problem is not an easy undertaking. But there is no substitute for this tedious and time-consuming task. The teacher is required to instill in pupil a respect for factual knowledge and an appetite for its acquisition.

The pupils must find out what others have done with the same or similar problems. Intelligent problem-solving is always based on whatever progress has already been made. Thus the pupils must be encouraged to make a brief record of sources of information on cards rather than on full sheets of paper. This way of gathering information makes the tedious task effective and interesting.

Formulating a Hypothesis

A hypothesis is simply a theory or a tentative solution. It is a tentative solution which may be accepted or rejected. It is not something which must be supported. One may take many hypotheses. One of them may turn out to be the correct solution. The worth of these possible solutions depends largely on the originality and intelligence of the problem solver.

Testing the Hypothesis

After some tentative solutions are accepted, the pupils can be asked to try or test the possible solutions and their consequences. Thus this is a step of judging and predicting. The pupils may test the possible solutions either in an actual situation or in the laboratory or through group discussions. This testing whether theoretical, situational or experimental gives additional information or data about the problem. The new information may result in an alternation of the hypothesis.

Making a Generalisation

Testing the hypothesis is often the final step in the solution of a problem. However, higher forms of reasoning demand still another step-making generalisation. This final step is an attempt to consolidate the conclusion in order to conserve the meaning. It is a verbal description of the salient information that has been obtained. The teacher must take the responsibility for impressing upon students the value of making sound generalisations. Making a generalisation will help the students in solving other problems in future.

However, these steps are not too difficult for children at the beginning of their school experiences. Small children may not find out correct solutions to problems. But they can feel the problem. They can gather data. They can make partially informed solutions. They can evaluate the solution and their knowledge. It is, therefore, gratifying to remember that the correct solution of specific problems is typically not more important than the process and interests involved.

10. TEACHING PROBLEM-SOLVING IN SCHOOLS

There are four different viewpoints regarding the chief purpose of teaching problem-solving in school. These are:

(i) Acquisition of knowledge of wide applicability;
(ii) Learning and using the techniques of problem-solving;
(iii) Learning and transfer of skills, concepts and principles, and
(iv) Development of the ability to transfer the skills acquired through problem-solving in schools to the solution of personal and community problems.

Whatever may be the purpose of teaching problem-solving, teachers must know the following points in providing instruction for problem-solving:

(i) The teacher must describe what the problem is and what constitutes the solution. This does not mean that the teacher will help the students in locating the problem. The students must construct the solution on their own through guided discovery.
(ii) A necessary condition for successful problem-solving is the acquisition of related concepts and principles. Thus

while presenting a problem and encouraging the student to find solutions — the student's entering behaviour the concepts and principles learned by the students which will be required in the solution of the problem should be assessed. If the students have not understood these concepts and principles, they will fail to solve the problem.

(iii) The teacher should help the students to recall all relevant concepts and principles. The students must recall these principles in the presence of the problem and discover the relationship between them which will result in the problem solution. By question and demonstration, the teacher can help the students recall the principles.

(iv) While helping students to recall the relevant principles, they should also be helped to apply these concepts and principles in the solution of the problem. Verbal direction and instruction by the teacher can help students apply the relevant principles in the problem situation.

(v) After trying and solving the problem, the students should be required to give a full demonstration of the problem solution. In order to test their real understanding of problem-solving, the teacher should use other problems of the same class and verify their learning and understanding. This will also lead to test their generalization and transfer.

(vi) Problem-solving behaviour can be fostered in children through the introduction of both general factors such as interest, persistence and self-confidence and specific factors such as ability in locating information, in formulating precise hypotheses and in defining terms, etc. Providing the child with a good background of information, particularly of principles and generalizations, can lead to improved problem-solving.

(vii) Some teachers think that children are inadequate in their reasoning capacity and problem-solving behaviour. This is partly true, primarily because of their lack of experience and understanding. Moreover, there are individual differences in reasoning capacity among children. Thus while encouraging problem-solving behaviour among children, the teacher should see that the problem is well within their understanding and experience. Problems should deal with the situations difficult enough to be challenging and yet simple and familiar enough for children to grasp.

11. CREATIVITY

1. Meaning and Nature of Creativity

So far as the concept of creativity is concerned, there is disagreement among psychologists about its definitions, nature and development. Definitions vary, models of identification vary, theories vary, research methods and results vary. In spite of all these disagreements, all agree that creative thinking is the highest of mental functions and creative production is the peak of human achievement.

There is no universally accepted definition of creativity just as there is no universally accepted definition of intelligence. Different definitions place emphasis on different aspects. Some place emphasis on creativity as a product. Some emphasize creativity as a process. Still others place emphasis on creativity as an experience.

Creativity as a product — It is novel and useful.

Creativity as a process — It is divergent, yet productive.

Creativity as an experience — It is subjective. It is inspired and immanent like a flash of insight.

A suggested definition of creative thinking is:

"The product has novelty and values for the thinker or the culture:

— the thinking is unconventional, highly motivated and persistent, or of great intensity;
— the task involves a clear formulation of an initially vague and unidentified problem." (Newell *et al.*, 1962)

(i) "Creative thinking applies to a thought process that constructs original answers, solutions, or ideas. Usually creativity is associated with responses that are novel to the society as well as to the individual. Problem-solving entails the correct answer. For creativity there is no correct response. It is new or original and unique" (Travers, 1982). But the goal of creativity is not mere novelty, because all novel responses do not reflect creative talent. False answers are novel, so are the bizarre statements and actions of the mentally ill, but we could hardly classify these as creativity. Originality is therefore not enough. The new idea must have some relevance to the solution of some problem. Usefulness is not quite so obvious because in science we often find that an original idea has no immediate application and must wait for advances in other fields before it becomes useful.

(ii) Creativity may be expressed in artistic, literary or scientific product. It may be of procedural or methodical nature, or a theoretical one.

(iii) Creativity is not the same as productivity or ingenuity. Productivity is shown by bringing together many ideas and solutions. It emphasises both quantity and contribution. Ingenuity is shown by inventing or discovering a solution to a problem. The emphasis is on the existence of a problem and the demonstration of originality in solving it in an unusually neat, clever and surprising way. Creativity is shown by bringing something new into being. The emphasis is on the newness and lack of previous existence of the idea or product.

(iv) All individuals are creative in diverse ways and in different degrees. Creativity is not restricted to a chosen few. Like the musical or artistic aptitude, creativity is a special aptitude. Every individual possesses some amount of creative abilities. He needs proper education, training and encouragement for expression of his creative abilities.

(v) Creativity is very often associated with giftedness. Although experimental evidence over this issue is not adequate, scores on creative thinking correlate high with scores on divergent thinking. Intelligence correlates high with convergent thinking. But creativity and intelligence have low correlation. This means that gifted individuals need not necessarily be creative thinkers. On the contrary, creative thinkers are not always gifted.

(vi) Creativity is not completely spontaneous. The individual must make conscious efforts to produce something creative. Understanding, discipline, hard work and patience are required to produce something creative.

(vii) Creativity does not involve any single trait or ability. It involves many abilities. These are fluency, flexibility, originality, elaboration, sensitivity to problems and openness to experience.

2. Characteristics of the Creative Individual

Who are the creative individuals? Do they possess any special characteristics? Calvin Taylor (1961) lists the following characteristics of creative individuals:

(i) Strong memory powers,
(ii) Tendency to evaluate the ideals and actions of self and others,
(iii) Originality,
(iv) Fluency,
(v) Flexibility,
(vi) Power of elaboration,
(vii) Sensitivity to problems,
(viii) Openness to new ideas and experiences,
(ix) Curiosity,
(x) Tendency to manipulate ideas,
(xi) High achievement motivation,
(xii) Intellectual persistence,
(xiii) Tendency to seek challenges,
(xiv) Preferring complex ideas,
(xv) Tolerance for ambiguity,
(xvi) Intense commitment to work,
(xvii) Independent,
(xviii) Inclination to take risks,
(xix) Resourceful,
(xx) Adventurous,
(xxi) Extroverted,
(xxii) Less tradition-bound,
(xxiii) More a perceiver than a judge,
(xxiv) Above average in intelligence.

3. Stages in Creative Thinking

There are four distinct stages in creative thinking. These are: (i) Preparation, (ii) Incubation, (iii) Illumination, and (vi) Verification.

(i) Preparation: This consists of purposeful study and enquiry in order to gather experience and information which are needed to solve the problem.

(ii) Incubation: Once the preparatory stage is complete, there seems to be a period of lull or rest period. The necessary facts are gathered and they are to be applied to the heart of the problem. This application of the idea may not appear immediately. A period of frustration in which the thinker may turn to other tasks attends each discovery. Somehow the mind continues its search; it seeks to uncover new relationships among familiar ones.

(iii) Illumination: Suddenly the idea, solution or the new relationship materialises. All the facts 'fall into place.' Vital new methods, data, or relationships become clear to the thinker.

(iv) Verification: The idea is new and appealing. It has exciting possibilities. But does it work? Here the idea must be tested and verified. During this stage, the thinker rethinks, revises and refines the solution.

4. Hindrances to the Promotion of Creativity

There are several unsatisfactory conditions, trends or blocks to creativity. Some of these conditions are unique to the individual while others are characteristics of the present day schools. James Adams has noticed four types of blocks to creativity which is unique to the individual.

(i) Fear of Taking a Risk: Children in schools have constantly been rewarded for the right answers. To propose something new may lead to disapproval, and ridicule of others. Novel ideas are always risky. So long as the child fears taking a risk, he cannot be creative.

(ii) Lack of Tolerance for Ambiguity: Some people are unable to tolerate ambiguity. They cannot endure vague and ill fitting ideas. They must have everything in proper place. But creative thinking presupposes a tolerance for ambiguity.

(iii) Quick Judging: Judging is basic to creativity. But some people judge too early in the process of solving a problem. As a result of this, many fragile ideas that could possibly lead to other ideas are lost.

(iv) Lack of Imagination: Creativity requires the manipulation or recombination of ideas based on imagination. Lack of imagination soon stifles creativity.

5. Promotion of Creativity

Teaching for creative thinking is the need of the day. Indian society needs creative thinkers and teachers can begin early to help youngsters think rationally, solve problems and search for the novel ideas. The following guidelines may help:

(i) Teachers should be certain that the material they use to encourage creativity in the classroom matches the developmental level of the children. Piaget's stages of cognitive development have made it clear that younger children cannot comprehend and use abstract subjects. So at these early stages, while encouraging children to be innovative, teachers must use content suitable to their mental ability.

(ii) Teachers must give children experience in deriving as many and different responses to a problem as possible. As for example, select a word "book" and ask them to think of as many uses as possible for it. List them on the board and then ask the children for more uses. You are then fostering divergent thinking and not just requiring one correct answer.

(iii) Teachers must encourage their pupils to search for relationships. Creativity tests often ask children to name one word that links three apparently unrelated items: stool, powder, and ball. Children should think of something that fits each of these.

(iv) The most important aspect of creativity is the ability to tolerate ambiguity. Fear of failure, or fear of the unknown makes people almost desperately desire some answer, suitable or not. Teachers should directly teach pupils that it is better to pause, to muse, to think of alternatives, and to search for the better way.

(v) Teachers should always remind students that true creativity rests squarely upon knowledge of subject, hard work and patience.

Don E. Hamachek (1979) suggests the following measures to encourage creative activity among children:

(i) *Learn to Value that which is Different:* The teacher should make explicitly clear that he values creative, different, novel, innovative and unique ways for doing projects, writing projects or conducting experiments. Sometimes students are hesitant to be different precisely because they are fearful of rejection, ridicule or low grades, and they need to be given permission by the teacher to be daring, adventuresome, novel or different. Of course, there will be times when doing things in a different way are not appropriate, and they need to be told that, too.

(ii) *Be Cautious Not to Reject Non-conformity*: Adventurousness, non-conformity and impulsiveness are traits that characterize the creative student. Hence teachers should be tolerant of such non-conformity of a student and should not emphasize too much on strict obedience. A teacher's effort to be creative is the very quality most likely to enhance the creativity of his students. If teachers can work on developing their own creative potential, they can be more tolerant of it in others.

(iii) *Teach Students to Ask Extending Questions*: Teachers should encourage students to ask extending questions. Extending questions are those that lead them from what they know to new and different ways to think about the problems.

(iv) *Be Willing to Accept That Which is New, Different and Even Imperfect*: Teachers should recognize that mistakes and imperfections are typically natural consequences of learning activities that are new, different, and original. If teachers and parents emphasize that one should be thoroughly competent and adequate in all possible respects, children will hesitate to talk about their imaginative ideas or display their creative products for fear of ridicule and censure.

An encouraging smile, a helping hand, a word of praise, an accepting attitude, alternative suggestions, each of these represents the sort of human touch necessary for helping a student experience the upper limits of his creative expression. Usually, motivation for learning is more effective, and creative effort more possible, if a teacher can help students concentrate on improvement rather than perfection.

(v) *Use Praise Liberally and Modify Assignments to Fit the Student:* The teacher is in a better position to encourage creativity, curiosity, independence and self-reliance. When a student shows some independent thinking, a teacher can praise him. When a student shows signs of boredom, a teacher can modify the assignment enough to include his interests.

6. Measurement of Creativity

Creativity is measured through tests of creativity. Creativity tests usually measure divergent thinking ability. The Torrance Test of creativity is one such test which can be used in primary and secondary schools. This test consists of verbal and figural activities and measures fluency, flexibility, originality and elaboration. Some of the tasks in this test are given below:

1. *Ask and Guess*: Given a sketch, a pupil is told to: (1) ask all the questions needed to know exactly what is happening in the drawing, (2) to guess as many causes as possible for the action in the picture, and also (3) to guess possible consequences of what is taking place in the picture.
2. *Product Improvement*: This task presents a picture of a stuffed animal and allow the pupils 10 minutes to list, "the cleverest, most interesting and unusual ways" they can think for changing the toy to make it more fun to play with as a toy, regardless of cost.
3. *Unusual Uses*: The respondent is given 10 minutes to list "interesting and unusual uses" for a common object, such as a tin can or a cardboard box.
4. *Just Suppose*: Here the respondent is asked to guess what would happen if a certain situation occurred. Here is an example. "Just suppose clouds had strings attached to them which hang to earth. What would happen?" Five minutes are allowed for the test.
5. *Picture Construction*: Here the respondent uses a shaped piece of coloured paper as the nucleus for a drawing. He

has 10 minutes to draw a picture of object "that no one else will think of," incorporating the piece of coloured paper, and to title his drawing.

6. *Incomplete Figures*: Ten incomplete figures are completed by the subject and each is given a title.
7. *Repeated Figures*: The subject is given 30 parallel lines or 40 circles and instructed to draw a picture, using the given elements as the main part of the picture.

SELECTED QUESTIONS

1. State the meaning and nature of intelligence.
2. What is intelligence? Discuss the theories of intelligence.
3. How is intelligence measured? Give examples of verbal and performance tests of intelligence.
4. What is problem-solving? State the conditions of problem-solving behaviour.
5. What is problem-solving? What strategies are to be adopted by the teacher for developing problem-solving behaviour among adolescents?
6. What is creativity? How can the teacher promote creative thinking abilities of adolescents?
7. Discuss the meaning and nature of creativity. State the characteristics of creative individuals.
8. What is creativity? Discuss the stages of creativity.
9. Write short notes:
   (a) Nature of intelligence,
   (b) Theory of Primary Mental Abilities,
   (c) Structure of Intellect,
   (d) Concept of Mental Age,
   (e) Concept of IQ,
   (f) Educational Significance of Intelligence Tests,
   (g) Steps of Problem-solving,
   (h) Characteristics of Creative Individuals,
   (i) Measurement of Creativity,
   (j) Hindrances to Creativity.

14
Theories of Learning

1. NEED OF A THEORY OF LEARNING

What happens when we learn? How does learning take place? Why do some people learn more readily than others? How can a teacher most effectively help people to learn? There are dozens of theories of learning which answer these questions. But none of them is adequate to have universal acceptance. Still, the search goes on. Theoretical questions about the nature of learning are ordinarily of more interest to psychologists than they are to classroom teachers. A teacher's main function is not to define learning or to explain how it occurs. His concern, rather, is with the more practical problems of guiding the student's learning activities whatever the nature of the learning process might be. Still, in order to carry out his responsibilities, a teacher needs at least tentative answers to the theoretical questions raised above. This is not to suggest that teachers need a profound understanding of the learning process, a systematic, comprehensive theory of learning. But they do need some set of principles and assumptions on which to base their practices.

2. VARIETIES OF THEORIES

When a teacher turns to psychology for information about the nature of learning, he is offered a choice of dozens of systematic theories. There are theories of learning developed by a number of psychologists like Guthrie, Hull, Pavlov, Skinner, Thorndike, Tolman, Wertheimer and others. In addition to these, there are various information processing theories. Some of these theories have little or no relevance to classroom instruction. Those theories which developed during the twentieth century and have the greatest and most direct implications for classroom learning can be grouped under two main headings: Association theories and Cognitive theories. Both of these "families" have their subdivisions, and splinter groups. Thus all of those who are classified as associationists, for example, are by no means in total agreement with one another on all details of the learning process. But their different views of the learning process do have enough in common to warrant them being grouped and discussed together.

Association (S-R) Theories

Association theories are so-called because they attempt to explain all learning in terms of the formation and strengthening of connection between stimuli acting on organisms and the responses they make accordingly. In other words, association theories emphasize the importance of association or connection between the stimulus and the response. Some association theories are, therefore, referred to as connectionism or Stimulus-response (S-R) theories. They are eager to analyse learning situations, to divide learning phenomena into small elements and to investigate the simplest possible S-R relationship in order to better understand the more complex total phenomena. Such theorists are thus said to be atomistic or molecular in their approach.

Modern association theories of learning were formulated in the early twentieth century largely through the efforts of I. Pavlov, John B. Watson and Edward L. Thorndike. More recently these theories have been refined and revised by such psychologists as Clark Hull, Edwin Guthrie and B.F. Skinner. In later sections of this chapter, some of these theories (Thorndike's Trial and Error Learning, Pavlov's Classical Conditioning and Skinner's Operant Conditioning) will be discussed in more detail.

Cognitive Theories

While association theories of learning centre around the concepts of stimuli and responses made by the learner, cognitive theories stress the variables that intervene between stimuli and the responses. Among these variables are the individual learner's purpose, aspiration, belief, ideas and his existing store of knowledge. Cognitive theorists point out that two students are likely to respond quite differently to the same stimuli because of what they have already learned, what they hope to achieve, what they feel are capable of achieving, because of differences in the ways their minds work or because of other differences which distinguish one person from another. Thus, according to cognitive psychologists, learning is a far more complex process than simply linking up connections between stimuli and responses. For cognitive psychologists learning is more of an individual matter involving perception, the processing and assimilation of information, the development of insight and discovery of meaning. Cognitive theorists generally prefer to describe and understand a whole, complex learning situation. That is, they prefer to view learning situation as one whole and complete phenomenon. Thus such an approach has been called a molar one. Cognitive theorists emphasize the cognitive reorganisation or the perceptual reorganisation in explaining learning. When S-R theories emphasize drill, bond or practice, cognitive theories emphasize the meaning or understanding in learning.

S-R theories make little or no reference to central or brain processes in explaining learning. These theories place heavy emphasis on the overt or observable behaviour of the organism. Thus these theories are said to be peripheral. Cognitive theorists are called central as opposed to peripheral in their orientation because they emphasize the central or brain processes as the integrators of behaviour.

Cognitive theories of learning, sometimes referred to as field theories are derivatives or modifications of Gestalt psychology. Gestalt psychology grew out of studies of perception conducted by Max Wertheimer, Wolfgang Kohler and Kurt Koffka. According to these Gestaltists, a person's sensory field is always organised or structured in such a way that an object is always perceived as standing out against a background and in relationship to other objects or stimuli. The manner in which an individual perceives these relationships determines what he sees in a situation and what he does as consequence. Among those who have contributed significantly to the development of cognitive theories are Kurt Lewin, John Dewy, Jean Piaget and Jerome Bruner. Just as associationists do not agree with one another on all of the particulars regarding the nature of the learning process, so are their differences of opinion among contemporary cognitive theorists. Still they generally agree that learning occurs when the learner understands the relationships involved in the learning situation, when he develops insights into the problem, or when there is reorganisation of the cognitive structure. In thinking about the learning processes of students, these theorists prefer the terms 'person' to organism, 'psychological environment' to physical or biological environment and 'interaction' to action, reaction or responses. There is a conviction that the concepts 'persons,' 'psychological environment' and 'interaction' are highly advantageous for teachers in describing learning processes. They enable a teacher to see the person, his environment and his interaction with his environment all occurring at once. In the later sections of this chapter, a detailed discussion of the theory of insightful learning will be presented.

3. IMPLICATIONS OF LEARNING THEORIES FOR THE TEACHER

S-R and cognitive theories agree in principle that the function of a teacher is to help people learn. But corresponding to the two basic theories of learning, there are two different concepts of how this help should be given,

(i) S-R theories emphasize the role of the teacher as a classroom manager or director of the learning process. Cognitive theories are more consistent with the idea of the teacher as a kind of guide or a facilitator for learning,

(ii) S-R theories lend support to a systematic, carefully preplanned, expository or programming approach to teaching while the cognitive theories support flexible, spontaneous and discovery methods of learning and teaching.

(iii) Association theories have implications for a classroom that is largely teacher-centered. Here, the student's interests, needs, goals and problems are taken into account, and there might be a concerted effort at

Table 6: Differences between S-R Theories and Cognitive Theories

Aspects	S-R Theories	Cognitive Theories
1. Thrust	Association or connection between stimulus and response.	Variables that intervene between stimulus and response.
2. Approach	Atomistic or molecular	Molar or whole
3. Emphasis	Drill, bond or practice in the learning situation.	Meaning or understanding of the learning situation.
4. Terms preferred	Physical or biological environment, organism, actions.	Psychological environment, interaction, persons (learners)
5. Learning process	Simple.	Complex.
6. Explanation of learning	Make little or no reference to central or brain processes in explaining learning.	Explain learning in terms of central brain processes.
7. Methods of learning and teaching	Systematic expository or programming approach.	Flexible, spontaneous and discovery methods.
8. Teacher's role	A classroom manager or a director of the learning process.	A kind of guide or a facilitator of learning.

individualising the instructional programmes. But by and large the teacher decides which particular kinds of changes are to be brought about in his students, what they will learn, and what kinds of responses they will eventually come to make. Then he proceeds to plan, organise and direct the work of the class in such a way that the desired responses will be made.

The role of the teacher, according to cognitive theories is broader than forming and strengthening connections or producing preplanned responses. His function is to organise the learning situation so that significant relationships emerge and personal understanding of the material results. The learning experiences are so structured that the learner is able to discover and generalize these relationships for himself.

For cognitive theories, the 'how' of learning is of greater importance than the 'what' of learning?

(iv) As discussed earlier, learning, to a cognitive theorist, is the student's personal discovery of meaning. If a teacher is to help his students make such discoveries, he must see the subject matter and the world through the eyes of the student. He must attempt to perceive the student's existing situation and knowledge so that he can make the material more meaningful to him in his present situation.

(v) In practice, teachers cannot accept either the cognitive theories or the S-R theories blindly. This assumption is made upon the fact that for certain types of learning, S-R theories offer more satisfactory explanations and that methods of teaching based on these theories are likely to be most effective. For other kinds of learning, cognitive theories and principles are more promising. Thus teachers should be flexible in selecting and adapting what they regard as the better features of each system. They must accept the better point, specific applications and implication of each theory for classroom learning rather than waste their time in applying all the conflicting views of all the theories.

4. LEARNING BY TRIAL AND ERROR

Learning is in some way a process of solving problems. When the problem is essentially new and difficult, the individual fails to solve it all at once. He tries one after the other ways of solving the problem until he arrives at the correct solution. Psychologists call this learning as trial and error. This type of learning is associated with the name of E.L. Thorndike, a pioneer experimental psychologist. To prove the occurrence of learning by trial and error, he conducted a large number of experiments on animals.

The Experiment

In one such experiment, Thorndike confined a hungry cat in a cage. The cage was closed by a door which could be opened by pulling a lever. Food (fish) was kept outside the cage visible to the cat. The problem for the cat was to open the door by pulling the lever and to come out to get the fish. When confronted with this situation, the cat, at first, failed to come out to get the food. The cat made a large number of random movements like crawling through the bars of the cage, biting and scratching at the walls. Sooner or later, by chance, she pulled the lever which opened the door and the cat came out. She was given a little bit of fish. Thorndike argued that one successful movement did not teach the cat the method of opening the door. Thus he placed that cat in the cage for the second time. This time also the cat went on performing random movements, and again hit upon the correct response by chance. But during the second trial, the number of incorrect responses was less than that of the first trial. In this way, as the trials increased, the number of incorrect responses decreased and at last the cat learned the correct response — pulling the lever to open the door. Thorndike argued that the cat was able to learn the correct response, not by reasoning or by imitation, but by trial and error.

Essential Features of Learning by Trial and Error

Learning by trial and error is a gradual process. In order that learning will occur, the learner must be definitely motivated — the learner must have a motive to reach the goal. The learner must make random and variable responses. Some of his responses will bring satisfaction whereas others will bring annoyance. With the increase in number of trials, the annoying responses will tend to be eliminated and the satisfying responses will be strengthened and repeated. Moreover the time taken to perform the task successfully will decrease with successive trials. Thus, through a process of trial and error, the animal will learn the correct response.

Laws of Learning

On the basis of his experimental findings, Thorndike suggested certain laws which govern learning by trial and error. We shall discuss three fundamental laws of learning in this section.

These laws are:

(a) Law of Exercise,

(b) Law of Readiness, and
(c) Law of Effect.

(a) Law of Exercise

This law means that learning becomes efficient through practice or exercise. This law is further split up into two parts, Law of Use and Law of Disuse.

Law of Use: This means that the native responses are strengthened by practice. Other things being equal, exercise of any action (walking, grasping, or of swimming) tends to make the action more prompt, more certain, and more easy. In other words, practice makes a man perfect.

Law of Disuse: Any act that is not practiced for sometime gradually decays. Use of exercise strengthens the connection between the stimulus and the response, disuse weakens the connection. This also means that anything that is not used, exercised or practiced for a certain period tends to be forgotten or weaken in strength, promptness and efficiency.

(b) Law of Readiness

This law refers to the fact that learning takes place only when the learner is prepared or ready to learn. Readiness may simply be physical as well as mental readiness. If the learner is not ready physically and mentally, no amount of efforts can make him learn. Learning failures are therefore the results of forcing the learner to learn when he is not ready to learn something.

(c) Law of Effect

This law states that learning is the result of forming a connection between the responses and their effects or consequences. A successful reaction gives satisfaction to the individual, tends to be repeated and is stamped in. An unsuccessful reaction gives annoyance to the individual, tends to be inhibited and is stamped out. The successful responses gradually acquire balance of greater frequency over the unsuccessful responses. Thus the responses which produce satisfaction or comfort for the learner are strengthened and responses which produce annoyance or discomfort to the learner are weakened.

Thorndike later revised some of his laws in the year 1930. According to the new revision, the law of exercise is not considered as an independent law. It is related to the law of effect. For example, if the practice is simply mechanical and lifeless, it has no effect. Practice itself does not lead to improvement in learning. Practice must always be followed by some reward or satisfaction to the learner. Another revision is about the law of effect — the role of reward and punishment in learning. Thorndike found that reward strengthened the response, but punishment did not always weaken the response. Thus, he placed more emphasis on the reward aspect than on the punishment aspect of the law of effect. He introduced a new concept 'belongingness' in the law of effect. According to the new concept, a response is more easily learnt if the response belongs to the situation or fits the situation. The reward must also fit or belong to the response situation. Similarly he also introduced another concept — spread of effect. This means that the effect of learning is not confined to a particular task but it also 'spreads' to other adjacent situations. Lastly, Thorndike introduced the principle of polarity. This means that 'connections' act more easily in the direction in which they were formed than in the opposite direction.

Subordinate Laws

In addition to the three main laws — law of exercise, law of readiness, and law of effect — Thorndike also gave the following five subordinate laws which are also equally important:

(i) Law of Multiple Response,
(ii) Law of Set or Disposition or Attitude,
(iii) Law of Selective Response,
(iv) Law of Analogy,
(v) Law of Associative shifting.

Law of Multiple Responses: This law states that when an organism is confronted with a new situation, he responds in a variety of ways — trying one response first, and then another before he makes the correct response.

Law of Set/Disposition/Attitude: This law states that learning is guided by a total attitude or set or disposition of the organism. The organism performs the task well if he has appropriate attitude towards the task.

Law of Selective Response: This law states that the organism reacts to the learning situation in a selective manner.

Law of Analogy: This law states that the organism responds to a new situation on the basis of the responses made by him in similar situations in the past. He makes responses by comparison or analogy between the present situation and situations in the past.

Law of Associative Shifting: This law states that any response may be elicited from the organism, of which he is capable, in association with any situation to which he is sensitive. In other words, any response which is possible can be linked with any stimulus.

Educational Implications

Learning by trial and error has significant implications for the classroom teacher:

(i) It implies that since learning is a gradual process, motor skills and other difficult skills need to be learned gradually, in a step by step manner. Whether learning involves verbal skills or motor skills, it needs practice or exercise. The more thoroughly a task is practiced, the better it is remembered. Thus in the learning of certain school subjects like mathematics and vocabulary of a new language, drill, practice and repetition are essential.

(ii) Mere practice is not enough. The learner must be motivated to learn. Thus before beginning teaching certain skills or some school subjects, the teacher must keep in view the motivational state of the students. Learning of students must be followed by rewards and other motivational strategies so that the students will be motivated to learn. Motivational techniques must be appropriate to the situation and the response of the students.

(iii) The teacher must consider the psycho-biological readiness of the students otherwise this may lead to learning failures.

The most significant contribution of Thorndike to modern educator is the law of effect or reinforcement in learning. This implies that learning trials must be associated with satisfying or annoying consequences. For this purpose, the teacher can use rewards to strengthen certain responses and punishment to weaken others. But on the whole, the use of reward is more desirable than the use of punishment in school learning.

5. LEARNING BY INSIGHT

A group of psychologists, known as the Gestalt psychologists, did a large number of experiments on how animals and human beings learn in the laboratory and outside. These psychologists were opposed to the contemporary psychologists, particularly Thorndike, in their explanations of learning phenomena. According to these psychologists, human beings, even animals also, learn not by trial and error or by conditioning but by reasoning, by insight. Thus, they developed a new learning phenomenon, insightful learning.

Gestalt psychologists were actually interested in the field of perception. Yet they made few significant contributions to learning theory. Three psychologists, namely, Kurt Koffka, Wolfgang Kohler and Max Wertheimer were the chief spokesmen of this group of psychologists. They conducted experiments on chimpanzees, human infants and other animals to prove the occurrence of learning by insight. Their experiments, particularly the experiments of Kohler on chimpanzees, were carried out at University of Berlin Anthropoid Station during the years 1913-17.

The Experiment

In one such experiment, Sultan, Kohler's brightest chimpanzee, was kept inside a cage. He was hungry for the last 24 hours. Banana was kept out of reach, outside the cage. Two hollow bamboo sticks were provided inside the cage. The problem for the chimpanzee was to get the banana with the help of sticks. Sultan, at first, failed to reach the banana. He raised one stick as far as it could go but failed. He was disappointed and left the idea of reaching the banana. He started playing with the sticks. While playing with the sticks he happened to push one stick into the other and with the help of both the sticks he reached the banana. Sultan exhibited considerable satisfaction at this actual contact with the fruit. In subsequent experiments, Sultan solved the problem quickly and was not confused even when three sticks were given, two of which could not be fitted together. But in this experiment Kohler had to give some 'hint' to the chimpanzee by putting his finger on the bamboo stick.

Kohler argues that the chimpanzee was actually confronted with two types of problems: (i) joining the sticks, and (ii) filling the gap between the banana and the floor. The first problem was solved by trial and error and by imitation; the second problem was solved by insight. This also means that the chimpanzee did not exhibit 'pure insight.' In solving the problem, some trial and error behaviour was necessary for the occurrence of learning by insight. Once the chimpanzee was able to solve the problem by insight, he exhibits a high degree of transfer and understanding.

Essential Features of Learning by Insight

Learning by insight requires that the animal must be able to understand the relationship involved among all parts of the problem. Only when the animal is able to perceive the relationships involved among various parts of the problem, insight can take place. This perception or understanding takes place suddenly. Thus, Gestalt psychologists defined insight as the sudden reorganisation in the perceptual process of the organism.

Secondly, insight is greatly facilitated by previous experience with similar problems. Third, once the problem is solved by insight there is a high degree of transfer to similar problems. Insight also involves little bit of trial and error behaviour. The most important feature of insightful learning is that insight is closely related to the intellectual development of the organism. Thus, all animals cannot learn by insight. The higher the intellectual level of a learner, the quicker will be the occurrence of insight. Insightful learning involves understanding and reasoning about the problem.

Differences between Trial and Error and Insightful Learning

Based on the above discussion on essential features of insightful learning, one usually tends to generalise that insightful learning is completely different from the trial and error learning. This is deduced from the fact that trial and error learning is gradual whereas insightful learning is sudden. Trial and error learning depends upon practice and insightful learning depends upon understanding. Since trial and error learning does not involve higher cognitive processes like reasoning, animals and young children usually learn by trial and error. Some psychologists, therefore, call this learning as a form of animal learning. By contrast, insightful learning involves higher cognitive abilities like reasoning, understanding and problem-solving behaviour which human beings are capable to demonstrate. Thus, it is a form of human learning. In reality trial and error learning and insightful learning are not completely different from one another. The differences between the two are matter of degree and not of kind. Let us take the case of sudden gradual nature of learning.

According to some investigators although insightful learning is sudden, this suddenness is not always important. The suddenness of learning depends on the nature of the problem, the way the problem is presented and previous experience of the learner. For example, if the problem is relatively easy and familiar, the learner tends to solve it by insight. By contrast, complex and unfamiliar problems are solved more by trial and error learning than by insight. If the difficulty level of a problem is gradually increased then the problem which was previously solved by insight tends to be solved now by trial and error. On the contrary, if the problem is made simpler then the problem which was solved gradually will now be solved little bit suddenly.

Insightful learning also involves little bit of trial and error behaviour. Without this trial and error behaviour, insight is difficult to occur. On the contrary, trial and error learning may also involve some amount of insight, although it does not appear outwardly. In trial and error learning, each successful response can be said to have occurred through 'partial insight,' so that it involves a series of partial insights.

Insightful learning necessitates the condition that the various parts or elements of the problem must be clear or open to the learner so that the learner can understand the relationships involved among all parts of the problem. If some elements of the problem are missing, hidden or not clear to the learner then insight cannot take place. Rather the learner will tend to solve it by trial and error. Similarly, the learner's previous experience with similar problems greatly facilitates the occurrence of insight. Lack of previous experience makes insightful learning time-taking which is characteristic of trial and error learning. Thus, it can be said that the differences between trial and error learning and insightful learning are a matter of degree, not of kind.

Educational Implications

Insightful learning has significant implications for classroom learning:

(i) As is true with other types of learning, learning by insight also implies that the learner must be properly motivated in the learning situation. Thus the teacher must see that the students have a desire, a motive and a certain purpose to learn. That is to say the learner's behaviour must be goal-directed.

(ii) Learning becomes meaningful when the learning tasks are properly structured. The various elements of the task must be clear and open to inspection.

(iii) Learning tasks must be properly graded according to the intellectual development of the learner.

(iv) In order that the learner will be able to solve problems by insight, meaningful learning, learning by understanding and reasoning must be encouraged in the school. Rote learning or blind drill or mechanical repetition of the tasks should be discouraged.

(v) The teacher must help learners generalise and transfer what has been learned in one situation to another. Generalization and transfer will be greatly facilitated only when the learners are helped to perceive similarities in the previous learning and the new learning situations.

(vi) Since insight depends upon the previous experience of the learner, the teacher must help learners recall what has been learned earlier, and relate them to the new learning. This can be facilitated by giving some 'hint,' verbal instruction and demonstration.

(vii) The teacher must encourage problem-solving attitude, attitude of enquiry and discovery in the learning situation where they are found appropriate. But the teacher should not have the wrong notion that insight can account for all types of learning. There are a large number of areas where insightful learning cannot be effective. For example, children cannot learn the names of people, places, events, dates, vocabulary of a new language, the names of plants, and stars by insight.

6. LEARNING BY CONDITIONING

When you are pinched, you feel pain, you react in some way that is involuntary and unlearned. Suppose, someone flashes a light and then pinches you; if he does this for several times, you will come to feel a facsimile of the pain when the light is flashed before you are pinched or even when you are not pinched. This latter reaction is a learned reaction. Psychologists, at present, explain this in terms of conditioning a simpler form of learning. Conditioning is of two types: Classical Conditioning and Instrumental Conditioning or Operant Conditioning.

Classical Conditioning

Classical conditioning is a form of learning in which two stimuli are presented together and the response originally elicited by one of them comes to be elicited by the other.

Classical conditioning had its origin in the experiments of I.P. Pavlov, a Russian physiologist. Its tradition is directly traceable in the writing of Greek philosophers like Locke and James, Russian physiologists like I.M. Sechenov and an American named Twitmeyer. Twitmeyer had made the same discovery by accident. When he reported his findings to the American Psychological Association in 1904, people looked at him indifferently. He was discouraged and dropped the idea. A year later Pavlov reported the findings not knowing of Twitmeyer. Pavlov had the credit of systematic experimentation. That is why classical conditioning has been associated with his name.

The Experiment

Pavlov encountered the phenomenon of conditioning in course of his studies on the digestive process for which he was awarded the Noble Prize in 1904. In course of his experiments, some problems in his laboratory gave rise to the most famous experiments ever done in psychology.

Food was a natural stimulus to evoke salivation in dog. But Pavlov noticed that the dog used to salivate at the sight of food. Even it salivated at the sound of the footsteps of the attendant, who used to present the food. The sight of food or the sound of footsteps of the experimenter was not natural stimuli to evoke salivation. This was a strange fact for Pavlov. He puzzled over this for a while, and then began to study it systematically.

In one experiment, a dog was kept hungry for the last 24 hours. It was trained to stand quietly in a loose harness on a table in a room which was insulated against any distracting noise or vibration. The experimenter occupied an adjoining room, observing the dog through a small window and presenting the stimuli by means of automatic device. A metronome was sounded and 7 or 8 seconds after the beginning of this stimulus, a plate containing small measured quantity of dry meat powder was presented within reach of the dog's mouth. No salivation was evoked at first by the tick-tock of the metronome. But during the eating there was a copious flow of salivation. Combinations of the metronome and food were presented three times during a daily session, separated by intervals of 5 to 35 minutes. Strength of salivation was recorded by means of special device. After several combinations of the metronome and the food, the dog started salivating at the tick-tock of the metronome. As the number of combinations increased, the number of drops of salivation also increased. The dog learned to salivate to the tick-tock of the metronome. That is to say, the tick-tock of the metronome also could cause the dog salivate.

This simple experiment established an important learning principle. When a dog expects food it automatically salivates. Salivation is a reflex action. But Pavlov discovered that the reflex action could be partly modified and associated with a new stimulus. Bell does not naturally cause salivating, but if it is associated with food it soon can stimulate the salivation response. For this reason, classical conditioning is also called stimulus substitution. Diagrammatically the experiment appears as follows:

Metronome Sound + Food		Salivation
(CS)	(UCS)	(URC)
Metronome Sound		Salivation
(CS)		(CR)
Metronome Sound		No Salivation
XXX		(Extinction)
Metronome Sound		Salivation
		(Spontaneous Recovery)

Essential Features

In the experiment cited above, food (the natural stimulus to evoke salivation) is called the unconditioned stimulus. The metronome sound (the neutral stimulus) is called the conditioned stimulus. Salivation to food is a natural response and is called the unconditioned response. Salivation to bell which is a learned response is called the conditioned response. It must be mentioned that bell alone does not cause salivation but being paired with food it causes salivation. Pavlov also encountered the occurrence of extinction in conditioning. When the bell is no longer followed by food for some trials, the dog stops salivating. In other words, when the CS is not followed by UCS it leads to extinction of the conditioned response. But extinction does not destroy permanently the CR. After some rest, a new trial will bring it out again and it will last for a few more trials even without reinforcement or pairing of the CS and the UCS. This is what is known as spontaneous recovery. Spontaneous recovery depends upon the strength and degree of extinction and the original strength of the CR. During the course of experiments on conditioning, Pavlov also demonstrated the possibility of second order conditioning and even higher order conditioning. In second order conditioning, the previously conditioned stimulus acquires the properties of the UCS as in the first order conditioning. Second order conditioning is defined as follows: "Whenever a neutral stimulus (CS) occurs in close time proximity with the natural stimulus (UCS) there is a tendency for the neutral stimulus (CS_1) to elicit the response which is originally elicited by the natural stimulus. Further, when a second neutral stimulus (CS_2) is presented along with the CS_1, the CS_2 tends to elicit the same response which is elicited by the CS_1 (now the U.C.S)." Diagrammatically it appears as follows:

Bell + Food..Salivation
(CS_1) (UCS) (UCR)
Bell...Salivation
(CS_1) (CR)
Red Light + Bell ....Salivation
(CS_2) (CS_1) (CR)
(now the UCS)
Red Light ....Salivation
(CS_2) (CR)

(Diagrammatic Representation of Second-order Conditioning)

Generalization and Discrimination

Pavlov and his followers demonstrated with considerable success that generalization and discrimination are possible in learning by conditioning. Generalization can be both stimulus generalization and response generalization. When an organism which has been conditioned to respond to one stimulus responds in the same fashion to other related stimuli without specific training, stimulus generalization is said to have occurred. In stimulus generalization, the organism responds to a class of related stimuli rather than to a single stimulus. Just as the tendency to respond to a class of stimuli in the same fashion is called stimulus generalization, the generalization of a CR is called response generalization. For example, a dog's CR of leg withdrawal in response to a shock can be generalized to all other legs even though none of the other legs received shock. Discrimination is the reverse of generalization. It is a tendency to respond differently to different stimuli. Through discrimination, the organism learns to discriminate between different stimuli. For example, a dog can be conditioned to respond when the light is on and not when the light is off, or to a red light but not to a yellow light.

Procedural Variations

Experiments on conditioning are not always conducted according to the procedure mentioned earlier. There are various procedures of conditioning and these procedures vary depending on the relationship between CS and UCS or the ordering and the temporal spacing of stimuli.

Conditioning is not limited to dogs and their salivary responses. Following Pavlov, other investigators conducted similar experiments on other animals and even on human subjects using different stimuli and different response patterns.

7. INSTRUMENTAL CONDITIONING

Instrumental conditioning is the learning of a response which is instrumental in securing a specific after-effect. When a child's response is instrumental to the production of reward or removal of punishment, such learning is called instrumental learning. In classical conditioning, a previously neutral stimulus elicits a response through repeated pairing with an UCS. By contrast, in instrumental conditioning, the response is made before a certain stimulus is presented. In other words, the child must make a response first before a reward (positive reinforcer) is given or a punishment (negative reinforcer) is removed.

A large number of investigators have conducted interesting experiments on instrumental learning. But instrumental learning had its origin in the experiments of E.L. Thorndike. Thorndike named his learning as trial and error learning because the name instrumental learning was not in use at that time. The operant conditioning of B.F. Skinner was a special arrangement within the type of instrumental conditioning. A discussion of Thorndike's experiment and Skinner's experiment is presented below.

Thorndike's Experiment

Thorndike was one of the first psychologists to study animal learning in controlled laboratory settings. His best known experiment was conducted on the cat in the 'Problem Box.' A cat was closed inside the box. Food was kept outside the box visible to the cat. The problem for the cat was to learn to press a lever that would allow the cat to escape from the box and get the food. In such situation, the cat displayed a good bit of random activities before more or less accidentally performing the correct response. In successive trials, the wrong responses were eliminated and it learned to respond correctly.

What factor was responsible for the cat making the correct response? As it has become clear to you now, as trials increased, errors decreased and the cat was able to form a bond between its response and the stimulus (food). Thorndike explained this in terms of law of effect or consequences of responding. The law of effect states, "Reactions that are followed by satisfying results are stamped in and those that are followed by annoying results are stamped out." Thorndikian learning is called instrumental learning because "in instrumental learning when a response is followed by a reinforcing event or positive reinforcer, there is a tendency for that response to be repeated." The cat made a number of random movements but only specific response (lever pressing) brought about the reinforcing stimulus (food) and thus it was repeated.

It must be remembered that not all events or stimuli strengthen the response or increase the probability of occurrence of a particular response. For example, a child touches a hot stove and gets pain. This response of the child "will not be repeated on subsequent trials, *i.e.*, the child will not touch hot stoves in future. Generally a stimulus that produces satisfaction or comfort strengthens the response. This stimulus is called the reinforcing stimulus or positive reinforcer. The stimulus increases the probability of the response. The reinforcing stimulus in instrumental conditioning is Thorndike's satisfier in trial and error learning. The aversive stimulus in instrumental conditioning is Thorndike's annoyer in trial and error learning. All later procedures of instrumental conditioning were based on Thorndike's annoyers and satisfiers.

Skinner's Experiment

Skinner made extensive research on operant conditioning, which is a special arrangement within the type of instrumental conditioning. Skinner distinguished between two types of behaviour — respondent behaviour and operant behaviour. Respondent behaviour is elicited by a specific stimulus. It depends on contiguity of stimulus conditions at the start of training. Respondent behaviour is involuntary behaviour. In case of respondent behaviour, the environment acts upon the organism. According to Skinner, Pavlov's conditioned response is an example of respondent behaviour. By contrast, operant behaviour is emitted by the organism. It is independent of stimulus conditions. It depends upon effects or consequences of responding. In operant behaviour what the organism does first is more important than what the environment does for the organism. Operant behaviour is voluntary behaviour. Thorndikian experiments deal with operant behaviour.

Skinner followed the traditions of Thorndike rather than of Pavlov. In other words, Skinner preferred operant behaviour instead of respondent behaviour.

Skinner designed an apparatus known as the 'Skinner Box.' A hungry rat was placed in the Skinner Box with three bare walls and one wall from which a bar projected. Food was kept outside the box. If the rat could press the bar, a plate of food was presented through automatic devices. When the rat was placed inside the box, it persisted in performing some exploratory behaviour. Sooner by accident, it pressed the bar and was given the food. On subsequent trials, the rat's movements centered on the release mechanism and gradually it learned to press the bar to get the food. In the experiment cited above, the response was emitted by the rat. It was not elicited by any specific stimulus. The rat's correct response depended on the consequences of responding. The rat made the response first.

Procedural Variations

Four different types of instrumental conditioning may be distinguished according to the kind of consequence that typically follows a given response:

1. *Reward Training.* A reward is given after the response, usually increasing the likelihood that the same response will occur again.
2. *Punishment Training.* An aversive or painful stimulus is given after the response, generally decreasing the likelihood that it will happen again.

3. *Escape Training.* After the response is given, the animal is permitted to escape from an aversive or painful stimulus. Escape from such a stimulus typically increases the likelihood that the response leading to escape will be given again when the painful stimulus recurs.
4. *Omission Training.* A reward is not given after the response that had produced it before. The omission of such a reward usually decreases the likelihood that the response will happen again, that is, omission training leads to extinction.

Discrimination and Generalization

As in classical conditioning, in instrumental learning also the animal tends to generalize and discriminate. The tendency to respond differently to different stimuli is called discrimination. The reverse of discrimination is called generalization. Generalization is the tendency to respond in the same manner to different stimuli. For example, an Eskimo living in Alaska can discriminate 36 different names for snow. An Indian will call any form of snow just plain 'snow.' The process of discrimination and generalization can be seen without going to Alaska. A young child who is taught to say 'horse' when exposed to either a live horse or picture of a horse will be very likely to call a donkey, even a cow, a 'horse.' The tendency is to respond in the same manner to stimuli similar to the original stimulus. If a horse is a large animal with four legs, then a donkey is similar to the original stimulus and may be responded to in the same manner. Usually the tendency to generalize from one stimulus to another depends on the similarity of the two stimuli. The more similar the new stimulus is to the original stimulus, the greater is the tendency to respond in the same manner to both stimuli.

Reinforcement

Skinner did extensive research on reinforcement. In classical conditioning, the pairing of the stimuli (UCS and the CS) or the association between stimuli is termed as reinforcement and it strengthens behaviour. In instrumental learning, the reinforcing stimulus is produced by or is the consequence of a response. Thus the association that is strengthened is that of a response and its consequence. That is why classical conditioning is termed as stimulus — stimulus learning and instrumental learning is known as response-stimulus learning. Reinforcement is necessary for the motivational state of the organism. Reinforcement requires the use of some reinforcer in the learning situation.

Primary Reinforcer and Secondary Reinforcer

Skinner distinguished between primary reinforcer and secondary reinforcer. In laboratory studies, incentives which interact directly with the motivational state of the organism such as food, water, and shock are used. These are primary reinforcers. Secondary reinforcers are stimuli which have acquired reinforcing properties. Stimuli regularly associated with primary reinforcers themselves acquire the power to strengthen behaviour. If the animal is always fed from a stainless steel plate or utensil, the utensil or the plate itself comes to acquire reinforcing properties because it is regularly associated with the food. Money has no intrinsic value but it acquires its value through repeated association with the necessities of life. In general, a primary reinforcer is one which is related to the organism's basic physiological system, *e.g.* hunger or thirst. Secondary reinforcers do not have intrinsic reinforcing properties for the organism. Rather their reinforcing values are learned because they are associated with some primary reinforcers. Thus, secondary reinforcers tend to supplement or substitute the primary reinforcers.

Positive Reinforcers and Negative Reinforcers

Skinner also distinguished between positive reinforcers and negative reinforcers. By a positive reinforcer is meant one which the animal does nothing to avoid, often doing such things as to attain and preserve it. A positive reinforcer strengthens the desired behaviour and increases the probability of the occurrence of that behaviour. By contrast, a negative reinforcer is one which the animal commonly avoids and abandons. It decreases the probability of the occurrence of the undesired response. Depending upon whether the investigator uses positive reinforcer or negative reinforcer in the learning situation, there are two types of reinforcement procedures: positive reinforcement and negative reinforcement. In positive reinforcement, a positive reinforcer is given after the response occurs and this increases the probability that the response will occur again. In negative reinforcement, an aversive stimulus is given after the response occurs and this decreases the probability of the occurrence of the response.

Schedules of Reinforcement

According to Skinner, there can be various schedules of reinforcement which influence learning and motivation in varying degrees. Broadly speaking there are two types of reinforcement schedules:

(a) Continuous Reinforcement Schedules, and
(b) Partial Reinforcement Schedules.

In continuous reinforcement schedule, the response produces reinforcement every time it occurs. For example, we can praise a young child each time he adds two numbers correctly. In partial reinforcement schedule, some but not all responses are reinforced. As for example, we can praise a child for correct addition only half the time or for every five correct responses. There are four basic schedules of partial reinforcement. These are:

1. Fixed Ratio Schedule (FR),
2. Variable Ratio Schedule (VR),
3. Fixed Interval Schedule (FI),
4. Variable Interval Schedule (VI).

***FR Schedule*:** A FR schedule of reinforcement requires the subject to make fixed number of responses in order to receive reinforcement. For example, a child may be praised for making five correct responses. The behaviour produced by using an FR schedule is usually very rapid.

***VR Schedule*:** A VR schedule requires the subject to respond some number of times in order to obtain reinforcement but the exact number of responses required at any one time changes and the subject does not know how many responses are required to produce the reinforcement. The rate of behaviour generated by this schedule is also very high.

Both the FR and VR schedules are based on the number of responses the subject makes. The other two schedules are based on time intervals.

FI Schedule: In FI schedule, reinforcement is available at regular time intervals; say a fixed interval of 30 seconds. The number of responses made by the subject will have no effect on reinforcement. Suppose, the rat pressed the bar 50 times in the first 30 seconds of the experiment and it did not result in reinforcement. Only the first response after 30 seconds would produce reinforcement. Behaviour in FI schedule is characterised by a period of no response early in the interval, but as the time for reinforcement approaches, the response rate increases until the subject finally receives the reinforcement.

VI Schedule: The VI schedule is similar to the VR schedule. In VI schedule, the time interval between the response and the reinforcement varies from trial to trial so that the subject never knows when a response will produce reinforcement. This type of schedule results in a moderate but extremely steady rate of responses.

Extinction

Another type of reinforcement schedule is an extinction schedule. It is the complement to the continuous reinforcement schedule. Extinction involves giving the subject no reinforcement for the response. When the subject is given no reinforcement for a response, the response tends to decrease in strength. Extinction is an alternative to punishment in decreasing the strength of a response or eliminating it. The smaller the amount of reinforcement given for a response, the more resistance to extinction the subject will exhibit. Usually partial reinforcement produces much greater resistance to extinction than continuous reinforcement.

Differences and Similarities between Instrumental Conditioning and Classical Conditioning

There are many aspects of the procedures used in each type of training that differentiate classical conditioning from instrumental conditioning:

(i) In classical conditioning, learning takes place when the subject establishes a bond between the CS and the UCS. Thus, classical conditioning is a form of learning in which two stimuli are presented together and the response originally elicited by one of them comes to be elicited by the other. For this purpose, classical conditioning is otherwise known as S-S learning.

In instrumental conditioning, learning occurs only when the subject establishes a relationship between the response and its consequences or the stimuli. Thus instrumental conditioning is a form of learning in which the response is instrumental in securing a specific after-effect such as the presentation of a reinforcing stimulus or the removal of an aversive stimulus. For this purpose, instrumental conditioning is otherwise known as R-S learning.

(ii) Classical conditioning measures respondent behaviour or involuntary behaviour of the autonomic nervous system. But instrumental conditioning measures operant behaviour or voluntary behaviour of the central nervous system. Respondent behaviour is elicited by known/specific stimulus. It depends upon contiguity or stimulus conditions at the start of training.

In classical conditioning, the environment acts upon the organism. By contrast, operant behaviour depends upon its consequences. It is emitted by the organism. The organism acts upon the environment.

(iii) The role of the stimulus which functions to strengthen learning is quite different in the two types of conditioning. Although the UCS in classical conditioning is designated as the reinforcing stimulus, it quite clearly functions in a different way from the reinforcing stimulus in instrumental conditioning. In the instrumental learning situation, the reinforcing stimulus is contingent upon the response. In a positive reinforcement situation, the operant response produces the reinforcing stimulus. In negative reinforcement procedure, the operant response serves to terminate the aversive stimulus. In either case, the subject's responses act upon the environment affecting the reinforcing events. Such is not the case with the UCR in classical conditioning. In classical conditioning, the UCS often called as the reinforcing stimulus, is presented first before the response is made.

Thus, the UCR does not act upon the environment. Rather it is seen as the end point in the learning trial. Instead of being a response that produces changes, it is a response that results from changes.

(iv) An important difference between the classical conditioning and instrumental conditioning lies in role of the subject in the two training procedures. In classical conditioning, the subject is a relatively passive responder to whom events happen. The CS occurs, the UCS occurs and the subject produces the response. The subject does not in any way control the stimuli. It may even be said that it does not control its own responses, for the response is automatically elicited by the UCS. When food is placed in the mouth, the dog does not salivate voluntarily, rather salivation occurs involuntarily. In instrumental conditioning, however, the subject is an active respondent. The subject is free to produce any response in instrumental learning situation. The production of the desired response depends upon the subject. That is why operant behaviour is said to be emitted by the organism.

(v) Some investigators argue that not only the training procedures are different but also both types of learning are governed by different laws of learning. According to these investigators, classical conditioning is governed by the law of contiguity. By contrast, instrumental conditioning is governed by the law of effect.

(vi) The essence of classical conditioning is stimulus substitution. But the essence of instrumental conditioning is behaviour modification. Classical conditioning is stimulus-oriented, but instrumental conditioning is response-oriented.

(vii) Kimble (1961) maintains the viewpoint that the original distinction between instrumental conditioning and classical conditioning is made on purely operational grounds. It is impossible on logical grounds to perform an instrumental conditioning experiment without also arranging the conditions of classical conditioning one.

> To obtain instrumental conditioning, it is essential to provide reinforcement to a subject for performing the act. Obviously this reinforcement must occur in some situation. Thus the situational clues are conditioned stimuli regularly associated with reinforcement after the manner of classical conditioning. It is also difficult, if not impossible, to perform a completely pure classical conditioning experiment with the result that the classically conditioned response may contain instrumental components. The appearance of an anticipatory CR often has an effect upon the UCS. In the Pavlovian experiment, the anticipatory salivary response no doubt changes the tastes of the food.

However, the differences which appear may be more a function of the differences that the experimenter chooses to measure than of the actual learning taking place. The rat in the Skinner Box is being instrumentally conditioned to press the bar. But at the same time, its salivary response is probably also being classically conditioned to various stimuli associated with delivery of the food. The experimenter, however, chooses to measure the operant response and ignores the respondent behaviour. Similarly, in the classical conditioning experiment, the focus is on the respondents so that the operants are not observed or measured.

However, whatever may be the differences between classical conditioning and instrumental conditioning, the two types of training have many similarities. The similarities between the two appear far greater than the differences. Both classical conditioning and instrumental conditioning involve the processes of discrimination and generalization, extinction, inhibition, reinforcement, second order and higher order conditioning. Similarly, whatever procedure may be followed in classical conditioning and instrumental conditioning, both aim at increasing the frequency of response or decreasing the strength of response.

In order to determine adequately whether the two types of learning are the same or different, more research is required. Thus, at present, the question of whether classical conditioning and instrumental conditioning are the same or different cannot be answered unequivocally. There are both similarities and differences between the two. Only further investigation can determine the relative importance of the similarities and differences.

Educational Implications of Conditioning

Conditioning, both classical and operant, was for many years attacked as being a lower or simpler form of learning, because learning by conditioning does not involve higher cognitive processes. It was thus identified with animal learning. Some psychologists hold the viewpoint that human beings learn more through insight and problem-solving, than through conditioning. Thus for these psychologists, conditioning cannot explain human learning. Consequently, principles of conditioning were not considered to be useful for teachers and teaching.

Bandura and Walters do not accept that principles of conditioning are sufficient for explaining the initial learning of all behaviours. They explain learning in terms of observation and imitation. Gagne accepts principles of conditioning as sufficient for explaining the simple types of learning but also indicates that they are not sufficient for explaining concept learning, principle learning and problem-solving behaviour. Ausubel also rejects the idea that human learning can be explained in terms of principles of conditioning.

Some other psychologists like Staats say that conditioning is too important for almost every aspect of human learning. It is the basis of all habits, skills, attitudes and all other learning. Even emotions are also learned through conditioning. Emotions such as fear and love can be acquired through conditioning. John B. Watson, a famous American psychologist, was successful in teaching an emotional reaction, like fear, to a small child through the principles of conditioning. Even language learning also occurs through a process of conditioning. Modern psychological researches reveal the fact that general feelings of helplessness, depression and psychosomatic illness are learned through conditioning. At present, many teaching techniques are based on the principles of conditioning.

Implications of Classical Conditioning

Classical conditioning does not have direct application to classroom learning. The principles of classical conditioning can be used in the following areas of human behaviour:

(i) Developing Good Habits and Breaking Bad Habits

Principles of classical conditioning can be used for developing good habits in children such as cleanliness, respect for elders and punctuality, etc. Habits, both good and bad, are all learned in a social environment. Consequently, bad habits can also be deconditioned by using the principles of classical conditioning. Classical conditioning can be used to develop favourable or unfavourable attitudes towards learning, teachers and the school.

(ii) Teaching an Emotional Response

We can teach an emotional response through the principles of classical conditioning. An example of this is teaching a child to avoid fire and hot stove. If the child sees the fire and then touches it, he will experience pain. The next time he sees the fire he will experience facsimile of that pain as he begins to reach for it. Contact with the fire is the UCS and sight of the fire is the CS, pain is the UCR and anticipation of pain is the CR.

(iii) Getting Rid of Emotional Responses

Principles of conditioning can be successfully applied in eliminating some emotional responses. If a student fears a learning situation, say a mathematics class, because failure or punishment has occurred in that class in the past, then the teacher can arrange things in such a way that the child will attend the class without fear or failure.

(a) ***Counter-conditioning***: In order to reduce an emotional response in a given situation, a teacher can make use of a procedure known as counter-conditioning. Counter-conditioning is a procedure which states that the particular situation should be accompanied by a stimulus which elicits a response which is the opposite to the one to be reduced.

(b) *Vicarious Conditioning*: Vicarious conditioning is a procedure which means that classical responses can be conditioned in a learner by having the learner observe another learner being conditioned or having the learner imagine the circumstance of conditioning rather than actually experiencing them.

(iv) Contiguity and Repetition

Principles of conditioning have definite implications for the classroom teacher for teaching certain subjects through contiguity and repetition. Contiguity and repetition are useful in the learning of factual information, names of numbers, letters, pronounciation, names of people, places and events and some other subjects specifically during the formative years of life.

Besides the various applications of classical conditioning mentioned above, classical conditioning has also implications for the readiness, motivation, and goals of the learners.

Implications of Instrumental (Operant) Conditioning

Principles of instrumental conditioning or operant conditioning have a large number of implications for the classroom teacher. In fact, many teachers consciously or unconsciously apply the technique of operant conditioning in the teaching — learning situation of the classroom and outside. The various applications of operant conditioning particularly those of extinction, reinforcement, shaping through successive approximation and behaviour modification programmes are discussed below:

(i) Successive Approximation

The exponents of operant conditioning believe that behaviour can be shaped through successive approximation. Successive approximation is a process which means that complicated behaviour patterns are learned gradually through successive steps which are rewarding for the learner. Suppose a child writes very poorly. The teacher in this case should pick out the best aspects of the existing writing and comment positively on them and even give rewards. As the writing improves slightly, the teacher should continue giving positive reinforcers. Every successful step of the child must be rewarded by the teacher, but the teacher should not punish the child for bad writing.

(ii) Eliminating Negative Behaviour through Extinction

When a learned response is repeated without reinforcement, the strength of the tendency to perform that response undergoes a progressive decrease. Extinction procedure can be successfully used by the classroom teacher in eliminating negative behaviour of students. It must be remembered that with the extinction techniques, the negative behaviour is likely to get worse before it gets better. The teacher must tolerate worsening of behaviour so that he will get the desired result. Consider, for example, the situation in which a teacher gives a child attention every time he behaves negatively. When the teacher decides to use extinction, it is necessary to withhold the attention. But, at first, this will only encourage the child to misbehave more in the hope of ultimately getting the attention (reinforcement) that is being withheld. This is why it is so important to decide what reinforcement actually can be withheld and to decide what alternative behaviours are going to be positively reinforced and how. In general, extinction is more effective if it is combined with a positive reinforcement programme (Belkin and Gray, 1977).

(iii) Reinforcement

Operant conditioning has very valuable implications for reinforcement techniques in the classroom. Positive reinforcement is perhaps the most widely used behavioural technique in the school setting. This technique simply involves providing a reward for positive behaviour. The reward can be anything ranging from a high grade to a pencil, to a smile, to a verbal compliment. The principle underlying positive reinforcement is that the tendency to repeat a response to a given stimulus will be strengthened as the response is positively rewarded.

One of the most debated questions among teachers, educational psychologists and concerned parents is, "To what extent is punishment an effective tool in classroom discipline? Punishment as a behavioural technique has been down rated from the time of Thorndike to the present. Thus, reward positive behaviour more than you punish negative behaviour."

While there may be some truth in this belief, evidence does indicate the efficacy of punishment as well. According to some educators, whenever a child is systematically punished for certain negative behaviour, that behaviour tends to decrease in strength. The researches of Macmillan, Horness and Trumbul (1973) suggest that the effectiveness of punishment as a reinforcement technique depends upon certain variables, such as: (i) the timing of punishment, (ii) consistency of punishment, (iii) intensity of punishment, (iv) adaptation to punishment, (v) alternatives to the goal, and (vi) relationship between the teacher and the child.

(i) To be effective, punishment should be administered immediately after the inappropriate behaviour. The longer the delay between the behaviour and the punishment, the less effective it will be.

(ii) If a student is punished sometimes for a certain behaviour but not punished at other times, then the punishment is less effective than if it is consistently administered.

(iii) Punishment may range from a disapproving look, to corporal punishment, to severe electrical shocks. But very strong aversive stimuli produce more permanent change than mildly aversive stimuli and that intense punishment is effective. But corporal punishment which is an intense aversive stimulus should be avoided and instead some other strong aversive punishing stimuli should be found.

(iv) If the child is continually subjected to punishment, he loses the ability to distinguish between aversive and non-aversive situations, between which behaviours are acceptable and which are not acceptable.

(v) One question the teacher must always ask when administering punishment is what alternative behaviours are available to the students? If a child is punished for a behaviour that has no alternatives, serious psychoneurotic side effects can be produced. By providing alternatives, a teacher also facilitates the child's discrimination between what is acceptable and what is unacceptable.

(vi) This variable can be simply stated, who can hurt us more — a person whom we deeply care about or one for whom we have only negative feeling? Clearly, the person about whom we care can hurt us more deeply. This has several implications for the teacher. If the teacher has a positive, highly motivating relationship with a student, the teacher is then more capable of dispensing punishment. Such a teacher must carefully weigh whether the administration of punishment will jeopardize the positive values of this relationship. One way of dealing with this dilemma for the teachers who wishes to punish a child with whom he has rapport is to combine some positive affection with that punishment — to make the student realise that, although he is being punished, the teacher still feels positively about him.

However, the teacher must realise that punishment by itself is not an effective tool for either correcting aberrant behaviour, facilitating emotional and intellectual growth, or maintaining classroom control. If at all punishment is used, it should be used advantageously to the benefit of the student, not simply as a retributive measure by the teacher.

The principles of operant conditioning have also another application for classroom learning. Since many responses and reinforcement events will likely be needed to attain the desired outcomes, it is often necessary to use programmed materials and mechanical devices such as computer-assisted instruction. The programmes should be linear or in small progressive steps from simple to more complex behaviours. Operant conditioning techniques also imply the use of behaviour modification programmes to shape desirable behaviour and to eliminate undesirable behaviour.

SELECTED QUESTIONS

1. Distinguish between association theories and cognitive theories of learning and state their educational implications.
2. Describe an experiment on learning by trial and error and state its implications for the teacher.

3. What do you mean by learning by insight? Describe an experiment and state its implications for the teacher.
4. Differentiate between trial and error learning and insightful learning and state their implications for classroom practice.
5. Discuss the essential features of learning by classical conditioning and state their educational implications.
6. What do you mean by instrumental learning? What are its implications for teachers?
7. Discuss the differences and similarities between classical and instrumental conditioning. State their implications for educational practice.
8. What do you mean by reinforcement? State its relationship to learning and motivation.
9. Write short note on Laws of Learning.

15
Teaching Learning Process

1. MEANING OF LEARNING

The popular belief is that "the mind is a storehouse for facts." Teaching is thus a process of filling the storehouse with facts and learning is the process of acquiring or absorbing facts. The more the facts, the more the learning. This concept of learning as a process of acquiring facts, knowledge or information is fallacious. Unless what we learn becomes a necessary or useful part of our functioning as individuals, unless there is a change in our behaviour as a result of learning, such learning cannot be called real learning. Contrary to the above traditional views, learning today is considered to be a process of change in behaviour or modification of behaviour. Look at the definitions given below; they all emphasize learning as change or modification of behaviour:

> "Learning, as we measure it, is a change in performance which occurs under conditions of practice."
>
> — *McGeoch and Irion* (1952)
>
> "Learning is more or less permanent incremental modification of behaviour which results from activity, special training or observation." — *Munn* (1955)
>
> "Learning may be defined more simply as profiting from experience." — *Hilgard, Atkinson and Alkinson* (1978)
>
> "Learning is a change in human disposition or capability, which persists over a period of time, and which is not simply ascribable to processes of growth."
>
> — *Gagne* (1976)

> "Learning is limited to those changes in behaviour which are a result of training or experience, and not a result of maturation or temporary physiological or psychological states of the organism."
>
> — *More, Manning and Smith* (1978)

The following points will help us to understand learning as modification behaviour:

(i) All learning is change in behaviour but all change in behaviour is not learning. Certain changes in behaviour occur due to maturation, drug and fatigue. For example, after long hours of continuous work, an individual shows deterioration in his performance. This change in the individual's performance is not due to learning but due to fatigue. When a man drinks alcohol or *bhang*, or takes some intoxicating drug his behaviour is changed. This change in behaviour is not due to learning but due to the effect of drug or alcohol. Similarly when a housewife is angry or depressed, she performs very poorly in her homework. This change in the performance of the housewife is due to her temporary mental state.

(ii) Changes in behaviour may be temporary or permanent. But any real learning leads to permanent changes in behaviour. Learning to speak a language or to write in the language is an instance of permanent change in behaviour. But most classroom learning situations do not support the idea that learning is permanent. Students learn a subject or a chapter; and after the examination they forget most of what they were taught. This happens so because what is learned does not become a part of their daily life. By learning they mean 'memorization' or being able to pass an examination on the subject; it does not matter whether they remember the facts permanently or forget them after the examination.

(iii) Changes in behaviour may take place in the desirable direction or in the undesirable direction. For example, children learn good habits as well as bad habits, desirable attitudes as well as undesirable attitudes. The concept of learning implies acquiring desirable habits, attitudes, and behaviours and modifying their undesirable habits, attitudes or behaviours.

(iv) Learning can be both incidental and intentional. The school curriculum, teaching methods and learning styles must be oriented to both intentional and incidental learning.

(v) Learning involves both overt acts and covert processes. Children learn attitudes and values which are covert processes. When we define learning as change in behaviour, it includes both overt acts and covert processes.

(vi) Learning results from reinforced practice. Practice makes a man perfect. Practice, training or experience lead to improvement in present learning. But practice alone does not cause improvement. Children will learn to do those things for which they are rewarded (praised, honoured, recognised) and will learn to avoid doing those things for which they are punished (blamed, or getting disapproval). Practice should therefore be followed by some type of reinforcement. Learning should always be associated with reinforcement.

(vii) Learning is both a process and a product. Learning as a process includes such things as how the child is learning (discovery learning, meaningful learning, rote learning, trial and error learning, conditioning, insightful learning, etc.), the nature of interaction between the child and the teacher, and many other factors such as coding and rehearsal which operate at the time of learning. Learning as a product includes the results or outcomes of learning. The outcomes of learning may be cognitive (learning a concept, a rule or principle, language, etc., affective (learning attitudes, emotions, values, etc.) or motor learning (learning skills such as typing, playing basketball, dancing). Outcomes of learning not only include the types of achievement but also the level of achievement such as mastery over the task, or learning just the essentials. In short, learning as a product includes the level and type of competencies attained by the child in relation to the learning task.

2. NATURE/GENERAL CHARACTERISTICS OF LEARNING

The nature and general characteristics of learning as conceived by modern psychologists may be summarised as follows:

(i) Learning is Growth

Learning is a process that results in modification of behaviour. It constantly enlarges the child's understanding of his environment. It leads to better understanding of life about him. It leads to growth of abilities, understanding, perceptions and intellect. Learning as growth depends upon a favourable environment and richer experiences. The child needs play constructive manual activities, aesthetic activities and social activities. By these means he should grow into a fully developed person. If the child is denied the richness of environment, he will inevitably be stunted in some aspect of growth or will develop the undesirable attitudes and traits. Effective education furnishes the controlled environment for favourable growth.

(ii) Learning is a Never-ending Process

Learning is a never-ending process. There is hardly anybody who has no more to learn. At each stage, the learner acquires new visions and achieves something new. Every achievement, then, becomes the basis for new achievements in future. In this way, the urge to acquire more and achieve something and noble is fulfilled.

(iii) Learning is Universal

Every creature that lives learns. Insects, mammals and human beings learn some form of behaviour. Animals learn more than the insects. But of all creatures, man learns most. Human children have the longest period of immaturity and helplessness and hence the longest period and opportunity for learning. Although learning is universal, the capacity to learn different forms of behaviour and the time required to learn vary from creature to creature.

(iv) Learning is always Purposeful

Learning is not aimless. It is purposeful. Young children learn behaviour patterns because they satisfy their needs and interests; they help them to fulfill their goals, purposes and expectations.

They work hard willingly only to fulfill these expectations, goals and purposes, because it is satisfying for them in some manner giving them a sense of accomplishment and power.

(v) Learning is Many-sided

Children acquire new knowledge, facts and ideas. They learn various types of skills. They learn attitudes and values, interests and emotions. They learn concepts, rules, problem-solving behaviour, etc. They also learn to learn. Thus psychologists have classified learning into various types — concept learning, rule learning, problem-solving, skill learning, verbal learning and non-verbal learning, learning of attitudes and values, etc. Learning, therefore, has many facets.

(vi) Learning comes only through Experience/Activity

Learning does not mean what parents and teachers do for the child or what they tell the child to do. It comes through the child's own activities and experiences. The child learns more by doings things by himself from his own experiences about things, people, objects, events and situations. Each activity or each experience modifies the learner's attitudes, ideals, knowledge, skills and habits. Each activity or experience develops in the child a new way of looking at things. The animal world changes its habits slowly. Human beings have the ability to profit from experience quickly and to readjust themselves to new situations rapidly. This distinguishes human beings from the animal world. In schools, children must have opportunity to learn by doing, activity, discovery and experience.

(vii) Learning is Adjustment

Learning involves the adjustment of the individual to the world in various ways. Even in a simple environment, the individual must learn to adjust himself to climate and weather in order to survive. In a complex environment, many intricate kinds of adjustment are necessary. The individual must learn to adjust himself to the changes that take place about him. It is the function of the school to teach the child how to meet and adjust himself to these new and complex elements in his environment. He must live in a world of change. While there is need for the development of independence and initiative in the individual to overcome undesirable conditions and make him better, there is also need for adjustment in the sense of conforming to the laws of the nature and other factors in the environment over which the individual has no control.

(viii) Learning as Problem-solving

In schools and colleges, students learn concepts, rules, and principles. Learning rules and principles helps them to learn new and higher order rules and principles in future. Learning rules and principles helps in solving problems of various types. The activity of problem-solving is thus an extension of learning rules. Problem-solving is a process by which the learner discovers a combination of previously learned rules which can be applied to achieve a solution for a novel situation.

Problem-solving is not simply a matter of applying learned rules. It is also a process that yields new learning. The learners are placed in a problem situation, or find themselves in one such situation. They recall previously acquired rules in the attempt to find a solution. In carrying out such a thinking process, they find a particular combination of rules that fits the situation. They not only solve the problem but also learn something new. In fact, all learning is problem-solving.

3. LEARNING CURVE

What is a Learning Curve?

The origin of learning curve is associated with the names of two telegraphists—Bryan and Harter. A learning curve is a graphic representation of the progress of learning of an individual in a given period. If we take the number of trials on X-axis of the graph and the scores or the amount of learning on the Y-axis of the graph and then join the points we get a learning curve. The slope of the curve indicates the rate of progress (increase or decrease) of learning.

Types of Learning Curve

The following types of curve are most commonly found in the learning situation:

1. *Straight Line Curve*: When the rate of progress is constant in successive trials we get a straight line curve.

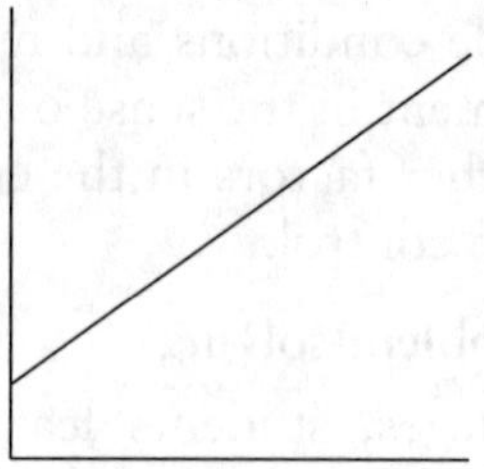

Fig. 3

2. *Negatively Accelerated Learning Curve or Convex Learning Curve*: When the rate of gain is rapid in the beginning and gradually lowers down or decreases in successive practice periods, we get a negatively accelerated curve or a convex curve.

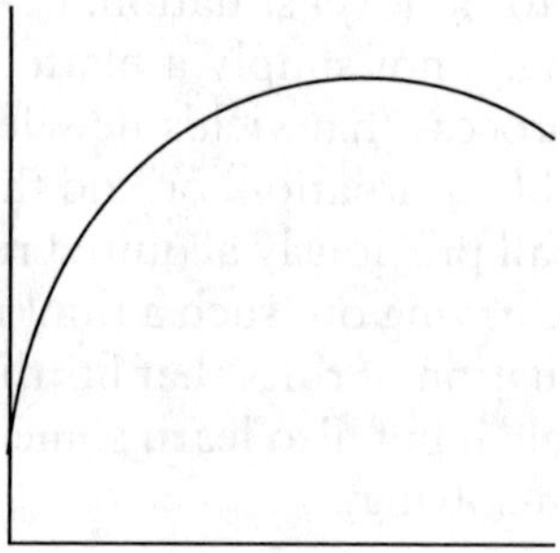

Fig. 4

3. *Positively Accelerated Learning Curve or Concave Learning Curve*: When there is a slow rate of gain in the beginning and the rate of gain gradually increases in successive trials, we get a positively accelerated curve or a concave learning curve (as in case of children's acquisition of vocabulary).

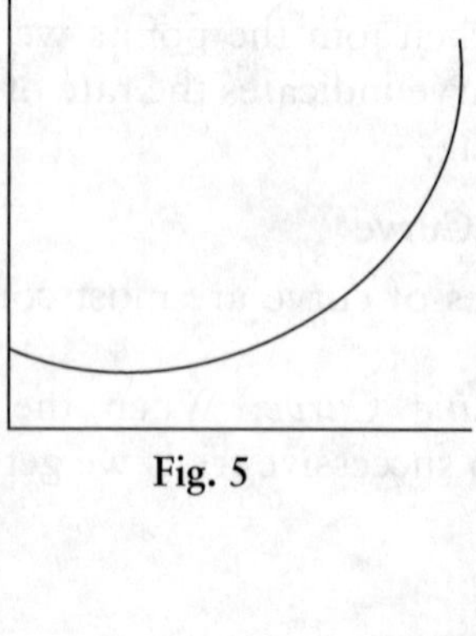

Fig. 5

4. *Combination of Convex and Concave Curves*: Sometimes we may get a combination of convex learning curve and concave learning curve. This type of learning curve is found when the initial slow rate of learning is followed by sudden rapid rate of learning.

The learning curve varies from learner to learner and from subject to subject. The type of curve which we may obtain depends on:

(i) Nature of the learning task (simple/complex, familiar/unfamiliar, interesting/uninteresting, meaningful/meaningless syllables, etc.),
(ii) Method of learning,
(iii) Learner's ability to perform a task,
(iv) Previous training/experience relating to the task,
(v) Level of enthusiasm, and
(vi) Learning environment.

Plateaus in Learning

What is a Plateau?

In learning trials, sometimes we notice a period of no progress or improvements. After a period of slow or rapid rise, the score or progress of learning remains almost constant for some trials. A straight but flat line appears in the learning curve. This is what we call plateau in learning.

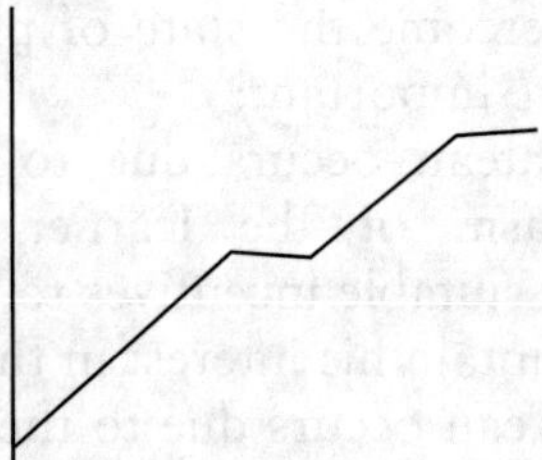

Fig. 6

It may also happen that the learner may again begin improving after a period of no progress. There will be again a rise in the curve after the plateau. After this rise, there may be a period of no progress again for some time, and again a rise, and then a plateau. In this way, the learning activity continues up to a point at which progress stops for ever.

Why do Plateaus Occur?

Plateaus occur due to the following reasons:

(i) Lapse of initial interest and enthusiasm;

(ii) Ineffective methods of work;

(iii) Shifting of attention from the learning task to some other task, or from one aspect to another aspect of the task (*e.g.* from speed to accuracy);

(iv) Transfer of errors from the earlier trials to the new trial;

(v) Lack of balance among various phases of the activity;

(vi) Inappropriate learning habits, fatigue and lack of rest periods, and

(vii) Complex nature or difficulty level of the learning task.

Implications for Teachers

Learning curves are of great value for teachers:

(i) Learning curves give an indication about the rate of progress in learning. They indicate where the learner stands in relation to learning task, the difficulty which a learner faces in learning the task, the shortcomings of teaching and help teachers plan their instruction in a better manner and to ensure appropriate progress by learners in the learning task.

(ii) Plateaus are common features in the learning curve. The teachers should take appropriate measures to help learners overcome the state of plateau. The following measures are important:

— If a plateau occurs due to lack of interest and enthusiasm of the learner, the teacher should provide suitable incentives to the learner to develop and maintain his interest in the task.

— If a plateau occurs due to the difficulty level of the subject-matter, the teacher should reorganise the subject matter suitably and avoid presenting the subject matter in quick succession.

— If a plateau occurs due to inappropriate methods of learning, teachers should guide children to adopt the appropriate method of learning.

— If a plateau occurs because the learner pays undue attention to some part and neglects other parts of the task, the teacher should help the learner to give a balanced treatment to all aspects of the task.

— If a plateau occurs at some unit because the learner has not mastered the prerequisites which are essential for learning the present unit, the teacher should help him to re-learn the previous units and then to attempt to learn the new unit.

— If a plateau occurs because the learner does not get sufficient rest periods to facilitate consolidation of the previously learnt materials, the teacher can avoid plateau by ensuring a proper combination of work and rest. Judicious distribution of curricular and co-curricular activities in the school time-table can help overcome plateaus in learning.

— Children vary from one another in respect of their abilities to learn. There is a limit beyond which a child cannot make any further progress in learning and plateaus are inevitable at such points. Hence, plateaus may be accepted as natural phenomena in the learning situation.

4. LEARNING AND MATURATION

Learning refers to change in behaviour. Maturation also plays an important role in bringing out change in behaviour. For example, the first time the child walks or talks are an indication that maturation is at work. The swimming of tadpoles and the flying of birds also demonstrate the effect of maturation on behaviour.

Whatever training you may provide to an infant of 6-month old he will not speak the language. The infant will speak only when his vocal organs mature. The child first creeps, then crawls, and then walks. But the first behaviour-creeping occurs only when the infant is mature to do so. All these examples make it clear that changes in behaviour also occur due to maturation. Maturation in this sense means development of anatomical and physiological structure of the body.

Certain changes in behaviour occur due to both maturation and learning. For example, a child cannot walk until his legs are strong enough to support the weight of his body and until the development of proper neural structure takes place. But children do not walk in the same manner. The manner of walking is learned. Similarly, a child cannot speak until the vocal organs develop. But children do not speak the same language. Those who speak the same language speak in different ways. Speech is also a learned behaviour.

Maturation helps in the learning process. We cannot learn anything without our bodies taking part. The things we learn, the speed with which we learn them, and our ability to retain them, all depend on the interaction between our maturation process and the learning experiences. There are different ages or stages of maturation and at each stage certain kinds of learning take place. Just as healthy maturation contributes to learning, delayed maturation or lack of maturation contributes to deficits in learning. For example, the muscles and other structures of the new-born baby are not sufficiently mature to permit walking. Since he cannot walk and get around in the world, he can obviously know very little about it. Thus, maturation determines learning.

5. PRINCIPLES OF LEARNING

There are no fixed principles of learning and psychologists are not in complete agreement about the principles which govern learning. Different theories of learning are based on different principles. Some principles are found to work best for some kinds of learning and in certain situations while other principles are most appropriate for some other kinds of learning and in some other situations. Some of these principles are as follows:

(i) The Principle of Trial and Error

This principle states that in any learning situation, the learner should try continuously and constantly to master the desired skill. While trying initially, he may commit errors. But as trials increase, errors will gradually decrease and in the long-run he will learn the skill. This principle is based on the contention that "practice makes a learner perfect". This principle is most appropriate for young learners and in the learning of skills such as riding a bicycle, driving an automobile, playing tennis, typing, etc.

(ii) The Principle of Reinforcement

This principle states that the learner learns a behaviour because he is rewarded for it or that he learns to give up a habit because he is punished for it. Any behaviour that is followed by satisfying consequences, reward, approval, honour or recognition is strengthened and tends to be repeated. Any behaviour that is followed by annoying consequences, punishment, disapproval or rejection is weakened and tends to be forgotten. On the whole, positive reinforcement is more effective than negative reinforcement. This principle also states that practice alone does not make learning perfect. Practice must be followed by reinforcers. This principle is useful for teaching children desirable habits and behaviour and breaking their undesirable habits.

(iii) The Principle of Wholeness and Understanding

This is based on the contention that learning is efficient when the learner adopts a 'whole' approach to the learning phenomena as opposed to a 'part' approach. The learner must try to understand the relationships involved among various elements in the learning phenomena; he must understand the 'whole,' first; and he must be able to reorganise his existing cognitive structure in the light of his understanding and the meaning he derives from the learning phenomena so that his learning will be efficient, effective and meaningful. Most often, children's learning becomes inefficient and ineffective because children fail to understand the meaning or the essence of what they are trying to learn, and that they learn by rote or drill. This is why children forget most of the facts they learnt by rote immediately after the examination.

(iv) The Principle of Learning by Doing

This is a very simple principle which states that the learner learns an activity or a skill by doing that activity himself. While performing an activity, he gains direct experiences and these experiences guide him in better performances on subsequent occasions. The principle of learning by doing or learning from one's own activities and experiences suggests that the school curriculum should be activity-centered.

(v) The Principle of Hierarchy and Sequence

This principle states that learning tasks should be organised in the hierarchical and sequential way. Learning task should be arranged from simple to complex, known to unknown, familiar to unfamiliar and in a graded way. Learning tasks should be so sequential that learning Task A should help in learning Task B and Task B helps in learning Task C and so on. The learner should first master Task A and then proceed to Task B, then to Task C and so on. Making learning sequential and hierarchical makes it easier and more effective. Learning of Mathematics, Language and Science and Psychomotor skills should be sequential in nature. For example, in learning of arithmetic, the learner should learn numbers first, then addition, then subtraction, then multiplication. In learning language, the child should first listen, then speak, then read and then write. The curriculum should be graded accordingly.

(vi) The Principle of Readiness

Learning proceeds along the path of development. There are different ages and stages of developments and at each stage or age, certain kinds of learning are possible. This means that the learner should be psychologically and biologically ready for the learning task. This principle of psycho-biological readiness suggests that the school curriculum should be based on the psycho-biological readiness of children at different stages of development.

(vii) The Principle of Assimilation and Accommodation

This principle states that the child's learning takes place as a result of assimilation and accommodation. Assimilation is the process of incorporating new ideas into an idea the child has already acquired. At each stage, the child has an existing set of ideas, actions or operations. When the child encounters an unfamiliar situation or a new situation, he tends to react to the situation in his existing style or in terms of his existing operations. If his actions are successful, he does not change his behaviour. This application of older ideas or actions to a new situation is called assimilation. In simple language, assimilation is applying old ideas and old habits to new situations. If the old ideas and old habits do not fit to the new situation, the child tends to adjust to the new situation by changing his old habits and old ideas. This is what we call accommodation. Learning takes place as a result of the child's assimilation and accommodation.

(viii) The Principle of Learning to Learn

This principle is based on the assumption that some learners, particularly the retarded ones do not know how to learn different skills or subjects as a result of which their learning becomes ineffective and inefficient. Children should therefore be told verbally how to learn and exposed to adult models or able classmates for learning how to learn.

6. FACTORS INFLUENCING LEARNING

There are several factors which influence learning. These factors can be grouped under four heads:

(i) Learner factors,
(ii) Teacher factors,
(iii) School factors,
(iv) Home factors.

(i) Learner Factors

Physical and Physiological factors: Learning is influenced by the child's maturity, age, sex, health conditions and his readiness to learn.

Intellectual factors: Learning in school is greatly influenced by the child's cognitive entry characteristics such as the ability to understand instruction, previous knowledge and experience in the subject, perseverance, time actively devoted by the child to learn, and his aptitude for particular kinds of learning.

Emotional and mental health factors: The child's level of motivation, level of aspiration, anxiety, interest, attitude and mental health conditions.

(ii) Teacher Factors

The teacher is the most influential figure in the teaching — learning process. It is the teacher who is mainly responsible for children's learning in schools. It is not so much his personality characteristics as his teaching style and the quality of his teaching which influence greatly learning in schools. Teachers who make their teaching systematic, sensitive and qualitative; who make use of alternative teaching methods and materials, and audio-visual aids; who provide guidance and encouragement to children; who provide extra time and remedial teaching; who expect children to learn well and provide corrective exercise for those who have learning difficulties, contribute significantly to excellent learning by children. Certain personality traits of the teacher also influence learning. Children learn better when a teacher is friendly, cooperative, enthusiastic and takes interest in children's learning. The techniques of classroom management and control (democratic, autocratic and *laissez-faire*), relationship of the teacher with the pupils, opportunities given by the teacher for pupils' participation in the teaching-learning process also influence learning.

(iii) School Factors

Just as the learner and the teacher are the two principal figures in the teaching—learning process, the school is the principal agency to promote learning. Schools are successful or unsuccessful to the extent they achieve the objectives, the most important objective being promotion of excellence in learning. "Fortunate are those children who have been blessed with the studentship in a school which is known for its excellent standard of academic achievement." A school with a record of brilliant and scholarly performance of its teachers and students attracts students and motivates them to learn excellently. The learning environment and the academic atmosphere of the school, continuous and comprehensive evaluation system of the school, its morale, emotional climate, interpersonal relationship, infrastructure facilities, quality of its staff, competitive and cooperative atmosphere, the ecosystem, the time allowed for learning, library facilities, provision of remedial instruction in the school, parent-teacher contact are some of the factors in the school which influence learning.

(iv) Home Factors

The home and not the school provides first the foundation of education of the child. Consciously or incidentally, parents provide a lot of educational experience to teach the child academic and non-academic skills, attitudes, values and knowledge. Previously it was believed that the education and occupation of parents are important factors which influence learning. Now it is believed that the home environment process is a powerful factor which influences learning. This includes the feelings the parents have towards the child, parents' attitude towards children's success and competition, the emotional climate in the home, the contribution of the home to the development of the child's mother tongue, the encouragement of parents to the children to learn well, the aspirations of the parents for their children, the provision of help in learning when the child most needs it, the way in which time and space are organised in the home, relationship among parents, relationship between parents and the child, etc.

7. SKILL LEARNING

Definition of Skill

Many important human activities require precision, timing and co-ordination of muscular movements. The acquisition of these qualities of action, precision, timing and co-ordination is required for all proficient performance and is known as skill learning. In other words, skill implies proficient performance or the level of proficiency needed for a specific task. Skill learning, motor learning and psychomotor learning are synonymous.

Skills Pertinent to Schools

Merril (1972) has proposed the following five categories of skills which are pertinent to schools:

(i) Physical education and recreation skills (sports, dance and exercise),
(ii) Communication skills (typing, handwriting, shorthand),
(iii) Language skills (speech and gestures),
(iv) Vocational skills (crafts, tool usage, machine usage) and
(v) Fine art skills (painting, singing, using musical instruments).

Characteristics of a Skill

Dececco and Crawford (1975) list three characteristics of a skill:

(i) A skill involves muscular or body movements. Some skills involve gross body movements as in walking, running, jumping, swimming, and dancing. Some other skills involve movement of a segment of the body as in holding and playing a musical instrument.

(ii) Skilled behaviour involves the co-ordination of hand and eye movements. For example, in typing there is co-ordination of hand (finger) and eye movement.

(iii) A skill involves a hierarchy of responses or organisation of individual sub-tasks or sub-routines. For example, swimming involves a number of sub-tasks like arm strokes, breathing and leg kicks. The individual must learn each of these sub-tasks in a hierarchical way before he becomes a swimmer. Like swimming, all complex skills are the result of learning subordinate skills.

Besides these three main characteristics, skills have also the following characteristics:

(a) A skill involves some amount of trial and error behaviour.

(b) Learning a skill depends upon development and experience.

(c) Different tasks require different combinations of abilities. For example, long distance running demands stamina, mechanical drawing requires precision, steadiness, aiming, etc.

Stages of Skill Learning

A skill is not learned all of a sudden. It is learned through stages or phases. Fitts and Posner (1967) observed learners during practice, and also interviewed some skill instructors. As a result of their observation and interview, they distinguished three phases or stages of skill learning. These are:

The Early or Cognitive Phase,

The Intermediate or Associative Phase, and

The Final or Autonomous Phase.

(i) The Early or Cognitive Phase

The beginning learner attempts to understand the task and what it demands. The instructor provides verbal guidance directing the learner's attention to the proper sequence of actions, the procedure of performing the action and putting together the various parts. This phase is also called the phase of instruction and intellectualisation. The duration of this phase varies from learner to learner depending upon one's capacity to intellectualise the task.

(ii) The Intermediate or Associative Phase

This is the second stage of learning skills. During this stage, the learner practices the skill. He practices the individual sub-skills, puts together, associates or co-ordinates the various part skills into a meaningful pattern. This phase may last for days or months.

(iii) The Final or Autonomous Stage

During the final stage, the skill becomes autonomous which means it can be executed while the individual is engaged in some other activity like conversing. Improvements in smoothness and precision of the skill continue to take place gradually. During the second stage, outside activities may interfere with the learning of a skill. But in the final stage, the skill becomes automatic and thus outside activities do not interfere with the present performance.

These three stages are not unrelated and discontinuous. On the contrary, each stage depends on its preceding one. For example, improvement in performance depends on practice and practice depends on effective instruction.

Conditions of Skill Learning

Like any other learning, skill learning also depends on certain conditions. Gagne (1976) recognises certain internal conditions and certain external conditions necessary for skill learning.

(i) Internal Conditions

Recall of Part Skills: In learning a skill, the child must first learn and practice over the part-skills. In order that a total skill is learned, these component skills or part-skills must be recalled. Even the execution of a simple skill such as the drawing of a square by a child depends on recall of part-skills of holding the pencil and marking directional marks on paper.

Recall of Sequence: The execution of a motor skill involves a pattern of movements, a sequence of movements. The child must be able to recall the sequence of various movements so that smoothness and precision are acquired. A bowler, in a cricket match, must follow a procedure of positioning the ball, approaching the release line, selecting and aiming a point, imparting a twist to the ball, and so on.

(ii) External Conditions

Verbal Instructions: Verbal instructions have an important role in the early phase of learning. The instructor has to explain what to do and what procedures to follow before the child has practice over the skill. Verbal instructions help to increase the distinctiveness of various features of the skill.

Pictures: Movies and still pictures of the movements involved in a motor performance may serve functions similar to those of verbal instructions. Often pictures can accomplish these purposes more effectively than words can. For example, diagrams which depict for children the separate steps in the procedure of writing E may be more effective than a verbal instructional sequence.

Demonstration: Actual demonstrations of the execution of a motor performance can serve useful purposes. The learner must observe the demonstration of the steps in performing the act and engage in mental practices after watching a demonstration.

Practice: An essential external condition of skill learning is the provision for repeated practice of the motor performance. A motor skill is acquired in a gradual fashion. Increasing degrees of smoothness, timing, and precision of movement are acquired in successive practice periods. Practice may be distributed or massed practice. Whether the learner has distributed practice or continuous practice, the amount of practice is very important. It is better to have a period of no practice or rest in between successive practice periods.

Feedback: Practice contributes to learning only when learners receive feedback relating to their performance. Thus, one of the most important external conditions for the learning of a motor skill is the provision of informative feedback, providing reinforcement for the motor performance. It is better to provide knowledge of results to a learner immediately after or during the practice about his performance. For example, a child has drawn a square and may view it as perfectly good. Feedback can be given by comparison of his square with a printed square on a paper. The degree of precision of his drawing becomes immediately apparent only when he gets direct feedback from the teacher.

Teaching Skill

Skill learning has definite part to play in education. During the pre-school years and elementary grades, skills are involved in many personal and social activities. The child learns to manipulate clothing, articles, furniture and equipment, and other physical objects. In addition, painting, writing, drawing and pronunciation of language are essential motor skills which children need to learn. Earlier in this chapter, the skills pertinent to schools have been mentioned. The teacher has the following important role in the teaching of skills.

Preparation

(i) The teacher has to analyse the skill to be taught. He should break it down into sub-tasks or part-skills.

(ii) He should then try to determine the extent of student's preparation, previous knowledge and abilities in respect of the skill to be taught.

Instruction

(iii) Now the teacher has to start formal instruction. He must explain what to do and what procedure to follow. It is better to teach basic skills or part-skills first and then the complex skills which are built on the earlier part-skills.

(iv) The teacher can use relevant pictures and films to explain difficult skills.

(v) Actual demonstration of the skill or the part-skill by the teacher helps in understanding learning. The teacher may also demonstrate with the help of a student. It is better to demonstrate the total skill first, then the part-skills individually and again the total skill.

Practice

(vi) The teacher should allow sufficient practice for students. The students can either have distributed practice or continuous practice, but not too much of it. There should be rest periods in between practice trials.

(vii) The teacher should devise a variety of ways for practising the same skill.

(viii) During and after practice, the teacher should provide feedback to the students about how well they are doing. Feedback can eliminate errors and increase the smoothness and precision. Too much practice without feedback spoils the spirit of learning.

8. CONCEPT LEARNING

What is Meant by Concept?

A concept is a mental image about objects, events, phenomena, etc. formed by generalizations from particulars. Concepts involve the ability of persons to distinguish between objects so that they are classified as belonging or not belonging to a particular group of objects. A concept represents a class of stimuli which have common characteristics. These stimuli may be objects, events or animals. Thus, we have the concepts of 'Book,' 'Man,' 'Chair,' 'Teacher', etc. These concepts do not refer to a particular stimulus but a class of stimuli having certain common characteristics. The process by which we organise and classify stimuli, by which we come to perceive sets of stimuli as unified wholes and by which we come to put a number of instances into a category such as 'Chair' is called concept formation or concept learning.

Characteristics of Concept

(i) Concepts are generalizations. The individual must have experience with a large number of objects, events or people of the same type. He must find the common elements or attributes so that he classifies them and forms the concept.

(ii) Concepts are learned more effectively by proceeding from simple to complex. The individual should not rush into complex experiences with the concept until they have been exposed to more simple experiences.

(iii) A combination of abstract and concrete examples results in greater functional efficiency than the use of either alone.

Telling an individual about the common elements in any concept is unsatisfactory. The individual must have concrete experiences with the concept as well.

(iv) Concepts have three attributes such as size, shape, and colour. These distinctive features vary from concept to concept. Every attribute must have several values. For example, colour may be red, white, blue; shape may be rectangular, square, etc.; size may be small, large or medium. A particular concept may have attributes with two or three values. There are concepts which do not have these attributes, *e.g.*, kindness, honesty, etc.

(v) Concepts may be two-dimensional or three-dimensional. For example, 'Blue square' is two-dimensional as it has two attributes — colour and shape. Similarly, 'Orange' has four dimensions such as colour, size, shape and texture. Complex concepts are multidimensional. As the number of dimensions increase, the difficulty of learning the concept also increases.

(vi) Concepts may have dominant attributes or obscure attributes. Dominant attributes are more easily learnt than the obscure attributes. But the obscure attributes can be made clear through aural or visual emphasis by the teacher.

(vii) Concepts are symbolic for human beings. Words, numbers, chemical symbols have symbolic significance. For the chemist, the symbol 'O' is not just a circle; it represents the element 'Oxygen.' Sometimes objects have complex symbolic meaning such as the crucifix, a V sign, or road sign.

(viii) Concepts can be formed horizontally or vertically. An example of horizontal classification would be if we give children some example of reptiles — snakes, lizards, crocodiles. They all belong to the same major group of animals because they possess certain attributes in common. Vertical classification results from the province of hierarchies, that is, categories which increase in complexity as we proceed through the classification. A dog belongs to the family of animals called Canis, which is subordinate to the order of animals called Carnivore, which is subordinate to the class of animals called mammals, which in turn are *vertebrates*, which are *animals*. Thus higher order concepts or vertical classification of objects is very complicated.

(ix) Concepts function in at least two ways—extensionally and intentionally. When we form a concept we give a meaning to the object. When the meaning given is the widely acknowledged one or universal one, we call it the extensional use of concepts. Sometimes an individual gives a meaning as a result of his personal or subjective experiences. Here the meaning is not universally accepted but it has a personal significance. We call this the intentional use of concept. A botanist might view the plant from a technical standpoint, an artist from a creative, aesthetic angle.

Development of Concept

L. Vygotsky (1962), who made a fascinating study in Russia on more than 300 children, adolescents and adults concluded that concept formation occurs in the following three basic steps:

(i) A Syncretic Form of Thinking

The first step in concept formation occurs when children group a number of disparate objects without any basis. They thus unite diverse elements into one articulated image because of some chance impressions.

(ii) A Complex Form of Thinking

Individual objects are combined in child's mind, not only by personal chance selection, but because of bonds actually existing between these objects. During this step, the bonds between objects are concrete and factual rather than abstract and logical.

(iii) The Formation of Potential and True Concepts

During this step, the single attributes are abstracted, the true concept appears when abstracted attributes are synthesized and this synthesis becomes the chief instrument of thought.

Vygotsky summarizes his study by stating that the process that results in concept formation begins in earliest childhood, but that the intellectual functions necessary for concept formation develop and ripen only at puberty. Thus Vygotsky recognises the relationship between concept formation and the maturation process. Piaget also holds a similar viewpoint. His stages of cognitive development clearly indicate how the child proceeds from sensory-motor experiences to concrete experiences, to logical thinking in learning concepts.

Klausmeir and his associates (1974) conducted laboratory experiments and classroom studies of children from 4 to 15 years. Based on their findings, they formed a model of conceptual learning and development (CLD). They recognized that the ability of children to acquire concepts depends on both external (appropriate instructions) and internal conditions (maturation and learning). This CLD model traces concept attainment through four successively higher levels: Concrete, Identity, Classificatory and Formal.

***(i) Concrete Level*:** Concept attainment at the concrete level means that the individual recognizes an object previously encountered. For example, recognizing a red ball implies the cognitive operations of attending to the ball, discriminating it from other environmental objects, forming an image of it and then remembering the attributes.

***(ii) Identity Level*:** Concept attainment at the identity level means that the individual recognizes an object when viewed from a different perspective or sensed in a different modality. For example, you can recognise the sound of temple bell which you originally saw in the temple.

***(iii) Classificatory Level*:** Concept attainment at the classificatory level means that the individual can generalize that two or more things are somehow alike. For example, a young child treats a toy-dog and an actual dog as dogs. We say that the child has attained the concept of dog at a basic classificatory level. But at this level, the child cannot define the word that represents the concept nor can he explain the basis of his classification.

***(iv) Formal Level*:** Concept attainment at the formal level means that individuals can define both the name and the attributes of the concept. For example, when presented with examples of trees, shrubs, and herbs, they identify the trees, call them by name, define a tree's attributes, give an accepted definition of tree and explain how trees, shrubs, and herbs differ.

The four levels of concept attainment emerge in an invariant sequence. The attainment of a particular concept varies among children. The same children acquire different concepts at different rates.

Klausmeir and his associates state that environmental conditions influence concept attainment. Instructional conditions can facilitate conceptual development. Teachers should identify those concepts that students are to learn in a specific subject and decide at what level each student should attain them. This means that instruction must match conceptual level and the maturation level of each student.

Teaching Concepts or Helping Children to Learn Concepts

Bruner and others say that it is possible to teach young children complicated concepts in simple manner without waiting for a magic number of years to pass to bring the child to a stage of logical thinking. These concepts can be reintroduced in later years in a more and more complex fashion:

(i) Planning Individualised Instruction

Sometimes teachers notice that some children tend to be abstract thinkers while others remain more concrete in their thinking even in higher grades. This is due to individual differences in conceptual styles. Teachers must be aware of these differences and plan individualised instruction.

(ii) Providing Opportunities for Experience

Learning of concepts varies with opportunities for experiences both at home and in the school. Thus, there is need to expose the child to a wide variety of stimuli during his early years. Since the early years are the foundation years of life, lack of opportunities during these critical stages may lead to retardation in child's thinking abilities. Teachers and parents must provide multiple of materials for manipulation and subsequent discovery by the child.

(iii) Demonstration and Questioning

Questions to learners about how two or more items are related and teacher's demonstrations with various objects and materials are important means for helping learners to acquire concepts.

(iv) Teaching with Examples

Concepts can be taught by both inductive and deductive methods. A purely inductive process (teaching purely by examples) is called the EG-EG approach while a purely deductive process (giving the rule or definition several different ways) is known as RUL-RUL approach. But a combination of both processes is often more effective. That is to say, a teacher can teach concepts by EG-RUL approach (examples followed by rule) and RUL-EG approach (rule followed by examples). In either case, the teacher has to teach with examples.

(v) Presenting Examples with Non-examples

In teaching a concept by examples or by a combination of rules and examples, it is important to present examples with non-examples, so that the students can identify examples from non-examples. But the teacher should not show too few or too many different examples and non-examples as too few or too many make learning difficult.

(vi) Proceeding from Simple to Complex

To make concept easier to learn initially, teachers should reduce the number of dimensions or attributes both relevant and irrelevant. As teaching progresses, these various dimensions should be increased. In other words, teachers should proceed from simple to complex examples as learning progresses.

(vii) Proceeding from Concrete to Abstract

Other things being equal, it is advisable to begin with concrete examples and move towards more abstract examples as learning progresses.

(viii) Varying Irrelevant Dimensions

In teaching concepts by examples, irrelevant dimensions of the concept should be varied from one example to another, so that the relevant dimensions common to the examples may be identified more easily.

(ix) Encouraging Independent Learning

To teach concepts with examples and non-examples, the teacher can encourage passive learning or active learning on the part of students. But it is more effective to seek active learning by the students. Active learning which is an important element of independent learning/learning by discovery must always be accompanied by feedback. Even if the students are learning independently or by discovery, the teacher should provide some amount of guidance to them through giving hints, simplifying the examples, assisting them to some degree in answering and other ways.

(x) Part to Whole Teaching

To teach a concept, it is important for the teacher to make sure that learners understand sub-concepts which make it up and if they do not understand the sub-concepts, he should teach those first.

9. MOTIVATION

What is Motivation?

Every behaviour is said to be motivated. There is a motive behind all our actions, behaviour and functioning. Sometimes the motives are obvious, and at other times they are not apparent. The motives cannot be seen directly. They are inferred from our behaviour.

Motivation refers to the 'why' of behaviour or 'go' of personality. It means what one wants to do. What a person wants to do can be a powerful factor in achieving his goals. Motivation is a process of arousing, directing, maintaining and controlling one's interest in a certain activity. It is the stimulation of actions towards a particular goal where previously there was little or no attraction towards that goal. It means to push the right button to get a desired reaction.

Motivation varies in degrees. It may be low, moderate or intense. Different degrees of motivation may be required for different levels of complexity of the task. For example, simple tasks require intense motivations; complex tasks require moderate motivation. It is easy to distinguish between highly motivated students and those having low motivation.

Motivation does not arise from any single factor. It is a very complex process and refers to a combination of forces. We are motivated in different ways at different times and for different purposes. The techniques of motivation should vary accordingly.

Functions of Motivation

Motivation has four functions in learning:

(i) It energizes the child and thus it initiates activity.

(ii) It directs the child's activity. Not all goals satisfy all needs. Particular goals are selected because of the nature of the guiding motives.

(iii) It controls behaviour determining if the consequences are satisfactory which influence later performance.

(iv) It sustains activity when a goal is not immediately available. The crying behaviour of a baby can be taken as an example to justify each function of motivation.

Types of Motivation

Motivation is a combination of forces which may arise from within the individual or outside the individual, in the environment. Consequently there are two approaches to motivation: Intrinsic Motivation and Extrinsic Motivation. Intrinsic motivation refers to forces within the individual and is not tied to the environment. Curiosity, level of aspiration, the desire to earn a name and a fame are forces within the individual that motivate the individual to perform some task or behave in a manner. These internal motivators push the individual into action.

Extrinsic motivation refers to forces outside the individual which are tied with the environment. Usually extrinsic motivation is provided by incentives. For this purpose, extrinsic motivation is also called incentive motivation. Praise, blame, rewards, marks, competition and co-operation are examples of extrinsic motivation. Extrinsic motivation pulls the individual towards a goal. Intrinsic motivation should be the goal of the teacher. But intrinsic motivation is very difficult to achieve. Teachers very rarely get children who are intrinsically motivated to learn. Thus they make use of some techniques of extrinsic motivation.

Techniques of Classroom Motivation

Motivation of behaviour is a complex phenomenon. It is one thing to motivate subjects in controlled laboratory experiments and it is another thing to motivate children in classrooms. Teachers should keep in mind the following guidelines for motivation in school:

(i) Motivation affects all aspects or behaviour — perception and attention, remembering and forgetting, problem-solving and creativity, learning and performance.

(ii) Intense motivation seems to facilitate learning simple tasks; moderate motivation aids learning complex tasks. This is called the Yerkes-Dodson Law, which states that ideal motivation for learning decreases with increasing task difficulty.

(iii) Motivation varies from child to child and in the same child at different times. Thus the teacher cannot be effective if he applies the same technique for all children and at all times.

(iv) There are definite sex differences in motivation. It is a fact that girls in elementary classes have more positive motivation than boys. It may be due to a predominant female influence during elementary stage.

(v) Motivation is linked to social class. Disadvantaged children have less motivation for academic learning than those more affluent.

(vi) Motivation to learn is enduring. While it is not fixed, motivation changes slowly. It is for this reason that the eager youngster is not easily discouraged — the reluctant scholar does not change overnight.

(vii) There is optimal motivation for individuals. Everyone has a personal, ideal, motivational level; beyond this, learning deteriorates. Thus too much motivation is bad; too little is undesirable.

(viii) Unmotivated students are easily distinguishable. Their arousal is limited, perhaps minimal, their behaviour is extinguished before objectives are attained, their attention is directed elsewhere and energy dissipated; the learning process had failed.

(ix) There are various techniques of motivation. But a combination of techniques is more effective than any single technique.

Curiosity: The Need to Explore and Manipulate

Teachers should not ignore the relationship between children's curiosity and their learning. Young children have a natural desire to explore the environment, to manipulate objects and learn about the environment. Teachers can create favourable opportunities so that children can satisfy their curiosity. Curiosity is an internal force that moves children to learn in school and outside.

Achievement Motivation: The Need to Achieve Excellence

Achievement motivation is also an internal force that motivates students to master challenging and difficult tasks and to derive satisfaction from their performance. It means a need a person feels within himself, to compete against an internal standard of excellence. In short, it means the pursuit of excellence. Students who have high achievement motivation work hard and perform well on tasks. Teachers must, therefore, encourage students to want to achieve. The need to achieve depends, among other things, on the probability of success and the incentive value of success. Thus, the learning situation should be so structured that every student will have a chance of success and that all success must be reinforced immediately.

Level of Aspiration: The Need to Meet One's Own Expectations

Every individual has certain goals. In many cases, these goals are of the immediate type which he reasonably expects to meet. Other goals will be of a long-range variety and attainment may be less sure. The success an individual has in reaching goals probably influences the future goals he sets. Thus, Kolesnik writes, "One's level of aspiration pertains to the goals he sets for himself, the amount and quality of work he believes he can do and is willing to try to do".

Level of aspiration is an intrinsic motivational variable in the classroom. Students establish expectations which may affect performance. Certainly, success or failure in performance appears to determine the expectations set. Children who have experienced success set realistic goals. Children who experience failure frequently set either too high or too low goals.

Level of aspiration is set informally by the student and formally by the teacher. Teachers should help students set goals which are neither too low nor too high, but realistic enough to be attainable.

Self-fulfilling Prophecy

Teacher's behaviour and expectations are motivating factors in school learning. A teacher may motivate children to learn more or perform better through his behaviour and expectations. A teacher may say to a child, "I expect that you will solve the problem," and the child may actually solve it. Some teachers expect a poor performance from some students and these students actually perform poorly on a given task. Research findings reveal that student's performances on task are simply attempts at fulfilling the expectations of the teachers for them individually. If teachers expect more, if they provide the help, time and material to learn more, most students can learn excellently.

Developing Interests

Interest corresponds to intrinsic motivation. A child is said to be interested in an activity, when his motives for engaging in that activity come from within himself. For example, if he is truly interested in music, no one has to motivate him to listen to it. But interests are not innate. They are acquired. A child is not born with an interest in sports or science. He learns to be interested in these fields. A child's existing interests, in turn, have an effect on his acquisition of new interests. Thus, interests can be thought of as both causes and effects of learning. Just as they are the products of previous learning so are they also a means of facilitating future learning. One of the things that teachers are expected to do is to make school work interesting.

Developing interest in a subject is primarily a matter of helping the student see how the learning material relates to him as an individual. The student must be helped to discover how the material can serve his purposes, how it can help to satisfy his needs, how it can help him directly or indirectly to fulfil his ambition to become a complete person. When the student realizes that learning is a means towards the achievement of his goal, he will be interested in and motivated towards learning it.

Competition and Co-operation

Competition has been widely used by teachers as a means of motivation towards scholastic achievement. Students have been encouraged to compete with one another to win some prize or to receive the highest grade in the examination. Competition has been regarded as a means for the students to satisfy their need for recognition or esteem. Sometimes students work as part of a team and compete with other teams. This is usually known as group competition. But several studies indicate that individual competition is better than group competition. Despite the tremendous utility in motivating scholastic achievement, objections have been raised about the possibility of adverse side-effects of competition on the personality development of children. Competition is especially harmful for slow learners. It contributes to feelings of superiority, selfishness or vanity on the part of winners or successful students, and frustration, discouragement and feeling of inferiority on the part of poor students. Moreover, competition also causes bitterness, jealousy and even hostility among the competitors. Thus while excessive pressure to achieve under highly competitive circumstances can be injurious to the students, self-concept as well as their scholastic progress and social relationship, a learning situation with no element of competition at all might be boring and ineffective. A middle of the road view is to encourage self-competition in which a student tries to surpass his own past performance or compete with his own pervious achievement. In self-competition, the student is not subject to unfavourable comparisons with others. Every student has a chance to achieve some degree of success. His abilities are taken into account, his self-concept is not threatened and he is permitted to advance at his own rate. Cooperation among students is better than competition among them. Encouraging small group discussion, team work and peer tutoring have motivating effects on learners.

Incentives

Although intrinsic motivation is most effective, it is very difficult and sometimes impossible for the teacher to manipulate it. Very often, teacher's efforts towards arousing and maintaining interest, developing curiosity or setting realistic goals do not bear fruits. Thus teachers probably want to use some sort of incentives.

Incentives correspond to outer direction and extrinsic motivation. They are means which are employed to induce a person to do something that he otherwise would not do, or would not do as well. Among the more common classroom incentives are grades and progress reports or feedback, prizes, honours, special privileges, rewards, approval, etc. These are also known as positive reinforcers. Negative reinforcers such as threat of failure, punishment, scolding and disapproval also serve as incentives. In most cases, students do not and will not learn for the sake of learning or for their interest in the learning material or to reach a remote goal. Of course, teachers should make effort to develop in their students an interest in the material to be learned. But in addition, they can also foster an interest in the incentives they are able to provide. Thus, they can motivate their students towards scholastic achievement indirectly when they are unable to do so directly.

(a) *Grades and Threat of Failure*

Most teachers try to motivate children by promising good grades or by the threat of failure. Promising good grades or the threat of failure may result in immediate achievement. But their ultimate outcomes are dissatisfying. Thus, grades and the threat of failure are not good motivational strategies.

(b) *Rewards and Punishment/Praise and Blame/Approval and Disapproval*

Rewards and punishments, praise and blame, approval and disapproval are the oldest motivational devices known to mankind. But on the whole, praise, reward and approval are more effective than their opposites as means of motivating students towards scholastic achievement. Students who are regularly and systematically rewarded for their good work or for improvement in the quality of their work tend to do better than those who are blamed or criticised or punished for their poor work. Frequent punishment and anxiety-producing threats have been found to inhibit rather than promote learning.

(c) *Feedback*

Providing feedback or knowledge of results to the students strengthens their motive to achieve success and also supplies the needed information so that an intended act may be completed. Periodical tests should be conducted at the end of a course and feedback should be provided to the student about his progress. The student should also be helped to correct his deficiencies in learning by re-learning the material adopting different methods and procedures.

10. TRANSFER OF LEARNING

What is Transfer of Learning?

At all levels of education, teachers expect students to transfer what they learn in one subject to another and from what they learn in school to their activity out of school. Traditional education developed in order to prepare a person for his role in later life and this is still important today. Teachers expect and hope that what they teach in their subjects will prove of benefit to the child when studying another subject. A mathematics teacher hopes that mathematics learned by the student will be useful to him when studying a science such as physics. This is referred to as lateral transfer. Similarly, a teacher in the infant school who teaches a child to read expects him to be able to use this skill in all other subjects throughout his later school life. This is referred to as vertical transfer. Students in the secondary schools expect that much of what is taught to them should be of value when they leave school. This naturally does not mean that they should be taught how to cope with each individual problem they might have to deal with in later life, as this would be an impossible task. Nevertheless, they should be taught the basic principles from which they will be able to transfer their knowledge to the problems they are likely to meet.

Transfer of learning is an important variable in learning. Transfer concerns how previous experience influences the acquisition of some specific material. It means carry-over of learning experiences from one situation to another. This effect of one learning upon another may be positive or negative. Consequently, there may be positive transfer or negative transfer.

Positive Transfer and Negative Transfer

Positive transfer occurs when prior learning facilitates subsequent learning. In other words, if what is learned in one situation helps one's performance in another situation, positive transfer is said to have occurred. For example, learning addition facilitates the learning of 'multiplication,' playing badminton helps in the learning of tennis. Sometimes what is learned in one situation may interfere with what is learned in another situation. Negative transfer of learning occurs when previous learning interferes with new learning. For example, a driver who has been trained in right-hand driving is prone to difficulty and accidents when he tries for left-hand driving. A sportsman experiences hindrance in trying to learn a second style of swimming after mastering one style. Thus, when the second task possesses content or requires procedures in conflict with the first tasks, negative transfer is likely to occur.

Theories of Transfer

One of the quarrels of the educational theorists concerns the extent to which special forms of training improve the general capacities of the mind. Does the study of mathematics improve one's general reasoning powers? Does laboratory work in science train the power of observation for all sorts of facts? How far does the training of any mental function improve other mental functions? Some educational theorists also ask, "Is transfer automatic?" Thus, the real question is, "To what extent and how does transfer take place?" We shall examine several theories of transfer to answer these questions:

(i) *Theory of Mental Discipline*

There was a belief among psychologists and teachers that some school subjects act as a training ground for exercising mental skills. For these psychologists, the mind is a unit and the faculties are simply phases or manifestations of its activity. Thus whatever strengthens one faculty indirectly strengthens all the others. This view became known as the doctrine of formal training or mental discipline. This view was maintained by a group of psychologists called faculty psychologists. Thus, mathematics was thought to develop children's powers of reasoning. Science was seen as training children to be observant; learning historical or geographical facts was thought to exercise the memory. These views are no longer held by the majority of psychologists and teachers today. This theory originated with the philosopher Wolff in 1734.

During the era when formal discipline theory was dominant, difficult courses comprised the curriculum both for the exercise that they provided for the various mental faculties and their supposed transfer value. But at the beginning of twentieth century as more and more psychologists questioned the formal discipline approach of learning, several studies were made that demonstrated that there was little actual transfer from geometry to general reasoning or from language to memory. These later studies did not accept the fact that transfer was automatic. The three psychologists who did the most to disprove the effects of formal discipline in relation to transfer of learning were William James, Edward Throndike (1906) and Charles Judd (1908).

William James started the first experimental work on this problem. He wanted to find out whether practices in memorising really improved one's memory powers in general. He conducted the experiment on himself. He tried to memorise 150 lines from one of the works of Victor Hugo. He noted the time taken to memorise the lines. Then he memorised Milton's 'Paradise Lost'. After mastering 'Paradise Lost' in about a month he tried to memorise other 150 lines of Victor. He found that this took more time than for learning the first 150 lines. From this he concluded that practice in memorising did not improve his memory power.

(ii) ***Theory of Identical Elements***

Thorndike also conducted many experiments under scientific conditions to test the hypothesis of formal discipline theory. As a result of his experiments in 1906, Thorndike concluded that "spread of practice occurs only where identical elements are concerned in the influenced functions." In other words, positive transfer occurs only when identical elements are present in the two learning situations. Later, these identical elements were called identities of substance (Matter) and identities of procedure (Method). For example, geography helps history because maps are common to both. Addition improves multiplication because multiplication is largely addition. Writing and spelling learned in connection with any subject transfer to all others in which writing and spelling are used. However, Thorndike found that the greater the number of these common elements, the greater will be the transfer effect.

Thorndike's work on transfer of training provided an entirely new basis for curriculum planning. No longer could subjects be included in the curriculum because of a belief that the subjects provide specific skills, knowledge, or understanding, in short, a general training for the various faculties of the mind.

(iii) *Theory of Generalisation*

Judd, through his theory of generalization, presented a different picture about positive transfer. Judd demonstrated that positive transfer would occur in so far as the individual is capable of forming generalization about principles or methods and to the extent of his success in applying his generalization to the new situation. In one experiment, one group of subjects was taught the principles of refraction and a second group was not given this instruction. Both the groups were required to hit an underwater target at different positions. It was found that the group which received knowledge about the principles of refraction was more successful in hitting the underwater target at different positions than the other group which had no such previous knowledge. Judd concluded that the first group experienced success because the subjects were capable of applying generalizations to a new but similar situation.

(iv) *Theory of Transposition*

A further refinement of the generalization theory is that of transposition. As an outgrowth of Gestalt theory, transfer is accounted for by the student's understanding of the structure or pattern of the problem. When the individual perceives, not only the facts or principles in any problem but also the relationship of facts to principles and principles to goals, then transfer occurs.

Modern psychologists do not accept the theory of formal discipline. They stress more on the application of learning experiences to new situations. John Dewey, probably the foremost American educator in the first half of the last century, stressed substantially this idea of applicability in his curriculum revisions and emphasis on 'learning by doing.' The Montessori approach to pre-school and primary education also emphasises learning through application. Increasingly today's students demand relevancy in their education. They want to be able to transfer the information and techniques learned in the classroom to the practical situations of everyday life. However, one to one transferability is virtually impossible because we do not know what problems any one will have to solve tomorrow and we possibly cannot teach solutions to all of todays. Despite such practical problems, however, it is obvious that the emphasis in curriculum design has been shifted from the formal discipline approach to one in which the applicability of one subject to another is demonstrated and stressed.

Conditions for Attaining Maximum Transfer

Principles of Transfer

A lot of research has been directed towards finding the conditions most necessary for transfer.

(i) *Similarity in Contents and Procedures*
As has been suggested earlier, transfer is clearly affected by the similarity in the content or in the procedures adopted in carrying out the two tasks. We can expect more transfer when the training task and the criterion task resemble each other in their overall characteristics. For example, the content of mathematics is useful in the solution of problems in physics. Some of the procedures of mathematics are helpful in statistics. Similarly, there is greater possibility of positive transfer in physical skills involving similar procedures.

(ii) *Amount of Practice*
A second condition for attaining maximum positive transfer is the amount of practice on the training task. The more thoroughly the first task is learnt, the more likely it is that transfer will occur.

For example, the more thoroughly and completely we memorise one list of nonsense syllables, the more likely we are to use that mastery in learning a similar list of nonsense syllables.

(iii) *Proceeding from Easy to Hard Tasks*

Another condition which affects the amount of positive transfer is the relative difficulty of training task. There is more transfer, for instance, from the learning of poetry to the learning of nonsense syllables than in the reverse direction. This comes from the fact that learning poetry is easier or that it is more natural to learn poetry than to learn nonsense syllables. There is some evidence that it makes no difference whether we go from easy to hard or from hard to easy task. But Lowrence and Goodwill claim an absolute advantage for practice on an easier training task. They found that those who had practiced on the easier task and then transfer to the difficult task were able, even on the first trial, to surpass those who had been practicing on the more difficult task itself. This reveals another possibility that the training task, whether difficult or easy, must permit some measure of success for the learner. Since difficult tasks in general prevent success, it is advisable to proceed from easy to hard tasks.

(iv) *Length of Training*

Length of training also has a long-term effect on transfer. For example, a person who has concentrated his efforts on science subjects at school and college levels may find that objectivity and conciseness begin to permeate into other aspects of his life requiring the assembly and dissemination of knowledge.

(v) *Generalization of Experience*

Generalization of experiences is an important condition for maximum transfer. The learner must be able to generalise his experiences and to apply them to a new but similar situation. This means that the learner must be able to develop insight into the new problem. In order that insight or generalization will occur, some verbalisation is necessary prior to its application.

(vi) *Intellectual Ability*

Intelligence has long been assumed to be an important factor in transfer, because it is found that intelligent children and adults are more likely to spot the relationship between tasks.

Related Teacher Behaviour or Teaching Strategies for Transfer

The amount of transfer induced can be increased by the method of teaching used. Although no set of principles can be expected to apply to all conditions, there are a few very general rules that cover a fairly wide range of situations:

(i) *Bring out the Feature to be Transferred:* The thing to be transferred from one experience to another may be a fact, a method, a general principle, an attitude or a way of life. In any case, the students must be made aware of the possibility of transfer.

(ii) *Develop Meaningful Generalization:* Transfer is more likely to occur when the thing to be transferred is a generalization or a rule that can be understood. There is some suggestion that it is better for the students themselves to work out this principle or formulate the rule or describe the essential method or approach. Of course, some verbalisation by the teacher is necessary to help students generalise or formulate the rule. But too much verbalisation may actually reduce the amount of transfer. In any case, it is important for the teacher to examine the generalisations suggested by the student and to suggest further exercises if those generalisations are not acceptable.

(iii) *Provide a Variety of Experiences*: Whenever it is a principle or generalization that is to be transferred, it is most important to use a variety of experiences to develop generalisation.

(iv) *Practice in Application in Other Fields*: Not only should the element to be transferred be brought into clear focus and, if possible, formulated and clearly structured, but it should also be applied to fields outside the subject-matter of the lesson. Contemporary research seems to indicate that learning will be more functional or relevant if it is originally presented with as many applications as possible. This application must be made from one subject to another and from school subject to out of school life.

(v) *Practice in Transfer*: There is some hope that, just as students can learn to learn, so they may have some success in learning to transfer. One experience of successful transfer may enable a student to extract more transfer from his next experience. This leads to another but a fundamental approach to transfer.

(vi) *Ascertain the Past Experience*: The teacher should ascertain as far as possible the past experience of children in relation to the new material he intends to teach. This will probably vary considerably and his approach will have to be modified for different groups of children. Thus, if one wishes to introduce a class to the division of fractions, this will be pointless if the children had not previously dealt with and understood the division of whole numbers and multiplication of fractions.

11. REMEMBERING AND FORGETTING REMEMBERING

What is Remembering?

Remembering plays an important part in our daily life. Our life becomes richer because we are able to remember past experiences which have made living pleasant and enjoyable. Our development as human beings depends to a large extent on how much we learn about our environment. Remembering plays an important part in this process of learning.

Remembering means that the effects of learning have been retained for a period of time and made available for subsequent behaviour. The effects of learning are retained in the form of memory traces in the brain. Memory traces are like impressions or marks established in the brain. Once these impressions are established, they need not necessarily continue to exist in their original form. Changes in these traces may occur and even many such traces disappear or get mutilated due to various reasons. Due to these changes in the memory traces, we fail to remember what was learned previously. We are said to have forgotten them. Thus the reverse of remembering is forgetting. Forgetting, in other words, means failure to remember what was learned previously.

According to the information processing model, information or the material first reaches the short-term-memory in the form of input. While in STM, the input must be processed in some way before it is passed on to the long-term-memory. While in STM, the input must be properly coded, rehearsed or given a meaning. Successfully coded information goes to the LTM and it remains there so that we can recall the information when we need it. In other words, we retain or remember that information which is properly coded and rehearsed. Information which is not properly coded while in STM is not allowed to go to the LTM. This is lost or forgotten.

Even when the information remains in the LTM we can recall it with the help of 'cues,' or reminders. These cues or reminders are sometimes not readily available to us as a result of which we fail to recall the information. We say that we have forgotten it. After an initial effort we may be able to recall the 'cues' and consequently the information. Thus, forgetting may take place either at the STM level due to lack of coding or rehearsal or at the LTM level due to unavailability of the 'cues' or reminders.

The process of remembering has four aspects such as learning, retention, recall and recognition.

Learning

Learning precedes remembering; remembering depends on learning. So there cannot be any remembering without learning. Learning is a general term which means profiting from life's experiences. The term 'learning' includes both verbal learning and motor learning. We learn verbal materials like words, prose pieces, etc. These are examples of verbal learning. We learn them with the purpose of memorising them. Learning to ride a cycle, typing, etc. are examples of motor learning. We learn meaningful materials and meaningless materials. Generally, meaningful materials are learnt better than meaningless materials like nonsense syllables. A nonsense syllable is a three-letter word which begins with a consonant and ends with a consonant. There is a vowel in between the two consonants. PIQ, XUZ are nonsense syllables. It must be remembered that anything that is learnt better is remembered well. There are various methods of learning or memorising. We shall discuss some of the economical methods of memorising later.

Retention

Retention follows learning. When what was learnt is preserved or stored in the brain, we say that retention has occurred. Retention, in other words, means permanence of what was learnt. Learning is an active process. So also retention is an active process. This comes from the fact that the material is retained when we are not at all thinking about it or even when we are in sleeping state. Had it been a passive process we would have forgotten the learnt material during sleep. Actually a great deal of mental activity goes on in connection with the process of retention. As we have discussed earlier, the material that is learnt is retained in the brain in the form of memory trace or impressions. So it is the memory trace of the learnt material that is being retained. If due to some reason, the memory trace fades away or disappears forgetting takes place. In later sections of this chapter, we will discuss the causes of forgetting and the methods of measuring retention.

Recall

We learn things in order to recall them at the time of necessity. If we fail to recall a material, it would mean that learning has not been efficient. Some people believe that when we fail to recall a material, it would mean that there is no retention. This is wrong. Rightly speaking without retention there cannot be recall. But there can be retention without recall. So failure to recall some lines or words should not always mean that there has been no retention. For example, you are enacting the role of prince or princess in your college drama. While enacting the role, you suddenly fail to recall some lines or words. Does it mean that the lines or words have not been retained? Actually you have memorised the lines perfectly during rehearsal. But due to some reasons like emotional factors or over consciousness, you failed to recall these lines at the time of need. After a few seconds you may be able to recall them. So failure to recall does not always mean that there has been no retention. Recall is affected by a number of factors and poor retention is only one such factor. When there has been perfect retention but we fail to recall the material, it is known as "recall amnesia." On the contrary when retention is very poor and so there is no recall, it is known as "retention amnesia."

Recognition

The fourth aspect of remembering is recognition. Recognition is related to recall. In recall, the learnt materials are not presented before us. We have to reproduce them from our memory. In recognition the process is different. The subject first learns a certain material, say a list of 10 words in a given order and sequence. Then after an interval of few minutes or hours or even months, the original words are shuffled and presented to the subject in a random manner along with some new words. The subject will be required to recognise the words that he learnt previously. In some cases, hundred per cent recognition may not be possible. Because recognition, like recall, is affected by a number of factors like attitude, set, emotional factors and motives of the subject. Recognition also depends on learning. Anything that has been learnt well will also be recognised easily.

However, all these four aspects of remembering are closely related to one another. Learning is closely related to retention. Retention is related to recall. Similarly recognition is related to recall.

Methods of Measuring Retention

Psychologists have developed certain methods for measuring the amount of material retained after learning. We have four such methods. These methods are:

(i) Recall Method,
(ii) Re-learning Method or Saving Method,
(iii) Recognition Method, and
(iv) Reconstruction Method.

Recall Method

We remember a certain material with the purpose of recalling it at the time of necessity. The amount that we are able to recall is certainly an indication of what has been retained. So the method of recall is a very direct method of testing retention. In the ordinary easy type of examination, recall method is used to test retention. The questions are so asked that the student has to recall or reproduce anything that he knows about it. This method is also known as the method of reproduction.

Re-learning Method

This method is also called 'the method of saving.' If you learned a particular assignment, it may happen that after six months you may be able to recall a part of it or nothing at all. Suppose, it took you 10 repetitions to learn that assignment during the first time and suppose now after two months you require only 5 repetitions to learn the same matter. This would mean that there has been 50% saving or gain at this second period of learning. This also means that there has been 50% retention. The saving must have been due to the retention of what has been learnt. The formula for finding the saving score is as follows:

$$\text{Saving Score} = \frac{(\text{Original Trials} - \text{Re-learning Trial})}{\text{Original Trials}} \times 100$$

Recognition Method

By this method it is tested whether a subject can recognise some particular material as having been learnt before. The act of recognition is definitely easier than the act of recall. In recent years, the method of testing retention by recognition is becoming more popular. The modern type of examination questions are based on this method of recognition. The student has to recognise the correct answer which is presented along with wrong answers. Either in the true — false type of questions or in the 'multiple choice' type of questions, the principle is the same. By the ability to recognise the familiar material or correct answer, the subject's retention of the material is tested. The formula for finding the recognition score is as follows :

$$\text{Recognition Score} = \frac{(\text{Right} - \text{Wrong})}{\text{Total}} \times 100$$

Reconstruction Method

Sometimes a fourth method is also mentioned by some psychologists to measure retention. This method is known as the method of reconstruction or rearrangement. But this method is used when we want to test a person's memory for a serial learning. The subject first learns a material in a serial order. Later the various items are all jumbled up and presented in a different order and the subject will be required to rearrange them in the original order.

Principles of Memorising

Learning or memorising is the first step in remembering. Attempts have been made to discover the most efficient principles of memorising. Some of these principles are discussed below:

(i) *Distributed Practice and Massed Practice*

Distributed practice and massed practice are the two common methods of learning. These two methods are also known as spaced practice and unspaced practice. Some students try to master the assignment at one continuous sitting. Others try to distribute their practice over a period of time with intervals of rest. The method of memorising the material at one continuous sitting is usually called the method of massed practice. The other method of memorising in which the material is learnt with intervals is usually called the method of 'distributed practice.' The question that is usually raised is: "Is distributed practice better than massed practice?" Several researches have been conducted on this issue. One such study is by C.I. Holland (1938) on learning of nonsense syllables using distributed practice and massed practice. All studies indicate that distributed practice is better than massed practice.

Why is distributed practice better than massed practice? Various explanations can be offered for this fact:

(a) When there are intervals between the attempts at learning, the learning process that has been set in motion at first goes on working below the threshold of awareness and thus fixing more durably whatever has been learnt.

(b) If learning a long assignment is attempted at one sitting naturally the factor of fatigue sets in. Intervals of rest reduce the fatigue.

(c) In a continuous sitting for a fairly long time, the 'law of diminishing returns' is bound to operate. Motivation for learning cannot be kept at a high level throughout the period.

(d) In distributed practice, interference of materials learned previously and those learned subsequently will be less.

When the learner takes intervals, such intervals should not be very short or too long. Moreover, if the materials are highly meaningful, then spaced practice will not be so much essential.

(ii) *Whole Learning and Part Learning*

In whole learning the learner memorises the task as one whole unit without separate attention to its parts. By contrast, in part learning the learner divides the lesson into parts and memorises each part separately. It is found that in general the whole method is more advantageous than the part method. But actually the appropriateness of the methods depends upon the nature of the material and the learner himself. Younger children or children with low intellectual development will learn faster with the part method. Similarly, when the material is long and difficult, part method is more economical. When an assignment is neither too long nor too difficult, whole learning is generally advantageous.

Why is whole learning superior to part learning? When we study the material as a whole, the material becomes meaningful and the significance can be grasped. Learning thus becomes easier. Dividing the material into parts may sometimes become artificial, spoiling the general meaning. Even if we study the material by part, the material must be divided carefully and meaningfully. If the material is really too difficult, part method gives greater confidence and enthusiasm. Sometimes a combination of whole learning and part learning will prove beneficial.

(iii) *Repetition and Recitation*

Repetition is another method of memorising materials. It has been experimentally proved that the more we repeat, the better will be the retention. Even after one gets a feeling of mastery over an assignment, it is advantageous to repeat the lessons for a few times more. Such extra amount of repetition is usually called 'over learning.' Over learning gradually reduces forgetting that would ordinarily take place. Over learning or repetition up to a certain point is useful from the point of view of retention. But beyond a certain point, over learning becomes uneconomical and does not produce proportionate advantage.

Recitation or review is also another method of memorising. One must review or recite to himself whatever material has been learnt. Recitation or review makes learning more efficient, quicker and permanent. It gives a certain amount of confidence, and ensures more concentration and attention on the material that is being memorised.

(iv) *Meaningful Learning/Rote Learning*

When a student learns or memorises a certain material by using the method of repetition without paying attention to its meaning or significance, he is adopting the method of rote learning. But mere repetition without paying any attention to the meaning will often prove to be a very inefficient way to learning. Materials so learned cannot be remembered for long. Thus, meaningful learning is more advantageous. In meaningful learning, the learner first understands the relationship between the different parts of the material itself. He then relates the meaning and the significance of the material with other things that he has learnt previously.

However, in learning or memorising a certain material, the learner must have a will to learn. But along with this will to learn, he must have a desire to remember. If the learner has a will to learn but no desire to remember, then he can learn the material but he soon forgets it. For this purpose, the learner must have a will to remember what he learns. The learner must have positive attitude and bias towards the contents of the material to be learned.

FORGETTING

Causes of Forgetting

Learning usually implies a relatively permanent change in behaviour that results from practice or activity. It involves a three-step sequence of initial acquisition, retention, and use or transfer. When children, for example, correctly spell a word or solve a problem for the first time, we say that they have then acquired the particular behaviour. If the same children correctly repeat the performance later, we say that they have remembered or retained what they acquired earlier. Transfer occurs when whatever is learned in one situation is used in a new or different situation. In a way, transfer depends upon retention. But in between acquisition and retention, certain factors operate to reduce the amount of retention. They fail to remember what they have learned earlier. They forget some amount of learned materials.

If you try to remember everything that happened during 5th, 12th, 16th, or 20th year of your life, you certainly cannot recall everything. But why have you forgotten so much? There are various explanations, none of which is completely satisfactory in itself.

(i) *Time*

Time has been recognised as an important cause of forgetting. With passage of time we tend to forget some amount of the learnt materials. But the rate of forgetting is not directly proportional to the time elapsed. In other words, if half the material learnt was forgotten during the first 24 hours, it does not mean that during another period of 24 hours the entire material would be forgotten. One of the earliest experiments on this problem was conducted by Ebbinghaus in 1885. On the basis of his

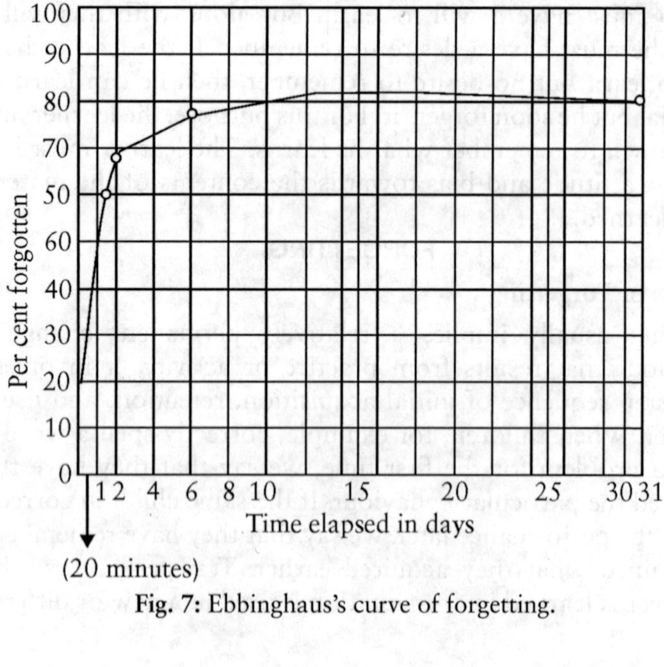

Fig. 7: Ebbinghaus's curve of forgetting.

finding, Ebbinghaus obtained a curve, which came to be called 'the curve of forgetting' or 'curve of retention.' He found that about 47 per cent of the material is forgotten within the first 20 minutes, 6 per cent within the first 24 hours, 75 per cent within 6 days, and 79 per cent in a month. Thus forgetting is very rapid in the initial period and as time lapses, the rate of forgetting becomes slower and slower.

It is possible that when we learn something, the memory traces that are formed take some time to get fixed or stabilised or consolidated.

Any activity during this time of consolidation disturbs that process and hence the memory traces. Thus psychologists now argue that time is definitely an important cause, but it is not the only cause of forgetting. What happens during the lapses of time may explain forgetting.

(ii) *Disuse*

When something is learned and used repeatedly, it is remembered, but when it is not used, it is forgotten. This explanation in terms of disuse suggests deterioration or decay of the connections in the brain as the reason for forgetting. Disuse is not satisfactory as the sole explanation, for we do not seem to forget while we are asleep. While we are awake there is a constant stream of new experience that would seem to produce interference and this results in forgetting.

(iii) *Interference*

Interference of present learning with what has been learned on other occasions leads to forgetting. When subsequent learning interferes with retention of previously learnt material, such interference is called 'retroactive inhibition.' Another kind of interference works in the opposite direction. Sometimes initial learning interferes with subsequent learning, as a result of which retention of the subsequent materials becomes weak and forgetting of such materials occurs. This phenomenon is called 'proactive inhibition.' Retroactive inhibition and proactive inhibition can be studied, for example, in the following two situations:

Retroactive inhibition		
Learn List A	Learn List B	Recall List A
Proactive inhibition		
Learn List A	Learn List B	Recall List B

(iv) ***Reorganisation***

Klausmeir and Goodwin (1975) argue that we may initially learn certain material or a skill, but do not learn it well and do not use it for sometime. We then need to use it, and in the process of recall, reorganise what we had previously acquired into some new patterns that make sense to us now. For example, we may have learned to spell 'believe,' but did not write it again for several weeks until we needed the word in writing a story. In the active reorganising process to meet the present situation, an incorrect spelling 'beleive' was accepted.

(v) ***Motivated Forgetting***

Sometimes we are motivated to forget something. Generally most human beings try to forget unpleasant experiences but are not successful; others sometimes forget so completely that 'amnesia' occurs. Amnesia means inability to recall past experiences which is not associated with any known damage to the brain or the central nervous system. In daily affairs, there is also some suggestion of motivated forgetting. Some adults forget appointments that will be unpleasant. Motivated forgetting may also occur in relation to school learning if the events surrounding the learning experiences are unpleasant for the student.

Although the basis of forgetting are not fully understood, the teacher or parents should not immediately conclude that children are deliberately lying when they say they forgot an appointment or forgot to carry out some activity. Such forgetting might have been actually motivated. Usually certain experiences involving guilt, shame, or frustration are repressed in the unconscious layer of the mind. As a result of this process of repression, the child fails to recall these experiences and we say that the child is motivated to forget these experiences.

At times, forgetting may take place which is caused by factors other than the ones we have discussed so far. For example, forgetting or complete amnesia may occur due to the severe injury to the brain or severe emotional shock.

Improving Retention: Role of the Teacher

Sometimes parents ask teachers to suggest ways of improving the memory power of their children. Even some parents seek the advice of doctors for possible capsules or tonic for improving the memory powers of their sons and daughters. Some children also tell that they are not able to remember dates, names of places or sequence of events. Some teachers are upset when they find that the students are not able to remember all that has been taught to them. Are there really any readymade ways of improving retention?

Retention depends on learning. Thus, the capacity to retain can never be improved in any appreciable manner other than by improving the methods of learning. Learning in schools is the result of systematic and sensitive instruction by the teacher. It is logical and psychological to assume that since retention depends on learning, and learning depends on instruction, retention can be improved by systematic instruction and effective guidance to children to improve learning. The teacher has to adopt the following strategy to systematise his instruction and ensure efficient learning by children so that their retention can be improved:

(i) The teacher should make children aware of the relationship between learning and retention. He should expect and develop in them a desire to learn well and remember.

(ii) He should make his teaching effective and their learning meaningful.

(iii) He should use the multi-sensory approach in the teaching — learning process to make his teaching more effective and thereby to ensure efficient learning by children.

(iv) He should make his teaching concrete. He should use pictures, recordings, spoken words and real objects. Children should be given the opportunity to touch, smell, manipulate and get a direct impression about concepts he is presenting.

(v) He should increase the intensity of what is given to the child. He should make it bigger, louder, more colourful, more imaginative, more exciting, and more interesting.

(vi) He should use different methods and materials to excite the child with stimulating experiences.

(vii) He should involve the child more actively in teaching — learning process.

(viii) While presenting his lesson he should emphasize important concepts and principles.

(ix) He should move sequentially in a step-by-step process.

(x) He should review objectively what he has taught and what the children have learnt. If necessary, he should repeat instruction.

(xi) He should create situations and encourage children to apply the acquired knowledge and skills in new situations.

(xii) The learning environment should be as pleasant as possible. Learning should be followed by satisfying consequences for children.

(xiii) The learning environment should be distraction-free.

(xiv) Children should be guided to learn with strong motivation and absorbing interest.

(xv) They should be guided to assimilate facts and learn with understanding. Initial learning should always be meaningful for them.

(xvi) Rote learning should always be discouraged.

(xvii) Children should be told when to use whole method of learning and when to use part method of learning.

(xviii) Children should be encouraged to review periodically what they have remembered and if necessary to re-learn the material. Periodical rehearsal, review, re-learning, making use of cues in learning and recall, a will to learn and remember, proper assimilation and understanding are some of the key strategies for improving retention.

12. MASTERY LEARNING

The Concept and Background

Bloom is unquestionably considered as the father of mastery learning strategy for his systematic investigation into the problem of helping each child to achieve mastery of a subject and thereby to remove individual differences among children. When Bloom was doing research in the field of learning, the prevailing construct was: *There are good learners and there are poor learners*. This was considered to be a relatively permanent attribute of the individual. Furthermore, it was believed that good learners could learn the more complex and abstract ideas, while poor learners could learn only the simplest and most concrete ideas.

In 1963, John Carroll came out with his model of school learning which was built on the construct: *There are faster learners and there are slower learners*. While Bloom and his associates were not entirely clear whether or not rate of learning was a permanent attribute of individuals, they dedicated themselves to finding ways by which the slow learners could be given the extra time and help they needed to attain some criterion of achievement.

Bloom's research led him to the view that most students become very similar with regard to learning ability, rate of learning and motivation for further learning when provided with favourable learning conditions. However, the research also demonstrated that when students are provided with unfavourable learning conditions, they become even more dissimilar with regard to learning ability, rate of learning and motivation for further learning. It is this idea which underlines Bloom's theory of school learning.

In this theory of school learning, Bloom advocated for mastery learning strategies with the main thrust of promoting excellence in learning under favourable learning conditions. At present there are many versions of mastery learning in existence. All begin with the notion that *Most students can attain a high level of learning capability if instruction is approached sensitively and systematically, if students are helped when and where they have learning difficulties, if they are given sufficient time to achieve mastery, and if there is some clear criterion of what constitutes mastery.*

Bloom's thinking was much influenced by John Carroll's Model of School Learning (1963). As Bloom interpreted it, the Carroll Model made it clear that *if students are normally distributed with respect to aptitude for some subject and all students are given exactly the same instruction (the same in terms of amount and quality of instruction and learning time allowed), then achievement measured at the completion of the subject will be normally distributed. Under such conditions the relationship (correlation) between aptitude and achievement will be relatively high.*

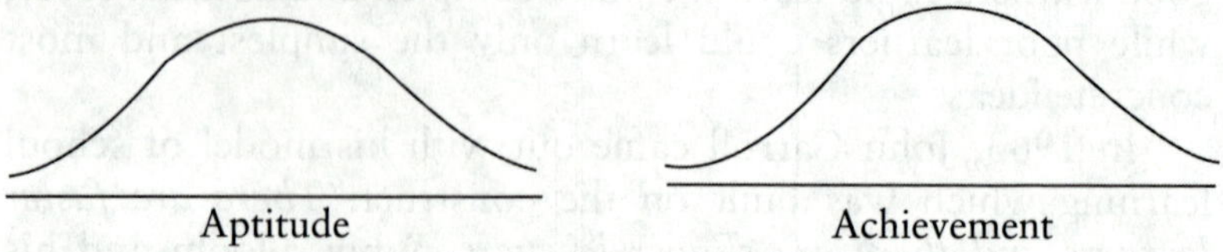

Fig. 8: Uniform Instruction for all Learners

Conversely, *if students are normally distributed with respect to aptitude, but the kind and quality of instruction are made appropriate to the characteristics and needs of each learner, the majority of students will achieve mastery of the subject. The correlation between aptitude and achievement in such cases should approach zero.*

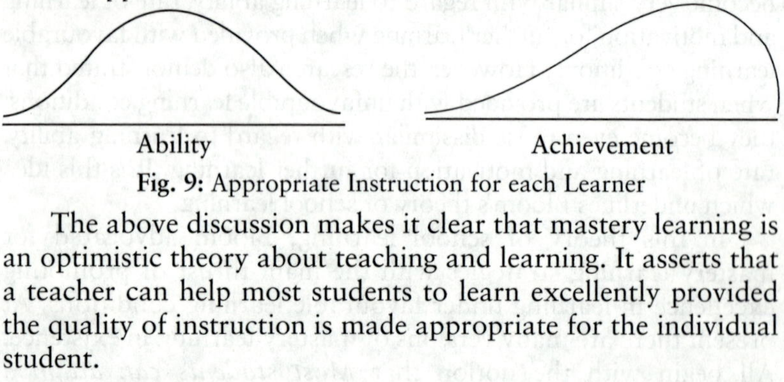

Fig. 9: Appropriate Instruction for each Learner

The above discussion makes it clear that mastery learning is an optimistic theory about teaching and learning. It asserts that a teacher can help most students to learn excellently provided the quality of instruction is made appropriate for the individual student.

How does it Work?

Fundamental Steps

There are two approaches of learning for mastery — the group-based teacher-paced approach, and the individual-based/ student-paced approach. In the former approach, students learn co-operatively with their classmates and the teacher controls the delivery and flow of instruction. In the latter approach, students learn independently of their classmates and each student controls the delivery and flow of instruction. The group-based/teacher-paced LFM strategy has proved to be one of the easiest mastery learning strategies. We shall examine now how it works.

Learning for mastery is accomplished through distinct sets of steps. One set occurs outside the classroom and prior to instruction; the second set takes place inside the classroom and during instruction.

(i) *Defining the Mastery*

The teacher who wishes to use a LFM approach begins by formulating what is meant by 'mastery' of the subject. Ideally the teacher may decide that scoring at least 80% to 90% in the final examination would indicate mastery of the subject. Students who perform better than this predetermined standard would be graded 'masters,' those who do not would be graded 'non-masters.' Some teachers have found it useful to fix an absolute grading scale wherein mastery corresponds to a grade of 'A' and non-mastery corresponds to a grade of 'B,' 'C,' 'D,' or 'E.' All students who achieve a particular level using mastery learning methods then receive the grade that corresponds to this level.

(ii) *Planning for Mastery*

Now the teacher breaks the course to be taught for mastery into a sequence of smaller learning units, each of which typically covers about two weeks' worth of material. In practice, these units correspond roughly to chapters in the course textbook or a set of topics. The various units of the course must be sequenced hierarchically so that the material in each unit transfers to a next unit. Then, for each unit, the teacher constructs a brief diagnostic progress test or formative evaluation instrument. These tests are explicitly designed to be an integral part of each unit's instruction and to provide specific information or feedback to both the teacher and the student about how the student is changing as a result of the group-based instruction. Next, the teacher specifies a score of performance standard on each formative test which, when met, will be indicative of unit mastery. Usually a score of 80 to 90 per cent correct on a formative test indicates that the student is not having learning problems. Finally the teacher develops a set of alternative instructional materials and procedures or correctives for each unit. Typically these correctives consist of co-operative small group study sessions, individual tutoring by classmates or alternative learning aids such as different textbooks, workbooks, audio-visual materials, etc. Each corrective is designed to re-teach the material in a different way, using different sensory mode or modes. Each corrective may be also used to supplement the material presented through group-based instruction. When a student encounters difficulty in learning certain material through group-based instruction, he can use the correctives to explore alternative ways of learning the unmastered materials, selecting those correctives best suited to his particular learning requirements, and overcome his learning problems before they impair subsequent learning.

(iii) *Orienting for Mastery*

After planning for mastery, the teacher is now ready to teach. But students are usually not accustomed to learning for mastery. The teacher must, therefore, spend some time at the beginning of the course, orienting them to the procedures to be used, what they are expected to learn, and how they are generally expected to learn.

(iv) *Teaching for Mastery*

Following the orientation period, the teacher teaches the first learning unit using his customary group-based teaching methods. When this instruction has been completed and before moving to the next unit, the teacher administers the unit's formative test to the entire class. Each student usually corrects his own test. Basing on the test scores, the teacher certifies those students who have achieved the unit mastery standard and identifies those who have not. The 'masters' are free to engage in enrichment activities and/or to serve as tutors for their 'slower' classmates. The 'non-masters' are asked to use the appropriate correctives to complete their unit learning. After all the students have mastered the unit, the teacher announces when the instruction for the next unit will commence. The teacher repeats the cycle of initial instruction, diagnostic progress testing, and certification or individual correction unit by unit until all units have been taught. The cycle is so paced that the teacher covers just as much material as would ordinarily be covered. The teacher can adjust the time by taking more time for the earlier units and less time for the later units.

(v) *Grading for Mastery*
After teaching all the units, the teacher finally administers the summative evaluation test and awards 'A's or their equivalents to all students whose test scores are at or above the predetermined mastery performance standard. Those students who score below this level are awarded grades appropriate to the level they have achieved.

The Variables for Mastery Learning

It was John Carroll (1963) who first identified the variables for mastery learning. Carroll identified five variables for mastery learning: These are:

1. Aptitude for particular kinds of learning.
   (This means the amount of time required by the learner to attain mastery of a learning task.)
2. Quality of Instruction.
   (This means the degree to which the presentation, explanation, and ordering of elements of the task to be learned approach the optimum for a given learner.)
3. Ability to understand instruction.
   (This means the ability of the learner to understand the nature of the task he is to learn and the procedure he is to follow in the learning of the task.)
4. Perseverance.
   (This means the time the learner is willing to spend in learning.)
5. Time allowed for learning.
   (This means the amount of time allowed by the teacher to each learner to learn a task. This is in contrast to the amount of time required by the learner to learn a given task.)

Bloom and other investigators studied these variables in different school conditions and, as a result of their research, Bloom identified two sets of variables which influence learning in school. These are: (i) alterable variables and (ii) non-alterable variables.

Non-alterable Variables	*versus*	Alterable Variables
1. Available time		1. Time on task
2. Intelligence		2. Cognitive entry characteristics
3. Summative testing		3. Formative testing
4. Characteristics of teachers		4. Quality of teaching
5. Parental status		5. Home environment process

(i) *Available Time versus Time on Task*

We have always recognised time as a central factor in all learning. The schools determine the number of hours per day or week that will be assigned to each part of the curriculum. Time in the sense of years, days, and hours available for school learning becomes a relatively fixed or stable variable. And since these times allocation are much the same for most of the students, they account for only small differences in the learning of individual students within a classroom or school.

Quite in contrast to the concept of time available for learning is the variable of time-on-task (*e.g.*, active learning time that students are engaged in learning). If two students are in the same classroom and one is actively engaged in the learning for 90% of the classroom hour while the other student is actively engaged for 30% of the classroom hour, there will be quantitative as well as qualitative differences in the learning during that hour for the two students.

Time-on-task is then one of the variables that account for learning differences among students. Time-on-task can be altered positively (or negatively) by the instructional process and this has direct consequences for the learning that will take place.

(ii) *Intelligence versus Cognitive Entry Characteristics*

Educators make use of intelligence and aptitude tests to predict later school achievement. There is some evidence that intelligence test scores are alterable in the early years (years 3-7) but there is little evidence of significant alternation in levels of intelligence as a result of school experiences in the later years. Little is known about the alterability of performance of specific aptitude tests. At least on the basis of present evidence, we may regard both intelligence and aptitude as highly stable characteristics.

Quite in contrast to intelligence and aptitude indices are cognitive entry characteristics. These are the specific knowledge, abilities, or skills which are the essential prerequisites for the learning of a particular school subject or a particular learning task. Such pre-requisites typically correlate +70 or higher with measures of achievement in a subject. Cognitive entry characteristics have high relations with achievement and they have an obvious causal effect on later achievement. Especially this is true when sequential learning tasks are involved, where it may be impossible to learn task B without prior adequate learning of task A.

Cognitive entry characteristics are highly alterable because they represent particular content and skills which may be learned if they are absent, which may be reviewed if they have been forgotten, and which may be learned to a criterion level if they have been learned to a lesser level.

(iii) *Summative versus Formative Testing*

In most classrooms, achievement tests are used for summative purposes. The summative test evidence is primarily used to classify or judge a student on the extent to which he has learned the content and objectives set for the course. Typically once the student has taken a test, he is marked and rarely he is given opportunities for correcting his errors or being retested.

In contrast to tests used for grading and judging is the use of tests and other evidence as an integral part of the formation of the learning. Formative tests are used primarily for feedback purposes in order to inform the student about what he has learned well and what he still needs to learn. When the feedback is provided in relation to corrective procedures to help the student correct the learning, then, with additional time and help, most students do reach the standard of achievement set by the teacher.

When formative tests and corrective procedures are used in this way over a series of learning tasks, the proportion of students reaching the mastery standard increases on each subsequent task until as high as 80% or 90% of the students are able to reach the mastery standard on the final learning tasks in the series. The amount of corrective help needed becomes smaller on successive learning tasks until only a few students need such corrective procedures.

Such formative tests are also useful in helping the teacher determine which aspects of the learning task were learned well by the majority of the students and which were learned poorly by most of students. This gives the teacher feedback in order to determine which ideas and skills need to be reviewed or re-taught in a different way if the majority of students are to learn them to a high standard. The major change is that teachers do less in the way of judging and grading, studying students on what they had learned by a particular date and they do more to see to it that each student learns what he or she needs as preparation for the next learning task(s).

(iv) *Teachers versus Teaching*

Over the past four decades there has been a great deal of research on teachers' characteristics and their relations with student learning. This research has been concerned with such variables as the age of the teacher, the training they have had, teaching experience, membership in teacher organisations, their personality and attitudes and even their performance on achievement tests related to their field of teaching.

Different from these studies of teacher characteristics is the more recent research on the qualities of teaching which have a direct causal relationship with student learning in the classroom.

Research studies indicate that qualities of teaching such as giving cues, reinforcement, active participation of students in the teaching-learning process or interactive teaching, providing favourable learning conditions to students, etc. are more important than the characteristics of teachers. Whereas teacher characteristics are more stable, the qualities of teaching are alterable as a result of in-service education programmes.

(v) *Parent Status versus Home Environment Processes*

Teachers and researchers have long known that children coming from some homes learn better in school than children coming from other homes in the same communities. In general, it has been found that learning in the schools is related to the education and occupations of the parents and to the social class and socio-economic status of the parents. But these characteristics are not alterable. There is little the school or the parents can do to alter their level of education, occupation, income, or ethnic characteristics.

Quite in contrast to those earlier studies of the characteristics of the parents are the more recent studies which emphasise what the parents do in interacting with their children and the home environment. Some of the home environment processes variables which appear to be most significant are the contribution of the home to the development of the mother tongue, the encouragement of parents to the children for learning when the children most need it, and the ways in which time and space are organised in the home. The home has greatest influence on the language development of the child, his general ability to learn, and his motivation to learn well in school.

Principles of Mastery Learning

We have already discussed the strategies of mastery learning in the section: How does it work? From what has been discussed earlier we can identify the principles of mastery learning.

(i) *Principle of Optimism*

Many teachers believe that mastery learning cannot work in our present school system. Students who work with such type of teachers having negative attitude may actually fail to attain mastery in their subjects. Mastery learning requires an optimistic attitude of teachers — an attitude and a belief that mastery learning does work well and that most students can attain mastery in the subject under favourable learning conditions.

(ii) *Principle of Systematic and Sensitive Instruction*

Simple optimism on the part of the teacher is not enough for mastery learning to work. The teacher needs to make his instruction systematic and sensitive to the needs and backgrounds of his students.

(iii) ***Principle of Clarity***

In order that mastery learning works, everything must be made clear from the very beginning of instruction. The students and the teacher must be clear about what constitutes mastery (the level of attainment or the score that will indicate mastery)- and the procedure to be followed for the purpose.

(iv) ***Principle of Unit-teaching and Unit-testing***

This principle demands unit approach to textbook preparation. The units in a textbook should be properly graded and sequential in nature. This will facilitate unit by unit teaching. At the end of each unit, there should be unit-testing or formative evaluation. Formative evaluation should be followed by immediate feedback to the learner about his progress and deficiencies in relation to that unit.

(v) ***Principle of Remedial Instruction***

Remedial instruction is essential for students to attain mastery in a particular subject. Remedial instruction means taking the child from where he is and leading him to greater achievement. It is concerned with two situations: (a) presence of bad habits and (b) absence of good habits. It has two objectives: (a) remediation of defects, elimination of ineffective habits, attitudes and skills which have been incorrectly learnt and (b) development of increased competencies, re-teaching skills which have not been learnt but should have been learnt earlier (*see* Flow Chart).

For purpose of remedial instruction, the teacher should make use of the following:

- Alternative learning materials (work books, different textbooks, audio-visual materials, encyclopaedia, dictionary, and remedial books).
- Alternative learning methods (small group discussion, library study, independent study, peer tutoring, cooperative learning and remedial teacher).

(vi) ***Principle of Time and Help***

This principle states that students should be given additional time and help on one-to-one basis by the teacher so that they will be able to attain mastery in the particular unit under study.

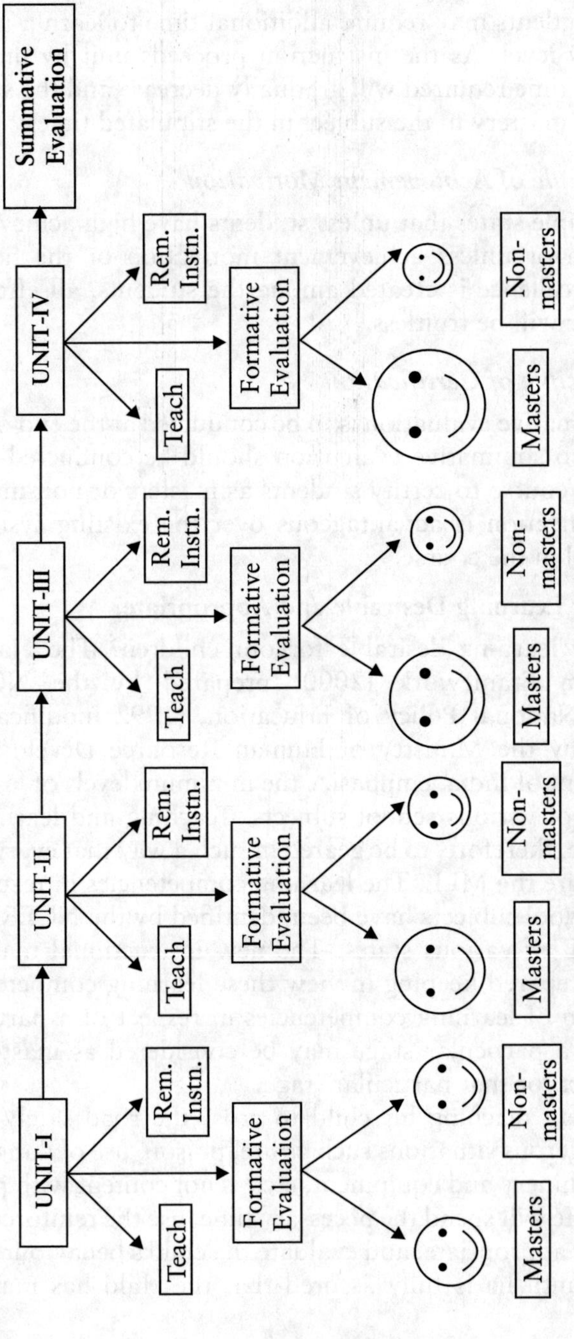

A Flow Chart of Mastery Learning Strategy (M. Dash, 2000).

Initially students may require additional time to learn a unit up to mastery level. As the instruction proceeds unit by unit, the additional time required will gradually decrease and the student will attain mastery in the subject in the stipulated time.

(vii) *Principle of Achievement Motivation*

This principle states that unless students have high achievement motivation or unless achievement motivation or the need to achieve excellence is created among the students, all efforts of the teacher will be fruitless.

(viii) Principle of Certification

Just as formative evaluation is to be conducted at the end of each unit so also summative evaluation should be conducted at the end of the course to certify students as masters or non-masters. Such certification is advantageous over the existing system of pass — fail in the course.

Is Mastery Learning Desirable and Appropriate?

Is mastery learning desirable for our children? The National Curriculum Framework (2000) prepared by the NCERT, and The National Policy of Education, (1992 modifications) prepared by the Ministry of Human Resource Development, Government of India, emphasize the minimum levels of learning in respect of various school subjects. Teaching and learning in schools are, therefore, to be geared in such a way that every child must acquire the MLL. The learning competencies in respect of various school subjects have been identified by the NCERT and SCERT/SIE of various states. The new instructional materials are also prepared keeping in view these learning competencies. Acquisition of learning competencies in respect of a particular subject at a particular stage may be considered as mastery of that subject for that particular stage.

A parent teaching his child to cross the road safely or to avoid dangerous situations such as fire, poison, use of dangerous tools, machinery and equipment, etc., is not content with partial learning. He will spend the necessary time, use the reinforcement he believes appropriate, and evaluate the child's behaviour in the situation until he is fully assured that the child has mastered the learning. One could cite many examples of mastery learning in the home, industry, and even in military training where the instructor insists that all learners reach an acceptable level of mastery before instruction ceases. These examples make it necessary for the teacher and the curriculum framers to insist on and plan for mastery learning in schools.

In a complex society such as ours, there are a variety of citizenship skills, understanding, interests and attitudes that may be necessary for the individual to lead a satisfying life and for the nation to survive as a democratic and open society. These behaviours require at least minimal levels of mastery.

The learner comes to view himself as adequate or inadequate in terms of his effectiveness in learning what the school or the curriculum expects of him. He is judged by teachers, examiners and his own peers on the basis of his success or lack of it in the learning tasks set by the school and the curriculum. These judgements are further reinforced by his parents. For the student who consistently gets low grades or performs poorly in school becomes frustrated and develops a negative self-concept. On the other hand, to do well in school consistently over a number of years is likely to lead to the development of a feeling of adequacy and positive self-concept in the student. Mastery learning helps to provide the individual with the basis for positive ego development and a sense of adequacy. Thus, mastery learning is desirable in terms of its opening up of interests in further learning and in developing a positive attitude towards school and school learning, as well as a healthy self-concept.

One objection against mastery learning strategies is the vast amount of time, money and labour that may be required to organise mastery learning strategies in the school. The other objection is that our teachers are not specially trained in mastery learning strategies. The third objection is that the curricula and the syllabi, the textbooks and other reading materials are not, in all cases, developed properly to emphasize mastery learning. However, if we are interested in children's welfare, if we insist that all or almost all children should acquire mastery of school subjects and if the national goals are to be achieved, then these objections raised against the desirability of mastery learning strategies will not count much.

At what stage and for which subjects is mastery learning appropriate? There are some fundamental considerations of where mastery learning is appropriate, or inappropriate. Clearly, not all school subjects need strive for mastery learning and perhaps not all students should strive for mastery learning in all subjects.

Mastery learning is relatively easy to achieve in school subjects with a minimum of pre-requisites. For example, first year course in English (as a second language) has a minimum of specific pre-requisite and, therefore, with a one-year course with appropriate feedback and corrective techniques, the teacher can bring a large majority of students up to a given standard of mastery. Similarly learning may be achieved in a course where a large portion of the learners have the minimal prerequisite learning at the time of entrance to the course.

Subjects which are *required, sequential, closed* and which emphasize *convergent thinking* should employ mastery learning strategies.

If a subject is required of the learners, and if some have regarded it as important for the learners or the society, then better or more adequate learning of such a subject is to be preferred to a lesser level of learning. If a subject is required then the learner should be given every opportunity to succeed in it and conversely, the learner's failure in a required subject should be seen as a defect in the curriculum and/or the instruction. A high rate of failure (or a low level of learning) in a required subject needlessly inflicts a negative self-concept on a group of learners who have no choice about being in learning situation or course.

An even better case can be made for mastery learning in sequential subjects. If learning of some set of school subjects (arithmetic, language, arts, mathematics, etc.) is sequential in the sense that the second course builds on and requires the first course and the third course builds on the first two courses, etc., then the student should be assured of successful progress through the sequence, in so far as this is possible. This, of course, places a very heavy burden on the first course, since inadequate learning in this course almost assures inadequate learning in each of the subsequent courses in the sequence. Mastery learning thus requires a greater concern on the part of the curriculum-maker about sequence and more careful consideration of what is truly sequential in learning and why.

By closed subjects we mean subjects where there is a finite set of ideas and behaviours to be learned about which there is considerable agreement among curriculum-makers and teachers. A closed subject is also one which is unlikely to change much over a decade or more. For example, arithmetic and mathematics may be regarded as relatively closed subjects. Even though there may be much change in the methods of teaching these subjects, their content and behaviours do not change fundamentally. History, many science courses, second language courses, and, to a lesser extent, mother tongue courses may also be regarded as closed subjects. Here the argument for mastery learning stems from the relative ease with which mastery learning standards can be developed, the general consensus about what learning is important for the students to acquire, and the great likelihood that once a mastery learning strategies have been adequately developed for one generation or group of learners, they can be employed for subsequent cycles of learners and teachers.

Finally, we believe that courses which emphasize convergent thinking, that is, thinking for which there are "right answers," "good solutions," and "appropriate thought processes" should employ mastery learning strategies. The argument here again stems from the case with which mastery learning standards can be derived and the availability of considerable consensus not only about the products of thinking (and learning) but also about the process of thinking that should be developed. Here again, subjects like mathematics, history, much of language, arts and second language courses are believed to be appropriate for mastery learning since convergent thinking appears to be the major behaviour which is emphasized in such courses.

We have now some idea about the desirability and appropriateness of mastery learning in schools. It is the curriculum-maker who must bear the burden of demonstrating what can and should be learned by the students. It is the curriculum-maker who must find the strategies which will ensure that the large proportion of students will learn adequately. It is the curriculum-maker who must develop the variety of alternative learning materials required for mastery learning. This also implies that suitable pre-service and in-service training should be provided to teachers to increase their effectiveness in the classroom.

13. HOW CHILDREN LEARN*

1. Active Involvement

Learning requires the active, constructive involvement of the learner. Learning at school requires students to pay attention, to observe, to memorize, to understand, to set goals and to assume responsibility for their own learning. These cognitive activities are not possible without the active involvement and engagement of the learner. Teachers must help students to become active and goal-oriented by building on their natural desire to explore, to understand new things and to master them.

It is a challenge for teachers to create interesting and challenging learning environments that encourage the active involvement of students. The following are some suggestions as to how this can be done:

- Avoid situations where the students are passive listeners for long periods of time.
- Provide students with hands-on activities, such as experiments, observations, projects, etc.
- Encourage participation in classroom discussions and other collaborative activities.
- Organize school visits to museums and technological parks.
- Allow students to take some control over their own learning. Taking control over one's learning means allowing students to make some decisions about what to learn and how.
- Assist students in creating learning goals that are consistent with their interests and future aspirations.

2. Social Participation

Learning is primarily a social activity and participation in the social life of the school is central for learning to occur. For many researchers, social participation is the main activity through

---

* Based on: *How children learn*, by Stella Vosniadou. Educational Practices Series-7, International Academy of Education, Geneva, 2001.

which learning occurs. Social activity and participation begin early on. Parents interact with their children and through these interactions children acquire the behaviours that enable them to become effective members of society. According to the psychologist, Lev Vygotsky, the way children learn is by internalizing the activities, habits, vocabulary and ideas of the members of the community in which they grow up.

Teachers can do many things to encourage social participation in ways that facilitate learning:

- They can assign students to work in groups and assume the role of a coach/co-ordinator who provides guidance and support to the groups.
- They can create a classroom environment that includes group work spaces where resources are shared.
- Through modelling and coaching, they can teach students how to co-operate with each other.
- They can create circumstances for students to interact with each other, to express their opinions and to evaluate other students' arguments.
- An important aspect of social learning is to link the school to the community at large. In this way, students' opportunities for social participation are enlarged.

3. Meaningful Activities

People learn best when they participate in activities that are perceived to be useful in real life and are culturally relevant. Many school activities are not meaningful since students understand neither why they are doing them nor what is their purpose and usefulness. Sometimes school activities are not meaningful because they are not culturally appropriate. Many schools are communities where children from diverse cultures learn together. There are systematic cultural differences in practices, in habits, in social roles, etc., that influence learning. Sometimes meaningful activities for students coming from one cultural group are not meaningful to students who are coming from another cultural group.

Teachers can make classroom activities more meaningful by situating them in an authentic context. An example of an authentic context is one in which the activity is typically used in real life. For example, students can improve their oral language and communication skills by participating in debates. They can improve their writing skills by being involved in the preparation of a classroom newspaper. Students can learn science by participating in a community or school environmental project. The school can be in contact with local scientists and invite them to lecture, or allow the students to visit their laboratories.

It is also important for teachers to be aware of the cultural differences of the children in their classroom and to respect these differences. They must see them as strengths to build on, rather than as defects. Children will feel differently in the classroom if their culture is reflected in the common activities.

4. Relating New Information to Prior Knowledge

New knowledge is constructed on the basis of what is already understood and believed. The idea that people's ability to learn something new follows from what they already know is not new, but more recent research findings have shown that the ability to relate new information to prior knowledge is critical for learning. It is not possible for someone to understand, remember or learn something that is completely unfamiliar. Some prior knowledge is necessary to understand the task at hand. But having the pre-requisite, prior knowledge is still not sufficient to ensure adequate results. People must activate their prior knowledge in order to be able to use it for understanding and for learning. Research shows that students do not consistently see the relationships between new material that they read and what they already know. Research also shows that learning is enhanced when teachers pay close attention to the prior knowledge of the learner and use this knowledge as the starting point for instruction.

Teachers can help students activate prior knowledge and use it for the task at hand. This can be done in a number of ways:

- Teachers can discuss the content of a lesson before starting in order to ensure that the students have the necessary prior knowledge and in order to activate this knowledge.
- Often students' prior knowledge is incomplete or there are false beliefs and critical misconceptions. Teachers do not simply need to know that students know something

about the topic to be introduced. They need to investigate students' prior knowledge in detail so that false beliefs and misconceptions can be identified.

- Teachers may need to go back to cover important pre-requisite material or ask the students to do some preparatory work on their own.
- Teachers can ask the kind of question that helps students see relationships between what they are reading and what they already know.

5. Being Strategic

People learn by employing effective and flexible strategies that help them to understand reason, memorize and solve problems. Children develop strategies to help themselves solve problems from an early age. For example, when pre-school children are told to go to the supermarket to buy a list of food items, they often repeat the items on their way to remember them better. These children have discovered rehearsal as a strategy to improve their memory without anybody telling them to do so. When they go to school, children need help from teachers to develop appropriate strategies for solving mathematics problems, when understanding texts, doing science, learning from other students, etc. Research shows that when teachers make systematic attempts to teach learning strategies to students, substantial gains can result.

Strategies are important because they help students understand and solve problems in ways that are appropriate for the situation at hand. Strategies can improve learning and make it faster. Strategies may differ in their accuracy, in their difficulty of execution, in their processing demands and in the range of problems to which they apply. The broader the range of strategies that children can use appropriately, the more successful they can be in problem-solving, in reading, in text comprehension and in memorizing.

Teachers must recognize the importance of students knowing and using a variety of strategies. The teaching of strategies can be done directly or indirectly. In the latter case, the teacher can give students a task and provide a model of the inquiry process or ask key questions. For example, in reading, teachers can explicitly show students how to outline the important points in a text and how to summarize them. Alternatively, they can ask a group of students to discuss a text and summarize it. They can help in this process by participating in the discussion and by asking critical questions. In science, teachers can show students how to conduct experiments, how to form hypotheses, how to keep a systematic record of their findings, and how to evaluate them.

It is important to ensure that students learn to use these strategies on their own and do not always rely on teachers to provide the necessary support. Teachers need to gradually fade their assistance and allow students to take greater responsibility for their learning.

6. Engaging in Self-regulation and Being Reflective

Learners must know how to plan and monitor their learning, how to set their own learning goals and how to correct errors. The term 'self-regulation' is used here to indicate students' ability to monitor their own learning, to understand when they are making errors, and to know-how to correct them.

Self-regulation requires reflection in the sense of being aware of one's own beliefs and strategies. Reflection can develop through discussion, debates and essays, where children are encouraged to express their opinions and defend them. Another important aspect of reflection is being able to distinguish appearance from reality, common beliefs from scientific knowledge, etc.

Teachers can help students become self-regulated and reflective by providing opportunities:

- To plan how to solve problems, design experiments and undertake tasks;
- To evaluate the statements, arguments, solutions to problems of others as well as of one's self;
- To check their thinking and ask themselves questions about their understanding — (Why am I doing what I am doing? How well am I doing? What remains to be done?);
- To develop realistic knowledge of themselves as learners — (I am good in reading, but need to work on my mathematics);

- To set their own learning goals and
- To know what are the most effective strategies to use and when to use them?

7. Restructuring Prior Knowledge

Sometimes prior knowledge can stand in the way of learning something new. Students must learn how to solve internal inconsistencies and restructure existing conceptions when necessary. Sometimes existing knowledge can stand in the way of understanding new information. While this is often the case in the learning of science and mathematics, it can apply to all subject-matter areas. It happens because our current understanding of the physical and social world, of history, of theorizing about numbers, etc. is the product of thousands of years of cultural activity that has radically changed intuitive ways of explaining phenomena. For example, in the area of mathematics, many children make mistakes when they use fractions because they use rules that apply to natural number only. Similarly, in the physical sciences, students form various misconceptions. The idea that the Earth is round like a pancake or like a sphere flattened on the top happens because it reconciles the scientific information that the Earth is round, with the intuitive belief that it is flat and that people live upon its top. Such misconceptions do not apply only in young children. They are common in high school and college students as well.

What can teachers do to facilitate the understanding of counter-intuitive information?

- Teachers need to be aware that students have prior beliefs and incomplete understandings that can conflict with what is being taught at school.
- It is important to create the circumstances where alternative beliefs and explanations can be externalized and expressed.
- Teachers need to build on the existing ideas of students and slowly lead them to more mature understanding. Ignoring prior beliefs can lead to the formation of misconceptions.
- Students must be provided with observations and experiments that have the potential of showing to them

that some of their beliefs can be wrong. Examples from the history of science can be used for this purpose.
- Scientific explanations must be presented with clarity and, when possible, exemplified with models.
- Students must be given enough time to restructure their prior conceptions. In order to do this, it is better to design curricula that deal with fewer topics in greater depth than attempting to cover a great deal of topics in a superficial manner.

8. Aiming Towards Understanding Rather Than Memorization

Learning is better when material is organized around general principles and explanations, rather than when it is based on the memorization of isolated facts and procedures. All teachers want their students to understand what they are learning and not to memorize facts in a superficial way. Research shows, that when information is superficially memorized, it is easily forgotten. On the contrary, when something is understood, it is not forgotten easily and it can be transferred to other situations (see also the next principle on transfer). In order to understand what they are being taught, students must be given the opportunity to think about what they are doing, to talk about it with other students and with teachers, to clarify it and to understand how it applies in many situations.

How does one teach for understanding? The following are some tasks teachers can carry out in order to promote understanding of the material that has been taught:

- Ask students to explain a phenomenon or a concept in their own words.
- Show students how to provide examples that illustrate how a principle applies or how a law works.
- Students must be able to solve characteristic problems in the subject-matter area. Problems can increase in difficulty as students acquire greater expertise.
- When students understand the material, they can see similarities and differences, they can compare and contrast, and they can understand and generate analogies.
- Teach students how to abstract general principles from specific cases and generalize from specific examples.

9. Helping Students Learn to Transfer

Learning becomes more meaningful when the lessons are applied to real-life situations. Students often cannot apply what they have learned at school to solve real-world problems. For example, they may learn about Newton's laws at school but fail to see how they apply in real-life situations. Transfer is very important. Why should someone want to go to school if what is learned there does not transfer to other situations and cannot be used outside the school?

Teachers can improve students' ability to transfer what they have learned at school by:

- Insisting on mastery of subject matter. Without an adequate degree of understanding, transfer cannot take place.
- Helping students see the transfer implications of the information they have learned.
- Applying what has been learned in one subject-matter area to other areas to which it may be related.
- Showing students how to abstract general principles from concrete examples.
- Helping students learn how to monitor their learning and how to see and use feedback about their progress.
- Teach for understanding rather than for memorization.

10. Taking Time to Practice

Learning is a complex cognitive activity that cannot be rushed. It requires considerable time and periods of practice to start building expertise in an area. Research shows that people must carry out a great deal of practice to acquire expertise in an area. Even small differences in the amount of time during which people are exposed to information can result in large differences in the information they have acquired. Cognitive psychologists Chase and Simon (1973) studied chess experts and found that they had often spent as many as 50,000 hours practicing chess. A 35-year old chess master who has spent 50,000 hours playing chess must have spent four to five hours on the chessboard from the age of 5 every day for thirty years! Less accomplished players have spent considerably less time playing chess.

Research shows that the reading and writing skills of high-school students relate to the hours they have spent on reading and writing.

Effective reading and writing requires a lot of practice. Students from disadvantaged environments who have fewer opportunities to learn and who miss school because of work or illness will not be expected to do as well at school compared to children who had more time to practice and acquire information.

Many educational programmes are designed to increase one's exposure to learning situations preferably at an early age. Here are some recommendations for teachers that can help students spend more time on learning tasks:

- Increase the amount of time students spend on learning in the classroom.
- Give students learning tasks that are consistent with what they already know.
- Do not try to cover too many topics at once. Give students time to understand the new information.
- Help students engage in 'deliberate practice' that includes active thinking and monitoring of their own learning.
- Give students access to books so that they can practise reading at home.
- Be in contact with parents so that they can learn to provide richer educational experiences for their children.

11. Developmental and Individual Differences

Children learn best when their individual differences are taken into consideration. Research shows that there are major developmental differences in learning. As children develop, they form new ways of representing the world and they also change the processes and strategies they use to manipulate these representations. In addition, there are important individual differences in learning. Developmental psychologist Howard Gardner has argued that there are many dimensions of human intelligence other than the logical and linguistic skills that are usually valued in most school environments. Some children are gifted in music, others have exceptional spatial skills (required, for example, by architects and artists), or bodily/kinesthetic abilities (required by athletes), or abilities to relate to other people, etc. Schools must create the best environment for the development of children taking into consideration such individual differences.

The following are recommendations for creating the best environment for the development of children, while recognizing their individual differences:

- Learn how to assess children's knowledge, strategies and modes of learning adequately.
- Introduce children to a wide range of materials, activities and learning tasks that include language, mathematics, natural sciences, social sciences, art, music, movement, social understanding, etc.
- Identify students' areas of strength, paying particular attention to the interest, persistence and confidence they demonstrate in different kinds of activities.
- Support students' areas of strength and utilize these areas to improve overall academic performance.
- Guide and challenge students' thinking and learning.
- Ask children thought-provoking questions and give them problems to solve. Urge children to test hypotheses in a variety of ways.
- Create connections to the real world by introducing problems and materials drawn from everyday situations.
- Show children how they can use their unique profiles of intelligence to solve real-world problems.
- Create circumstances for students to interact with people in the community, and particularly with adults who are knowledgeable and enthusiastic about the kinds of things that are of interest to the students.

12. Creating Motivated Learners

Learning is critically influenced by learner motivation. Teachers can help students become more motivated learners by their behaviour and the statements they make. Motivated learners are easy to recognize because they have a passion for achieving their goals and are ready to expend a great deal of effort. They also show considerable determination and persistence. This influences the amount and quality of what is learned. All teachers want to have motivated learners in their classrooms. How can they achieve this?

Psychologists distinguish between two kinds of motivation: extrinsic motivation and intrinsic motivation. Extrinsic motivation results when positive rewards are used to increase the frequency of a target behaviour. Praise, high grades, awards, money and food can be used for that effect. Intrinsic motivation is when learners actively participate in activities without having to be rewarded for it. The child who likes to put together puzzles for the fun of it is intrinsically motivated.

An important characteristic of intrinsically motivated learners is their belief that effort is important for success. Teachers can influence students' determination to achieve by their behaviour and the statements they make.

Teachers must use encouraging statements that reflect an honest evaluation of learner performance:

- Recognize student accomplishments.
- Attribute student achievement to internal and not external factors (*e.g.*, 'You have good ideas').
- Help students believe in themselves (*e.g.*, 'You are putting a lot of effort on math and your grades have much improved').
- Provide feedback to children about the strategies they use and instruction as to how to improve them.
- Help learners set realistic goals.

It is also important to:

- Refrain from grouping students according to their ability. Ability grouping gives the message that ability is valued more than effort.
- Promote co-operation rather than competition. Research suggests that competitive arrangements that encourage students to work alone to achieve high grades and rewards tend to give the message that what is valued is ability and diminish intrinsic motivation.
- Provide novel and interesting tasks that challenge learners' curiosity and higher-order thinking skills at the appropriate level of difficulty.

SELECTED QUESTIONS

1. Learning is the modification of behaviour. Explain.
2. Discuss the role of maturation in learning.

3. Discuss the principles of learning.
4. What is learning? State its nature.
5. Discuss the factors influencing learning.
6. Discuss the concept and nature of skill learning.
7. State and explain the various phases of skill learning.
8. Discuss the various conditions of skill learning.
9. How can the teacher teach skills to children? Discuss.
10. What do you mean by concept? How do children learn concepts?
11. What is concept formation? How can the teacher teach concepts to children?
12. What do you mean by problem-solving? How can the teacher develop problem-solving behaviour among children?
13. Discuss the various techniques of classroom motivation.
14. Discuss the role of motivation in learning.
15. What is transfer of learning? Discuss the various theories of transfer.
16. Discuss the various strategies to be adopted by the teacher to facilitate transfer of learning.
17. What is retention? What strategies are to be adopted by the teacher to improve retention of students?
18. What is mastery learning? Discuss the variables of mastery learning.
19. What is mastery learning? Is mastery learning desirable and appropriate? If so, why and at what stage of instruction? Explain.
20. How do children learn? State briefly the roles of the teacher in helping children learn.
21. Explain the different types of learning curve. What are their implications for the teacher?

16
Teacher Effectiveness

1. TEACHER EFFECTIVENESS: ITS DETERMINANTS

Teacher effectiveness means perfection or the optimum level of efficiency and productivity on the part of the teacher. It refers to the height of maturity during the lifespan of a teacher. This concept of effectiveness as the height of maturity and learning indicates that as the teacher grows with experience and learns more he is able to perform his best in the process of education, Anand (1983) reports, "... effectiveness is considered to be the finest trait of a person. As an attribute, it represents his personality in the best of his form." Teacher effectiveness is an area of research which is concerned with relationships between the characteristics of teachers, teaching acts, and their effects on the educational outcomes of classroom teaching.

Teacher effectiveness is assessed using three types of criteria such as: (a) process, (b) product, and (c) presage.

Process as a Criterion

Process refers to the performance and behaviour of the teacher, student behaviour, and the student-teacher interaction in the classroom. Individuals who prefer this criterion think that the best indicator of teacher effectiveness is what the teacher does in the classroom, what the students do, the interaction that occurs between the teacher and the students or all these. Thus, teacher effectiveness according to this criterion, is assessed through observation of teacher behaviour and student behaviour.

Product as a Criterion

Product refers to what is learned or the outcomes of learning. Individuals who prefer this criterion think that the best test of teacher effectiveness is how well students achieve. Achievement tests and other measures in the cognitive, psychomotor and affective domains are used to measure teacher effectiveness according to this criterion.

Presage as a Criterion

A third type of criterion is presage which refers to the academic background and personal characteristics of teachers. Individuals who prefer this criterion think that the best test of teacher effectiveness is the intellectual abilities of the teacher, the training and education received by him, his personal characteristics or all these. Thus, according to this criterion, teacher effectiveness is assessed from the teacher's college records/marks, test scores and ratings usually made outside the classroom.

It must be noted here that there are both direct and indirect ways of determining teacher effectiveness. Product and process are direct determinants of teacher effectiveness, presage being the indirect determinant. But while assessing teacher effectiveness, it is advisable to use all the three criteria than to use any one criterion.

2. CHARACTERISTICS OF EFFECTIVE TEACHERS

Effective teachers possess certain characteristics which are markedly different from those possessed by ineffective or 'poor' teachers. Research findings of characteristics of effective teachers are accumulating day by day, but still the search goes on. The findings bear testimony to the fact that effective teachers are different from ineffective teachers on certain fundamental characteristics. While some researchers have dealt with personality and affective characteristics, other researchers have studied the interaction styles of teachers.

Personality Component

Learning aims at the moulding of behaviour of students in a preconceived and desired direction. Such modification of behaviour is ultimately to be found in healthy attitudes, good habits, standard values, fine temperaments and as a whole in the sound character development of students. Within the school periphery, the teacher is the recognized organiser of learning environment and stimulant conditions. The teacher is expected to create the set-up to enable the students to 'pick' up the goals of learning. In this performance of their duty, teachers cannot be effective merely by 'telling' the students whatever is written in the books.

The inculcation or the modification of attitudes and values in one's character is a matter of reinforced practice. In other words, development of character depends on the nature of experience one is exposed to or one comes across in one's daily routine. Moreover, the experiences are found to be more vulnerable and penetrating when they are actually provided by someone through his mode of living. Thus, teacher's personality remains the mainspring of vital experiences for children. The effectiveness of teachers in the character formation of students essentially depends upon the teacher's own character. The truth of the maxim, "Example is better than precept," goes absolutely unchallenged and true here than anywhere else. Teachers need fundamentally to practice those traits which the society wants to instill amongst the incoming citizens through the school. To present children with a pattern of traits worthy of emulation, teachers will have to observe the highest standards of conduct in public and private life.

Behaviour of Teachers

Behaviour is the mirror of personality. It is the personality in action. The teacher's relationship with his pupils is of prime importance in effective teaching. The research findings uniformly confirm that sympathetic, kind, loving, affectionate, and impartial behaviour of teacher towards his students establishes rapport with them and is a probable factor in teacher's effectiveness. Teachers are required to be acceptable to their students. To be effective, teachers have to show due 'respect' for every child with concern for the uniqueness of each of them. Conversely, rude, whimsical, and unpleasant behaviour on the part of teachers is a formidable barrier between them and their pupils. A consistently sound and warm attitude of teachers towards students is essential for a purposeful teaching-learning situation. Working on the interests and aptitudes of students and initiating their motivation for learning ensures teacher's effectiveness.

The teacher has been very rightly seen as a group leader for students. He is to demonstrate his leadership role in the right spirit of democratic principles. Being sought by his students for guidance to make appropriate and accurate choices, plans and adjustments in their life is an indication of teacher's effectiveness. Once the teacher gains the respect and trust of students, his effectiveness is fairly ensured.

Qualification of Teachers

Teachers' qualifications essential for their being effective may be discussed under three heads:

(a) General Qualifications,
(b) Special Qualifications, and
(c) Professional Qualifications

(a) General Qualifications

A teacher must possess the minimum of the required general qualifications. He should at least be a graduate for all levels of school teaching. However, the researchers have yet to establish the relationship between academic attainments and teacher effectiveness. But obviously a teacher who teaches should be reasonably expected to have a good academic record to set an example for his students. He must be the custodian of general knowledge relating to various disciplines. He should be able to answer the diversified queries of students. This should not be taken as if we want a teacher to be jack of all trades but master of none. The main idea behind this thinking is that a teacher should be in touch with the current affairs concerning our life.

(b) Special Qualifications

In this age of specialization and intensive studies in all spheres of life, it is very essential that the teacher must claim his specialization at least in one of the school subjects. He should be the master of one or two subjects of teaching. This makes his personality all the more influential and impressive.

The teacher must feel intrinsically interested in keeping himself abreast of the latest advances in his area of specialization. He should remain constantly in touch with the growing knowledge and always maintain the claim to be the master of his subject. This widened area of knowledge broadens the teacher's scope of effectiveness over his students.

(c) Professional Qualifications

Besides academic qualifications both general as well as specific, the teacher must earn his professional qualifications before making an entry into the teaching profession. This aspect of qualification relates to his professional training which is popularly known as teacher training programme. Before embarking on the profession, the professional must internalize the skills of his profession. He should be in the know of different methods of teaching and by virtue of his practice, should evolve his own efficient and competent style of working. Professional competency and efficiency are directly and very closely linked with the effectiveness of teachers. Furthermore, once taken, professional degrees and qualifications should not lead to complacency in teachers. The active participation of a teacher in the orientation courses, workshops and seminars is very necessary to keep his professional acumen and skill up to the required mark.

Teacher's Job Satisfaction

Teacher's satisfaction in his job is so self-explanatory that it hardly needs a detailed discussion. This relates to his identification with the profession and his willingness to be effective. It is his involvement in the job which will determine the effectiveness of his efforts. Taking school teaching as a matter of joy and pride sharpens his teaching skill and refines his performance. The feelings of being unfortunate to be in the teaching profession because of reasonable or unreasonable excuses are very much likely to jeopardise teacher's potential effectiveness. Teacher's style of enjoying his job may compensate for the lack of required personality traits and qualifications for his effectiveness in his job.

Teaching is not a mechanical process. It is an intricate, exciting, challenging job. Teacher's satisfaction and contentment being found and derived from the profession may be an index of effectiveness. The total commitment to the teaching profession, and enjoying being fully wedded to it, enhances teacher's effectiveness.

Student's Success

The teacher functions for the development of desirable behaviour patterns among the students. He works on the attitudes, values, habits and temperaments already acquired by students from homes. That means pupils themselves provide the starting point of teacher's mission. The teacher has to understand the entering behaviour of students to mend, mould and enrich it with the attitudes and values of men of character of the society. The success the students exhibit in these respects indicates the effectiveness of teachers.

3. THE TEACHER AS A LEADER OF THE GROUP AND FACILITATOR OF LEARNING

An effective teacher is a leader of the group and facilitator of learning. An effective leader possesses certain competencies such as the ability to utilise the authority of a leadership position in a beneficial way. Authority refers to the power to make decisions that affect students. The ways in which the teacher demonstrates power and authority produce differing results and either contributes to the teacher's effectiveness in the classroom or are detrimental to it.

As a leader of the group, the teacher may be either authoritarian, or democratic, or *laissez-faire* leader. These various forms of leadership have differing effects on the individual and group behaviour.

Authoritarian Leader

When a teacher plays the role of an authoritarian leader, practically all policies and procedures are determined by him. He remains aloof from active group participation, except in demonstrating. He dictates orders, gives disruptive commands and non-constructive criticism. The students are not to ask 'why' for a certain order or decision. Whatever the teacher thinks, feels or says must be carried out by the students.

Democratic Leader

Under the democratic leadership, the teacher guides, gives suggestions, extends knowledge and stimulates self-guidance. The teacher as a democratic leader is jovial, self-confident. All policies and procedures are a matter of group decision. There is an element of freedom and acceptance. Division of responsibility is a matter of accepted principle. The teacher also actively participates in the activities of the group.

Laissez-faire Leader

Under the *laissez-faire* leadership, the teacher plays a rather passive role in social participation and leaves complete freedom for group or individual decisions in relation to the activity and group procedures. He takes minimum initiative in making suggestions. But he supplies information and help when asked. He makes no attempt to evaluate negatively or positively the behaviour or productions of the individuals or the group.

Effect of Leadership Style

These three styles of leadership create different emotional and attitudinal characteristics of group in a learning situation. Since the psycho-social climate differs from one style to another style of leadership, these three styles produce different results and behaviour patterns among students. For example, the authoritarian role brings better discipline, less confusion and more production when the leader is present in the group. But when the leader is absent, there is a breakdown in order. Moreover, authoritarian leadership brings reactions such as aggressiveness and scapegoating. The democratic role results in less order and productivity generally, but even when the leader is not present, order, discipline and production are not disrupted or hampered. Such a role also produces less aggressive and scapegoating tendencies among the members. Generally students prefer a democratic leader to an authoritarian one.

A teacher who is able to control classes and to structure learning environment for individual learners is an effective leader. Although students have power and the right to set their own rules and goals, the presence of a leader remains necessary, if goals are to be defined, energies rooted, values examined, tasks set and motivation maintained. Successful leadership style contributes to the success of the teacher as a facilitator of learning. The nature of teacher-student interaction, the type of teacher behaviour, methods of teaching and characteristics of teachers are all related to student learning.

Facilitator of Learning

As a facilitator of learning, the teacher must be warm, understanding and self-controlling. He must listen attentively and accept students' feelings and ideas. He must observe students' reactions skillfully. He may ask questions to the students and praise and encourage when necessary. In his planning and execution of work, he must be responsible, business-like, systematic, flexible and work-oriented. He must explain things clearly and reward fairly. Whenever he criticizes a student, he must explain the reasons for criticism. He must be stimulating and imaginative in his approach to classroom behaviour and subject. For facilitating learning, the teacher must encourage classroom discussion, panel discussion and question and answer session. Whenever necessary, he must lecture, demonstrate and explain things with examples. He must encourage independent study habits. If the teacher selects procedures and materials in terms of instructional objectives and student characteristics, achievement of students becomes high and consistent. Emotional security of students is high when the teacher maintains balance of direction and freedom in various activities.

As a leader of the group and facilitator of learning, the teacher cannot function in the air. The physical conditions, *i.e.*, school building, laboratories, library, sports fields, availability of appropriate amounts of funds, etc. go to activate the wheels of teacher effectiveness. The physical provisions are needed to provide the infrastructure for the working teachers. These are the facilities required to be provided to the teachers to make the best of their knowledge and skills. Moreover, the nature of leadership rendered by the head of the school can prove to be a pace-setter or deterrent to the teacher's willingness to work and show the expected results. The relationship of the society and the schools with teachers also accounts for the quality of teacher's work. The respect enjoyed by teachers in the teaching profession cannot be ignored in accounting for their effectiveness. The pay scales, opportunities for professional and academic advancement along with a ladder of promotional avenues also contribute towards teachers' effort for effectiveness.

4. ROLE OF PERCEPTION

The effectiveness of a teacher depends as much on his understanding of himself as it does on his understanding of his students. Hence it is essential that teachers study and try to understand the psychological factors and forces in their own lives. Understanding the psychology of being a teacher — the numerous roles one has to play — contributes to effectiveness in the profession.

Teachers play many roles. They interlock and overlap. Some are complementary and some are contradictory. They differ with the kind of school and the subject, and they differ with the individual teacher.

The varied duties, functions, and problems for which the teacher is responsible require him to enact a number of psychological roles. We shall discuss below some of the roles of effective teachers as perceived by the teachers themselves, the community and the students as related to pupil's learning.

Instructor

The teacher is the person who initiates, directs and evaluates learning. Presumably, this is the chief reason why teachers are employed, to see that learning takes place. The role of the teacher as the instructor is a kind of core role for some other subordinate roles.

Representative of Society

As the representative of society, the teacher is concerned with transmitting the values and standards of the culture and the community. The teacher should be perceived by his students as representing or embodying those values. By precept and example, the teacher should try to develop the moral attitudes, the thinking patterns, the life goals which he feels make for good citizens living a good life. In this role, the teacher should perceive himself as more or less a faithful mirror of the society in which he lives.

Subject-matter Expert

The teacher should be the person who has studied and mastered certain areas of learning. With this background, the teacher should perceive himself as the man to guide the experiences of students, help them at their difficult stages of learning and suggest enriching experiences for those who learn more rapidly than others.

Disciplinarian

The teacher is the person to see that the classroom group and its members stay within the limits set by society, the school and the needs of the group. As a disciplinarian, the teacher should not perceive himself as the person to 'set everything right' with a long stick in his hand. Rather this role calls for the teacher to help children and classroom groups to become self-disciplined.

Clerk

For a teacher, there are marks to be entered, tests to be scored, reports to be made, letters to be written, files to be maintained, papers to be corrected, and so on. Most teachers perceive their clerical role unfavourably, partly because it gives them less time and energy to spend on their chief role of helping children learn. Most teachers also feel that, after all, they are teachers, not clerks. But teachers must understand that most professional jobs require a large amount of clerical work, and teaching is no exception.

Youth Group Worker

Most teachers are required to participate in one or more school activities outside of class or in co-curricular activities. This is one of the main roles of a teacher. However, many teachers perceive this role as something extra, separate and distinct and an added burden. If teachers hold this perception, there would be no one else to take their place as youth group leaders, as organisers of learning in out-of-class activities. Co-curricular activities should not be perceived as extras, rather they should be considered as an integral part of learning experiences.

Interpreter to the Public

Parents and community members continuously ask teachers to comment on some aspects of the school programme or the education system in general. Teachers have to interpret to the public about school's programme, the country's plan and the educational policies. For this purpose, teachers need to be familiar with all changes and developments in educational policies and programmes. This will earn them the respect and status they deserve in the society. But many teachers show reluctance in carrying out the duties of this role. Even some think that it is the head teacher who should be asked to perform this duty. Effective teachers seize the opportunities to carry out their function as public interpreters through participation in community organisations, home visits, formal and informal meeting with parents, etc.

Artist in Human Relations

The teacher must perceive himself as an artist in human relations — the person who works with a variety of techniques and forces to produce situations that will stimulate learning.

Group Builder

Teachers know from their experiences that groups can knowingly or unknowingly block the progress of learning and that there are factors or forces within the group that can be used to stimulate learning. Effective teachers perceive their job as one of building the classroom group through helping students understand and accept one another, work together co-operatively, share experiences and materials, and communicate more effectively with one another as well as with the teacher.

Mental Hygiene Worker

In this role, the teacher may function as a referral agent to a counsellor or some other kinds of guidance worker. He may give reassurance and emotional support to students when they are experiencing difficulties or problems. The teacher can do a lot of things to improve the mental health of the classroom group or of the individual student.

Most teachers do not see this as their chief role. Yet if a teacher ignores the mental health aspects of his work, he will be much less effective than he should be.

Learner and Scholar

The most effective teachers are those who are able to grow not only in the knowledge of their subject but in their understanding of both in and out of the classroom. Effective teachers perceive the classroom as a fascinating laboratory of life, wherein they grow in their ability to understand more about their subject, more about children and how they learn, and more about themselves as teachers and as individuals. The teacher who is a learner and a scholar is perceived by his students, parents, and community favourably.

Parent Figure

Children tend to look upon teachers as parent figures. Their attitudes towards teachers tend to be somewhat similar to the attitudes they have towards their own parents and they expect teachers to react and behave more or less as their parents do.

Conflicts in Roles, Expectations and Loyalties

Teaching is a strenuous work. Some of the strain comes from the need to play many different roles, particularly roles that are in conflict with one another. One of the key problems that faces the teacher, therefore, is that of integrating his roles organizing them around the values in life that are most important to him, and playing them in ways that are not in basic conflict with his self-concept or his self-ideal.

In addition to conflict in roles, there are also conflicts in expectations. There is often a discrepancy between what people expect of teachers and what teachers expect of themselves. One example of conflict in expectation is that teachers may be expected to maintain high academic standards in their class, but to promote all students automatically.

Unfortunately, the teacher cannot succeed in all of these roles. He tries to satisfy everybody. What happens actually is that most teachers fail.

There are also conflicts in loyalties. Teachers are said to be loyal to children, loyal to community, loyal to the administration, loyal to themselves and their profession and loyal to their own families. Teachers are very often the targets for hostility, agitation, blame and criticism for many a time.

These conflicts in roles, expectations and loyalties create anxiety, boredom and tension among teachers. Teachers who fail to meet the conflicting demands and expectation may withdraw from the profession, or if they continue to remain in the profession they become ineffective and they lose the respect and status which they naturally deserve in the society. Effective teachers, on the other hand, are not frustrated by the disintegrative factors and forces in the profession. Further they perceive their conflicting roles, expectations and loyalties as challenging and yet stimulating for functioning in their best form. Teaching provides a broad range of satisfactions, ranging from those that are personal and practical to those that are idealistic and humanitarian. It provides opportunities to do work that is creative and important, to achieve status and prestige, to give something of oneself, to attain financial security, to contribute something of value to the lives of children and youth, and to attain greater personal growth. The effectiveness of the teacher depends on how he perceives his profession and his various roles and how he integrates the various conflicting roles, expectations and loyalties.

SELECTED QUESTIONS

1. What is teacher effectiveness? How is teacher effectiveness determined?
2. Discuss the characteristics of effective teachers.
3. The teacher is a leader of the group and facilitator of learning. Discuss.
4. State the various roles to be played by a teacher.

17
Core Teaching Skills

1. WHAT ARE THE CORE TEACHING SKILLS?

The National Policy on Education (1986) states: "The status of the teacher reflects the socio-cultural ethos of a society. It is said that no people can rise above the level of its teachers." This frank admittance of the policy makers about the dignity which teachers command from the society is only one side of the golden coin. The other relates to the crucial role which teachers play in the education of young children and in nation-building. The preamble of the Education Commission (1964-66) is extremely meaningful and significant for understanding the crucial role which teachers play. It states, "The destiny of India is now being shaped in her classrooms." Who is shaping the destiny of the country in the classroom? It is the teacher. If the teachers fail to impart the right type of knowledge, skills and ideals to the students, the country will be in darkness. Teachers have to develop their ability and skill of teaching effectively in the classroom. They have to learn the art and craft of teaching. They have to make right use of various skills of teaching at different situations and for various purposes. The art and craft of teaching make teaching systematic, sensitive, effective and joyful.

Teaching refers to the sum total of teacher behaviours in the classroom. A teacher introduces a lesson; he asks questions; he explains; he illustrates with examples; he motivates students by reinforcing their performance; and he does many other things in the classroom so that students will learn what is desirable and valuable to the nation. With training, experience and maturity, the teacher acquires proficiency in relation to these behaviours. The proficient performance and behaviour of teachers in the classroom are called teaching skills. There are various teaching skills which are needed for teaching various lessons. But some teaching skills are the most important ones and these skills are central in the teaching of all types of lessons. The central and the most important teaching skills are called the core teaching skills. The skill of introducing a lesson, the skill of using the blackboard, the skill of explaining, the skill of illustrating with examples, the skill of questioning, and the skill of reinforcement are central in the teaching of all types of lessons and are called core teaching skills.

2. THE SKILL OF INTRODUCING A LESSON

The skill of introducing a lesson appears very simple and easy to deal with, although, in reality, it requires clear thought, imagination and ingenuity of the teacher. The importance of this skill in the teaching — learning process is evident from the fact that pupil's learning of a new lesson depends largely on the way the lesson is introduced in the class.

When a teacher enters a classroom, he should not start the lesson abruptly and in a hurry. He should create a favourable setting, an atmosphere and readiness of students to learn a new lesson. He should first introduce the lesson in some way or the other. Introducing a lesson means what the teacher does (with or without the help of students) from the beginning of the period up to the statement of aim of the lesson or declaration of the topic. The skill of introducing a lesson serves the following purposes:

- (i) This is a stage when students are made ready to receive new knowledge or ideas.
- (ii) This is a stage for motivating students for the new lesson.
- (iii) This is a stage for drawing the attention of the class and focusing their attention on the topic for discussion. For this reason, introducing a lesson is regarded mostly as an attention-drawing behaviour.
- (iv) In case of continuous lesson, introducing a lesson serves the purpose of testing students' previous knowledge

and understanding of the units taught earlier and grounding the instruction on such knowledge and understanding.

Ways of Introducing a Lesson

There is no fixed procedure to introduce a lesson. Introduction varies from lesson to lesson depending upon the nature of the lesson (new lesson or continuous lesson), subject matter (history, science, mathematics), nature of the learners (beginners or students of higher classes), teacher's creative talents, experience and success in using specific ways.' Thus, a lesson may be introduced in any one of the following ways:

(i) by telling an interesting story which has relevance to the lesson to be taught;
(ii) by showing an experiment to create their curiosity;
(iii) by showing a picture or series of pictures which will stimulate their interest to know more about them;
(iv) by asking questions on previous knowledge;
(v) by reading a newspaper cutting, a portion of magazine about an incident;
(vi) by reporting about an event which took place very recently to arouse their curiosity;
(vii) by using any other devices, and
(viii) by a combination of two or more devices or ways mentioned above.

Examples of Introducing a Lesson

Example 1

Suppose a teacher has to teach a new lesson "Flying Fishes" in Class V of an English medium school. He can introduce the lesson by asking questions relating to their own knowledge about fishes of different kinds and then stimulating their curiosity to know more about fishes:

1. How many of you eat fish?
2. Can you tell the names of different kinds of fishes?
3. Where do fishes live?
4. Can fishes fly?

After getting answers from the students (either yes or no), the teacher will say, "Well boys and girls, there are some fishes that can fly. They live in sea, and they can fly in the air. But how can they fly? Let us read a lesson on flying fishes."

Example 2

Suppose a teacher has to teach about carbon dioxide. He may introduce the lesson by telling about an event which most of the students may not be knowing, and then asking questions to arouse their curiosity about the event and gradually to lead to the topic:

1. Who can tell me about the Valley of death?
   (No response from the students)
2. Nabin, will you tell me about the Valley of death?
   (No response from Nabin)

The question is repeated to two or three students and again there is no response. The teacher says: All right — listen, I will tell you about the Valley of death. The teacher then tells about it.

"There is a mountain cave in Java where thousands of skeletons of birds and animals have been lying for hundreds of years. If you throw a bird into a cave, it will die before it touches the ground. If you throw a dog it will die in few seconds. This Valley is called the Valley of death."

3. What could be the reason for this?
   (No response from students)
4. Mohan, you tell me why does it happen so?
   (Mohan says, "Due to the presence of ghost").
5. Any other reasons, Nina?
   (Nina says: "Due to some poisonous gas").
6. What is that poisonous gas?
   (No response from students)

The teacher says: That gas is carbon dioxide. Carbon dioxide is heavier than air. It has accumulated there for thousands of years and is so concentrated that whenever an animal or a bird is enveloped with the gas it dies immediately.

7. Do you know about the properties of carbon dioxide?
   (No response from the students)
8. Do you know how is carbon dioxide prepared?
   (No response from the students)

The teacher says all right, today we will learn about the preparation and properties of carbon dioxide.

Desirable and Undesirable Behaviours

From the above two examples, it becomes clear that lessons may be introduced in a number of different ways depending upon the nature and type of the lesson, characteristics of the learners, and creativity of the teacher. There are some teacher behaviours which are desirable in introducing a lesson. These desirable behaviours are given below.

Desirable Behaviours

(i) To use the previous knowledge of the students as the starting point in introducing a lesson, and

(ii) To use different devices such as story-telling, questions, using examples, analogies, similarities, describing, narrating, illustrating, role playing, demonstration, dramatisation, experimentation, and audio-visual aids.

Undesirable Behaviours

There are some undersirable behaviours which teachers should try to avoid. These are:

(i) devoting more time to introduce a lesson,

(ii) lack of continuity in ideas or information being presented or questions being asked, and

(iii) using irrelevant statements and questions which have no relation to the topic to be taught.

3. THE SKILL OF USING THE BLACKBOARD

The blackboard, now called the chalkboard, is known as the teacher's old and dependable friend. The blackboard is found almost in every classroom in our country. The blackboard does not have the glamour of many of the new devices, but it has two qualities which give it solid value as an item of teaching equipment. It is cheap to use, and in skilful hands it is amazingly flexible. Even though the blackboard is the cheapest and the best, very few teachers make the right use of its vast range of possibilities in teaching and learning. Use of a blackboard serves the following purposes:

(i) It draws attention of the class to teaching items or points which are significant.

(ii) It helps in making teaching systematic and orderly.

(iii) It helps teachers to draw sketches, diagrams and figures as and when required during instruction.
(iv) It helps in clear understanding of facts which would be otherwise confusing or difficult for the students.
(v) It gives opportunity to students for participation, performance and a sense of achievement in the class.

Even though the blackboard is a valuable asset for the teacher, very few teachers make use of it. Some are ignorant about its use, some feel incompetent, and still some forget to use it while teaching. Thus, some teachers struggle hard, to explain a difficult concept which would have been made easier by a simple diagram on the board. Using the blackboard is an art in itself, a skill to be mastered by every teacher, no matter who he is and what subject he teaches. The skill of using the blackboard effectively can be developed by focusing the attention of the teacher on certain desirable behaviours.

Desirable Behaviours in Using the Blackboard

The desirable behaviours in using the blackboard are:
(i) Legibility of handwriting,
(ii) Neatness of writing,
(iii) Appropriateness of the blackboard work.

The behaviours are mentioned in detail below:
(i) Every letter, word or sentence written on the board should be distinct.
(ii) There should be equal spacing between letters in a word, in a sentence and between different sentences. It should not be too short or too long. If the spacing is too short, it becomes difficult for the students to read the writings. If the spacing is too long, very few words or sentences can be written on the board at one time and it will take a lot of time of the teacher to clean the board and write something more.
(iii) The size of the letter should be large enough to be read easily by the students in the last bench of the class.
(iv) All small letters and all capital letters should be of the same size.
(v) Thickness of lines should be of the same width.

(vi) Words and sentences should be written in horizontal lines parallel to the base of the blackboard.

(vii) One should not stretch too much to the top of the board or cramp too much to bottom, as this will cause bad writing.

(viii) One should stand to one side of the board (at an angle of 45° to the board) while writing, so that students see what is being written on the board.

(ix) One should talk while writing on the board. The voice of the teacher will reinforce writing on the board.

(x) The surface of the board should be kept clean, so that the writing will be clear and visible.

(xi) Only relevant matters should be written on the board.

(xii) Only one point should be written on the board at a given time. When that point has been explained, the other point be written on the board. In this way, continuity should be maintained on the board.

(xiii) Blackboard work should be clear, brief and in simple language.

(xiv) Important words or points should be underlined, preferably in coloured chalks, to put emphasis, bring contrast with other points, and to draw students' attention on those points.

Undesirable Behaviours in Using the Blackboard

There are some undesirable behaviours which every teacher should try to avoid while using the blackboard:

(i) Overwriting on the board.

(ii) Not cleaning the board before and after teaching.

(iii) Writing too much at the top, too much at the bottom, and stretched too far to the sides of the board.

(iv) Disfiguring the board by encircling some words or sentences, a jungle of words, disorderly writing and pressing the chalkboard while writing.

(v) Standing back to the class while writing.

(vi) Ignoring the headings and sub-headings of points written on the board.

(vii) Using the chalk in a way and on a surface which creates peculiar sounds while writing on the board.

(viii) Committing mistakes while writing on the board.

(ix) Polluting the air inside the classroom with chalk dust by moving the duster from one side to the other (The right way is to move the duster upward and downward).

4. THE SKILL OF EXPLAINING

Explanation by the teacher is a commonly used teaching skill. In fact, it is the essence of instruction. Explaining means describing 'how', 'why' or 'what' of a concept, phenomenon, event, action, condition, etc. It is an activity that fills in the gap in students' understanding.

This gap in students' understanding is filled in by relating present knowledge with their past experiences, by citing cause-effect relationship, by making inter-related statements about the concept, principles, event or idea. Explanation is, therefore, like a bridge that connects antecedents and the result, experiences and present knowledge.

Explanation serves the following purposes:

(i) It brings about understanding of students about an event or a phenomenon.

(ii) It increases their understanding by relating a phenomenon to its causes, an idea with similar other ideas, new knowledge with previous experiences.

(iii) It leads to a conclusion about the event, phenomenon or idea being studied.

Desirable Behaviours for the Skill of Explaining

The skill of explaining depends upon certain desirable behaviours of the teacher. These are:

(i) Using beginning and concluding statements,

(ii) Using explaining links, and

(iii) Testing pupils' understanding:

(a) Before explanation is given, the teacher should make few beginning or introductory statements about the phenomenon, concept, event or action. Beginning statements create mental readiness on the part of pupils to listen to what is going to be explained. After explanation has been given, the teacher should make few concluding or summarizing statements about the event, phenomenon, action or concept. Concluding statements help in consolidation of ideas explained to them.

(b) While explaining about an event, action, phenomenon, or concept, the teacher should make use of certain linking words or phrases, such as because, therefore, hence, as a result of, consequently, that is why, this is how, but, why, thus, next, then, after, before, by, due to, in order to, etc. Such linking words make the explanation more clear by bringing continuity in the statements.

(c) After explaining the idea, the teacher should put three or four questions to the students to test their understanding of the idea. Actually testing pupils' understanding is not a part of the skill of explaining, but it helps in knowing whether the purpose of explaining has been achieved or not.

Undesirable Behaviours for the Skill of Explaining

While explaining an event, phenomenon, concept or action, teachers sometimes show certain undesirable behaviours. In order that explanation be effective, teachers should avoid these undesirable behaviours. These undesirable behaviours for the skill of explaining are as follows:

(i) Stating irrelevant statements which do not contribute to the understanding of the concept but which distract their attention from the topic to some other ideas and thus cause confusion.

(ii) Lacking in continuity of statement of ideas presented, lack of sequence of ideas, failure to relate present knowledge with previous experience or information.

(iii) Using vocabulary-words, terms, definitions, sentences not appropriate to the age, grade, and the level of understanding of the students which make ideas more difficult to comprehend.

(iv) Lack of fluency in narration of facts such as speaking half sentences, reformulating the sentences, taking unnecessary pause in between statements which make explanation dull and uninteresting.

(v) Using vague words and phrases—as you see, probably, you know, correct, I mean, obviously, etc. which hinder understanding of concepts.

5. THE SKILL OF ILLUSTRATING WITH EXAMPLES

While teaching abstract ideas or concepts to students, some teachers feel difficulty in explaining in simple, clear and concrete form. The skill of illustrating with examples aims at teaching difficult concepts or ideas in simple, clear and interesting way. For example, while teaching about the "force of gravity," the teacher may present a long verbal description of the concept of gravity. But that will be uninteresting and difficult for students to comprehend the concept. The teacher can teach the same concept by illustrating with example. He may hold a piece of chalk or a small ball and throw it high in the air. The chalk or the ball will return to the ground. He may then ask students to tell the reasons. From this illustration, the teacher can introduce the famous discovery of Sir Isaac Newton about the force of gravity. He can ask students to give other similar examples — fruits and leaves falling from the tree, raindrops falling from the sky, etc. Thus, the skill of illustrating with examples serves the following purposes:

(i) It brings clarity and simplicity in teaching.
(ii) It creates interest in the lesson.
(iii) It takes the pupils from the known to the unknown.
(iv) It secures and sustains their attention.
(v) It arouses their curiosity to know about things, events or phenomena.

The skill of illustrating with examples involves two processes:

(i) Clarifying the idea or concept to the students by giving various examples and through classroom demonstration, and
(ii) verifying whether students have really understood the concept by asking students to give similar other examples relating to the concept.

The important components of the skill of illustrating with examples are as follows:

(i) To formulate simple examples.
(ii) To formulate interesting examples.

(iii) To formulate examples relevant to the concept, idea, topic or subject.
(iv) To use appropriate media (verbal and non-verbal) for examples.
(v) To use appropriate media (verbal and non-verbal, auditory and tactual) suited to the subject.
(vi) To use examples by inductive or deductive approach.

When the teacher illustrates a concept, the examples should be simple, interesting, relevant to the students, and suited to their previous knowledge and experience. He may give visual examples, auditory examples, and tactual examples. Visual examples are objects, models, pictures, charts, and specimens. Auditory examples are those presented orally or verbally by the teacher. Tactual examples involve the use of objects which the students can touch and feel and understand it. In a second way, examples can be presented verbally or in a non-verbal way. Verbal examples are presented orally by the teacher through story-telling, analogies, etc. Non-verbal examples are objects, models, pictures, diagrams, maps and charts, etc. Whether the teacher presents visual, auditory or tactual examples, in a verbal or non-verbal way, they must be appropriate to the topic or the subject.

Examples can be used through inductive and deductive approach. In inductive approach the teacher first presents a number of different examples relating to the concept and on the basis of these examples, he helps students to arrive at a conclusion. For example, the teacher may proceed in the following way:

Teacher : What happens when copper is heated?
Pupil : It expands.
Teacher : What happens when iron is heated?
Pupil : It expands.
Teacher : What happens when gold is heated?
Pupil : It expands.

Now the teacher comes to the conclusion:

"A substance expands when heated." In deductive approach, the teacher proceeds from general to particular. First, he states a general principle and then cites different examples to verify and substantiate the idea. For example, the teacher states that the angles of a triangle are equal to two right angles. He then asks students to draw different triangles and measure the angles of the triangles. They verify and find that the angles of a triangle are equal to two right angles.

6. THE SKILL OF QUESTIONING

What is Meant by Questioning?

Questioning is an important teaching skill which every teacher needs to possess. In fact, the ability to ask questions has long been regarded as one of the chief qualifications for successful teaching. It is sometimes said that the teacher who never questions never teaches. Questioning plays a very important part in all learning, teaching and testing. It is the key of all educative activity.

Questions are interrogative statements which are asked to stimulate the learner's mental activities, to search for the answer, to solve a problem, to clarify a doubt, or to provoke the thinking process of the child.

Classification of Questions

Questions are classified into various categories for various purposes:

(i) *Natural and Formal Questions*: In one way, questions are classified into two major categories: natural questions and formal questions. A natural question is one which is asked because the questioner wants to know the answer. Children's spontaneous questions are of this type. The formal question is the type asked by the teacher in his attempt to stimulate some type of response on the part of the pupil. In this book, we are concerned with the formal questions of the teacher.

(ii) *Fact and Interpretational Questions*: Questions are also classified as fact and interpretational (thought) questions. A fact question calls for the ability to answer in terms of data already in existence which may be known or unknown. "Which is the largest wheat producing State in India?" is a definite fact question. An interpretational question, on the other hand, requires the student to draw an inference from data which are known but which cannot yield the answer to the question without interpretation. "Why do you like this story?" is a question which requires thought and interpretation on the part of the pupil while "Do you like this story?" is a mere question of fact and can be answered without thought.

(iii) ***Memory and Recognition Questions***: Questions are also classified into two types: memory and recognition questions. Memory questions are those which must be answered with reference to something that has been learned in past. Recognition questions are those which can be answered by observation or examination of data presented to the students.

(iv) ***Detailed and Topical Questions***: Questions may be also spoken of as detailed questions or topical questions. A detailed question asks for a simple fact: "What happened on August 15, 1947?" The topical question asks for a connected statement: "What were the causes of the Quit India Movement?" Thus, the detailed question may require a single statement for the answer while the topical question requires a discussion of topic.

(v) ***Gatto's Classification***: F.M. Gatto (1929) worked out a classification of questions according to the mental processes involved in answering the question. This classification seems sufficiently fine for practical use. Gatto's classification of questions is given below:

(a) Memory Question
(Where is Lord Jagannath Temple?)

(b) Organisation Question
(How did people in ancient days travel?)

(c) Causal Reasoning Question
(Why is a blast furnace never allowed getting cold?)

(d) Evaluation Question (Is it a true story?)

(e) Inference Type Question
(Would you like to go to Kashmir in winter?)

(f) Information Type Question (What makes leaves green?)

(g) Comparison Type Question
(Whose fields were the best — Lambkin's or Granny's?)

(h) Analysis Type Question
(What makes this flower beautiful?)

(i) Interpretation Type Question (What does census mean?)

Components of the Skill of Questioning

What is a good question? What are its characteristics? How should questions be asked? How should the answers be treated?

The skill of questioning implies three aspects or components. These are the (i) Structure, (ii) Process and (iii) Product.

(i) *Structure of a Question*

The structure of a question indicates the framing and organisation of the question. Questions should be structured on the basis of the following characteristics.

(a) *Clarity*: The question must be constructed in such a fashion that the child easily understands what is wanted even though he may not know the answer to the question. The same qualities that make a sentence clear make a question clear. For example, "Who was the queen of England?" is a question that cannot be answered until the child knows what period is meant.

(b) *Simplicity*: A question may be a good question for adults and a very poor question for children. "What is the nature of the theory of relativity?" is perfectly a good question for an advanced student of mathematics but not a question a child can answer. The language of the child must be used in formulating questions.

(c) *Challenge*: A good question stimulates the child to think, that is, to compare, evaluate and draw inferences and conclusions. For example, "Do you think New Delhi is well-located to be the capital of India?" is a question that stimulates the reasoning powers of the child and leads to further thinking.

(d) *Specificity*: Questions should require specific rather than general answers. The child should not be encouraged to bluff and generalize without some data on which to base his answer. The child should not be permitted to give vague and general answers to specific questions.

(e) *Definiteness*: The question must be so stated that it permits one answer only. The definiteness of a question indicates its objectivity.

(f) *Conciseness*: The question should be short and concise as far as possible. A concise question is that which does not contain any unnecessary or redundant words like 'Who can tell me?' 'Does any one know?' 'Can you tell me?' etc.

(g) Relevancy: The question should be related to be topic being discussed and the objectives of teaching the lesson.

(h) *Grammatical Correctness*: Questions should be asked in language which is grammatically correct; grammatically wrong sentences will confuse students to organise their answer. For example, the question "Have you went to Nandan Kanan?" will elicit the answer "Yes, I have went to Nandan Kanan."

(ii) Process of Asking Questions

Process refers to the way the questions are asked. This usually includes:

(a) The number of questions asked,
(b) Repetition of questions,
(c) Distributing and directing questions,
(d) Speed of asking question,
(e) The voice of the teacher.

(a) *The Number of Questions Asked*: Good technique in questioning involves asking a sufficient number of questions so that pupils will be stimulated to activity, but not a barrage of questions which require a minimum of thought and the giving of short or one-word answers. Too many questions lead to too much teacher activity and not enough activity on the part of pupils.

(b) *Repetition of Questions*: Sometimes teachers repeat the question unnecessarily. When students become used to repetition of questions by the teacher, they develop a habit of attempting to the questions only at the second time. Much time is wasted in repetition of questions for which fluency is decreased and pupils become inattentive.

(c) *Distributing and Directing Questions*: Some teachers follow a fixed order of giving out questions to the class, such as proceeding alphabetically or row by row, as a result of which all children cannot participate in the discussion. Ideally the teacher should distribute the questions in such a manner that the majority of the pupils in a class will take part in a discussion. The teacher should distribute his questions among the bright and dull students, those who raise their hands or those who do not, those who are attentive and those who are not attentive so that each and every student will have the opportunity to participate in the discussion. He should first ask a question, take a pause and call on a student to answer it.

(d) *The Speed of Asking a Question*: Questions should be put not too hurriedly or too slowly. If the question is put too slowly it becomes time-consuming resulting in decrease in fluency. On the other hand, if it is put too hurriedly or rapidly, students find it difficult to comprehend the question properly resulting in failure to answer the question even if the answer is known by them. When a question is asked, there should be a pause to enable the students to understand, think and answer.

(e) *The Voice of the Teacher:* Questions should be asked in a pleasant manner, not in a fashion likely to create a nervous tension in the pupil or block his thinking. Nervous haste on the part of the teacher will encourage the same attitude among the pupils. The voice of the teacher should be clear and distinctly audible to the students in the last benches. When this is not done, students in the last benches ask the teacher to repeat the question. This consumes more time of the teacher and decreases his fluency.

(iii) Product of Questioning

Product refers to student's answers. If the discussion has been effective, if students have the interest and previous knowledge, if they are attentive, if the structure and process for questioning are free from faults, students will answer the questions. It may so happen that even if there is nothing wrong in the structure and process of questions, students fail to respond. The failure of students to respond may be due to various factors, such as:

(a) Students may not be intelligent enough to understand the question.
(b) Questions may be of higher order of difficulty for the class.
(c) The lesson may not be interesting to them and lack of interest causes inattention.
(d) Students may be lacking in appropriate previous knowledge to answer the question.
(e) There may not be any rapport between the students and the teacher.

When students fail to answer the question, the teacher should try to know the underlying causes. If necessary, he may re-teach the topic or provide remedial teaching. When a student has given the correct answer, the teacher should not repeat it. If a student has given a wrong answer, the teacher should not use bad language or harsh language to criticise him or make fun of his answer. In such cases, some other students should be asked to tell the answer. Students' answers should be treated positively or negatively by using various reinforcement techniques.

7. THE SKILL OF REINFORCEMENT

What is Reinforcement?

In the classroom, a teacher teaches a subject, he discusses, he asks questions, he expects his students to answer his questions and participate in discussion and other classroom activities. When a student answers a question or performs an activity, he wants to know whether his answer is right, whether he has performed the activity in the correct manner. He needs the approval and attention of his teacher and his classmates. The teacher has to reinforce the student's answer and his performance as right or wrong, desirable or undesirable. Such information, knowledge, or feedback about a student's answer should be provided by the teacher immediately. If the student's answer is right, the teacher motivates him by approving his answer, by praise, recognition, reward, by a pat on-his-back and other encouraging words. This strengthens the student's response. If the student's answer is found wrong, the teacher disapproves his answer and uses discouraging words, he shakes his head, pays attention to some other student, punishes, scolds, etc. This weakens the student's response. In fact, when a student behaves in the desirable way, and when he makes a correct response, it should not be reinforced negatively. Reinforcement is a technique of strengthening the desirable behaviour and weakening the undesirable behaviour. It is a condition of motivating or encouraging students to behave in the desirable way, or to give correct answer and discouraging them to behave in the undesirable way or to give wrong answers.

Types of Reinforcement

The above discussion suggests that reinforcement is of two types — positive reinforcement and negative reinforcement. Positive reinforcement is given to strengthen a behaviour or a response and to motivate students to behave in the desirable way. Praise, recognition, approval, reward, encouraging words, grades and marks, certificate of proficiency, notifying the name on the school notice board, paying attention, drawing others' attention to the answer, etc., are used for providing positive reinforcement to students. On the contrary, negative reinforcement is given to weaken a behaviour or a response and to discourage students to behave in the undesirable way. Reproof, blame, punishment, threat of failure, warning, rebuke, moving away from the responding student, discouraging and angry looks, etc., are used by the teacher for providing negative reinforcement to students. Even though the teacher can use positive reinforcement techniques or negative reinforcement techniques to strengthen or weaken a behaviour respectively, the effect of positive reinforcement in strengthening a behaviour is greater than the effect of negative reinforcement in weakening a behaviour. In order to reinforce a behaviour either positively or negatively, the teacher makes use of some reinforcers. There are four types of reinforcers, such as: (i) positive verbal reinforcer (ii) positive non-verbal reinforcer, (iii) negative verbal reinforcer, and (iv) negative non-verbal reinforcer.

These types are based on the purpose served by a reinforcer (strengthening or weakening the behaviour) and the mode of its presentation (verbal and non-verbal).

Examples of each type of reinforcers are given below:

Types of Reinforcer	Purpose Served	Mode of Presentation	Examples
Positive verbal reinforcer	Strengthens behaviour	Verbal expressions	Saying good, OK, praising, approving, all types of encouraging words.
Positive non-verbal reinforcer	Strengthens behaviour	Non-verbal expression and ways	Giving reward, grades, marks, certificate of proficiency, smiling, pat-on-the back, nodding his head, moving closer to the student, paying attention to him, writing encouraging words in his notebook, etc.

(*Contd.*)

Types of Reinforcer	Purpose Served	Mode of Presentation	Examples
Negative verbal reinforcer	Weakens behaviour	Verbal expression	Rebuking, threatening, warning, and other discouraging words.
Negative non-verbal reinforcer	Weakens behaviour	Non-verbal expressions and ways	Punishing, moving away from the student, discouraging and angry look, etc.

The skill of reinforcement has tremendous value for motivating students in the learning situation. But reinforcement techniques should not be used indiscriminately. The following care should be taken in the use of reinforcers:

(i) The teacher should not reinforce the behaviour of responding students only. Students who are shy, withdrawn, and who do not participate in the classroom activities or answer the questions need to be encouraged by the teacher.

(ii) Reinforcers lose their value if they are used too frequently by the teacher. If a teacher says "good," "all right," "OK," etc., every time a student makes a correct answer, the student will be accustomed with that reinforcing word and such word will lose its motivational value. Thus, the teacher has to use different positive reinforcers or negative reinforcers on different occasions.

(iii) The impact of reinforcers varies from child to child. One student may be encouraged by the teacher saying 'good' when he makes correct answer, while another student may be encouraged by a pat on the back by the teacher.

(iv) Teachers should remember that the impact of positive reinforcer in strengthening a desirable behaviour is greater than that of the negative reinforcer in weakening undesirable behaviour. Along with encouraging the responding pupils, the teacher should also encourage the non-responding pupils and the pupils who give wrong answers to work hard and answer the questions correctly.

SELECTED QUESTIONS

1. What are the core teaching skills? Explain the skill of questioning with examples.
2. Write short notes:
   (a) Components of questioning.
   (b) The skill of reinforcement.
   (c) The skill of introducing a lesson.
   (d) The skill of illustrating with examples.
   (e) The skill of using the blackboard.
3. Explain the skill of reinforcement.
4. Explain the skill of using the blackboard.
5. Explain the skill of illustrating with examples.
6. Explain the skill of introducing a lesson.

18

Personality

1. THE CONCEPT AND NATURE OF PERSONALITY

Ordinarily, the term 'personality' refers to the impressions which an individual makes on others. Personality, as a term, is used to mean the configuration of individual characteristics and ways of behaving which determine an individual's unique adjustment to his environment. The term 'personality' is a very inclusive one. Thus any description of an individual's personality must take into account his appearance, abilities, motives, emotional reactions, his values and attitudes and his distinctive traits.

In defining personality, the psychologists employ the indispensable ideas of integration and uniqueness. Personality invariably signifies the functioning of the whole person and the unique organisation of the individual that distinguishes him from his fellows. Allport says that, "Personality is the dynamic organisation within the individual of those psycho-biological systems which determine his unique adjustment to the environment."

Guilford (1959) similarly defines personality as an individual's unique pattern of traits. Guilford, like Allport, stresses the integration of traits when he discusses the individual's pattern of traits. By trait Guilford means any distinguishable, relatively enduring way in which one individual differs from others. He groups traits into seven modalities or classes. These modalities or traits are as follows: interest, attitude, needs, temperament, aptitude, morphology or the body structure, and physiology (basic bodily functions).

2. CHARACTERISTICS OF MATURE PERSONALITY

The young individual with immature personality gradually grows into a mature adult through successive stages of development. What are, then, the characteristics of a mature personality? In order to understand the characteristics of mature personality, it is advisable to compare the behaviour patterns of infants and adults:

(i) The infant is passive whereas the adult shows increasing activity. The mature adult shows self-initiative and possesses self-determination for various activities relating to his life.

(ii) The infant is dependent upon others to meet his basic needs. By contrast, the adult is relatively independent of others. Relative independence means to "stand on one's own feet." The mature adult develops his own sets of behaviour and his behaviour is no longer determined by his family as in case of an infant.

(iii) The infant is capable of behaving only in a few ways. But the adult is capable of behaving in many different ways in a particular situation.

(iv) The infant has erratic, casual, shallow and quickly-dropped interests. But the adult has deeper interests. Mature personality is characterized by an endless series of challenges, and the reward comes from doing something for its own sake.

(v) The infant possesses a short-time perspective. His behaviour is determined largely by the present. But the mature adult possesses a much longer time perspective. His behaviour is determined by the past experiences and future consequences.

(vi) The infant occupies a subordinate position in the family and the society. But the mature person aspires to occupy an equal and/or superior position relative to others.

(vii) The infant lacks awareness of self. But the adult is conscious of his self — his abilities and limitations, integrity and worth.

In addition to these characteristics, there are several other criteria of maturity as suggested by Allport (1961). These are as follows:

(viii) There is an extension of the sense of self that grows with experience until the welfare of others becomes as important as one's own.

(ix) The mature personality is capable of intimacy and compassion. The adult possesses a capacity for love and also a respect for the worth and dignity of others.

(x) Emotional security characterizes the mature personality. There is a growing ability to tolerate frustration and to express convictions and feelings with consideration for others.

(xi) Mature personalities are realistic in their judgment of people and situations, and they are in touch with the real world.

(xii) Mature persons know themselves. They possess self-insight.

(xiii) Mature persons have a clear comprehension of life's purposes. They develop a philosophy of life.

3. FACTORS INFLUENCING PERSONALITY

How does personality develop? What are the factors which influence the development of personality? What are the causes of individual differences in personality development?

Personality develops as a result of hereditary endowments or biological givens. Early experiences of a child also influence his personality. Culture has tremendous influence on the development of a child's personality. The interaction of heredity, experiences and culture causes individual differences in personality development.

Influence of Biological Givens (Heredity)

Biological givens refer to what nature contributes to the person. The biological make-up of a person is received from the parents. The process of passing on biological characteristics from one generation to another is called heredity. The influence of heredity may commonly be observed in the physical resemblance of children to their parents. We shall discuss the relationship between certain given biological factors and corresponding personality factors.

Hormones

Modern medical science has identified chemicals, produced by a number of glands that stimulate the body to various behaviours. They are called hormones. Numerous hormones influence various physical functions and account for differences in temperaments.

Glandular excesses or deficiencies can have great direct or indirect effects on the personality structure. An excess of insulin causes fatigue, nervousness and anxiety. Deficiency of thyroxin or under activity of the thyroid gland may cause restlessness, nervousness, irritability and general hyperactivity. The adrenal glands are related to cardiac activity, and increased secretion of adrenaline is characteristic of emotional activity. Similarly sex gland secretion affects masculinity and feminity.

Physique

Physical characteristics of the individual contribute to the total personality and are designated as physique. Kretschmer and Sheldon described various types of physique and the corresponding personality types.

Body build has both direct and indirect influences on personality. The direct influence of body build on personality is seen in the manner in which it determines what a person can and cannot do, his energy level and his reactions to other people whose body builds are superior or inferior to his own body build. Indirectly body build influences personality through body cathartic — the degree of satisfaction a person feels about himself. If a person is satisfied with his body, his positive attitude is expressed in self-confidence, self-assurance and a generally wholesome self-concept. A person's adjustment to life is influenced by the way he perceives his body in relation to the bodies of others, his ideal as well as culturally approved standards, by the evaluation of his physical abilities and stabilities by others.

Temperaments

Everyday experiences also provide numerous examples of the relationship between biology and personality. Temperamental differences are noticed among infants after few days of birth.

Some infants are placid, others are fretful. Some are passive, others are active; some are more readily upset by outside noise than others. During the first few days, the social environment has little or no influence on the infants. Temperamental differences noticed among them during the first few days are mainly due to heredity. Perhaps with this idea in mind, some psychologists say that 'personality is structured on the delivery table'.

Influence of Culture

Culture in simple terms is a way of life. A way of life includes many things — social institutions, traditions, ideas, art, morals and much more. There are no absolute standards of the proper or correct way of life. Propriety can be judged only in relation to a given culture at a given time. As cultures differ, so do the personalities embedded in these cultures. Regarding cultural influences on personality development, Allport maintains the following viewpoints:

(a) Cultural traditions determine the lessons the parents will teach the child and the way in which the lessons are taught;
(b) Different cultures have different ways of training the child and different lessons to teach;
(c) Child's early experiences in a given culture exert a lasting effect upon his personality, and
(d) Similar experiences will tend to produce similar personalities.

The views of Allport provide guidelines to understand why the personalities of a bushman and a modern businessman are different and why one bushman is similar to another bushman.

Even cultures which are similar in many respects put varying degrees of emphasis on commonly held values. The French, for example, put more emphasis on thrift and individuality than Americans. The Germans put more emphasis on work and discipline than Americans. The American child is expected to develop 'marketable personality' with emphasis on ambition, getting ahead, popularity, initiative and friendliness.

Sub-cultures

In our study of personality we must be aware not only of the whole culture, but also of smaller unit of culture called subculture. Sub-cultures, while sharing most of the ways of life of the general culture, also have a way of life of their own. Both the general culture and the sub-cultures to which we belong contribute to our personality development. Two such sub-cultures are family and the peer group.

The Family

The family is like a small culture. Each family tends to be somewhat unique just as people are unique. The importance of family on children's personality development is evident from the fact that about half of the child's personality is formed by the time the child enters kindergarten. It is an observed fact that attitudes and values tend to be similar among members of a family. The same is often true of political beliefs and views on important social issues.

Such tendencies for ways of life to run in families come about largely through imitation, learning and identification. The younger children in a family simply imitate their parents and older siblings. Thus to some extent they do things and think about matters as the older members of family do. This process is aided when the child identifies with a parent or older sibling. But children do not always behave as their parents do not do, nor do they always approve their parent's opinions and beliefs. Sometimes children develop quite opposite tendencies; they experience counter-identification. For example, the young man may have political beliefs that are contrary to those of the parents. Such an opposition or the reaction by the young man is called 'adolescent rebellion.' Adolescent rebellion is an indication that the adolescent is trying to be independent of his parents and conform to peer-group standards.

The Peer Group

Peer groups have great influence on personality development. Almost everybody belongs to at least one group of equals. Sociologists and psychologists refer to such components of our society as peer-groups. This term generally refers to people of similar age who have in common certain experiences, interests and way of understanding events. Most of us informally learn a great deal, especially about social conduct from our peers. From our peers we learn some of our values — what is right and what is wrong. The teenage peer group is very powerful in moulding behaviour patterns of teenagers.

The general culture and the sub-cultures refer to the environment in which personality development takes place. The child's environment moulds his personality through modelling and opportunity for imitation learning. Through its child training methods, every cultural group tries to produce group members whose personality patterns conform to the standards of the culture. There are different methods of child training and each method leads to a particular pattern of personality development.

Studies by Baumrind (1966) show that authoritarian methods produce a child who is quiet, well-behaved, non-resistant, socially unaggressive, and restricted in curiosity, originality and fancifulness. Strict treatment and demands for rigid conformity in the early years of life often lead to the development of authoritarian personality syndromes.

Sears (1957) is of the opinion that democratic child training results in greater independence in thinking and acting and in a healthy, positive, confident self-concept. This leads to better personal and social adjustments and to more outgoing, active and spontaneous behaviour.

Effects of Modelling

Albert Bandura, one of the chief architects of social learning theory, has stressed the potent influence of modelling on personality development. Bandura and Walters (1963) note that children do not do what adults tell them to do but rather what they see adults do. The importance of models is seen in what happens as a result of observing others:

1. The observer may acquire new responses.
2. Observation of models may strengthen or weaken existing responses.
3. Observation of model may cause the reappearance of responses that were apparently forgotten.

If children witness undesirable behaviour, which is either rewarded or goes unpunished, they develop undesirable behaviour pattern. The reverse is also true. Bandura, Ross and Ross (1963) studied the effect of live models, filmed human aggression, and film cartoon aggression on pre-school children's aggressive behaviour. They noted that all the children exhibited significantly more aggression than youngsters in a control group. Also filmed models were as effective as live models in transmitting aggression. Research by Bandura and Walters (1963) suggests that prestigious, powerful, competent models are more readily imitated than models who, lack these qualities.

The preceding discussion on various factors contributing to individual differences in personality development indicates that personality is neither the result of hereditary endowments only nor of environmental influences alone. Heredity is responsible for the raw materials of personality. It also sets the limit for the development of these raw materials. Environment also exerts powerful influences on personality development.

4. VARIOUS APPROACHES TO THE STUDY OF PERSONALITY

There are various approaches to the study of personality and all these approaches can be helpful in personality evaluation. These approaches are:

(a) The Normative Approach,
(b) The Projective Approach,
(c) The Intuitive Approach, and
(d) The Phenomenological Approach (Norman Tallent 1978).

The Normative Approach

To describe the degree to which an individual has some particular quality, we often compare that person with another. Thus, we may say that "Mili is as intelligent as Lily," "Riku is more intelligent than Mitu" or "Nina is less imaginative than Bina." Using the normative approach, we can compare a given individual with the average for a group — the norm. For example, in the MMPI there is a scale for measuring depression: 50 is the average score in that scale and scores below 70 are regarded as in the average range. A person, who scores 90 or higher is appreciably depressed.

The Projective Approach

This approach is based on the fact that in most life situations, you have some amount of freedom to choose what you will do. What you do is an expression of your own personality. Your total behaviour is unique, different from that of any one else on earth. As for example, if you decide to spend some time reading, you may choose between a humour magazine, a novel with some social implications or a classical literature. What you choose is a reflection of your personality. Suppose, an artist is provided with a blank canvas or the poet with the blank sheet of paper. What appears on these blank forms is largely a projection of the personality of the individual. If the new production is highly conventional and unoriginal, this fact too reflects the personality of the individual who created it. Psychoanalysts believe in this approach to the study of personality. According to these psychologists, an individual's personality is projected through his style of life, his behaviours, manners, talks, walks, thoughts and feelings. Thus, we can study an individual's personality by observing his style of life, his behaviour, etc. Basing on this ideology, psychologists have devised certain 'projective techniques' like TAT, Rorschach Test, CAT to study personality.

The Intuitive Approach

The intuitive approach is highly important in our everyday understanding of people. When we are able to understand an individual without significant reflection, we are studying personality through intuition. Intuition can be understood as an approach that is facilitated by life's experiences and learning. People develop different forms of intuition based on their experiences and interests. Those who have a keen interest in people may understand others intuitively. Sports fans intuitively pick up subtle actions of players that have significance, but are missed by less experienced observers. Highly skilled people of many callings seem to develop a 'sixth sense' for many matters pertaining to their work. We call all such understanding intuitive, because they occur immediately without any reflection. Generally, clinical psychologists and other mental health workers are good in intuition.

The Phenomenological Approach

The phenomenological approach may be useful in understanding others. It is simply a matter of putting ourselves in the other person's shoes. Psychologists frequently find it helpful to understand people in terms of their perceptions, how they see their world. This is because much of our behaviour is determined by our understanding. As for example, if a man believes that a secret organisation is out to 'get' him, he may take action appropriate to his understanding; he may buy a gun or hide in a basement. If an individual has a feeling of inferiority or fear of failure, he may not enroll in a course because of fear of failing even though objectively he has all the needed abilities. To this individual, "things are what they seem."

These various approaches have significance for assessing personality through various techniques. Sometimes we may use a number of these techniques in combination. Such a combination is called a 'battery.' In evaluating an individual's personality we may conduct an interview, administer three or four psychological tests, and perhaps have the individual's behaviour judged or rated by some of the people who know the person best. Through this battery approach we can combine, for example, the normative approach, the projective approach, and the intuitive approach. We may first administer the MMPI, and then a projective test like the TAT. While the person is taking the tests we can also study his reactions and personality patterns through intuitions. The battery approach permits us to cross-check the results of one technique against another. Evaluation techniques overlap in the information they provide about an individual's personality. We can thus place more confidence in our conclusion than if we had used only one technique. The various techniques that comprise the battery also tend to supplement one another. That is why, they may yield information on different aspects of the same behaviours. An obvious example is the manner in which a test of intelligence and teacher's ratings may supplement each other.

5. TYPES AND TRAITS OF PERSONALITY

Some psychologists are of the opinion that personality can be studied through a somewhat different approach — type approach. Thus, there are various type of theories of personality.

Type theories of personality were among the first to be found in recorded history. The ancient type theories were based upon the idea that people could be divided into a relatively small number of types according to their personalities and that one could predict a person's behaviour with reasonable accuracy by simply knowing his 'type.' The type theories of personality can be divided into three categories such as:

(a) Types based on body,
(b) Types based on endocrine glands and
(c) Types based on behaviour or psychological types.

These type theories are discussed later in this chapter. It is here to re-emphasize the fact that the type approach groups individuals into distinct types. Although some type theories are valid in some way, there remain two dangers in type theories. One danger is that the type descriptions tend to assert too much about the individual. As soon as a person is tagged to a type, he is expected to have all the characteristics belonging to that type. This may lead to stereotypes about the person. But actually a person may not possess all the characteristics of a particular type. The determiners of personality are too many and the various characteristics combine into something both too rich and too unusual to be described with a single general term. The second danger is that type description tends to maintain outmoded conceptions of personality and neglect cultural influences. Type theories are sponsored primarily by those who see human characteristics as chiefly the result of biological inheritance. That is why many type theories refer to body forms. The body is an important locus of personality — but personality is also dependent on childhood experiences, later opportunities and on the relations to other people.

While the type approach appears to account for some of the major differences among people, it is also clear that people differ in more ways than can be encompassed by a small number of classifications. Thus a new approach called the trait approach attempts to distinguish between personality types using a large number of characteristics. The trait approach is in some respect at the opposite extreme of a type approach. At present, more interest is shown in trait approach which has become more popular than type approach.

A trait is a relatively permanent quality or attribute of an individual which is sufficiently general to manifest itself in a variety of situations. Instead of grouping people according to a few types, the trait approach classifies people according to the degree to which they can be characterized in terms of traits. According to the trait approach, one can describe a person by his position on a number of scales each of which represents a trait. Thus, we may place the person on a scale of intelligence as indicating one personality trait, on a scale of emotional sensitivity as another trait, on a scale of ascendance — submission as a third. Several theories of personality have been based on this trait approach, two of which were advanced by Allport and Cattel. These two theories are discussed later in this chapter. Let us first discuss the type theories of personality.

Body Types of Personality

This theory classifies personalities according to physique or body-types. This theory believes that body types give rise to or correlate with types of personalities. One such theory was propounded by a German psychiatrist, E. Kretschmer. After making careful physical examinations of approximately 400 psychiatric patients, Kretschmer concluded that there were three basic physiques: asthenic, athletic and pyknic, as well as some unusual body types known as dysplastic.

Kretschmer described the pyknic as one with a broad trunk, relatively short limbs, round face and a short and fat body. He described the asthenic as one having a narrow trunk, long limbs, long narrow face and generally a tall and thin body. He described the athletic as one with broad shoulders, well proportioned limbs and good muscular development. Kretschmer endeavoured to illustrate the sharp differences in these body types by securing photograph of typical individuals in each category.

Kretschmer's purpose was not simply to identify body types. He wanted to show that these types were significantly related to the particular psychiatric disorders of the patients. The two major diagnostic categories of these patients were schizophrenia and manic depressive psychosis. Schizophrenia characterizes those who show disordered thought and loss of emotional reactions, while manic depressive psychosis typifies those who demonstrate extreme elation (mania) or extreme depression or sometimes a periodic shift from one to the other.

Kretschmer found dramatic differences in frequency of schizophrenia and manic depressive psychosis as a function of body type. As can be seen from table 7, asthenic, athletic and dysplastic body types were associated almost exclusively with a diagnosis of schizophrenia, while the pyknic type was nearly always diagnosed as manic depressive psychosis.

Table 7: The Relationship between Physique and Psychiatric Diagnosis of 243 Patients

	Schizophrenic	Manic-depressive	Total
Asthenic and Athletic	91.2%	8.8%	100%
Dysplastic	100%	-	100%
Pyknic	6.5%	93.5%	100%

Although Kretschmer had considered the possibility of extending these findings to the normal population, it was an American, William Sheldon, who actually did so. After extensive independent research, Sheldon identified three primary components of body structure — endomorphy, mesomorphy and ectomorphy, which correspond quite closely to Kretschmer's pyknic, athletic and asthenic body types respectively. However, whereas Kretschmer believed that each individual could be typed as belonging to one of the categories in most cases, Sheldon argued that individuals cannot be grouped into distinct types rigidly. An individual may possess more characteristics of one type and less of other types. An individual may be rated in a seven-point scale as to whether he is endomorphic, mesomorphic or ectomorphic.

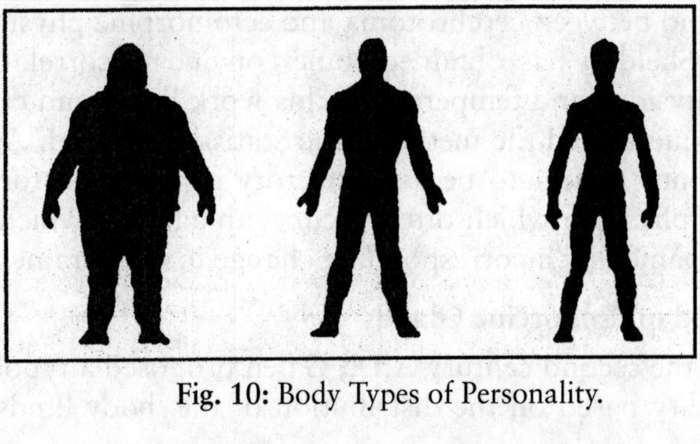

Fig. 10: Body Types of Personality.

An individual may be rated 7-1-1 which means he is predominantly endomorphic and possesses other characteristics in negligible amount. An average rating in this scale will be 4-4-4. Sheldon also identified three components of temperament called Viscerotonia, Somatotonia, and Cerebrotonia. The characteristics of these components are given in table 8.

Table 8: Sheldon's Scale of Temperament (Abbreviated)

Viscerotonia	Somatotonia	Cerebrotonia
Love of physical comfort, slow reaction, enjoyment in being with the others, tolerance, smooth easy communication of feeling, extroversion.	Love of physical adventure, need for and enjoyment of exercise, love of risk and chance, bold, directness of manner, physical courage for combat.	Overly fast reactions, love of privacy, apprehensiveness, dislike for being with others, secretiveness of feeling, emotional restraint.

Sheldon also found correlations between body types and temperaments as given in table 9.

Table 9: Correlations of Body Types and Temperaments

Viscerotonia	Somatotonia	Cerebrotonia
Endomorphy +.76	–.29	–.32
Mesomorphy –.23	+.82	–.83
Ectomorphy –.40	–.53	+.83

It can be seen that viscerotonia tends to be positively associated with an endomorphic physique and negatively associated with mesomorphic and ectomorphic physique. There is a similar relationship between somatotania and mesomorphic physique and between cerebrotonia and ectomorphic physique.

While Sheldon has obtained some convincing correlations between physique and temperament, his work has found critics who have questioned the methods and statistics he used. Again there does not appear to be a satisfactory explanation for the changes in physique which often occur with age and which are not accompanied by a corresponding change in temperament.

Types Based on Endorcine Glands

As long as the second century A.D., Galen proposed a typology of personality based on the distribution of the 'body fluids' or 'humours' first suggested by Hippocrates (Greece, fifth century B.C.). The personality types were called the melancholic, sanguine, phlegmatic and choleric. The corresponding 'homours' and characteristics are given in table 10.

Table 10

Humour	**Personality Type**	**Characteristic Behaviour**
Black bile	Melancholic	Pessimistic, suspicious, depressed
Blood	Sanguine	Optimistic, sociable, easy-going
Phlegm	Phlegmatic	Calm, controlled, lethargic
Yellow bile	Choleric	Active, irritable, egocentric

However, at present, such functions of personality are assigned to the secretions of the endocrine glands. It is now found that over activity of the thyroid gland results in nervousness, irritability and the like. Under activity of the thyroid will bring about apparent mental deficiency and indifference to emotional stimuli. Sex gland secretions markedly affect masculinity and faminity in physique and personality. Other biological maladjustments can lead to serious disturbance in the individual.

Psychological Types

Personalities can be grouped into types basing on the behaviour or the psychological characteristics of the individuals. Perhaps, the best known of the psychological type theories is Jung's classification of personalities into introverts and extroverts. According to Carl J. Jung, the introverted person likes solitude, tends to withdraw into himself at the time of emotional stress and conflict. His attention and interest are directed to within. But the extrovert takes interest in the outside word. He is likely to be conventional, orthodox, well-dressed and outgoing. But in reality, it is very difficult to find a typical extrovert or a typical introvert. Rather most people are ambiverts, a mixture of introversion and extroversion.

E. Spranger, a German philosopher, divided human beings on the basis of interests in the following categories:

(a) *Theoretical*: Persons who are theoretical in nature, neglect social and political participation.

(b) *Economic*: Those persons who are interested in money hoarding.
(c) *Aesthetic*: Those persons who are lovers of beauty and are busy in sensuous gratification.
(d) *Social*: Persons who are interested in social activities.
(e) *Political*: Dominating and desirous of power.
(f) *Religious*: Persons who devote themselves to religious activities and mysticism.

Locus of Control and Personality Types

Some people believe that they have little control over the outcome of their actions. For example, a student may believe that the poor marks obtained in a subject in a particular examination were due to the reason that the teacher disliked him; or that the good marks were due to luck. If you believe in similar ways, you may be an 'external' — the locus of control is outside you. On the contrary, if you believe that you can control what happens to you, you may be an 'internal' — the locus of control is within you.

The locus of control concept is usually associated with Julian Rotter (1966, 1971) and E. Jerry Phares (1973). If individuals believe that behaviour is rewarded not because of skill but because of luck, they believe in the external control of their actions. If they believe that their behaviour deserves success or reward, they believe in the internal control of their actions. But people are neither all internal, nor all external but, more or less, internal.

Internals seem to have more self-confidence and self-control, work better with others, and have better mental health. Phares notes that internals are more energetic in their efforts to control the environment.

Investigations of the roots of internal-external have concentrated upon social and family origin. Evidence suggests that lower class children are external, while children from more affluent, educated background are internal. Phares (1973) believes that this is only logical since lower-class individuals have little access to power and material gains and have limited social mobility.

The family also strongly influences the internal-external continuum. Parental acceptance, encouragement and support are associated with internals; hostility and rejection produce more externals; inconsistent parental behaviour, that is uncertainty about appropriate child behaviour, also was linked to external; internal children saw their parents as more consistent in their expectations. Internals and externals seemed to have experienced different child rearing patterns: internals have parents who encouraged independence; externals have parents who foster dependency, hostility and aggression.

Allport's Trait Theory

For more than 40 years, Allport was the dean of American trait theorists. His view which influenced many psychologists and inspired considerable research was that personality truly exists within the individual and that the psychologist's job is to discover it by identifying each person's enduring characteristics or traits. The traits may be either unique to the individual or sufficiently common so that comparison could be made between people. For example, two persons may both be aggressive, but each will be aggressive in his own way, depending upon individual experiences and capabilities.

One of Allport's most widely accepted propositions is that a person's traits can be classified according to the extent to which they pervade his personality. Thus he distinguished between cardinal traits or dispositions, central traits or dispositions, and secondary traits or dispositions. A cardinal trait is one which is so pervasive and central that it dominates an individual's every action. Some individuals stand out because they are dominated by a single cardinal trait. Such persons become 'reference personalities' by which we describe others. While few people are dominated by cardinal traits, many are guided by a few central traits. Central traits or dispositions are those traits that are uniquely characteristic of the individual. These consist of a relatively small number of traits which manifest themselves in a wide range of situations. They all have a common core but are variable in their expression. The last important characteristics — those that appear only in limited settings — are called secondary dispositions. They would include preferences for particular kinds of food, attitudes on specific issues and enjoyment of certain leisure time activities.

Functional Autonomy

A final aspect of Allport's trait theory is his concept of functional autonomy. This refers to the idea that a person may begin to act in a certain way because of one or more 'outside reasons' and then continue that behaviour even when the original reason no longer exists. Thus, certain personality characteristics become autonomous despite their origins in childhood.

Functional autonomy regards adult motives as varied and self-sustaining contemporary systems, growing out of antecedent systems, but functionally independent of them. Just as a child gradually outgrows dependence on his parents, becomes self-determining and outlives his parents so it is with many motives. The transition may be gradual but it is nonetheless drastic. As the individual or the motive matures, the bond with the past is broken. The tie is historical, not functional.

Functional autonomy clearly means that a given form of behaviour may become an end or goal in itself despite the fact that it may have been originally adopted for some other reasons. The original motives are lost. What was formerly a means to an end has now become an end in itself. In other words, the original reason for behaviour is missing, yet the behaviour persists. This is the essence of functional autonomy.

Motivation is always contemporary. The life of modern Athens is continuous with the life of the ancient city, but in no sense depends upon it for its present 'go.' The life of a tree is continuous with that of its seed, but the seed no longer sustains and nourishes the full-grown tree. Earlier purposes lead into later purposes, but are abandoned in the latter's favour. An ex-sailor has a craving for the sea. The sailor may have first acquired his love for the sea as an incident in his struggle to earn a living. The sea was secondary reinforcement for his hunger drive. But now the ex-sailor is perhaps a wealthy banker: the original motive is destroyed and yet the hunger for the sea persists and even increases. Similarly hard work of a carpenter, once a means to an end, becomes an end in itself. A student who first undertook a field of a study did so merely to please his parents or because it was required. But now the original motives are no longer functioning, still he continues in that filed for the sake of knowledge or for life. Thus, a motive which was instrumental in carrying out a work initially becomes a habit subsequently. In other words, the activity that later became motivational was at first instrumental to some other end. What was once extrinsic and instrumental becomes intrinsic and impelling. The activity once served a drive or some simple need; it now serves itself or in a larger sense serves the self-image of the person.

Functional autonomy, then, refers to any acquired system of motivation in which the tensions involved are not of the same kind as the antecedent tension from which the acquired system developed.

Functional autonomy has been acknowledged by many writers. Many years ago F. Brentano called it a well-known psychological law. What at first was desired merely as a means to something also comes at last from habit to be desired for its own sake? Similarly, R.S. Woodworth said, "The fundamental drive towards a certain end may be hunger, sex, pugnacity or what not, but once the activity is started, the means to the end becomes an object of interest on its own accounts."

Allport says that human purposes are not limited by a strict list of drives or instincts, but that they change in time, with varying conditions and keep pace with one's course of becoming. This view is definitely an advance over the earlier theories of unchanging energies. Freud spoke of the autonomy of ego. According to Freud, much motivation is unconscious, infantile and hidden from oneself. Allport's view is that motivation is conscious and contemporary and changing in nature. Thus motives undergo a change of functions. The young man who once wanted to become a politician because of his early father fixation or identification may become interested in politics for its own sake as a means of carrying out his own style of being, as a way of actualizing his own potentiality. Since motives are the dynamics of personality, we must expect motives also to grow and to change.

What educational implications can be derived from the short and simple account of functional autonomy of motivation? The doctrine of functional autonomy of motives implies that the teacher should provide motivation for developing in children the habits of punctuality, neatness and honesty. Once these habits are sustained for sometime they would quite become automatic in course of time. In other words, extrinsic motivation should be provided to children for learning desirable behaviours, but ultimately the task of the teacher should be to encourage intrinsic motivation.

Cattell's Trait Theory

More recently by means of factor analysis, clusters or groups of personality traits have been identified. One of the best known and most widely accepted classification of personality clusters is that of Ramnond Cattell (1965). Cattell has argued: "The trouble with measuring traits is that there are too many of them. Thus, what is needed is a method that will allow us to relate various aspects of personality in such a way that unifying and systematic patterns can emerge." Starting out with 4,000 trait names, Cattell, therefore, reduced the list to 171 by eliminating overlapping and rare qualities. Then, by factor analysis, he reduced the traits into two categories: Surface traits and Source traits.

Cattell has argued that certain trait-like factors lie behind all human behaviour and that they can be discovered by examining common relationship among various measures of the individual. These underlying and presumably causal personality structures are called source traits. Surface traits are those which show the influence of environment and which, therefore, vary in different cultures. It must be remembered that Allport's secondary traits are comparable to Cattell's surface traits, his cardinal traits are close to Cattell's source traits and his central traits are intermediate between the two. Cattell identified 12 clusters of source traits and 20 clusters of surface traits.

6. TESTS OF PERSONALITY

Although they are called personality tests, most of these tests are concerned with evaluating only a portion of the total personality. Typically they do not evaluate intelligence, vocational interests, aptitudes and achievements, though, by definition, these are all aspects of personality. Personality tests focus on such topics as life's interests and goals and how effectively these are pursued, perception of self and others, interpersonal relationship, problems of everyday life and how these are coped with and deviations from adequate normal functioning of the personality.

Five personality tests have been selected for discussion. They are the Rorschach test (commonly referred to as the "ink blot test"), the Thematic Apperception Test (usually abbreviated to TAT), the Minnesota Multiphasic Personality Inventory (usually abbreviated to MMPI), the Sentence Completion Method, and the Money Problem Check List. All these tests of personality can be grouped under two heads, such as Projective tests and Non-projective tests.

Projective Tests

1. The Rorschach Test

The Rorschach test introduced in 1921 by Herman Rorschach, a Swiss psychiatrist, consists of ten cards. On each card there is an ink blot. Five blots are in black and white and five are in colour. Each blot is made by dipping an old-fashioned quill-type pen in ink; shaking the ink out on a sheet of paper and then folding the paper in half. When the paper is opened a blot appears. The blot may suggest interesting things to people. Try it.

Because the Rorschach evaluates personality and because every person has a unique personality, no two people give the same answers in responding to all the cards, although some people may see the same things that others see on some of the cards. If you make some of your own ink blots — you may find that you and your classmates see some things in a blot-perhaps a butterfly, a person, or an animal. You may also find that some of the things that you see are not seen by your classmates at least not until you point them out.

The Rorschach test has proved to be a highly useful instrument particularly: in the hands of clinical psychologists. The psychologist first asks me test subject what she or he sees in the ten blots. The psychologist asks what aspect of the blot caused the subject to see whatever was seen. For example, was it the colour of the blot, the way in which different parts are related to one another, or the shape of the blot which caused the subject to say "an angle," "a prehistoric animal," part of the body, etc.

The part of the blot in which the test subject reports seeing something is also significant. "A butterfly" may be an excellent response when seen in one blot area. But it may be suggestive of disordered mental functioning when seen in another area or it is visualized in some peculiar way, as for example, "an electrical butterfly." Even though the shape of the blot suggests a well-formed butterfly that many people see, the fact that one subject calls it "an electrical butterfly" — a bizarre concept — introduces further data to be interpreted by the psychologist.

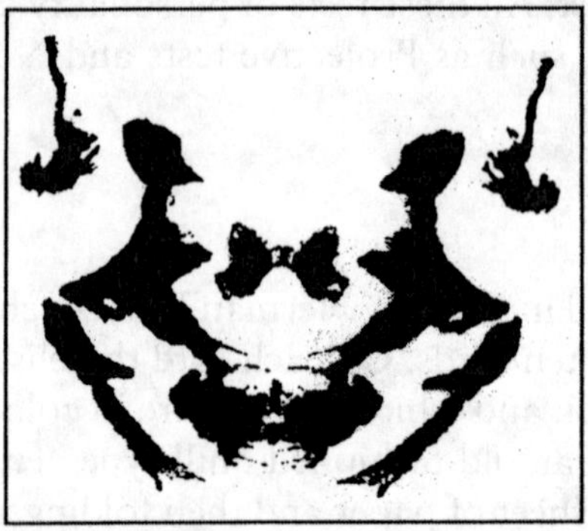

Figs. 11 & 12: Rorschach Test.

From the psychologist's interpretation we obtain a general picture of the personality — a picture which does not include IQ, vocational interests, and many of the subject's aptitudes and achievements. Even though the Rorschach Test does not measure intelligence, the approximate level of a subject's intellectual functioning may be seen. How effectively the subject uses intelligence may also be apparent.

From this test we sometimes also learn about the subject's imagination and fantasy life. We can determine the extent to which the subject is an intellectual person or an emotional person. We can get an idea of the subject's life goals: perceptions of self and others, inter-personal relationships, feeling of anxiety and guilt, and problems and ways of coping with these and present mental disorders. The diagnostic powers of the test are broad. The test is particularly useful as part of a battery of tests, which is the typical practice. Because the test can penetrate below the surface personality, the Rorschach Test is sometimes referred to as a "depth instrument."

2. *The Thematic Apperception Test*

The Thematic Apperception Test is another projective technique and consists of a series of cards on which pictures are printed, plus one blank card on which the test subject is asked to imagine a picture. In the TAT, the subject is shown a number of pictures, sometimes as many as twenty but ordinarily fewer. For each picture shown, the subject is asked to make up a story-telling what led up to the scene, what the character or characters shown in the picture are thinking or feeling, and finally, how the story is likely to turn out. If the subject does not give a full length story, the examiner asks for additional details.

A basic premise of TAT interpretation is that the test subject identifies with a character in the picture and, in effect, becomes that character, whether `male or female. This character is called

Fig. 13: A Sample Picture from TAT

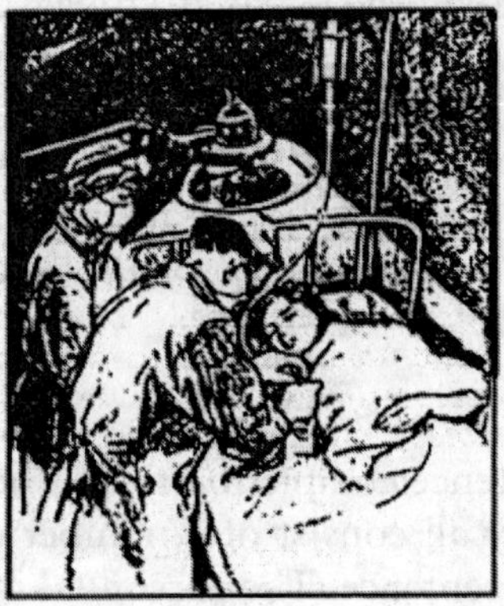

Fig. 14: TAT (Japan).

the hero. We find that, through the hero, the test subject reveals personal feelings, wishes, striving, problems and frustrations. Subjects may reveal how they cope with problems and how they get along or do not get along with others, and things they may possibly feel anxious or guilt about. From this list, you can see that TAT may reveal much the same information as the Rorschach Test. Findings from either test can be used to reinforce the findings of the other. However, to some extent, the two tests yielded different information. The Rorschach test is more likely to identify the presence of certain mental disorders. The TAT is superior in showing how a person relates to others.

Non-projective Tests

1. *The MMPI*

The Minnesota Multiphasic Personality Inventory is a psychometric test of personality. It may be administered to a group or to one individual at a time. It consists of an inventory, or a list of 550 assorted items. To each test item, the test subject is asked to respond "True" or "False" or "Cannot say." The following items are similar to those that appear on the test:

I like to walk in the rain.
I become upset when a cat crosses my path.
Sometimes I do things that I know I should not.
I have a good sense of humour.
Most people can't be trusted.

The test is scored by a key — a device that sorts the responses into various categories. The interpretation is based largely on statistical computations, but involves some clinical judgement as well. Computers are sometimes used to obtain a statistical interpretation. The test was designed as an aid to the diagnosis of particular mental disorders. It is also useful as an instrument to evaluate numerous important features of the personality such as the presence or absence of anxiety.

2. *Sentence Completion Tests*

There are a number of different sentence completion tests. They are all similar, however, in that they all consist of a number of words that form the beginning of a sentence. The person taking the test is asked to add words, complete the sentence, and in so doing supplies what may be important personal information. Examples of the sort of items used are:

When I get angry ....

Death is ....

People are ....

The worst time of life is ....

Next year ....

From the manner in which these sentences are completed, the psychologist learns something of such matters as the person's goals, conflicts, attitudes towards people and towards various situations — for example, job, school, environmental stresses, personal worries and ways of coping with problems.

3. The Mooney Problem Check List

The Mooney Problem Check List, like the MMPI, is an inventory of problems that many people have. The list consists of 288 items similar to the following:

Wondering if my sex urges are normal.

Worried about using drugs.

Having compulsion to gamble.

Feeling that people do not like me.

Not living up to my aspirations for myself.

Having secret thoughts that trouble me.

To respond to this list, the person is instructed to underline those statements that are applicable to the self. This is a simple direct way for the person to communicate to the psychologists his or her problems, as perceived, or as many of them as the person may wish to communicate.

7. ROLE OF THE TEACHER IN FOSTERING GOOD PERSONALITY

One of the aims of education is the development of harmonious, well-adjusted and successful personality of children. Personality, as we have studied, is the result of hereditary endowments and environmental influences. A teacher has nothing or very little to do with the heredity of children. But he can ensure a favourable environment to foster the development of good personality of children.

What is good personality? There is no specific answer to this complex phenomenon of 'good personality.' It is much easier to describe the various qualities which make up a good personality than to define the term 'good personality.' Individuals who are said to have good personality possess the following qualities:

Harmonious functioning of all aspects of the individual: physical, intellectual, social, moral, spiritual and emotional.
Positive attitude towards life:
Self-confident,
Self-assured,
Wholesome self-concept,
Vigorous, energetic and active,
Emotional balance, control and stability,
Satisfaction in life,
Well-adjusted in social, occupational and family situations,
Stress tolerance,
A philosophy of life and an ambition in life and striving to achieve it,
Healthy interpersonal relationship, and
Freedom from worries, anxieties, tension and disease.

A teacher has to develop these qualities among children in three ways:

(i) Projecting these qualities through his own personality,
(ii) Projecting selected personalities through films or television, books and other instructional aids, and
(iii) Creating a conducive environment in the school and the classroom for developing these qualities.

Teacher's own personality is a powerful force for fostering the development of good personality of children. The way the teacher behaves, his manners and habits, his style of interaction with students, colleagues and community members, the way he dresses himself up, the way he talks and walks, all these influence young children's way of living and behaving. Teachers who have developed a positive attitude towards life, a wholesome self-concept, a good philosophy of life and a realistic ambition in life who are self-confident, self-assured, energetic, active and smart; who are emotionally stable under stressful and happy moments; who have found satisfaction in their life are successful in fostering similar qualities among children. The reverse is also true. That is why frustrated teachers have usually frustrated students.

Teachers can also make use of films, and video-recordings which depict good personality characteristics of eminent men, artists, and other persons from various walks of life. Films and video-recordings are very powerful. Personality characteristics of eminent men and women can also be presented through books and other instructional aids.

Most teachers are capable of creating a conducive classroom and school environment for fostering good personality characteristics in their students. Healthy, social and emotional climate and interpersonal relationship among students, among teachers and between students and teachers should be ensured in the school. There should be an atmosphere of mutual love, acceptance and respect in the school.

The three strategies just mentioned above are based on the conviction that young students learn personality characteristics through observation, modelling and imitation.

SELECTED QUESTIONS

1. Explain the concept and nature of personality. What are the determinants of personality?
2. Discuss the causes of individual differences in personality development of individuals. Cite experimental findings.
3. What is personality? Discuss the various approaches to study of personality.
4. Differentiate between types and traits of personality.
5. Define personality. How is personality measured? Describe any one test of personality.
6. Write a brief note on functional autonomy of motives.
7. What are the qualities of good personality? Discuss the role of the teacher in fostering good personality.
8. Discuss the characteristics of mature personality.

19
Mental Health, Adjustment and Maladjustment

1. MENTAL HEALTH OF PUPILS

What is Mental Health?

The term mental health or mental hygiene is of recent origin. The concept and the objectives of mental health have been explained differently by different authorities. Authorities have not yet found a definition of mental health which is unanimously accepted. It is, therefore, advisable to describe the characteristics of mentally healthy individuals than to define the term. However, Jahoda (1950) presented a definition of mentally healthy individual which may be noted here. According to Jahoda, "A mentally healthy person is one, who actively masters his environment, demonstrates a considerable unity or consistency of personality and is able to perceive self and the world realistically. Such a person is also able to function effectively without making undue demands upon others."

Just as physical health refers to absence of disease and physical well-being of the individual, mental health refers to freedom from psychological stress, absence of mental illness, and socio-psychological and emotional well-being of the individual. It refers to perfect functioning of the individual at psychological, social and emotional levels.

Jahoda (1963) proposes six characteristics of the mentally healthy individual. These are as follows:

(i) *Environmental Mastery*: This includes the
ability to love,
adequacy in interpersonal relationships,
efficiency in meeting the requirements of the situation,
capacity for adaptation and adjustment,
efficiency in problem-solving, and
adequacy in love, work and play.

(ii) *Perception of Reality*: This includes understanding the
reality,
empathy, and
social sensitiveness.

(iii) *Integration*: This means,
a balance of psychic forces in the individual,
a unifying outlook on life and
resistance to stress.

(iv) *Autonomy*: This refers to the
capacity to make a decision independently,
regulation of one's behaviour from within and
capacity to act independently.

(v) *Growth*: This means,
self-development,
self-actualisation, and
self-motivation.

(vi) *Attitude Towards Self:* This includes,
awareness about self,
self-acceptance,
self-correction, and
a sense of identity.

Factors Influencing Mental Health and Adjustment of Pupils

Every pupil should have sound mental health. But some children experience mental ill-health due to certain conditions in the home and the school. This adversely affects their learning and adjustment. The factors in the home and the school which influence the mental health and adjustment of children have been discussed in the chapter on Adolescent Development. The reader is advised to refer to the concerned chapter of this book to understand the factors which influence the mental health of children.

Role of the Teacher in Fostering Good Mental Health of Pupils

Teachers have a crucial role to play in fostering good mental health of pupils. Teacher's intervention may be designed to change the individual pupil or his environment. Teacher's intervention may be of three types, such as:

Remedial Intervention,
Preventive Intervention, and
Developmental Intervention.

The remedial intervention intends to resolve a problem that already exists. The preventive approach is designed to develop skills that keep a problem from occurring. The developmental approach aims at teaching normal children to increase their functioning level. Among these three approaches, the preventive and developmental approaches are more important than the remedial approach. Teacher's role in promoting adjustment has already been discussed in a previous chapter. We shall again return to this discussion on teacher's role later in this chapter when we will discuss maladjustments among children.

It is noteworthy here that the teacher should perceive the child as a human being, and not as a patient. The programme of psycho-education which teaches children skills that equip them to manage their lives more intelligently proves very useful for children. The programme of psycho-education covers every aspect of community life and emphasizes employment opportunities, recreational programmes, psychiatric services, community health care, mental health services, and supportive emotional environment.

2. MENTAL HEALTH OF THE TEACHER

Importance of Mental Health of the Teacher

The keystone of entire educational enterprise is the teacher. Undoubtedly the teacher is the greatest single determinant of whether the school programme will be beneficial to the mental health of children. But unless the teacher has sound mental health, unless he is free from worries, anxieties, tensions and mental abnormalities, he cannot discharge his most important duty of promoting the mental health of children. Thus, the mental health of the teacher is no less important than the mental health of children.

If a psychiatric examination is made on teachers, most teachers will be found internally maladjusted even though they do not appear to be so outwardly. The very nature of the profession with its continual demands for dealing with children of varying adjustment problems and the complex nature of the society at present have caused maladjustment among teachers. Maladjusted teachers, generally, tend to have maladjusted pupils. It is so because the teachers' maladjustment may be reflected in their behaviour, teaching and interaction which may affect children's adjustment. The teacher's mental health is directly related to the work of the classroom. The good mental health of the teacher should be as important a qualification as academic competence. This is particularly important in the elementary school where children may be stuck with the same teacher day in and day out for a whole year.

Factors Affecting the Mental Health of the Teacher

Teaching like any other occupation incorporates favourable and unfavourable mental health factors. Some of the favourable factors are the following:

(i) Teaching presents ample opportunities for satisfying one's needs. The teacher doing the job has the satisfaction of seeing children grow, feeling their respect and affection and obtaining the recognition of parents and the community. Thus, teaching is probably the most rewarding profession.

(ii) Teaching involves a variety of work and a constant challenge for the teacher interested in children and their growth. Every child is unique and presents unique problems calling for the highest level of professional competence. For the imaginative and successful teacher, each day is a whole new adventure.

(iii) Teaching offers a steady employment and numerous vacations throughout the year.

(iv) Teaching offers opportunity for association with educated people of like interest, clean work and contact with youth. It is this association with the youth that the teacher really never grows old.

Teaching also incorporates certain factors which affect unfavourably the mental health of the teacher. These are the following:

(i) For some teachers, the major hazard in teaching is monotony — using the same methods, the same outlines, the same illustrations, the same aids and wearing the same style of clothes, etc. Presenting the same material year after year is bound to get boring.

(ii) Teaching is a profession where there is no immediate reward or recognition. A teacher has to work for months or for a year with no observable immediate results. It is also true that some teachers try too hard but they expect too much too soon and, as a result, end up disappointed and discouraged.

(iii) Teaching involves a great deal of stress and strain. Teachers have to deal with youth always who create various problems of motivation, learning and adjustment. The classroom and the school campus remain very often emotionally charged. If the teacher fails to begin with successfully, he has to face unbearable, stressful and strainful situation in future.

(iv) The teacher needs time to collect his wits and his energy. But very often teachers are overburdened with extra responsibility in co-curricular activities, examination work and similar other work. Thus, they don't have time to stand and stare and to entertain themselves.

(v) Teaching is a profession where more than any other, rivalry, jealousy, conflicts and misunderstanding occur most frequently. Conflicts between teachers, rivalry and jealousy among teachers and the administrator, and teacher and the pupils are important hazards for teacher's good mental health.

(vi) The salary of the teacher is also an important factor for the mental health of teachers. If teachers are not well-paid according to their qualification and the responsibility, they will naturally look for other means of income. Consequently they devote most of their time and energy in secondary sources and neglect their duty in school. This latter leads to resentment among parents and students and disciplinary measures by the authority. Once this situation arises, the peace of the profession is lost.

Suggestions for Promoting the Mental Health of the Teacher

The most effective way of improving the mental health of the teacher is to select emotionally stable individuals as teachers. Individuals who possess most of the personal and affective characteristics of effective teachers or who promise to be so, who have interest and liking for children should be selected as teachers. The headmaster and the administrator have this responsibility for choosing good teachers.

The headmaster must see that high moral efficiency is maintained in the school. In order to do that, a democratic atmosphere must be ensured in the school. Discussion, rather the dictations of policies, constructive supervision and group action on school problems must be the guiding principle of the school. Adequate salary, equipments and other facilities that befit the dignity of the teaching profession must be available to the teacher. Cordial relations among administrators, teachers, pupils and parents must be maintained in the school and outside.

The teacher himself has the primary responsibility for his own mental health.

The teacher must have genuine liking for the children and be interested to help them. He must acquaint himself with the principles of psychology so that he can understand children better. He should concentrate on developing positive relationship with pupils, fellow teachers, parents and administrators. He must be sensitive and resourceful in dealing with people. He also needs to understand and accept himself — his own strengths and shortcomings. He should be true to his profession and strive for competence in both his subject area and teaching methods.

When all these and similar other conditions are present one expects a relatively good mental health in teachers. If in spite of all these provisions, opportunities, and conditions, a teacher fails to have a good mental health then it is better for the teacher to resign from the profession than to despair.

3. WHAT IS ADJUSTMENT?

Essentially adjustment refers to the ability of an individual to satisfy the demands of his surrounding as well as his own needs.

Originally, the meaning of adjustment was borrowed and changed from the concept of 'adaptation' in biology. Adaptation refers to the biological changes that facilitate the survival of a species. At the psychological level, adjustment means the individual's struggle to survive in his or her surroundings. The emphasis is on the functional or learned changes the individual must make to achieve a harmonious relationship with the environment.

The Dictionary of Behaviour Science (by B.B. Wolman, 1973) defines adjustment as follows: A harmonious relationship with the environment involving the ability to satisfy most of one's needs and meet most of the demands that are put upon one. It refers to the variations and changes in behaviour that are necessary to satisfy needs and meet demand so that one can establish a harmonious relationship with the environment.

Some people think that adjustment involves a great deal of social conformity because, in order to survive socially, one has to become normal or like everyone else. Actually adjustment consists of two kinds of processes — fitting oneself into given circumstances and changing the circumstances to fit one's needs. A good adjustment in this sense involves more than a passive relationship with one's surroundings. It involves taking the initiative, taking risks, and learning to make the most of a situation. It may even lead to an active involvement in social change. In other words, adjustment is an active, two-way relationship between the individual and his or her surroundings.

Adjustment may be of three types, such as: (1) biological adjustment, (2) adjustment to the social environment, and (3) adjustment to the self. Human biological adjustments are basic in the sense that they are life functions and have their equivalents in animals. We breathe in air perhaps eighteen or over twenty times a minute, usually with little or no awareness. We build shelter against the cold and other elements. Such biological adjustments are usually called adaptations. Adjustment to the social environments usually refers to other people or interpersonal relations. In popular usage we are likely to regard a person as well-adjusted who 'gets along' with other people. The social adjustment that people make varies from situation to situation. For example, conversation and manner among a group of girls may change abruptly when a boy approaches.

Sometimes the words we use to describe a person's most typical social adjustment patterns are highly descriptive or forceful. People may be characterized as passive, aggressive, dominating, considerate or withdrawn. All of these suggest the most typical sort of adjustment a person makes in relating to others. Adjustment to one's self is certainly no less a challenge than is adjustment to other people. Our greatest battles, commonly, are with ourselves. Personal needs that we hold frequently are inconsistent with one another and lead to internal psychological conflict and strain. One cannot get a full night's sleep before an important examination for which preparation has been inadequate. Many of the goals we seek are, in fact, thwarted or frustrated and we must somehow adjust to those failures. We must also adjust to our shortcomings as we understand them. All these indicate adjustment to self. Positive adjustment to the self means greater satisfaction in living and smoother functioning of personality.

What constitutes good adjustment is a matter on which psychologists differ. Further, different people may reasonably have different views of adjustment based on different views on life on different life situations. What may be very good adjustment for a hospitalized mental patient would be very poor adjustment for yourself. Thus adjustment or maladjustment should be considered in relation to the individual, the particular situation, the values or the view of life.

4. MALADJUSTMENT

What is Maladjustment?

Maladjustment refers to the failure of the individual to adjust to the needs of self and demands of the environment.

Adjustment or maladjustment is inferred from the behaviour an individual shows in a given situation. Behaviour that is in conformity with the demands and expectations of others, peers, teachers, parents, siblings and community members is called adaptive behaviour. Behaviour that fails to meet the social and cultural patterns is called maladjusted behaviour.

The term maladjustment has two aspects: emotional disturbance and social maladjustment. Although social maladjustment and emotional disturbance in children are not necessarily synonymous, there is a considerable overlap between them. Social maladjustment refers to behaviour of children which is not within the range of the culturally permissible either at home, in the school, or in the community. These children are unmanageable in the home, causing difficulties for the parents and siblings. They are generally problems in school, retarded in educational achievements, destructive, quarrelsome and often socially immature. In the community they may seek undesirable companions or be isolates. Delinquents are a sub-group of the socially maladjusted.

The term 'emotionally disturbed children' refers to those who have inner tensions and show anxiety, neuroticism, or psychotic behaviour. Emotional disturbance does not always cause social maladjustment. For example, the isolate, or withdrawn child may be considered emotionally disturbed but not necessarily socially maladjusted, since his behaviour or lack of it does not come in conflict with the lives of others.

Socially, maladjusted children are usually emotionally disturbed, but not always. Similarly emotional disturbance may lead to social maladjustment, but not always. Social maladjustment may lead to delinquency but not always. But all delinquents have some form of social maladjustment. It appears then that maladjustment may first appear as emotional disturbance. When emotionally disturbed children have conflict with parents and siblings at home and with classmates and teachers in school, they are considered socially maladjusted. When maladjustment leads to aggressive behaviour, stealing, or destruction of property and causes conflict with the law, such a child is called a delinquent. Thus the three levels of maladjustment are emotional disturbance, social maladjustment and delinquency.

Dennis Child (1972) holds a similar viewpoint. He states, "When emotional handicaps reach the stage of being so grave as to affect social development leading to the behaviour disorders and frequently influencing school work, we term this maladjustment." Dennis quotes the definition adopted by the Handicapped Pupils School Health Service Regulations of 1945 which suggests that "Maladjustment is exemplified by pupils who show evidence of emotional instability or psychological disturbance and requires special educational treatment in order to effect their personal and educational readjustment."

Signs of Maladjustment

The Underwood Committee, London (1955) set out six groups of symptoms commonly associated with maladjustment. Examples of the six groups of symptoms are:

(a) *Nervous Disorders*: Fears and anxiety; marked solitariness and timidity; depression and obsession; excitability and apathy; hysteria and amnesia.

(b) *Habit Disorders*: Speech defects and stammering (other than those caused by physical defect); excessive day-dreaming, sleeplessness and nightmares, facial and body tics, nail-biting, rocking, bed-wetting and physical symptoms such as asthma and allergies.

(c) *Behaviour Disorders*: Temper tantrums, destructive, defiant or cruel, stealing, lying, truancy; sex aberrations.

(d) *Organic Disorders*: Neurological dysfunctioning, head injuries, brain tumours, epilepsy.

(e) *Psychotic Disorder*: Hallucinations, delusions, bizarre behaviour.

(f) *Educational and Vocational Difficulties*: Lacking concentration; unable to hold down a job, irregular response to school discipline, slow teaming, retarded in reading particularly.

The appearance of any of these symptoms does not of itself signify maladjustment. These symptoms may not be also necessarily permanent. These symptoms range from mild to severe and many mild cases can be dealt within the normal school setting by teachers.

Maladjusted behaviour is to be judged in terms of a society's existing standards. Thus, what is commonly acceptable to a society at one time might be thought of as quite unacceptable at another time. Again changes in attitude as a result of the process of maturity should not be taken as signs of maladjustment. Adolescents in search of adult standards, values and privileges may appear to some parents to be suffering from behaviour disorders, whereas, in fact, the onset of these attitudes is a healthy developmental sign.

Causes of Maladjustment

There is no single factor which causes maladjustment among children. The causes of maladjustment are many and varied. Again some children are predisposed to maladjustment. That is to say, some children tend to be easily maladjusted under certain situations whereas others do not. The causes of maladjustment can be grouped under three heads:

1. Psychological Factors,
2. Psycho-social Factors, and
3. Physiological Factors.

Psychological Factors

Maladjustment is very often caused by life's frustrations. When a child is placed in situations in which his capacities are strained, or in which he is unable to satisfy his motives and drives, behaviour deviations of aggression, regression, compulsive behaviour or other abnormal reactions may result. When a child is unable to choose between one of two courses of action, or when the course of action does not reduce his tensions, he reacts in an emotional way — by temper tantrums, fighting, and other bizarre types of behaviour. Thus, maladjustment is the outcome of frustration resulting from the discrepancy between the child's capacity to behave and the requirements of the environment.

In some cases, the child is forced to attempt a task which he cannot perform. He becomes tense and excited and may get angry at object or people. In many such situations, he escapes the requirements. For example, truancy from school is prevalent among slow learners and among the educationally retarded than among those who are succeeding in school. Although other factors operate in truancy, when the school and the home require of the child certain achievements which he cannot accomplish, he tends to run away from the situation or becomes aggressive and hostile. Maladjustment is common among children whose parents are over ambitious or expect too much of them in school without due regard for their capacities.

Psychosocial Factors

Not all maladjustments arise from frustrations in an immediate situation or from the discrepancy between the child's capacity to behave and the requirements of the environment. Other factors include (a) early home experiences, and (b) social and economic aspects of the child's environment.

Different types of maladjustment are caused due to specific home situations. Some children defy all authority, are hostile towards authority figures, are cruel, malicious, and assaulter and have inadequate guilt feelings. Such children are jealous, deceitful, and blameful of others. Such children are known as *unsocialized aggressive children*. Children of this type come from broken homes where they receive no love and attention. Many such children are illegitimate or the products of forced marriage. They were unwanted by their mothers in infancy. It is presumed that these children had no opportunity at an early age to form positive interpersonal attachments, especially with their mothers.

There are some children who are known as *socialized aggressive*. Such children are aggressive and hostile to authority figures, but they are socialized within their peer groups, the gang or companions. This group defy authority but at the same time show attachment and loyalty to the gang. Their activities consist of stealing with others, truancy from the school and other forms of gang activities. These children also come from broken homes. They were loved by their mother during early infancy but were later rejected.

Maladjusted children also fall into a third category called *over-inhibited*. They lack close friendships, are over dependent and easily depressed. They have frequent physical complaints. This type of child usually comes from a family of a higher economic level where he was overprotected. His home atmosphere is likely to be restrictive.

The three categories of maladjusted children and their home background indicate that maladjustment is caused at home by such factors as overprotection, rejection, hostility, and inconsistent discipline, unhealthy relationship between the father and the mother, frequent quarrels between parents, failure of the parents to meet the basic demands of the child, etc. The relationship between economic status of parents and maladjustments is evident from the fact that a majority of delinquents come from homes with low economic status.

Physiological Factors

Just as the mind has effect on the body, so also the body has effect on the mind. Neither psychological factors nor the psycho-social factors explain all forms of maladjustment. There may be some physiological factors which might have caused maladjustment. Prolonged illness of a child, or chronic diseases of various types, brain damage, etc. have adverse effects on a child's behaviour and interaction with others. We call such behaviours maladjustment even though we do not know the physiological factors which might have caused it.

Remedial Measures

Just as there is no single cause of maladjustment, so also no one can prescribe a ready-made solution to the problems of maladjusted children. Maladjustment may be caused due to a multiple of causes. The remedies also depend upon the collaborative efforts of a number of persons — teachers, guidance workers, psychologists and health officers.

Maladjustment may be mild or severe. It may appear in the form of emotional disturbance, social maladjustment or delinquency. The remedy also can vary from mental health practices in the regular schools to treatment in residential schools.

The teacher is not a professional personnel to deed with maladjusted children. Remedial measures for maladjustment fall under the sphere of psychologists and psychiatrists. But the teacher can do a lot to help the maladjusted child live a happier life in the school and overcome some of his difficulties. Here we will only mention the specific measures the teacher can take to help the maladjusted children:

(i) The teacher should try to understand the cause behind the defiant behaviour of the child.

(ii) He should try to ascertain the seriousness of the problem by studying the symptoms of maladjustment.

(iii) He may educate the parents about effective child-rearing practices and healthy relationship between parents and their children.

(iv) He must ensure that the atmosphere in the school, interpersonal relationships between the teacher and the child, teacher's expectations and behaviour patterns, quality of teaching, etc., are all conducive to the well-being of the child.

(v) The teacher, in collaboration with his colleagues, should adopt good mental health practices in the school.

(vi) He should refer the child to appropriate professional personnel for treatment, if the child is found not curable in the regular school programmes.

5. ADJUSTMENT MECHANISM

Life is largely a process of satisfying needs and desires. Needs give rise to goal-oriented behaviour in an organism. Obstacles in the path of need fulfillment lead to frustration. Frustration produces worries and anxieties. But freedom from worries and anxieties promotes physical and mental health. Thus, any need is bound to produce some tension and tension will automatically upset the equilibrium of the organism. To restore the equilibrium, the self-adopts some mental mechanisms. All of us at one or other time in our life use these mental mechanisms to adjust ourselves to the environment. These mechanisms are also called adjustment mechanisms. In other words, adjustment is the chief purpose of these mechanisms. The self or the ego is the integrating core of personality and threat to its worth due to frustration is a threat to the individual's very existence. These mechanisms defend the ego against the consequences of frustration. This is why these mental mechanisms are also known as defence mechanisms.

Adjustment mechanisms take many forms. A brief discussion of some of the adjustment mechanisms is given below:

Projection

Projection is an adjustment mechanism by means of which we transfer the blame for our shortcomings, mistakes and misdeeds to others. Through projection, we attribute to others our own unacceptable impulses, thoughts and desires. For example, the student who fails in the examination blames the examiner. Fate and bad luck are particularly overworked objects of projection. Individuals who are constantly found criticizing others for their foolishness and selfishness are, in reality, foolish and selfish. Projection helps the projector to avoid social disapproval and punishment and protect his self-esteem.

Rationalization

Rationalization involves thinking of logically and socially approved reasons for our past, present and proposed behaviour. Through rationalization we try to justify our past deeds and present tendency, and thereby to soften the disappointment. The individual who fails to reach the unattainable goals rationalizes that actually he does not want it. The so-called 'sour grapes and sweet lemon' is an example of rationalization. Rationalization has become an important adjustive reaction in helping us to avoid unnecessary frustrations. But these are self-deceptive reactions and may lead to the development of false belief and delusion when used in excess.

Repression

Repression is a mental mechanism by means of which the individual's painful thoughts, ideas, experiences and memories are excluded from his consciousness without the person's awareness of it. Repression differs from suppression in that while the individual consciously suppresses some desire, repression is an unconscious process. All our immoral, anti-social and irrational desires are repressed in the unconscious part of the mind. Repressed desires are frequently revealed in dreams, jokes, slip of tongue and slip of pen. Generally speaking, repression is not harmful when used occasionally.

Withdrawal

Some students react to their problems by refusing to face them. Habitual withdrawal responses to life's problems are serious for several reasons. Because children who withdraw do not cause social annoyance, their problems may go unnoticed and unsolved until they have become so numbered by life's shock and disappointments that they resign themselves to a world of inner living.

Regression

An unconscious backtracking in behaviour to an earlier adjustment which might have been successful in the past without due regard to its appropriateness at the present moment is called regression. A woman who cries like a child when her slightest wants are denied or the old man who tells about the successful achievements of his earlier years are examples of regression.

Acting Out

Acting out involves relieving the tension of unacceptable impulses by expressing them directly or symbolically. People with inadequate self-control or a weakly developed conscience may choose acting out as the most convenient way to discharge their anxieties. For example, an adolescent struggling with feelings of independence towards parents may act out in moodiness, procrastination, and failure at school. Such negativistic behaviour serves as an attempt at communicating one's underlying feelings or resentment towards parents or other adults. Acts of school vandalism may be expression of the frustration and resentment associated with having to attend school. Similarly, delinquent behaviour is sometimes a means of release from pent-up aggressive tendencies.

A person who displays acting-out behaviour will often say afterwards, 'I don't know why I did that.' Acting-out behaviour helps a person achieve temporary relief from the painful awareness of unacceptable impulses, but does not lead to the self-insight needed for a satisfying resolution of the problem.

Sublimation

Sublimation is an important adjustment mechanism. It means acceptance of a socially approved substitute goal for a drive whose channel of expression is blocked. The girl who fails to marry may find a substitute emotional outlet in teaching or nursing. A student who cannot do well in games and sports may find study as a substitute goal in which he can show his merit. It is one of the important duties of a teacher to provide opportunity to the students to sublimate their sex instinct through participation in creative work, games and sports, dramatics and other co-curricular activities.

Fantasy

Fantasy is another defensive reaction in which the individual gratifies his frustrated desires in the world of belief and in imaginary achievements.

Identification

In identification, the individual increases his feelings of worth and adequacy by identifying himself with the person or institutions of an outstanding nature.

However, it is worth re-emphasizing that these defence mechanisms are learned adjustive reactions. They are motivated by the driving force of anxiety aroused by the threats to the self. They function in both individual and group situations. They operate on relatively habitual and unconscious level. But they involve self-deception. These mechanisms are essential for the maintenance of ego, integrity and we use them in various degrees and ways. They lie in between a stage of health and disease. They are good when used in moderation but harmful when used to an extreme degree.

SELECTED QUESTIONS

1. What is mental health? Discuss the factors in the school which affect the mental health of pupils.
2. What are the factors which influence mental health and adjustment of pupils? Discuss the role of the teacher in fostering good mental health of pupils.
3. Discuss the factors affecting the mental health of the teacher. What suggestions do you have for promoting the mental health of the teacher?
4. What is maladjustment? State the signs of maladjustment.
5. What are the causes of maladjustment? Discuss remedial measures for maladjusted children.
6. What is adjustment? Explain any three adjustment mechanisms with examples.

20
Frustration and Conflict

1. WHAT IS FRUSTRATION?

Frustration refers to the situation, or the event that blocks the way to a goal. It also means a sense of disappointment that is the result of being blocked. The course of life is not always smooth. In our daily goal-seeking effort, we encounter barriers between ourselves and our goals. There are more or less minor frustrations which we encounter everyday — a person misses the bus, causing a late arrival for an appointment; the office assistant is ill, delaying the preparation of an important report. There are, of course, much greater frustrations in life. A boy who aspires to be a football player loses a leg. A boy who always wanted to marry his childhood sweetheart is jilted for another. A student fails in the college entrance examination and is denied admission. A sense of psychological disorder interrupts a brilliant career.

2. SOURCES OF FRUSTRATION

Frustration is encountered in myriad forms ranging from petty annoyances to the thwarting of life-goals. These sources of frustration or the barriers to the attainment of goal, and satisfaction of a motive may be of three types, such as:

(i) Environmental obstacles,
(ii) Personal limitations, and
(iii) Conflict.

Environmental obstacles are major sources of frustration. The physical environment may present such obstacles as intemperate weather, droughts, and flood. The social environment may present obstacles through the restrictions imposed by other people and the customs of social living. In fact, any society, no matter how simple, places restrictions on its members.

Sometimes the barriers to goal satisfaction lie within the individual's own deficiencies or limitations. Some people are handicapped by blindness, deafness, or paralysis. Not everyone can become a great singer like Anuradha Podwal or a number one hero like Hrithik Roshan or pass the examinations necessary to become a doctor. If goals are set beyond one's ability, then frustrations will inevitably result.

Conflict between two opposing motives is a major source of frustration. When two motives conflict, the satisfaction of one leads to the frustration of the other. For example, a student may not be able to gain the recognition as the president of the college community and still secure the marks needed to be the best student of the college. Even when one motive is involved, there may be various ways of approaching the goal and conflict arises when the paths to the goal diverge. For example, a student can get post-graduate education at any one of a number of colleges, but choosing which one to enter presents a conflicting situation. Sometimes conflict arises between a motive and a person's internal standards, rather than between two external goals. For example, a woman's motives for achievement may conflict with her standards for appropriate feminine behaviour. Conflict between motives and internal standards can often be more difficult to resolve than conflict between external goals. Conflicts may be of various types. We shall again return to a discussion on conflict after we discuss the reactions to frustration.

Reactions to Frustration

Frustration — whether it is the result of environmental obstacle, personal limitation or conflict — has a number of possible consequences or reactions. Some of the immediate reactions to frustration are given below. These reactions have been studied by Banker, Dembo, and Lewin (1941) through their experiments on effects of frustration on children's play behaviour.

One of the immediate reactions to frustration is restlessness in behaviour. Restlessness is associated with many actions indicating unhappiness and an increase in tension, or the level of excitement. Restlessness and tension are noticed in both children and adults.

Closely related to increased tension and restless movements are feelings of anger that lead to destructiveness and hostile attacks. Aggression may be direct aggression or displaced aggression. Sometimes aggression is expressed directly against the individual or object that is the source of frustration. For example, when a small child takes a toy from another child, the second child is likely to attack the first child in an attempt to regain the toy. In case of adults, aggression may be verbal rather than physical. Frequently, the frustrated individual cannot satisfactorily express aggression against the sources of frustration. Sometimes the source is vague and intangible. The person does not know what to attack, yet feels angry and seeks something to attack. Sometimes the person responsible for frustration is so powerful that an attack would be dangerous. When circumstances block direct attack on the cause of frustration, aggression may be displaced. Displaced aggression is an aggressive action against an innocent person or object rather than against the actual cause of frustration. For example, the husband who fails to attack his wife expresses his resentment on his office staff. The child who is not getting along well with his playmates may pull the tail of his cat. The practice of 'scapegoating' is an example of displaced aggression. An innocent victim is blamed for one's troubles and becomes the object of aggression. An experiment by Miller and Bugelski (1948) with boys at a summer camp shows the relationship between frustration and scapegoating. The boys were required to participate in lengthy and boring testing session which ran

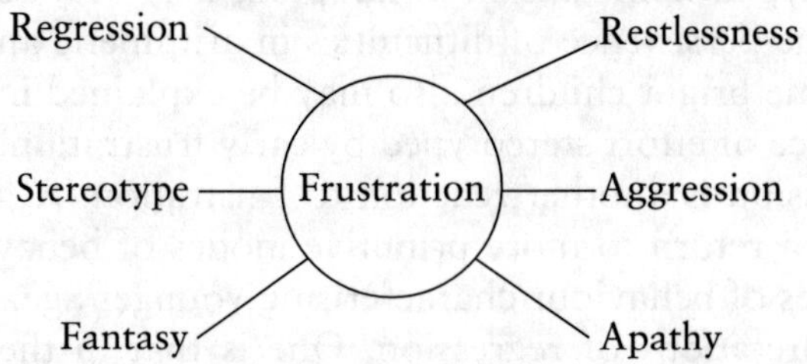

Fig 15: Some Reactions to Frustration.

overtime so that they missed their weekly outing to the local movie. A survey measuring attitudes towards Japanese and Mexicans given before and after the testing session showed a significant increase in friendly feelings. The boys displaced their anger verbally towards remote people rather than expressing it directly towards the administration of the tests.

Although a common reaction to frustration is active aggression, another reaction is its opposite — apathy, indifference, withdrawal. A girl who has been frustrated in love affairs with her boyfriend may later show indifference towards all other boys even though the other boys may be really good and reliable. An extreme form of such indifference may be avoiding men and living as a spinster.

When problems become too much for us, we sometimes seek the 'solution' of escape into a dream-world, a solution based in fantasy rather than reality. The pin-up girls in soldiers' barrack symbolize a fantasy life that goes on when normal social life with women is frustrated. Men on a starvation diet lose their interest in women, and instead hang on their walls pictures of prepared food cut-out from magazines. Severe and continuous frustration may produce such complete escape into fantasy that the individual loses the ability to distinguish between fantasy and the real world.

Another consequence of frustration is stereotype in behaviour, that is a tendency to exhibit repetitive, fixated behaviour. Ordinary problem-solving requires flexibility, striking out in new directions when the original path to the goal is blocked. When repeated frustration baffles a person, some flexibility appears to be lost and the person will stupidly make the same effort again and again though experience has shown its futility. Once the stereotyped habit has been adopted, it is very resistant to change. The persistence of difficulties in arithmetic and reading among some bright children also may be explained in part as a consequence of effort stereotyped by early frustration.

Regression is another reaction to frustration. Regression is defined as a return to more primitive modes of behaviour, that is, to modes of behaviour characterising younger age. There are two interpretations of regression. One is that in the midst of insecurity, the individual attempts to return to a period of past security. An older child seeks the love and affection bestowed upon him in childhood by behaving again as he did during younger ages. This type of regression is called retrogressive behaviour. The second interpretation of regression is that the childish behaviour following frustration is simply a more primitive kind of behaviour, not actually a return to earlier behaviour. For example, the adult accustomed to the restraints of civilized behaviour may become so upset by frustration as to lose control and start a fist fight even though he did no fist fight as a child. Both forms of regression may, of course, occur together.

We have discussed a number of observable reactions to frustration. In order to explain these reactions, psychologists have introduced the concept of anxiety. By anxiety we mean the unpleasant emotion characterised by the terms 'worry,' 'apprehension,' and 'fear' that we all experience at times in varying degrees. Because anxiety is a very uncomfortable emotion that threatens our well-being, it cannot be tolerated for long. We are strongly motivated to avoid or to reduce it. Sometimes we attempt to deal directly with the anxiety producing situation by appraising the situation and then doing something to change or avoid it. These are direct methods of coping with anxiety. For example, a student is experiencing anxiety about failure in the examination. He may be able to take a direction — consult with his teacher to find out what can be done to pass the examination, devise a work schedule that will fulfil the requirements and then start it. Sometimes the individual, instead of dealing directly, adopts defensive coping or defence mechanism to defend himself against anxious feelings.

It is noteworthy that different individuals react to similar frustrating situations in a variety of ways. For example, one individual may react to the frustrating situation by aggressive behaviour, whereas another individual may react by apathy or indifference, still a third by regression. The reason is that reactions to frustration are learned tendencies. A child who cries when frustrated and finds that his needs are then satisfied will probably resort to the same behaviour the next time his motives are thwarted. On the contrary, a child whose crying behaviour is never successful may react differently in subsequent frustrating situations. Defence mechanisms are also learned behavioural tendencies.

3. CONFLICT

1. What is Conflict?

Another threat to successful adjustment is conflict. Conflict refers to the existence of compatible goals. Such a state of affairs is commonplace in psychological life. Conflict may be illustrated by ambivalence — a situation in which the person finds the self-attracted in opposite directions. It is not impossible to love and hate the same person at the same time — or to find a person simultaneously attractive and unattractive. Many people seek both dependence on parents and independence of them.

The concepts of frustration and conflict are closely linked, often one leads to another, or both frustration and conflict may be induced in a vicious circle. In any situation involving incompatible goals, the reaching of one goal necessarily means that the individual is frustrated with regard to the other.

When people are in conflict over their ability, on the one hand perceiving themselves as capable and on the other hand perceiving themselves as inadequate or inferior, their perceptions may be resolved in favour of the latter. In this way, they may perceive their strength and set the stage for failure. The ensuing experience of failure further deteriorates self-perception and paves the way for further failure.

2. Real Goals and False Goals

Conflicts are often described in terms of the goals a person tries to achieve and those that the person tries to avoid. Consequently there are two goals in any conflict situation. The goals which the person tries to achieve are known as plus goals (+) or approach or real goals and the goals which the person tries to avoid are known as minus goals (-) or avoidance or false goals. There may be various types of conflict depending upon whether the two goals are equally attractive, equally repelling, or attractive and repelling simultaneously. Thus, we have: (1) an approach-approach conflict (2) avoidance-avoidance conflict, and (3) an approach-avoidance conflict. There may be also a fourth type of conflict known as double-approach — avoidance conflict.

Conflicts occur and are later resolved depending on how the individual perceives goals. Suppose there are two goals before the individual. If the individual perceives both the goals as 'real goals,' he experiences a conflict. In other words, the conflict is resolved in favour of the stronger goal or the goal having greater valence.

Due to lack of adequate knowledge, complete ignorance or misunderstanding, the individual may perceive both goals as 'real goals.' But once the individual is made aware of the essential features of both the goals, once he has adequate knowledge about both goals and develops insight, he tends to perceive one goal as his 'real goal' — the goal that is desirable and acceptable for him, and the other goal is perceived by him as the false goal — the goal that is undesirable or unacceptable for him. Conflict is thus resolved in favour of real goal.

3. Types of Conflict

Approach — Approach Conflict

An approach — approach conflict arises, when the two goals are equally attractive to the individual and the individual wants to achieve both. As for example, two boys may be in love with the same girl. The girl regards both boys as attractive. The girl is in conflict to decide whom to accept and whom to reject. She is, thus, experiencing an approach-approach conflict. A student may be attracted towards courses in Engineering and course in Medicine at a given time. Both the courses are attractive for the student. Which one should the student pursue? The student is experiencing an approach-approach conflict.

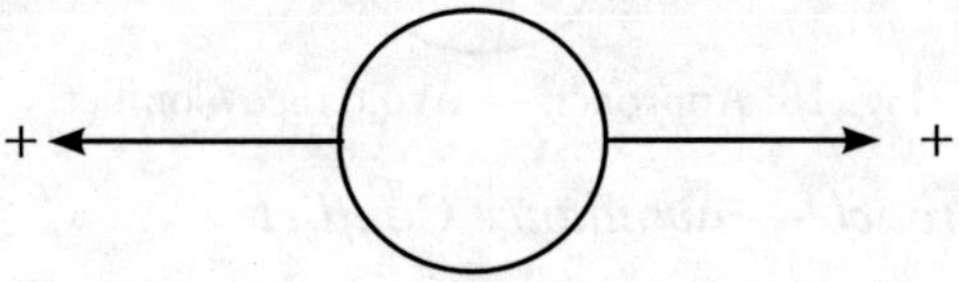

Fig 16: Approach — Approach Conflict.

Avoidance — Avoidance Conflict

This involves a situation in which the individual has two goals and he wants to avoid both the goals. The child may be asked to read in his study room or else to go to bed. The child neither wants to read nor go to bed. He wants to play. Thus the child is experiencing avoidance — avoidance conflict. A girl may be asked by her parents to choose between two young men as her life partner. She wants to avoid both the young men. She is thus said to be experiencing avoidance — avoidance conflict. This type of conflict is sometimes called 'devil and the deep blue sea' conflict.

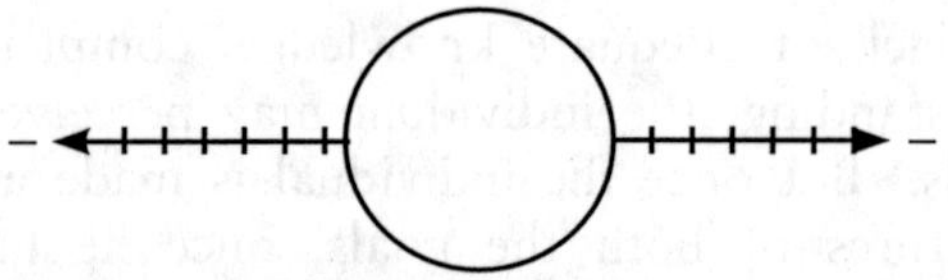

Fig. 17: Avoidance — Avoidance Conflict.

Approach — Avoidance Conflict

An approach — avoidance conflict exists when attainment of the goals is perceived as both positive and negative. The person may be both attracted and repelled by the same goal. This type of conflict is known as "dieter's dilemma". A man suffering from diabetes is attracted towards and at the same time also wants to avoid sweets because of their ill-effects on his body. Thus, he is both attracted and repelled by the same goal-eating sweets. A little child may be attracted towards a lonely dog, and he wants to reach for the dog. At the same time he is also afraid of the dog. A student may be attracted towards a particular subject in college education, but he is repelled by its dark future or prospects.

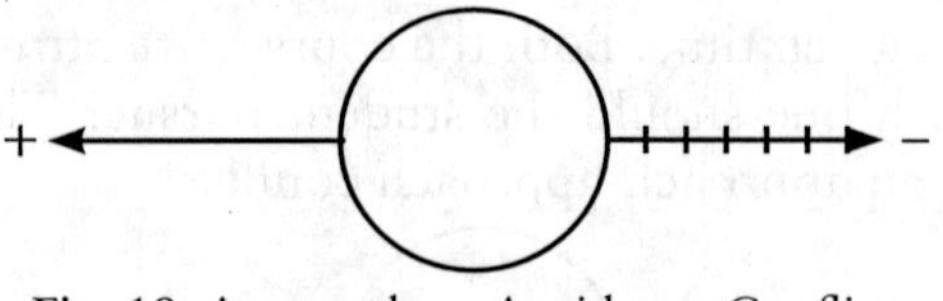

Fig. 18: Approach — Avoidance Conflict.

Double-Approach — Avoidance Conflict

This is a more complex type of conflict situation. Here the individual is drawn to incompatible goals each of which is partly positive or attractive and partly negative or repelling. As for example, a student may be in conflict to choose between two universities — University 'A' and University 'B'. At University A, the demands of the students are not granted and they are disenchanted. But it is famous for its high standards of scholarships. At University 'B', the administration is sympathetic. Students enjoy a great deal of freedom and are not subject to the usual college regulations. But its records of achievements are not so high. Thus, for the student, each university has both positive and negative valences, *i.e.*, each university is partly attractive and partly repelling. But he has to choose between the two. He is thus experiencing a double, approach — avoidance conflict.

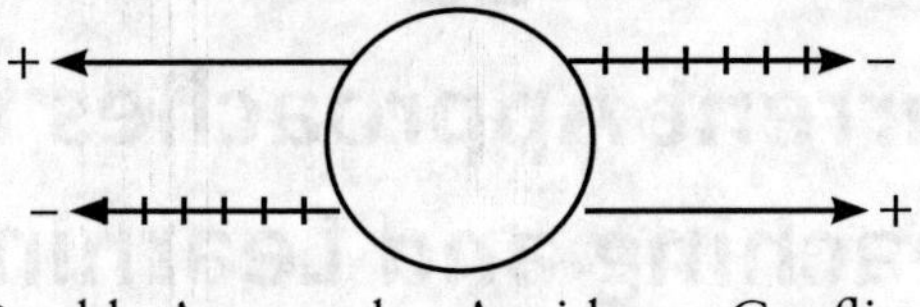

Fig 19: Double Approach—Avoidance Conflict.

As you have understood now, each conflict situation demands that the individual has to choose in favour of one of the goals and resolve the conflict. The conflict as resolved contributes to adjustment or maladjustment. Successful resolution of the conflict leads to adjustment and healthy functioning of the personality. Failure to resolve the conflict causes maladjustment.

SELECTED QUESTIONS

1. What are the sources of frustration? Discuss the reactions to frustration.
2. Why do children experience conflict? Discuss the various types of conflict.

21
Current Approaches to Teaching and Learning

1. GAGNE'S HIERARCHY OF LEARNING

R.M. Gagne is a prominent educational psychologist who has developed an eclectic approach to the psychology of learning. His approach to learning is eclectic because it is based on behaviouristic explanation and at the same time Gestalt explanation.

Gagne on the Concept of Learning

According to Gagne, learning is a change in human disposition or capacity which can be retained and which is not due to the process of growth. Since learning is something that takes place in the individual's brain, it cannot be observed directly. Learning is inferred from observable behaviour or from change in one's capacity to perform a certain action. Learning is not only inferred from change in performance but also from change in attitudes, interests or values. This inference is made by comparing the individual's behaviour before learning and his behaviour after learning.

Gagne on the Types of Learning and the Hierarchy of Learning

Gagne specifies eight types of learning. These are as follows:

(i) Signal Learning ,
(ii) Stimulus-response Learning,
(iii) Chaining (Motor Chaining),
(iv) Verbal Association,

(v) Multiple Discrimination Learning,
(vi) Concept Learning,
(vii) Principle Learning,
(viii) Problem-solving.

These types of learning can be arranged in a hierarchical way from the most simplest type (signal learning) to the most complex type (problem-solving):

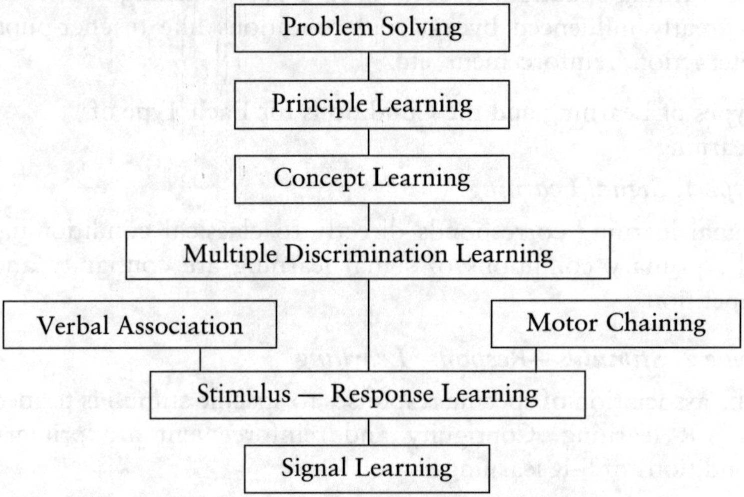

Fig 20: Gagne's Model of Hierarchy of Learning.

Gagne's model of learning is also known as the Cumulative Model of Learning. The various types of learning are inter-related. Each type is built upon its preceding type and is more complex. For example, problem-solving is the most complex type and depends upon principle learning. Principle learning depends upon concept learning. Concept learning depends upon discrimination learning, and so on. The individual must have mastered a lower level of skill or learning before he learns a task in the next higher order. For example, the individual must learn to discriminate various objects before he learns a concept. Principle learning requires that the learner must have learnt concepts and based on two or three concepts he will learn a principle. In other words, learning proceeds from simple to complex form and the experience accumulates gradually. An individual who fails to learn one type will also fail to learn the other types in the hierarchical order.

Conditions of Learning

All learning depends upon certain conditions. There are internal conditions and external conditions. Motivation, attention, self-confidence and previous experience are internal conditions. Contiguity, repetition and reinforcement are external conditions. For Gagne, external conditions are of primary importance in the learning situation. According to Gagne, learning in schools is greatly influenced by external conditions like teacher-pupil interaction, reinforcement, etc.

Types of Learning and the Conditions for Each Type of Learning

Type 1. Signal Learning

Signal learning corresponds directly to classical conditioning. The primary conditions of signal learning are contiguity and repetition.

Type 2. Stimulus—Response Learning

The association of specific responses to specific stimuli is termed as S-R learning. Contiguity and reinforcement are primary conditions of S-R learning.

Type 3 and Type 4. Motor Chaining and Verbal Chaining

Motor chaining refers to combining or chaining two or more separate motor responses to develop a more complex motor skill. Verbal chaining or verbal association refers to combining two or more verbal responses, such as words to form a more complex verbal behaviour, such as a sentence. The primary internal condition of chaining is the ability of the individual to recall the various sub-skills and to combine them into a meaningful pattern. The primary external conditions are contiguity, repetition and reinforcement.

Type 5. Multiple Discrimination Learning

Discrimination of a specific stimulus from some other stimuli or one object from other objects is called discrimination learning. In multiple discrimination learning, the discrimination is among already learned stimulus-response connections. The essential internal conditions are acquisition of chains and the capacity to discriminate among chains. The external conditions required for multiple discrimination learning are contiguity, repetition and reinforcement.

Type 6. Concept Learning

Concept learning refers to the process of making a common response to a number of stimuli that are similar in some ways and dissimilar in other ways. The important feature of concept learning is that, having learned a concept, one is able to identify other examples of the concept without further learning. The internal conditions of concept learning are ability to discriminate between objects and the ability to notice commonalities in them. Contiguity, repetition, and feedback are some external conditions.

Type 7. Principle Learning

Principle learning involves chain of two or more concepts. A principle is a relationship between two or more concepts. Thus, the essential conditions for principle learning are learning concepts and forming a relationship between these concepts to form a rule or principle. Verbal instruction, and asking the student to give an example of the principle and to state it are external conditions.

Type 8. Problem-solving

Problem-solving is the highest form of learning. It enables a person to secure new ideas independently of others. Learning of rules, the ability to recall and apply these rules in the solution of a problem are essential internal conditions of problem-solving. The external conditions are verbal instruction and guidance to the learner.

Implications for School Learning

Gagne's model of hierarchy of learning or the model of cumulative learning has significant implications for school learning:

(i) Learning in schools should be sequential and a step-by-step process. Today every child is required to master the minimum levels of learning. These minimum levels of learning or minimum learning competencies are arranged in hierarchical way or in a graded way. The child must master the competencies specified for a particular grade before he is allowed to learn and master the competencies specified for the next higher grade.

Gagne's types of learning and his conditions of learning have also important implications for the teaching — learning process.

(ii) Children's likes and dislikes may be acquired through signal learning. In securing attention of noisy students in the class, a teacher can shout a word that acts as a signal to control behaviour.

(iii) S-R implies that children have acquired many S-R responses before starting school and, thus, they can acquire other S-R responses with relative ease during their school years.

(iv) Many examples of learning chains — motor and verbal chains — are found in the schools. Learning to write the letters of the alphabet and to write words, learning Oriya language equivalents of English vocabulary, recalling definitions of words, memorizing a date are examples of learning of chains. Repetition and memory or rote learning are important in learning verbal and motor chain.

(v) Children have already learned to discriminate between objects, events or persons before starting school. Such discrimination among things continues after schooling starts. Discrimination learning can be applied in the learning of sounds of letters or words.

(vi) Concept learning has a central position in school situations, particularly in the teaching of Mathematics, Science, Geography and English.

(vii) Rule learning or principle learning probably ranks above concept learning in terms of its importance in the school setting. Teaching of Mathematics, Science and Grammar depends on rule learning.

(viii) Gagne's model of cumulative learning has also implications for curriculum planning. Gagne's model calls for instruction to be varied according to the type of learning and individual student's performances required in the learning situation. Schools and teachers must be capable of implementing a design for instruction that considers the individual student rather than the classroom group as the basic unit of instruction.

(ix) Gagne accepts principles of classical conditioning and operant conditioning as sufficient for explaining the simple types of learning but also indicates that they are not sufficient for explaining concept learning, the learning of principles or rules and problem-solving. Gagne recognised four conditions for problem-solving, such as:

(a) The learner must have a goal or that the learner must be able to identify the essential features of the responses that will be the solution before he arrives at it.

(b) The learner must be able to recall relevant principles previously learnt.

(c) Then recalled principles are combined to form a new principle.

(d) Then the solution is arrived at suddenly as if by insight.

In the classroom situation, then, the teacher must ensure that the children's past experience is known and utilised. The child must be able to recall all the relevant information he has previously learned as and when required. He must be able to relate these units of knowledge to one another and to apply them to the new principles he is attempting to understand. To facilitate these processes, it would appear that some verbal instruction is essential.

(x) For Gagne, insight cannot be a prototype for a vast amount of learning that human beings ordinarily undertake. He says that there are areas in education where insightful learning cannot take place. A child cannot learn the names of planets or stars in an insightful manner. He cannot learn to read by insight nor to learn a foreign language. A student of biology does not learn the structure and functions of animal by insight. For those who accept Gagne's views on insight, the 'look and say' method of teaching reading is more desirable.

(xi) Like Skinner, Gagne also realises the importance of reinforcement in learning. But he says that verbal reinforcers are not always necessary. In a classroom setting, for example, when the correct response is supplied by a student, the teacher may simply move to the next point. The respondent and other members of the classroom learn that this signifies a correct response and it bears consequent reinforcement value. All kinds of subtle cues may acquire reinforcement value — smiles, glimpses, and the like.

2. AUSUBEL'S THEORY OF MEANINGFUL LEARNING

D.P. Ausubel is a cognitive psychologist. His book *School Learning* is a valuable asset for teachers of today. His theory of learning is known as the 'Theory of Meaningful Learning.' In his theory of learning Ausubel distinguishes between two dimensions of the learning, process. One dimension of learning deals with the ways by which knowledge is made available to the learner. There are two such ways — reception and discovery. The second dimension of learning deals with the ways by which learners incorporate new information into their existing cognitive structure. There are two ways — meaningful learning and rote learning.

Reception and Discovery

In reception learning, the learning materials are presented to the learner through books, audio-visual aids, reference books and other instructional aids. The learner has merely to receive what is presented to him.

In discovery learning, some information is presented to the learner by the instructor or the teacher and the learner is required to get additional information independently through discovery. The learner then relates the information obtained through discovery to the information already presented to him by the teacher. If necessary, he has to reorganise his cognitive structure to arrive at the final form of the information or knowledge.

Meaningful Learning and Rote Learning

Reception and discovery enable the learner to acquire new knowledge or information. This is the first stage of learning. In the second stage of learning, the learner tries to remember the information so that it will be recalled as and when necessary. There are two ways of remembering the learnt material. If the learner tries to retain the information with understanding and relating the new information with his prior learning or with what he has learnt previously meaningful learning occurs. If the learner tries to memorize the new information by mechanical drill or rote without any understanding, rote learning occurs.

Types of Learning

Based on the dimensions and ways of learning discussed above, Ausubel proposed four types of learning, such as:

(i) Meaningful Reception,
(ii) Rote Reception,
(iii) Meaningful Discovery, and
(iv) Rote Discovery.

In meaningful reception, new knowledge or information is presented in the final form through books, audio-visual aids and other instructional aids. The learner relates this knowledge or information to what he already knows or his previous knowledge and assimilates the new knowledge.

In rote reception, new knowledge is presented to the learner in the final form. The learner simply memorizes this knowledge or information.

In meaningful discovery, the learner is required to learn independently. He relates the information obtained through discovery to his existing knowledge.

In rote discovery, the learner has to memorize the information obtained through discovery.

Ausubel recognises the importance of meaningful reception and to lesser degree meaningful discovery. Rote learning is abandoned in favour of meaningful learning.

Cognitive Structure and the Process of Subsumption

According to Ausubel, as an individual acquires knowledge in a particular field, he develops a cognitive structure related to that field. The cognitive structure of the individual is like a pyramid. General propositions and concepts form the apex of the pyramid. Sub-concepts form the middle level and specific information forms the base:

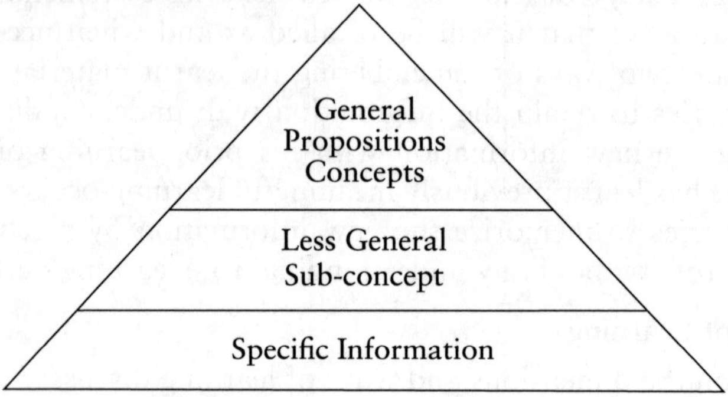

Fig 21: Gagne's Pyramid Model of Cognitive Structure.

According to Ausubel, the principal way to get new information into the cognitive structure is to assimilate it as part of the existing structure. This process of assimilating new information as part of the existing cognitive structure is called 'subsumption'. Subsumption, in other words, means relating a new idea to an existing one and if necessary modifying the new idea and the existing idea meaningfully. Ausubel recognises three types of subsumption:

(i) Derivative subsumption,
(ii) Correlative subsumption, and
(iii) Combinational subsumption.

Derivative subsumption is the process through which the new idea is derived from the existing idea. For example, the child has already learnt the proposition that "Cats climb trees." The new and specific proposition "The neighbour's cat is climbing the tree" can be derived from the existing proposition "Cats climb trees."

Sometimes the new idea extends or modifies the existing idea. When this happens, correlative subsumption occurs. For example, the child has already learnt that, "An equilateral triangle is a closed, plain and simple figure with three sides of equal length." Now he learns that "Equilateral triangles have three angles which are equal" to one another. By correlating the new idea with the existing idea, he modifies his cognitive structure that, "Equilateral triangles have three equal angles as well as three sides of equal length." He develops a new idea that "If three sides of a triangle are equal in length, then the three angles are also equal." It is either through derivative subsumption or correlative subsumption that new subordinate concepts and propositions are related to the more abstract ones already in the cognitive structure.

Sometimes related subordinate concepts and propositions are not available in the cognitive structure. When the child learns new concepts and propositions but related concepts and propositions are not available in his existing cognitive structure, it is called combinational subsumption. For example, a child may learn how atoms function by observing a physical model. But he had no such knowledge or idea previously. He will obtain this knowledge by relating concepts to one another, concepts to propositions, etc.

Ausubel also explains the phenomenon of forgetting in the light of subsumption process. He says that with the passage of time and lack of use, the various concepts already learnt become less distinct and eventually these concepts cannot be recalled as and when required. We can recall for sometime what we have learned but are not using. With the passage of time we can only recognize but we cannot recall it. Later we can neither recall nor recognize. But we can re-learn it in less time than originally. Thus, in order to avoid the occurrence of forgetting re-learning or practice is essential.

Educational Implications

(i) Ausubel's theory gives primary importance to meaningful reception learning. This implies that the teacher should guide children to relate the material presented in the textbooks, reference books or through classroom instruction to their existing knowledge, derive meaning from what they learn and this will enable them to remember the learned facts for long. His theory also implies that children should have periodical review at reasonable intervals to avoid forgetting.

(ii) His theory of meaningful learning also implies that curriculum planners and teachers should take care to see that whatever is presented to the child is meaningful for him. Meaningful materials are learnt and remembered better than meaningless materials.

(iii) His combinational subsumption is a very valuable contribution to the process of instruction. While learning scientific concepts and propositions, children should be guided properly to understand the relationship involved among various concepts, between concepts and propositions and among propositions. This will facilitate efficiency in learning and permanence of retention.

(iv) Ausubel's idea of advance organisers has significant implications for the teacher. When the teacher plans to teach new concepts or ideas, he should present short, expository passages, synopsis or brief handouts to children in advance so that children can come prepared and participate in classroom discussion enthusiastically.

3. LEARNING BY OBSERVATION AND MODELLING (ALBERT BANDURA)

What is Learning by Modelling?

Albert Bandura is known for his extensive research on how children learn by observation or watching and imitating a model. Bandura and his associates have also conducted extensive research on how problem behaviour can be modified by modelling techniques.

At every moment, children watch and observe the behaviour, actions, reactions and manners of parents, teachers, and other adults. They also watch and observe the TV personalities and film stars. Parents, teachers, other adults, TV personalities and film stars act as models for children. Children not only watch and observe them but they also imitate the behaviours of the model. Learning that takes place in this way is not deliberate and conscious. Children can also be trained deliberately to watch, observe and imitate the behaviour of a model. Problem behaviour of children can also be modified by deliberate efforts to expose them to live models and filmed models. This is in essence the concept of learning by observation and modelling.

Processes Involved in Modelling

Learning by modelling is not as simple as it appears to be. It involves a number of psychological processes, such as:

Attention,
Recognition,
Identification,
Retention,
Reproduction,
Internalisation,
Reinforcement.

A child watches the model. He attends to the behaviour or characteristics of the model. Gradually he recognises the specific qualities or characteristics of the model. He tries to identify himself with the model. He retains in his memory whatever qualities he has recognised. Later in a similar situation he reproduces those qualities or characteristics of the model. Modelling is said to be effective only if the child is influenced by the characteristics of the model, if he has been able to imitate and reproduce those characteristic, and if he has been able to internalise those behaviour patterns of the model. If imitated behaviour is followed by pleasant experiences, reward, recognition or approval that behaviour is strengthened and repeated on subsequent occasions. If imitated behaviour is followed by unpleasant experiences, disapproval, ridicule or punishment that behaviour is weakened and forgotten.

Effects of Modelling

When a child is exposed to a model, three types of effects are possible:

(i) The child may copy an entirely new behaviour. For example, children who watch film or television programmes involving aggression, violence, etc. show similar behaviour more often than children who are not exposed to such programmes.

(ii) The child may alter his own established behaviour by strengthening or inhibiting it. For example, if a child sees a certain kind of behaviour going unpunished which he previously regarded as punishable, he is less likely to inhibit his problem behaviour on subsequent similar occasion.

(iii) Observation of a model may cause the reappearance of behaviours which were apparently forgotten. The child matches the behaviour he observes in others with his present behaviour. The behaviour of the model acts as a releaser for parallel behaviour in the child. For example, in dance lessons, a girl observes the movements of her master and quickly picks up the movements she has forgotten.

Bandura (1970) developed the modelling technique for modifying problem behaviour. His technique consists of allowing individuals to observe and imitate appropriate models. In the first stage, a client learns by watching another person perform the desired behaviour including the consequences or reinforcement experienced by the model. Then, in a second stage, the client may be reinforced externally for doing the behaviour in addition to the intrinsic reward of performing the behaviour itself.

Bandura and his associates applied this technique to four groups of people with a fear of snakes. Each group was treated differently. Individuals in the first group watched a film showing children and adults fearlessly handling a king snake. This was called "symbolic modelling". Those in the second group saw a live model handling a king snake and then were told to imitate the model's actions. They did this through graduated steps, such as first touching the snake with gloved hands, then with bare skin, later letting the snake coil around their arms, and finally allowing the snake to crawl over their bodies. This second procedure was called the "live modelling with participation." A third group of people were taught to relax while they imagined handling snakes, and a fourth group received no training at all. While all individuals performed better than those in the fourth group, individuals in the participant modelling group improved the most of all. Eleven out of the 12 people in this group overcame their fear of snakes.

Modelling techniques have been used for people of all ages and all types of problems, including phobias, alcoholism, delinquency, schizophrenia as well as for the training of professional delinquency personnel.

Bandura, Ross and Ross (1963) studied the effects of live models, filmed human aggression, and filmed cartoon aggression on pre-school children's aggressive behaviour. They noticed that all the children exhibited significantly more aggression than children in the control group. Also filmed models were as effective as live models in transmitting aggression. Research by Bandura and Walters (1963) suggests that prestigious, powerful, popular, attractive persons and persons, who are warmly disposed to the child can be effective models for children.

Educational Implications

Learning by observation and modelling has significant implications for parents and teachers:

(i) The home, the elementary school and the pre-school centres are the prime sites for children to learn by observation, modelling and imitation. Children who are dependent and less competent should be exposed to models. By watching others in activities about which the child feels unsure, he frequently reassures himself and also acquires the skills needed to handle the situation. Children who are very fearful and less confident may need direct help from the parents and teachers.

(ii) Learning by modelling, observation and imitation is very appropriate for learning language, attitudes, personality traits, sex-appropriate roles, modification of problem behaviour and all types of social learning.

(iii) It is very important to note that children do not do what adults tell them to do, but rather what they see adults do as in case of punctuality, discipline, toileting, smoking, dining manners, etc. Thus, adults should be very careful in their words and actions.

(iv) Every teacher is a live model of social behaviour for children. A teacher can initiate new behaviours in children or modify their existing behaviours. All this depends on how he interacts with children, how he behaves with his colleagues and students and what manners he exhibits. Aggression, hostility, friendliness, aloofness, co-operativeness and many other traits are learned by observation and modelling. The teacher should show consistency in his behaviour and reinforcement techniques to avoid any confusion and ambiguity among children.

(vi) Models can be live models, filmed models, pictorial models or verbal models. In general, live models are most effective. Filmed models are also effective. Filmed models can be used only when live models are not readily available and unsuccessful. Verbal models can be used only after children have acquired language. Pictorial and cartoon models are effective for young children.

4. BRUNER AND MENTAL GROWTH

Born in 1915, Jerome Bruner remains a potent figure in developmental psychology, cognitive studies, and education. Bruner's interests range over many disciplines. Whenever he champions a new idea, it is sure to generate excitement and enthusiasm. Yet, as productive and innovative as Bruner is, he has had much less influence than either Piaget or Skinner. His varied interests are perhaps the reason. Bruner, unlike many of his colleagues, has investigated rat behaviour, German propaganda, perception, cognitive styles, sensory deprivation, learning, child development, innate behaviour, and education. Bruner's valuable insights deserve our consideration because his view of the child as an information processor, thinker, and creator emphasizes both rationality and dignity.

The Pattern of Cognitive Growth

One of Bruner's major assumptions is that teaching is an effort to assist growth. He believes that intellectual growth has several discernible characteristics:

1. Freedom from Environmental Control

Increasing independence of response from an immediate stimulus distinguishes mental growth. We can predict much of young children's behaviour from knowing the stimuli around them. But as children grow mentally, they are able to maintain a desired response although conditions (stimuli) change. A good example is the proficiency to give the right response in a multiple-choice examination. The youngster maintains the response in spite of assorted stimuli. Children also can change their response to meet unchanging environmental demands. For example, if an answer is incorrect, and children know it is incorrect, they change their answer (response) to the same question (stimulus).

2. A Model of the World

Intellectual growth depends upon the child's mental construction or model of the world. The child actively constructs a mental picture of the world. Building this mental image of the world permits a child to use the information to compare, judge, and predict. It is similar to Piaget's explanation of a child's ability to go from the real to the possible.

3. Symbolism

Growing skill in symbolic activity features intellectual development. Youngsters can say what they have done or will do; they begin to use proposition or statements and thus reflect a logico-mathematical capacity that did not previously exist.

4. Interactions

Intellectual development depends on a close interaction between a teacher and learner. There are many tutors in a child's environment, school teachers, father, mother, friends, heroes and there is still considerable uncertainty about the details of the different relationship. For example, different individuals possess different personalities and thus do things differently. Is the relationship between a permissive teacher and her pupils radically different from the relationship between a firm teacher and her pupils? What is the ideal learning environment for these two examples? Are they identical? More data are needed before confident decisions are possible.

5. Language

Language facilitates teaching and learning, but a child gradually uses it not only for communication but also to bring order to the environment. For example, while the young child uses language to inform others of needs or to identify objects, the older child uses language to represent things or events not present: "Tomorrow I must bring my notebook home to study for the weekend."

6. Competence

Finally, intellectual development is marked by increasing competence in attending to several possibilities. For example, in Piaget's conservation experiments, when youngsters are no longer distracted by the length or width of the glass but realizes that the liquid remains intact, they are attending to several things.

Modes of Representation

How can these ideas help us in teaching? Bruner believes that the mental growth characteristics aid a youngster in achieving three levels of representation, that is, a child passes through three distinct cognitive phases:

(i) Bruner calls the first level "the enactive mode of representation." The infant knows the world only by acting on it; otherwise the object does not exist. As Bruner notes, there are times in the adult's life when words simply cannot express what is meant. For example, how can you tell someone about "the feel" of the golf or tennis swing?

(ii) The second level is "the iconic mode of representation," Bruner's expression for perceptual organization. Faced with a series of apparently unrelated tasks, discovering a pattern makes the work easier.

(iii) The third level is "the symbolic mode of representation." Here the child engages in symbolic activities, such as language and mathematics. Bruner (1966) states that when children translate experience into language, they enter the world of possibilities, enabling them to solve problems and engage in creative thinking.

Youngsters learn according to their mode of representation. For example, youngsters at the iconic level need concrete objects and activities so that they can absorb them perceptually. Bruner (1960) states that learning a subject involves three almost simultaneous processes:

(i) Acquisition of new information, which replaces or expands what the child already knows, is the initial phase. Here the child incorporates environmental stimuli according to the existing mode of representation: by physical action, by forming images, or by abstracting, comparing, and judging.

(ii) Transformation is the second phase. Once youngsters or adults acquire new information then they must manipulate or change it to meet new tasks. Bruner often uses the illustration, "going beyond the information given." For example, your girl friend passes by the door and says, "Hi, Mitu." You do not see her, but immediately think. "There goes Swapna." You manipulated verbal stimuli to form the idea of your friend.

(iii) Evaluation is the final phase. Have they successfully manipulated the information? Was it adequate? Correct?

Bruner joins mental growth, modes of representation, and learning processes to introduce his idea of the spiral curriculum. He states that if teachers respect a child's thinking process and translate material into meaningful units (that is, if they match the subject-matter to the child's mode of representation) they can introduce great ideas to children at different times and with increasing abstractness. For example, freedom discussed in the first grade differs from a junior high school discussion of slavery, which differs from a high school discussion of the meaning of the Constitution hence the spiral curriculum.

Bruner and Piaget

Bruner and Piaget share many ideas, and Bruner has often acknowledged his debt to Piaget. Recently, however, Bruner has stated that he differs from Piaget in emphasizing a culture's influence on intellectual development. Anglin (1973) has summarized the similarities and differences between the two. Both believe that mental development involves qualitative rather than quantitative changes in cognitive structures. Both believe that mental development occurs in phases:

Similarities in Levels of Mental Development

Piaget	Bruner
Sensorimotor	Enactive
Pre-operational	Iconic
Concrete operations	
Formal operations	Symbolic

Their interpretations of the levels are almost identical. Both believe that action in infancy is critical for normal intellectual growth.

Differences

Anglin (1973) states that there are also important differences. Piaget's work, highly mathematical and logical, is quite formal. Bruner emphasizes more psychological concepts, for example, cognitive conflict hastens mental development. Bruner believes that his interpretation of language's role in development differs from Piaget's. Bruner states that language facilitates mental performance. It is causally linked to increased mental competence while Piaget believes that language is an outcome of growing mental competence. Finally, Bruner stresses more than Piaget a culture's role. He states that mental development is as much "from the outside in as from the inside out" due to language.

How real are these differences? Probably minimal, since both basically agree about mental development. Bruner questions Piaget's interpretation of maturation and experience, but Piaget believes that two of the four agents that aid cognitive development are cultural: experience and social transmission. Piaget questions Bruner's interpretation of culture, but Bruner believes that the material must match the growth of child's changing capacities. His famous readiness statement — any subject can be taught effectively in some intellectually honest form to any child at any stage of development — reflects recognition of maturation's importance. He states that his interpretation of readiness depends on three general ideas: the path of intellectual development (which is essentially Piaget's), the act of learning (which must match the level of intellectual development), and the spiral curriculum.

SELECTED QUESTIONS

1. Discuss Gagne's hierarchy of learning.
2. Explain Gagne's conditions of learning.
3. Explain Ausubel's theory of meaningful learning. What are their implications for the teacher?
4. Explain learning by observation and modelling.
5. Discuss Bruner's views on mental development of children.
6. Discuss the similarities and differences between Piaget and Bruner.

22
Organisational Climate

1. WHAT IS ORGANISATIONAL CLIMATE?

The school is an organisation. Every organisation has its own goals, plans and programmes. The success or failure of any organisation in implementing its plans and programmes to reach its goals depends to a great extent upon its climate. The term "climate" refers to the conditions of a school in respect of its plans and programmes. It refers to the physical, social and emotional conditions of the school in relation to its academic programmes. Thus the term "organisational climate" refers to the overall characteristic atmosphere in a school. It refers to the sum of all physical, social, emotional and instructional factors which contribute to the total teaching — learning situations in the school.

Organisational climate may mean inter-school climate or intra-school climate. In other words, it may mean the atmosphere prevailing in a cluster of schools in a particular locality or it may mean the atmosphere within a school. The school climate may be open climate or autonomous climate. It is open in the sense that the atmosphere of the school is determined, influenced or modified by external agencies such as government and public. It is autonomous in the sense that the school has autonomy in deciding its atmosphere and independent of external influences.

Factors Influencing Organisational Climate

The following factors influence organisational climate:

(a) Emotional climate of the school,

(b) Social climate of the school,
(c) Physical environment of the school, and
(d) Instructional climate of the school.

Emotional Climate of the School

The emotional climate of the school is a basic condition for healthy organisational climate. In certain schools there is free exchange of ideas, feelings and experiences. There is mutual trust and respect among its members. Love, appreciation and permissive atmosphere are characteristic features of such schools. Performance of students is better in such schools than in other schools. By contrast, there are schools where there are frequent quarrels and fights among its members. Distrust, disrespect, confusion, unpleasant atmosphere, anxious moments and lack of appreciation of each other's difficulties and contributions are day-to-day features of such schools. Performance of students is adversely affected in such schools.

Social Climate of the School

The social climate of the school is linked directly with its emotional climate. It relates to the human relations and interaction among its members. Such relations and interactions refer to the following:

Teacher — Student Interaction
Student — Student Interaction
Headmaster — Staff Interaction
Teacher — Parent Interaction
Teacher — Teacher Interaction

The social climate of the school also refers to the leadership style adopted by the headmaster and teachers. Leadership style is of three types such as:

Autocratic or authoritarian style,
Democratic style, and
Laissez-faire style.

The overall performance of the school is better under democratic leadership than under other styles. The general feeling about the school is better when the headmaster is a democratic leader.

Physical Environment of the School

The physical environment of the school contributes positively or adversely to the total functioning of the school. It refers to the location of the school (rural, urban, slum area, crowded market-place or sensitive spot), type of school building, space and equipments of the school for proper education and the ecosystem.

Instructional or Academic Climate of the School

The effectiveness of a school depends upon its instructional climate. The instructional climate of the school refers to the qualities and qualification of teachers, teaching styles, learning environment, organisation of co-curricular activities, evaluation system, academic records of the school and the school policy.

The factors which influence the organisational climate are not mutually exclusive or independent of each other. Each is linked with and influences the other. For example, the emotional climate of the school is linked with its social climate. The psycho-social climate depends on the physical environment of the school which influences the academic performance of the school. Thus, the organisational climate of the school is the result of interaction and interplay of its physical, social, emotional and academic atmosphere.

2. LEADERSHIP STYLES

What is Leadership?

The New Webster's *Comprehensive Dictionary of English Language* defines the leader as "someone who acts as a guide." Thus, the headmaster, the leader of the school, is a guide — a guide for total quality education in the school, a guide for total quality management of his school. J. Case (1993) defines the leader as the chief coach-cum-coordinator.

An effective teacher is a leader of the group. Leadership is an interactive process. It is an interaction between the teacher as the leader and the members of the group. Thus leadership is found in some kind of group and the leader functions in relation to his followers.

Groups differ in terms of specific characteristics such as size, homogeneity, stability, viscidity, and hedonic tone. Since groups differ from each other, leadership behaviours also differ from group to group. Behaviours effective in one situation may not be effective in others. In addition to the situational factors, leadership also depends on certain personal traits. It is generally believed that intelligence, imagination, self-confidence, tolerance for ambiguity, impartiality, objectivity, perseverance, and emotional stability are among the many personal traits which characterize the teacher to exercise leadership.

Styles of Leadership and their Effects on the Group

As a leader of the group, the teacher may be either authoritarian, democratic, *laissez-faire* or charismatic. Consequently there are four styles of leadership such as:

Authoritarian Leadership,
Democratic Leadership,
Laissez-faire Leadership, and
Charismatic Leadership.

Authoritarian Leader

When a teacher plays the role of an authoritarian leader, all policies and procedures are dictated by him. He dictates orders, gives disruptive commands and makes non-constructive criticisms. He remains aloof from the group participation. The students are not expected to ask 'why' for a certain order or decision. Whatever the teacher thinks, feels or says must be carried out by the students.

Democratic Leader

Under the democratic leadership, the teacher guides, gives suggestion, extends knowledge and stimulates self-guidance. All policies and procedures are matters of group decision. There is an element of freedom and acceptance. Division of responsibility is a matter of accepted principle. The teacher also actively participates in the activities of the group.

Laissez-faire Leader

Under the *laissez-faire* leadership, the teacher plays a rather passive role in social activities and leaves complete freedom for the group. He takes minimum initiative in making suggestions.

But he supplies information and provides help when asked. He makes no attempt to evaluate the activities of the group or individual members.

Charismatic Leader

Charismatic leadership is characterized by the personal charm and inner qualities of the leader. It is due to this personal charm and inner qualities that the leader can influence the group activities, procedures, decision and the outcome. His very presence in the group acts as a magic for the group. There are very few teachers who are endowed with charismatic personalities.

These styles of leadership create different social, emotional and attitudinal climate of the group. These styles produce different results and behaviour patterns among students. For example, the authoritarian role brings better discipline, less confusion and more production when the leader is present in the group. But when the leader is absent there is a breakdown in order. Moreover, authoritarian leadership brings reaction such as aggressiveness, and scapegoating. The democratic leadership results in less order and productivity generally, but even when the leader is not present, order, discipline and production are not disrupted or hampered. Such leadership also produces less aggressive and scapegoating tendencies among the members. Democratic leadership facilitates learning. Generally speaking, students prefer democratic leadership to authoritarian leadership.

Laissez-faire leadership is ineffective leadership. Neither it causes order and discipline, nor does it produces any significant results. Charismatic leadership is ideal but very rarely noticed among teachers.

Another categorization of leadership is designated leadership and ascribed leadership (Mukhopadhyaya, 2002):

Designated Leadership and Ascribed Leadership

Designated leadership means somebody occupies leadership position because of his designation. Thus, the headmaster is a designated leader. When an individual is chosen by his peers and other staff members as the leader, it is called ascribed leadership. The real leader is the one who is ascribed to lead. The headmaster should, therefore, emerge as an ascribed leader.

Authority and Power

Leadership can also be viewed in terms of authority and power. Authority flows from official position or the designation which a person holds. Power flows from personal qualities of influencing others. Thus, the designated, leader can use authority whereas the ascribed leader uses power. Some headmasters are high on power but low on authority. They depend much more on their personal influence than on official position. They get most of their tasks accomplished by their followers without invoking official rules, procedures, etc. Some headmasters are high on both. They can use power as well as authority. Some headmasters are high on authority but low on power. This is noticed among autocratic headmasters. Some headmasters are low on authority and low on power. This is noticed among headmasters who are *laissez-faire* in their style.

Leadership can also be categorized under four heads, depending upon the leader's (i) concern for tasks, and (ii) concern for relationship. These are:

Telling Style,
Selling Style,
Participating Style,
Delegating Style,
(Hersey and Blanchard, 1991).

Mukhopadhyaya (2002) explains these styles as follows:

Telling Style Leadership

This style of leadership is characterized by high concern for task but low concern for relationship. Usually, the headmaster as the leader instructs his colleagues to carry out a task. He specifies the time, method of carrying out the task, and the quality of the task he intends. He is not concerned with relationship as much as he is concerned with task accomplishment. This style is often considered as the dictatorial style and the leader is nick-named as "hard task master." This style is generally effective with teachers who have low task motivation and in crisis situations.

Selling Style Leadership

This style of leadership is characterized by high concern for task and high concern for relationship. In this style, the headmaster ensures task accomplishment with the defined quality and within specified time period. While emphasizing the task accomplishment, he also ensures that the relationship is not disturbed or that the members of the group have healthy interpersonal relationships and a trusting relationship with the leader. This style is most effective when the headmaster introduces an innovation in the school.

Participating Style Leadership

This style of leadership is characterized by high concern for relationship but low concern for task. This style is the reverse of the telling style. In this style, the headmaster may ignore task accomplishment for the sake of maintaining good relationship with his followers. In other words, he values his relationship with the group more than he values task accomplishment. These leaders are called 'Mr. Nice man' or 'Nice Madam.' In this style, the leader participates in task accomplishment. This style is relevant when routine, monotonous but necessary work have to be done, *e.g.*, calculation of attendance, tabulation of marks, etc.

Delegating Style Leadership

This style of leadership is characterized by low concern for relationship and low concern for task. In this style, the leader allows things to happen as in case of *laissez-faire* leadership. He does not take responsibility for anything. Rather he delegates purposefully the responsibilities on others. This style is most effective when the members of the group are extremely competent and mature to accomplish the task.

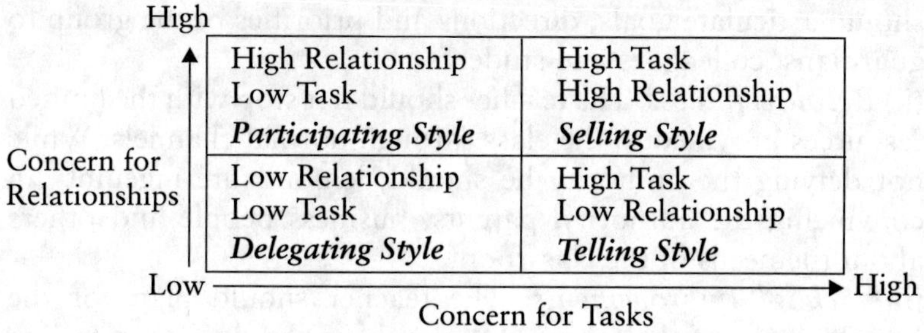

Fig. 22: Leadership Styles.

Some headmasters have a preference for a particular style. Some headmasters are flexible in their style. They adopt a style as required by the situation. The effectiveness of a headmaster depends on adopting a particular style as the situation demands.

There are also important differences that exist in various classrooms managed by various types of leaders. Classrooms managed by incompetent leaders simply don't get the job done. Typically such classrooms are characterized by confusion and inefficiency in operation and malaise in human relations. Students' achievement is lower in such classrooms. Student absenteeism, discipline and violence may be problems faced by the leader in such classrooms. Parents may feel isolated from the school. Classrooms managed by competent leader's measure up to these standards. The group gets the job done in a satisfactory manner. Classrooms managed by excellent leaders exceed the expectations. Students in such classrooms accomplish far more and teachers work much harder than can ordinarily be expected.

Behaviour of Effective Leaders

Role of the Teacher

Although effective leadership depends on certain situational factors, there are some behaviours which characterize effective leadership. In other words, the teacher must demonstrate the following behaviour patterns in order to function as an effective leader:

(i) *Vision*: The teacher should have a sense of vision as to the kind of classroom and learning environment he intends to create. He should articulate goals, directions and priorities of the group to guardians, colleagues and students.

(ii) *Resourcefulness*: The teacher should not stop with the limited resources provided to the class through normal channels. While not defying the authority he should demonstrate ingenuity in convincing the authority, parents, business people and others about the needs of the classroom.

(iii) *School Improvements*: The teacher should plan for the improvement of the school. He should try to develop a feeling among the people that the school cares for its students and values their contributions.

(iv) *Instructional Support*: The teacher should be a visible entity in all aspects of school life and provide active instructional support to students. He should spend much time in discussing academic matters with students and provide help as and when needed.

(v) *Monitoring*: The teacher should know more about how students are doing in various subjects. Such information should be the basis for giving feedback to students and other teachers and for setting priorities in various subject areas.

(vi) *Optimism*: The teacher should be optimistic that improvement of the school and change in students' behaviour are possible. Lack of optimism on the part of the teacher may be a hindrance to all change and improvements that are likely to occur.

(vii) *Clarity of Role*: The teacher should define group activities and his relation to the group. He should define the role he expects each member to assume, assign tasks, plan ahead, establish the ways of getting things done and motivate for performance.

(viii) *Consideration*: There should be mutual trust and respect and certain warmth and rapport between the teacher and the students. This does not mean a superficial 'pat-on-the-back' or 'first-name-calling' kind of human relation behaviour but a deeper understanding and concern for needs of students and a two-way communication process.

3. ECOLOGY OF EDUCATION

What is Ecology of Education?

Ecology of education is a newly developed science. The term ecology has been borrowed from the field of biology and is now applied in the field of education. Ecology is a scientific study of interaction between environment and the organism. Just as the environment influences the organism, the organism affects the environment and education. So ecology of education means a systematic study of how the school environment affects education, learning and growth of learners, how education improves the environment, and how environment and education interact with each other. In short, ecology of education means the educational environment of a particular institution as related to children's learning (Although the home environment is equally important, we are concerned with the school environment here).

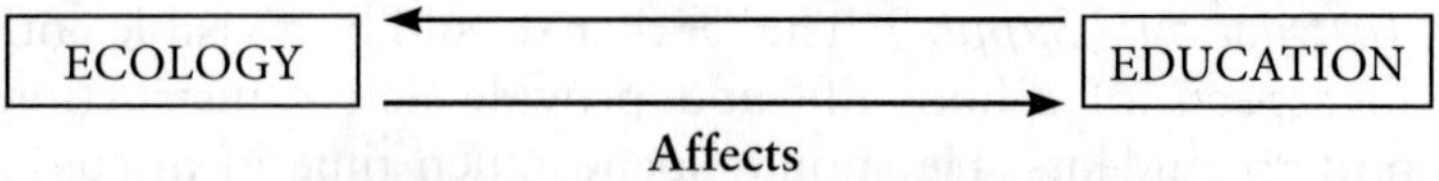

A Model of Ecology of Education

Ecological Factors Influencing Education

The overall growth, development and behavioural changes of a learner in a particular institution entirely depend on environmental factors and conditions of that institution. These factors are of two types: Biotic factors and Abiotic factors.

(i) Biotic factors are living components such as teachers, students and the administrator. The number of teachers, their qualification, experience and behaviour influence what and how much students can learn. Similarly, the number of students, their socio-economic background, and interaction pattern among them also influence education and development. For example, if the classroom is overcrowded it leads to low standard of education. Similarly, if the administration is autocratic and unsympathetic, it may lead to a number of problems. Teacher — pupil interaction is a significant factor which influences learning.

(ii) Abiotic factors are non-living components. They may be physical or chemical factors. Physical factors include temperature, light, location and type of the building, furniture, laboratory, library, playground, aids and equipments, etc. Chemical factors include sanitation, ventilation, pollutant gases, etc. These abiotic factors influence children's learning. For example, in ancient "Gurukula" system, classes were held in the open air under the tree as there was no formal school building. Sophisticated aids and equipments were not available at that time. Teaching style and the ability of analysis and expression of the *guru* were the basis of education. Emphasis on rote learning in the ancient schools in India was due to the environmental factors like non-availability of paper and ink, absence of books and printing press. Teacher — pupil interaction was ideal and healthiest as the number of students was very less. Today with the advancement of science and technology, education is provided through computer, television and multi-media package. Emphasis is now given on independent study, self-learning strategies, discovery learning and problem-solving ability. In addition to these improvements, a large number of educational problems are noticed today due to financial constraints, overcrowded classrooms, and certain political factors.

The sum of all these biotic and abiotic factors makes the educational environment of an institution. These factors are inter-related. Variation in one factor may affect the other factors.

Just as environmental factors mould education so also education can improve the environment. This consciousness about the role of education in improving the environment has led to the development of environmental education programme. It is through a programme of environmental education in schools that we can create awareness among the younger generation about the environment, its resources and limitations, environmental pollution and control, its effect on quality of life, develop in them a rational and responsible attitude towards their environment; and help them develop the skills and competencies needed to take a decision relating to their environment in future.

4. STRESS MANAGEMENT

What is Stress?

Sometimes when we don't perform well, we say "It is because of stress." When we have difficulty in interacting with our friends and relatives, we say "I am under a lot of stress." Various events in our life cause stress for us. Some of these events are:

Death of a family member
Personal injury or illness
Sex difficulties
Death of a close friend
Separation or divorce of parents
Outstanding work
Attending a marriage ceremony
Change of residence
Change of living conditions

Change in sleeping habits, etc.

Certain events relating to schooling are also stressful for children. These are:

The first and the last day in a school
Change of school
Change of courses of study
Change of school time
Difficulties with classmates
Change of seats
New responsibilities assigned
Ensuing examination
Obtaining a poor grade
Failure in the examination
Minor violation of school discipline
Joining of a new teacher
Outstanding home tasks

Teachers also experience stress in schools. The following situations are stressful for teachers:

Inter-role distance
Role stagnation
Role ambiguity
Role overload
Role inadequacy
Inefficient administration
Poor academic, emotional and social climate
Student vandalism

Everyone experiences stress but stress is experienced more by boys than girls. Women teachers experience stress more than male teachers.

Stress refers to any adjustive demand that requires an adaptive response from us. As such, it is not always harmful. At times stress is beneficial for the individual as it stimulates the individual to action appropriate for the situation. How stress affects the individual depends on how the individual perceives the stressful situation and his tolerance for stress. The term "distress" would be reserved for the harmful effects of stress, such as excessive pressure on work which makes an individual ill.

Whether stress is harmful or beneficial, it is an inevitable part of one's life. Since stress is built into life itself, it is not so much whether we will experience stress or not but 'what kind,' 'how much,' and 'how to tolerate.'

Types of Psychological Stress

Since the human organism responds to stressful forces as a whole, we can distinguish but cannot separate the various forms of stress. Stress may be biological, such as a bacterial infection, or it may be psychological, such as failure in an examination. We will discuss here the various types of psychological stress. There are four types of psychological stress, such as:

Pressure,
Frustration,
Conflict, and
Anxiety.

We may experience pressure from inner sources or outer sources. Our own ambitions and the social pressure to compete or to complete work in time are examples. Frustration results from the thwarting of our motives either through unnecessary delays or because of social and personal obstacles. The experience of conflict comes about when we have to respond to two incompatible forces at the same time. Anxiety is an unsettling feeling that serves to alert us against impending danger or threat.

Managing Stress: Role of the Teacher

Stress is common in everyone's life. Men and women, boys and girls, rich and the poor, young and the old, all experience some form of stress in their life. It is not important to consider what kind of stress or how much one has experienced. The important thing is how one manages a stressful situation.

In the modern complex society with its rapidly changing values, stress is an inevitable event in the life of young children and adolescents. The social — emotional climate of the school, the instructional programme having complicated textbooks, heavy demands of home tasks, failure of instruction to meet individual needs, undue emphasis on examination, etc. are very stressful for most adolescents.

Under the stressful situations in the home and the school, most adolescents respond by resorting to defence mechanisms. Defence mechanisms are spontaneous reactions to stress which alleviate or reduce some of the tensions of stress. But they do not modify the overall stressful situations nor do they help the adolescents to gain relief from their stress permanently. Many adolescents simply talk, laugh or cry under stress. Talking it out, laughing or crying give temporary relief but the stress continues to affect the adolescent.

Teachers in schools can provide a great deal of help to adolescents to increase their tolerance of stress and manage their stress successfully. The following approaches are useful:

(i) Children should be helped to learn to increase their tolerance for stress. Tolerance for stress refers to the degree and duration of stress one can tolerate without becoming irrational and disorganized. In other words, it refers to the point beyond which one's behaviour becomes inefficient and thinking irrational. Stress tolerance varies from individual to individual and from situation to situation.

(ii) Children can increase their tolerance for pressure with greater experience and skill in a particular activity.

(iii) Children should be helped to understand themselves, their worth and their abilities. When children fail to succeed in a competition, they may blame others and be harsh themselves. They should be told that success is not dependent totally on one's performance and occasional failure is an inevitable part of life. Children should learn from the experiences of failure and try to improve the skills needed for success. They should be made aware of the fact that many outstanding persons have become that way partly from what they learned from earlier failure.

(iv) Frustration tolerance can be improved by understanding the nature and source of frustration, selecting appropriate tasks keeping in view one's abilities, strong motivation to be successful and adjusting one's expectations to the demands of the task.

(v) Children should be guided properly to be independent of others and to tolerate criticism, disappointment and rejection up to a point. Of course, this requires emotional maturity.

(vi) When children experience conflict, they should be guided not to approach any goal hurriedly. They should persist in examining all the alternatives more rationally until they are able to reach an acceptable decision.

(vii) Children should be helped to develop their ability to function while feeling anxious. In no case they should sacrifice their performance in anxious moments. This is possible by knowing more and more about the unknown threat or danger, achieving self-control and increasing self-confidence. Mild anxiety stimulates the child to action while excess of anxiety is disruptive. Most anxious moments pass away when children learn to relax naturally in a quiet environment, shifting attention away from the surroundings, adopting a passive attitude towards distracting thoughts and assuming a comfortable position.

(viii) The child should be helped to take an assertive approach to cope with stress whenever there is a reasonable possibility of success. This consists of attempts to modify the stress in a direct, constructive way. Even when one's response does not directly modify the stress-provoking agent, taking action diminishes one's feeling of stress. Blindly reacting in an aggressive, destructive way usually aggravates the situation and intensifies the stress. Simply speaking up promptly and clearly about the problem to the teacher, thinking of various possible solutions to the problem before acting on a solution, sharing one's problems with an interested person and seeking support from others, and joining the action-group to take appropriate action to solve the problem are helpful techniques.

(ix) Whenever a stressful situation cannot be successfully modified in the above-said ways, withdrawal from the field of stress may be the wisest way to reduce the harmful effect of stress. For example, being disturbed by the pressure of work, some employees proceed on leave for sometime.

(x) Very often, when children are made aware of their ability to do something to avoid stress, it helps them to reduce the stress itself. Teachers need to create a sense of confidence among children which reduces stress.

(xi) Stress is also reduced by compromise, conformity to the demands, adopting a substitute goal and by negotiation.

SELECTED QUESTIONS

1. What is organizational climate? What are the factors which influence the organizational climate of the school?
2. What is leadership? Discuss the effects of different styles of leadership on the group.
3. What is leadership? What behaviour patterns should the teacher demonstrate to function as an effective leader?
4. What is ecology of education? Discuss the ecological factors which influence education.
5. What is stress? Discuss the role of the teacher in helping students manage their stress.
6. Write short notes on:
   (a) The Concept of Organisational Climate,
   (b) Leadership Styles,
   (c) Ecology of Education,
   (d) Stress Management.

23
Inclusive Education

In a democratic country like ours every child has the right to education. All children should be given equal opportunity to learn to the limits of their capacities. We have to devise a classroom for all — an inclusive classroom — a classroom which welcomes all children with and without disabilities, a classroom which meets the special educational and other related needs of children.

Few educational topics have attracted as much recent attention as inclusion. Inclusion has been the subject of heated debate in professional journals. Inclusion has emerged as a reform in the education of children with disabilities which gained momentum since 1994 UNESCO World Conference on Special Educational Needs (Salamanca).

1. PRESENT PRACTICE OF EDUCATING CHILDREN WITH SPECIAL NEEDS

(i) Education of CSN in Special Schools

At present children with severe-disabilities are educated in special schools being segregated from their peers. They may be placed in residential schools and may be segregated from their parents, communities etc. Special schools/residential

* Based on:

1. "Inclusive Education," a paper presented in the Seminar organised by the Department of Education, Kurukshetra University (2001) by Neena Dash under the guidance of Prof. (Dr.) D.S. Yadav.
2. A Module on "Classroom for All" by M. Dash submitted to the Department of Groups of Children with Special Needs, NCERT, for use in Training Programmes (2002).

schools sometimes provide the most restrictive environment for education of children with special needs. This is because the children stay with other children, who have disabilities and may not be able to achieve as much as they can because of no exposure to competition.

(ii) Education of CSN in Regular Schools

Children with mild to moderate disabilities are enrolled in regular schools. They are educated in common schools with non-disabled children in the regular classrooms. Although children with disabilities are educated in physical proximity with non-disabled children in the regular classroom, social and academic integration of such children is not taken care of. The social distance between children with disabilities and their counterparts is still very large. Academically they are integrated only for a part of the day. Even when these children receive education in common schools with others in the regular classroom care is not taken to ensure quality education for them. Thus the academic achievements and progress of these children in terms of minimum levels of learning as compared to non-disabled children are far from being satisfactory. Of course there are instances where children with disabilities (particularly children with low vision, orthopaedic handicap and mild hearing loss) excel their counterparts in academic achievements. But these are rare cases.

(iii) The Problems Faced *Acceptance and Respect*

It has been seen that in the present practice of integration, children with SEN are enrolled in regular classroom, but they are not accepted and respected by their age-peers and the regular teachers.

Labelling: In most cases these children are teased and labelled by their peers. Although these children have their own name and identity regular teachers are in the habit of categorizing and addressing them by a label. Labelling itself is not a healthy practice for a number of reasons:

- Labels usually focus on a child's negative aspects. Once a child is labelled, teachers tend to think about the child only in terms of his inadequacies or defects.

- Teachers and parents tend to have low expectations about what a child can do.
- Teachers tend to explain the child's poor performance only in terms of his disability and not in terms of instructional failure.
- A labelled child develops a poor self-concept.
- Labels lead to rejection by the peers.
- Labels create a sense of helplessness, inferiority and stigmatization.

Responsibility: When a child having special educational needs is studying in the regular school whose responsibility is he/she? Is he/she the sole responsibility of the resource teacher, if such a teacher has been posted in the school implementing the scheme of integration, or of the general teacher? If the school does not have a resource teacher for education of such children then are they nobody's responsibility? Do you think regular teachers are involved in any decision-making or in giving remedial help to those children who need such help? Are the regular teachers accountable for the education of children with special educational needs?

Partnership: We must realize here that the whole foundation of inclusion of children having special educational needs in the community and community institutions like schools rests on building partnerships. No one person can achieve as much as can be achieved through team effort that adopts a problem-solving approach. Partnerships between the parents, resource teachers, general teachers, school administrators and other community members is an essential requirement of any effort to include children with special educational needs. This essential requirement is missing in the present practice of integration.

Traditionally-oriented Teaching: It has been seen that teachers' approach to teaching children with special educational needs is traditionally-oriented. They transmit information, no matter whether the special child is benefited or not. They follow the whole class lecture method with a fixed time-table, a single textbook, and rigid age grouping. Their instruction is focused on the whole class and individual attention is not paid to children with special needs. Instead of adapting the curriculum to fit to the needs of children with special needs teachers try to fit these children to the existing curriculum.

Personnel and Resources Not Integrated: It has also been seen that when children with special educational needs are integrated into the mainstream of regular school the personnel and the resources are not integrated. An unhealthy division between special education personnel and resources and the regular education personnel and resources still exists in schools implementing the scheme of integration.

Lack of Support: Children with disabilities studying in regular classrooms do not get the support of regular teachers and peers. Mutual support between regular teachers and the resource teachers is missing in most of the schools.

No Collaboration/Consultation: There is no collaboration and consultation among teachers about educating children with disabilities in the regular classrooms.

Parents Not Involved: In most of the cases parents feel alienated from the school. They are not involved in planning, preparation, implementation or any decision-making process. In some cases parents are not aware about the provision of educating children with disabilities in the regular schools.

Lack of Leadership of Headmasters: To a great extent quality education for children with special educational needs in the regular schools depends on the leadership, initiative and resourcefulness of the head teacher. The IED units in most schools are functioning so — so because of lack of vision, monitoring and proper leadership of the head teacher. Headmasters lack conceptual clarity about integration, the objectives to be achieved and the programmes or activities to be organised in their schools.

Lack of Linkage: One significant difficulty at present is the lack of linkage between special schools and regular schools. In an ideal situation the special school should function as a resource centre for the regular schools or a cluster of regular schools located in the area. But this is not the case. As per the provision contained in the NPE (1986) and the Programme of Action, children with severe disabilities who have completed their preparation in special school should be encouraged to go to the regular schools. But this may not be the case at all.

Conversely there are instances where special schools enroll mildly and moderately handicapped children who can be better educated in regular schools.

Inadequate Training of Resource Teachers: The resource teachers working in regular schools sometimes fail to design activities to meet the special educational needs of children with disabilities enrolled in regular schools. This happens so because of their inadequate training. They were not properly oriented about the mechanism of integration/inclusion. Thus real integration does not occur due to faulty training of resource teachers.

2. CHANGES TO BE BROUGHT ABOUT IN THE EDUCATION OF CHILDREN WITH SPECIAL NEEDS

In the previous section, we made an assessment of the current practices in integrating/including children with SEN in the regular classrooms. This assessment indicates that we have not been able to achieve what is intended in terms of:

(i) Coverage of children with SEN;
(ii) Perception of teachers about educability of SEN children;
(iii) Attitude, acceptance and respect of teachers and peers;
(iv) Administrative support and quality education for such children, and
(v) Linkage between special education personnel and regular education personnel.

There is, at present, a growing feeling to change our focus from integration to inclusion.

Inclusion — What is it?

Inclusion is the provision of services to students with disabilities in their neighbourhood schools with necessary support services and supplementary aids for both children and teachers. It means meeting the needs of children with disabilities for a free and quality public education in the least restrictive and most effective environment. The goal of inclusion is to prepare students to participate as full and contributing members of the society.

Inclusion does not mean 'dumping.' Inclusion is a basic value that extends to all children. Inclusion gives a message: "Everyone belongs to the school; everyone is welcome to the school."

A school that promotes inclusive education is called an inclusive school. "An inclusive school is a place where everyone belongs, is accepted, supports and is supported by his or her peers and other members of the school community in the course of having his or her educational needs met" (Stainback, Stainback and Forest, 1989).

Inclusive schooling is the process of carrying out the operation of supportive schools — a process of operating a classroom or school as a supportive community where the needs of all members are met and people support and accept responsibility for each other.

Inclusion is not a new label for mainstreaming or integration. It is related to but different from the movement to integrate or mainstream students with disabilities into their regular neighbourhood schools. Mainstreaming was an educational philosophy and practice which assumed the existence of two separate systems — regular education and special education — in which integration was largely limited to non-academic activities for a part of the day. In the existing system of integration students with disabilities are educated in physical proximity to their age-peers, yet without significant attention paid to the qualitative features of this arrangement. In integrated settings the focus is on how to fit students into the regular education programmes. In inclusive settings the focus is on how to develop supportive classrooms and schools that fit, nurture and support the educational and social needs of every student in attendance. Integrated education focuses on the deficiencies of the child. Inclusive education focuses on the quality of schooling.

An inclusive school or the process of inclusive schooling is the ultimate goal of integration and mainstreaming process. Once inclusive schooling and inclusive schools are achieved integration and mainstreaming will no longer be necessary since there will be no longer anyone left out to be integrated or mainstreamed into the regular educational settings.

In the background of the preceding discussion, the following changes in the school system seem appropriate for providing free and quality education to children with disabilities:

(i) Every primary school should follow the principle of zero reject and admit all children irrespective of caste, religion, sex, home background, disability etc. The school's philosophy should be: "Everyone belongs to the school. Everyone is welcome to the school."

(ii) Education of children with SEN in the regular classrooms should be the responsibility of each and every teacher.

(iii) Education should be viewed as a basic right of the child and care must be taken to ensure quality education for children with SEN.

(iv) Teachers should develop respect and a positive attitude towards SEN children and expect a high-level performance from such children. Teachers' expectations are reflected in children's performance and progress.

(v) Children with SEN should be accepted as equal members of the school community and their individuality and diversity should be respected by teachers and peers. Such children should be given opportunity to participate in classroom activities and school programmes.

(vi) Teachers should avoid labelling the child. Not only that, they should also discourage other children to label such children. Children usually imitate their teachers. Peers will interact and behave with the child with SEN in the way teachers do. Non-categorization and non-labelling are the starting points for respecting the child with SEN.

(vii) Parents should be made aware about their own involvement and responsibility in the education and care of their children with SEN. They should be involved in all decision-making in the school.

(viii) There should be continuous linkage between special schools and the regular schools. Special schools situated in the locality should act as a resource centre for the regular schools. They can help in preparation of daily living skills, self-help skills, communication and social skills and pre-academic skills. The specially trained teachers in special schools may provide technical resource support to teachers of regular schools when such support is needed by regular classroom teachers.

(ix) The training inputs provided in Training Centres and various National Institutes should be redesigned to equip teacher-trainees with the knowledge, skills and attitudes required for successful inclusion programme.

(x) Teachers should also keep themselves abreast of the latest developments in the field and keep collecting experiences of good practices from the field. They can pressurize for administrative support to schools for operating inclusive classrooms. They can also make the administrators of the school aware of the need for provision of adequate grant to meet the expenditure on material resources, aids, mobilisation of the community leaders, parent-teacher meetings and for meeting the exigencies.

3. INCLUSION: WHY IT MATTERS?

Education is a human rights issue and children with SEN should be part of schools which should modify their operations to include all students. The PWD ACT (1995) of Government of India clearly stipulates:

> *The appropriate Government and the local authorities shall (a) ensure that every child with a disability has access to free education in an appropriate environment till he attains the age of 18 years; (b) endeavour to promote the integration of students with disabilities in the normal schools.* (*Article — 26 a & b*)

The rationale for inclusive education can be discussed in terms of benefits to students, teachers and society:

(i) In inclusive classrooms all children are enriched by having the opportunity to learn from one another, grow to care for one another, and gain the attitudes, skills and values necessary for our communities. When proper arrangements are present, inclusion works for all students with and without SEN in terms of mutually held positive attitudes, gains in academic and social skills, and preparation for community living.

(ii) When these positive effects are contrasted with the negative effects of exclusion, the benefits of inclusive schools become even more prominent. Academically, socially and occupationally segregated placements are damaging to students. Segregated classes do not lead to independence and competence but instead foster an unrealistic sense of insulation. Separate education can generate a feeling of inferiority as to their status in the community that may affect their hearts and minds. This sense of inferiority affects the motivation of the child to learn.

(iii) In inclusive system teachers develop their professional skills through collaborative consultation and team teaching. Peer collaboration and consultation not only provides psychological support to teachers, it also leads to better student learning.

(iv) Inclusive schooling empowers teachers. Teachers keep themselves informed of changes occurring in their fields, participate in decision-making process and receive in-service education programme from time to time. The initial negative reactions of teachers about inclusive education strikingly change after active exposure to the practice of inclusion.

The most important reason for inclusive schooling is the social value of equality. Despite differences, we all have equal rights. But separate is not equal. In contrast to the past experiences of segregation, inclusion reinforces the practice of the idea that differences are accepted and respected. It is important that we avoid the mistakes of the past. We need schools that promote wider social acceptance, peace and cooperation. When schools include all students then equality is respected and promoted as a value in society. When schools exclude some students, prejudice is entrenched in the consciousness of many students when they become adults, with the result of increased social conflict and dehumanizing competition.

The Benefits of Inclusive Classroom

Children with Special Needs	General Education	Teachers	Society
Affords a sense of belonging to the diverse human family.	Provides opportunities to experience diversity of society on a small scale in the classroom.	Helps teachers appreciate the diversity of the human family.	Promotes the civil rights of all individuals.

(Contd.)

Children with Special Needs	General Education	Teachers	Society
Provides a diverse stimulating environment in which to grow and learn.	Develops an appreciation that everyone has unique and beautiful characteristics and abilities.	Helps teachers recognize that all students have strengths.	Supports the social value of equality.
Evolves a feeling of being a member of a diverse community.	Develops respect for others with diverse characteristics.	Creates an awareness of the importance of direct individualized instruction.	Teaches Socialization and collaborative skills.
Enables development of friendships.	Develops sensitivity towards others' limitations.	Increases ways of creatively addressing challenges.	Builds Supportiveness and independence
Provides opportunities to develop neighbourhood friends.	Develops feelings of empowerment and the ability to make a difference.	Teaches collaborative problem-solving skills.	Maximizes social peace.
Enhances self-respect.	Increases abilities to help and teach all classmates.	Develops team-work skills.	Provides children a miniature model of the democratic process.
Provides affirmations of individuality.	Develops empathetic skills.	Acquires different ways of perceiving challenges as a result of being on a multi-disciplinary team.	
Provides peer models.	Provides opportunities to vicariously put their feet in another child's shoes.	Enhances Accountability skills.	
Provides opportunities to be educated with same age peers.	Enhances appreciation, for diversity of human family.	Combats monotony.	

The philosophy of inclusion hinges on helping students and teachers become better members of a community by creating new visions for communities and for schools. Inclusion is about membership and belonging to a community. Inclusion involves all kinds of practices that are ultimately practices of good teaching. What good teachers do is to think thoughtfully about children and develop ways to reach all children.

Inclusive education is based on the belief that people/adults work in inclusive communities, work with people of different races, religions, aspirations and disabilities. In the same vein, children of all ages should learn and grow in environments that resemble the environment that they will eventually work in.

4. STRATEGIES FOR MAKING INCLUSIVE SCHOOL EFFECTIVE

An inclusive school is one that educates all students in the mainstream. Educating all students in the mainstream does not mean merely dumping them into regular classes without having any strategies. The following strategies are useful for creating a quality inclusive school:

(i) Establish a School Philosophy

An inclusive school works successfully when it has a philosophy based on democratic and egalitarian principles. Inclusion is not an experiment to be tested, but a value to be followed or an attitude to be developed. Inclusive schools focus not only on academic achievement, but also social, emotional development, community spirit, collective responsibility and citizenship. The school philosophy should reflect this clearly. Administrators, teachers, parents, students with and without SEN, community leaders and support personnel should be involved in the planning and decision-making process.

(ii) Follow the Principle of Natural Proportions

The second strategy for creating an inclusive school is to accept all students who are natural part of the neighbourhood. There should not be any unhealthy competition between special schools and regular schools to admit children with disabilities. In fact all childfen irrespective of caste, religion, sex and disability should belong to the regular school. Children with severe disabilities may be referred to special schools when needed.

(iii) Develop Network of Support

Inclusive school does not work unless students with SEN and teachers get the needed support. For example, a student with SEN may be benefited by the support of peer tutor, a teacher may require the support of team teachers or inclusion facilitator.

Thus, the school should develop a network of support services. A network of support is a group of people who come together to brainstorm, problem-solve, and exchange ideas, methods, techniques and activities in order to assist teachers and/or students requiring support to be successful in their roles.

(a) Peer Tutoring

Tutoring is a process that typically involves one-to-one instruction. It can involve a peer, an older student or an adult in the tutoring role. The tutor is the individual who provides instruction, and the tutee is the one who receives instruction. Tutoring can be used to meet the individual needs of students with disabilities by providing remedial or supportive instruction. Of all types of tutoring peer tutoring is the most effective in inclusive situations.

Peer tutoring is instruction provided by the peers of students and involves children teaching other children usually on a one-to-one basis. Cross-age and same age tutoring can be adopted in peer tutoring. Cross age tutoring refers to instructional situations in which the student tutor provides instruction to younger students of a lower grade. Same age tutoring is instruction that involves students of the same age or grade in the tutoring process. Whatever type of peer tutoring is adopted-cross-age or same-age tutoring— it can be used for teaching spelling, handwriting, arithmetic and social behaviour in the last period and twice a week.

In peer tutoring the tutor should perform four acts, such as:

Monitoring : which means supervision and regulation of the performance of a tutee;

Reinforcing : which means providing appropriate contingencies for approved behaviour. He may praise the tutee if he has completed the work to a required standard;

Modelling : which means the demonstration of a particular activity or behaviour by the peer tutor, and

Explaining : which means the peer tutor should expose the relationships on a topic and provide appropriate examples to clarify doubts.

The success of peer tutoring depends upon the interpersonal and communicative relationships between peers. In peer tutoring, although the tutor plays an important role in the instructional process, it is the teacher who virtually retains overall responsibility for selecting the tutors, orienting them about their crucial role, matching the tutor with the tutee, directing, organizing, coordinating and evaluating the performance of the tutorial project. The teacher should follow the guidelines noted below for establishing a peer-tutoring programme:

Guidelines for Peer-Tutoring Programme

(i) Make a careful diagnosis of the tutee's weakness in the subject area.

(ii) Inform the tutor about the levels of mastery expected for the tutee and the time-frame (Tutoring should not be viewed as a time-filling exercise).

(iii) Match the tutor and the tutee (The tutor must have mastery over the subject and skills to be learned by the tutee. Pairing of tutor and the tutee should be based on similar interests and background and sometimes on sex. It may be a good practice to give both the tutor and the tutee some choice in the selection of partners).

(iv) Develop appropriate instructional packages, worksheets, games and learning activities, charts, record sheets and other practice materials in advance that can be used by the tutor.

(v) Arrange a short training programme for tutors which should include tutoring skills, giving feedback, questioning, student management etc. (This can be done through explicit instruction, guidance, modelling or watching experts).

(vi) Establish a practical work routine and suitable work environment for tutoring.

(vii) Reinforce both the tutor and the tutee and encourage, them to persist at the prescribed task.

(viii) Monitor the progress of tutoring in terms of concepts and skills to be learned, quality of relationship and communication between the tutor and the tutee, attendance and completion of tasks.

(ix) Change the tutor, if there is conflict between the tutor and the tutee or if there is personal animosity or dissatisfaction in the tutoring situations.

(x) Give certificate of merit to the tutor and some incentives to the tutee if the tutoring programme has been completed successfully.

(b) Cooperative Learning

In an inclusive classroom where a large number of children with and without SEN have been enrolled, children can be taught with the help of cooperative learning techniques in which they help each other learn, they work together to seek solutions to problems and to complete the assignment. The children should be encouraged to learn cooperatively.

Cooperative learning is a procedure used by a mixed ability group to achieve a common goal with mutual collaboration and support. Cooperative learning provides opportunities to children to learn academic skills and pro-social skills of listening, taking turns, asking questions, seeking assistance, answering questions, offering suggestions, good manners, speaking positively about others and correcting others. The teacher operates as a planner, facilitator and evaluator:

(i) The teacher specifies the instructional objectives of the lesson.

(ii) He/she places children in groups.

(iii) Each group should be small in size and heterogeneous. Each group may have one child with high ability, one child with SEN and three or four children of various abilities.

(iv) He/she arranges the room or the learning environment in such a way that groups are not too close or too far. The members of any group sit together facing each other to facilitate interaction.

(v) He/she assigns roles to each member of the group-leader, recorder, performer and evaluator.

(vi) He/she rotates roles by lesson so that each member of the group has the opportunity to lead, record, perform and evaluate.

(vii) He/she explains the task to the group and distributes materials.

(viii) He/she ensures individual accountability. That is, even if children work cooperatively, each child has to take responsibility for his/her own learning.

(ix) He/she has to ensure inter group interaction without which cooperative learning is meaningless.

(x) He/she has to monitor the progress of individual children and the group and provide assistance to the group when needed.

(xi) He/she has to evaluate the performance of individual children and the group as a whole in terms of:

- Level of mastery,
- Completion of task,
- Quality and quantity of work done,
- Peer interaction and collaboration,
- Satisfaction of the group as a whole.

(xii) Cooperative learning should begin with younger children so that they learn collaborative skills early and progress effectively in later grades.

Cooperative learning is an innovation not only in meeting the special educational needs of children with disabilities, but also in teaching in a situation where a large number of children are on the roll. It benefits children with special educational needs and all other children. It promotes academic achievement, develops problem-solving skills, leadership skills and pro-social skills, increased motivation, understanding, retention and transfer. It provides opportunity to peer interaction and social integration of children with disabilities.

(c) Personnel Support

Some students with special educational needs will require personnel support to benefit from placement in inclusive settings. When teachers are asked to implement educational practices that represent a significant departure from their traditional approaches they may feel the need of training, information and support from others. Particularly in the beginning a teacher cannot be expected to have all the expertise necessary to meet the needs of all students in a heterogeneous classroom. In such cases the special education teacher, and regular teachers should collaborate and carry on the task of providing support to students. After a while, with gained experience he/she can develop skills to educate all children together in a common classroom.

Supportive service for students in inclusive settings may work in various ways from direct collaboration to indirect collaboration.

Direct Collaboration: Cooperative teaching or team teaching is an example of direct collaboration. In this approach a group of teachers, say two or three teachers, join together, plan together, teach together and evaluate together. In inclusive settings the regular education teacher and the special education teacher work together in providing direct service to students in the classroom. In such cases meeting the special educational needs of children becomes the joint responsibility of the regular teacher and the special teacher. After planning jointly the regular teacher or the special teacher takes the responsibility of teaching a particular topic or subject and evaluation depending upon his or her expertise, experience and confidence. When the school does not have a special education teacher, a teacher of the school may be designated as inclusion facilitator or support teacher and he/she collaborates with other teachers in team teaching.

Indirect Collaboration: The special education teacher or the inclusion facilitator and the regular education teacher can provide academic support to children with special educational needs through indirect collaboration outside of the classroom. Indirect collaboration can be possible in three ways:

Collaborative Consultation: The regular education teacher requests the services of special education teacher (consultant) to help generate ideas for addressing an ongoing situation. Collaborative consultation is interactive in nature.

Peer Consultation: Two regular education teachers work together to identify effective solutions to classroom situations such as developing friendships, gaining peer acceptance, solving academic difficulties etc.

Teacher Assistance Team: A team of teachers provides support to regular education teachers. The team may be made up of core members plus the teacher seeking assistance. It emphasizes analyzing the problem situation and developing potential solutions.

Whether the teachers collaborate directly or indirectly, personnel support ensures high academic gains, development of friendship and peer interaction, and acceptance among children. It also increases professional competence of teachers. Regular teachers should be given encouragement by team members and the inclusion facilitator or special education teacher to meet the needs of all children in inclusive settings. Adequate literature should be supplied to teachers and in service education and opportunity to visit inclusive schools in operation should be provided to them so that teachers can be made more competent to provide personnel support to children with special education needs.

(iv) Integrate Students, Personnel and Resources

Inclusive schooling becomes effective when students, personnel and resources are included in the mainstream. When all students are included in the mainstream there will be no necessity of any division between special education personnel and regular education personnel, between special education resources and regular education resources. In such a setting every student, every teacher and each resource belongs to the mainstream.

(v) Adapt the Curriculum

In inclusive schools the focus is not on how to help all students to gain access to the existing curriculum of the school. Rather the focus is on adapting the curriculum to fit to the needs of any student. In other words, the instructional objectives may be same for all students, but the learning experiences may be different for different children when needed. For example, while most students in a science unit on temperature may focus on learning to understand Fahrenheit and Celsius temperature scales, one student with special educational needs might learn to recognize and point to items that are hot and cold. That is, while all students can pursue the same basic educational goals (what is temperature) and learn together in the same regular education class activities, it may be necessary for some children to pursue the same goal by a different approach and be evaluated differently. The teacher should plan creatively to adapt the contents, teaching strategies, evaluation procedure and time allowed for completing an assignment to fit to the needs of children:

Adapting the Contents: The teacher may adapt the number of items that the learner is expected to complete. For example, the teacher may reduce the number of concepts in Social Studies a learner must learn at any one time.

Substituting the Curriculum: He/she may substitute the curriculum by allowing a child with hearing loss to learn computer skills during language test.

Adapting Teaching Strategies: He/she may adapt teaching strategies to fit to the needs of some learners. For example, he/she may use different audio-aids for children with visual problems; visual aids for children with hearing problems, plan more concrete examples for children with mental retardation, provide multi-sensory experiences for children with learning disabilities and organize small group work for all children.

Adapting the Level of Support: The teacher may adapt the level of support by increasing the amount of personal assistance for a specific learner. He/she may assign peer tutors to provide academic support to a child.

Adapting the Rules: He/she may adapt the rules on how a learner should approach the work by allowing the use of a calculator to solve problems in Mathematics, changing or simplifying directions or allowing the child to respond to questions orally instead of answering the question in writing. He/she may also allow extra time for some children during examination if there is a need. Thus, the teacher has to adapt the curriculum depending upon the specific needs of children.

(vi) Provide Strong Leadership

The Headmaster must recognize his or her responsibility to set the tone of the school. He/she must ensure that decisions are made, challenges are met and interactions and processes are supported that are consistent with the school's philosophy. To lead an inclusive school requires a personal belief that all children can learn, a commitment to providing all children equal access to a rich core curriculum and quality instruction, and maintaining the school as a supportive and caring community.

The school must move beyond its traditional sole focus on basic academic learning. Schools are microcosms of society, they mirror both positive and negative aspects, values, priorities, and practices of the culture that exist outside of the school's walls. Schools are also training grounds where the younger members of the society develop attitudes, interests and skills that they will use throughout their lives. Therefore, schools must assume responsibility for improving negative societal conditions. In other words, if we want the society to be a place where an increasing diverse groups of people get along with each other, where all people are valued as contributors to national development, where all people share the basic rights, then schools must reflect those values by providing environments in which the values are modelled by adults and students and in which the very structures, teaching practices and curricula reflect and model those same values. The school should help children realize that they are part of a caring community. Such a realization will not occur unless the school itself becomes a community.

For schools to become caring communities requires much more than providing quality education or support services to help children cope with the problems. Developing a caring learning community necessitates a pervasive school culture that communicates clearly, publicly, and intentionally that the school philosophy is based on principles of equity, justice and fairness for everyone, that the school personnel attend to children's needs for acceptance, belonging, respect and friendship.

(vii) Celebrate Successes and Learn from Challenges

The school personnel should cultivate the habit of acknowledging, celebrating, and building on success. The teachers must celebrate the small successes they are achieving, introspect what they are doing to generate these successes and what they could be doing more, better or differently to achieve greater success and institutionalize the new practices which brought success.

(viii) Maintain Flexibility

The final strategy to promote inclusive schooling is, to maintain flexibility. Flexibility is necessary as even the most thoughtfully designed strategies and plans sometimes are not successful and need revision. Thus, the educators should adopt a problem-solving approach.

5. CHARACTERISTICS OF TEACHERS IN AN INCLUSIVE SCHOOL

Every teacher in an inclusive school is a key person who is responsible for the success or failure of inclusion. The teachers should possess the following characteristics/competencies to be effective in their classrooms:

(i) Ability to problem solve, to be able to informally assess the skills a student needs (rather-than relying solely on standardized curriculum).

(ii) Ability to take advantage of children's individual interests and use their internal motivation for developing needed skills.

(iii) Ability to set high but alternative expectations that are suitable for the students; this means developing alternative assessments.

(iv) Ability to make appropriate expectations for each student, regardless of the student's capabilities. If teachers can do this, it allows all students to be included in a class and school.

(v) Ability to determine how to modify assignments for students, how to design classroom activities with so many levels that all students have a part. This teaching skill can apply not just at the elementary or secondary level, but at the college level as well. It will mean more activity-based teaching rather than seat-based teaching.

(vi) Ability to learn how to value all kinds of skills that students bring to a class, not just the academic skills.

In doing this, teachers will make it explicit that in their classrooms they value all skills, even if that is not a clear value of a whole school.

(vii) Ability to provide daily success for all students. Teachers have to work to counteract the message all students get when certain students are taken out of class for special work.

(viii) Ability to make learning joyful.

Other competencies that will help teachers in an inclusive environment include:

(i) A realization that every child in the class is their responsibility. Teachers need to find out how to work with each child rather than assuming someone else will tell them how to educate a child.

(ii) Knowing a variety of instructional strategies and how to use them effectively. This includes the ability to adopt materials and rewrite objectives for a child's needs.

(iii) Working as a team with parents and special education teachers to learn what skills a child needs and to provide the best teaching approach.

(iv) Viewing each child in the class as an opportunity to become a better teacher rather than a problem to be coped with or have someone else fix.

(v) Flexibility and a high tolerance for ambiguity.

Only a few years ago it was considered unrealistic by most people to even discuss the possibility of educating all students, with and without disabilities, in regular schools and classes. Now this is being done successfully in a small but growing number of schools in United States, Canada, Italy, Australia and other countries. In our country also policy decision has been made; selected resource teachers of existing schools implementing IEDC in different States have been exposed to inclusive schooling system in Australia; the first ever Workshop on Development of Modules on Inclusive Schooling has been organised by NCERT on 12-13, February, 2001 at New Delhi; and advocacy programmes have been organised for administrators and planners of different States. The stage is thus ready for the teachers to play their roles in the background of their earlier achievements and failures in implementing the Centrally Sponsored Scheme of

Integrated Education for Disabled Children. Let us be optimistic that inclusive schooling will be successful under conditions specified below:

(i) Practicing teachers are oriented about the theory and practice of inclusion;
(ii) Head teachers provide instructional leadership to teachers;
(iii) Pre-service education programme for teachers are reoriented to incorporate inclusive education into their course contents;
(iv) Teachers have commitment and competence;
(v) There is adequate monitoring and supervision;
(vi) There is adequate provision in the budget to meet the financial requirement of operating an inclusive school.

Bibliography

Allport, Gardan (1961): *Pattern and Growth of Personality*, New York, Holt, Rinehart and Winston.

Anglin, Jeremy (1973): *Beyond the Information Given*, New York, Norton.

Ausubel, David (1978): *Educational Psychology: A Cognitive View*, New York, Holt.

Ausubel, D.P. & Robinson, F.G. (1969): *School Learning: An Introduction to Educational Psychology*, New York, Holt.

Bandura, Albert & Richard, Walters (1963): *Social Learning and Personality Development*, New York, Holt.

Bigge, Moris (1976): *Learning Theories for Teachers*, New York, Harper & Row.

Block, J.H., ed. (1970): *Mastery Learning: Theory and Practice*, N.Y., Holt.

Block, J.H. and Anderson, Lorin (1975): *Mastery Learning in Classroom Instruction*, N.Y., Mcmillan.

Bloom, B.S. (1975): *Human Characteristics and School Learning*, N.Y., McGraw Hill.

—— (1979): *Alterable Variables: The New Direction in Educational Research*, Edinburgh, SCRE.

Bruner, Jerome (1960): *The Process of Education*, Cambridge, Mass, HUP.

—— (1966): *Toward a Theory of Instruction*, Cambridge, Mass, HUP.

Chaplin, J.P. and Krawiec, T.S. (1974): *Systems and Theories of Psychology*, 3rd ed. New York, Holt, Rinehart and Winston.

Child, Dennis (1976): *Psychology and the Teacher*, 2nd ed., N.Y., Holt.

Dash, M. (1995): *Educational Psychology*, New Delhi, Deep and Deep.

——(2000): *Education of Exceptional Children*, New Delhi, Atlantic.

Dececco, J.P. and Crawford, W. (1975): *The Psychology of Learning and Instruction*, N.Y., Prentice Hall.

Elkind, D. (1970): *Children and Adolescent; Interpretive Essays on Jean Piaget*, London, OUP.

Ellis, H.C. (1965): *The Transfer of Learning*, N.Y., McMillan.

Elmore, R.F., Peterson, P.L., and Mc Carthy, S.J. (1996): *Restructuring in the Classroom Teaching, Learning and School Organisation*, San Francisco, C.A. Jossey, Bass.

Gagne, R.M. (1970): *The Conditions of Learning*, N.Y., Holt.

Gardner, H. (1991): *The Unschooled Mind: How Children Think and how Schools should Teach*, N.Y., Basic Books.

—— (1993): *Multiple Intelligence: The Theory in Practice*, N.Y., Basic Books.

Heward, W.L. and Orlansky, M.D. (1992): *Exceptional Children* (4th ed.), N.Y., McMillan.

Hilgard, E.R. and Bower, G.H. (1975): *Theories of Learning*, Englewood, Prentice Hall.

Hilgard, E., Atkinson, R., and Atkinson, R. (1975): *Introduction to Psychology*, N.Y., Harcourt Bace Jovanovich.

Hurlock, E.B. (1974): *Developmental Psychology*, New Delhi, TMH.

——(1976): *Personality Development*, New Delhi, TMH.

Kerlinger, Fred (1973): *Foundations of Behavioural Research*, N.Y., Holt.

Kimble, G. (1961): *Conditioning and Learning*, Englewood Cliffs, Prentice Hall.

Kirk, S., Gallagher, J.S., and Anastasia, N.J. (1996): *Educating Exceptional Children* (8th ed.), Boston, Houghton Mifflin.

Klausmeier, H., Ghatala, E., and Frayer, D. (1974): *Conceptual Learning and Development*, N.Y., Academic Press.

Klausmeier, H.J. and Goodwin, W. (1978): *Learning and Human Abilities*, N.Y., Harper & Row.

Kolesnik, W. (1976): *Learning: Educational Applications*, Boston, Allyn & Bacon.

Lindgren, H.C. (1962): *Educational Psychology in the Classrooms*, London, Wiley.

Mayer, R.E. (1937): *Educational Psychology: A Cognitive Approach*, Boston, M.A., Little Brown.

Morgan, C.T. and King, R.A. (1978): *Introduction to Psychology*, N.Y., Harper & Row.

Mouly, G.J. (1960): *Psychology of Effective Teaching*, N.Y., Holt.

Mukhopadhyay, M. (2001): *Total Quality Management in Education*, New Delhi, NIEPA.

Piaget, J. (1978): *Success and Understanding*, Cambridge, M.A., HUP.

Spaulding, C.L. (1992): *Motivation in the Classroom*, N.Y., McGraw Hill.

Stainback, S. and Stainback, W. (1995): *Inclusion—A Guide for Educators*, London: Paul Brookes.

—— (1990): *Inclusive Education, Baltimore*; Paul Brookes.

Tallent, Norman: *Psychology of Adjustment*.

Travers, J.F. (1982): *Educational Psychology*, N.Y., Harper & Row.

Woodworth, R.S. (1976): *Contemporary Schools of Psychology*, London, Methuen.

Index